THE POLITICS OF THE YORKSHIRE MINERS

The Politics of the Yorkshire Miners

ANDREW TAYLOR

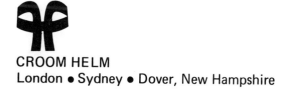

CROOM HELM
London ● Sydney ● Dover, New Hampshire

© 1984 A.J. Taylor
Croom Helm Ltd, Provident House, Burrell Row,
Beckenham, Kent BR3 1AT

Croom Helm Australia Pty Ltd, First Floor, 139 Kings Street,
Sydney, NSW 2001, Australia

Croom Helm, 51 Washington Street, Dover, New Hampshire, 03820 USA

British Library Cataloguing in Publication Data

Taylor, *Andrew, 1954–*
   The politics of the Yorkshire miners.
   1. National Union of Mineworkers. *Yorkshire Area*
   –History. 2. Trade-unions–Great Britain–
   Political activity–History–20th century
   3. Great Britain–Politics and government–
   1945-
   I. Title
   322'.2   HD6668.M6152N3

ISBN 0-7099-2447-X

Printed and bound in Great Britain by
Biddles Ltd, Guildford and King's Lynn

CONTENTS

LIST OF ABBREVIATIONS

AS Circular	Circular to all Area NUM Secretaries
BACM	British Association of Colliery Management
BS Circular	Circular to all Branch Secretaries
CLP	Constituency Labour Party
DLP	District Labour Party
DCC	District Consultative Committee
JNNC	Joint National Negotiating Committee
LPEC	Labour Party National Executive Committee
LPCR	Labour Party Annual Conference Report
MFGB	Miners Federation of Great Britain
MFGB (EC)	Miners Federation of Great Britain, Executive Committee
NACODS	National Association of Colliery Overmen, Deputies and Shotfirers
NCB	National Coal Board
NUM	National Union of Mineworkers
NUM (EC)	National Union of Mineworkers, National Executive Committee

List of Abbreviations

TUC	Trades Union Congress
YMA	Yorkshire Miners Association
YMWA	Yorkshire Minerworkers Association
YA (NUM)	National Union of Mineworkers (Yorkshire Area)
YRCL	Yorkshire Regional Council of Labour

LIST OF TABLES

PREFACE

The research for this work began in 1975 with the
miners triumphant: at the time of publication
they, their union and the industry are passing
through a major crisis, arguably their most severe
since 1926. The events described in this book are
the pre-history of this situation written from the
standpoint of the Yorkshire miners. It was the
political transformation of the Yorkshire Area (NUM)
as a result of the crisis of the 1960s which, in
a large part, pulled the NUM as a whole to the
left, a movement which perhaps culminated with the
election of Arthur Scargill as President of the
NUM.
     This book is in no sense an official history
of the Yorkshire Area, though it is plain where
my sympathies lie. The betrayal of the miners by
the Government and by 'their' leaders made a
shift to the left inevitable. The Officials of
the Yorkshire Area granted me virtually free access
to research the doctoral thesis on which this book
is based. I cannot hope to express my gratitude
to them for their help and kindness, I hope they
feel the book does their members justice.
     Many of the events described in this book were
part of my childhood, my youth and my experience as
a research student, this in a large part accounts
for my passionate interest in miners and mining.
Anyone who did not work or live in the coalfields
cannot imagine the uncertainty generated by pit
closures in the mining communities, the relief
caused by the unofficial strikes of 1969 and 1970,
the triumph and elation of 1972 and 1974, or the
frustration of the 1970s and 1980s, but these
events must be understood if the present dispute
and the role of the Yorkshire miners in it are to
be fully understood.

Preface

I began work on the Yorkshire miners in 1975 and
since that time I have received considerable help
from many people. My original dissertation was
supervised by Pat Seyd and Jim MacFarlane of the
University of Sheffield. I benefitted greatly
from their help and encouragement, I owe them a
great deal of personal and intellectual debt.
Also, thanks are due to Lewis Minkin who examined
the dissertation and made many useful suggestions
during the course of writing. A work of this
kind relies heavily on oral evidence and I would
like to express my thanks and deep appreciation
to those members of the Yorkshire Area (NUM) who
so freely gave of their time in answering my
queries and providing interviews. Peter Sowden
of Croom Helm guided an inexperienced author
through the publication process, Mrs Chatoo
speedily and efficiently typed the manuscript and
Steve Pratt drew the maps. Dr B J Evans and my
colleagues at the Polytechnic provided both support
and encouragement. Finally, my greatest debt is
owed to my wife, Dawn, who uncomplainingly put up
with me and the Yorkshire miners since 1975. It
is to her that I dedicate this book.

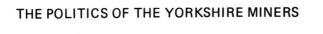

THE POLITICS OF THE YORKSHIRE MINERS

INTRODUCTION

How influential are the Yorkshire miners and the
National Union of Mineworkers (Yorkshire Area) over
the Labour Party and Labour Governments? What is
their role in coalfield Constituency Labour Parties
(CLPs) and in the recruitment of MPs? Why did the
Yorkshire miners and subsequently the Yorkshire
Area, become identified as the militant core of the
NUM? What was the role of the Yorkshire miners in
the national coal strikes of 1972 and 1974? These
are the questions answered in this book.
    The miners are politically and industrially
conscious, they enjoy a close relationship with the
Labour Party and in the 1970s were transformed
from a relic of Britain's industrial and political
past in one of the most important groups of workers
in the political system. The Yorkshire miners are
the largest group in the NUM and they played a
major role in this renascence. The period
1944 - 1974 begins with the nationalisation of the
Miners' Federation of Great Britain (MFGB) into the
NUM and ends with the entry into office of a Labour
Government as a consequence of a miners' strike.
During these thirty years the Yorkshire Area moved
from the political and industrial right to being
the leading left-wing Area in the NUM, a
transformation symbolised by the rise of Arthur
Scargill.[1]

The Political Development of the Miners
The prime function of a trade union is to defend
and improve the wages and conditions of its
members.[2] The Yorkshire miners, indeed miners in
general adopted political activity to avoid the
limits placed on their activities by the weakness of
union organisation, and party-political activity
and pressure group politics were seen as the only

1

way of circumventing employer resistance. The
Mines Act (1842) legitimised government regulation
of the mines but it was never as extensive as the
miners desired.[3]   The subsequent political history
of the miners is concerned with extending State
regulation, culminating in the nationalisation of
the mines.

The political strategy pursued by the miners
from the 1870s -- Lib-Labism -- sought to give the
miners a foothold in the political process by
exchanging miners' votes (which increased
considerably after the Third Reform Act) for Liberal
parliamentary seats.[4]   The direct representation of
labour under the Liberal Party banner appeared to
offer the best available opportunity for miners'
influence to enter the political process.   However,
by the 1890s and 1900s increasing numbers of miners
and other commentators were suggesting that the
Liberals' concession of a few seats was mere
'tokenism' and that Lib-Labism had given the miners
little for their loyalty and should be abandoned.
In 1908 the MFGB conceded and affiliated to the
Labour Party, although Lib-Labism remained a potent
force in some districts.[5]

Affiliation to the Labour Party was important
as it linked the miners to a broader political
strategy -- parliamentary socialism.   By 1914
nationalisation of the mines was the MFGB's prime
aim, socialistic by definition it was more likely
to come from the Labour Party.   This meant that the
miners were dependent on the election of a majority
Labour Government and this contributed to the
tendency of the Union to defer to the Party's
definition of its electoral interests and draw a
distinction between 'political' and 'industrial'
activity.   Both Party and Union Leaders were at one
in their belief that the Union should do nothing
which might damage the electoral advance of the
Labour Party.   After 1918 mines nationalisation
became subsumed within parliamentary socialism, and
therefore within the electoral strategy of the
Labour Party.[6]

The General Strike and lockout of 1926 had two
crucial effects on the political development of the
miners.   First, it convinced the miners' leaders
that strike action should only be used in the very
last resort and never with any political intent.
This was to amount to a self-denying ordinance
over strike action.   Second, it reinforced the
already strong commitment of the Union and the miners
to the election of a majority Labour Government

which would nationalise the mines.[7]

Nationalisation was seen as the panacea for the ills of the industry, and union leaders regarded its achievement as a matter of "practical politics", not direct industrial action. They recognised that party political action could not be used to defend all the miners' interests so a powerful union was essential for collective bargaining. Union leaders emphasised that the miners should not damage the electoral prospects of the Labour Party.[8] After 1926 the MFGB and the district unions virtually surrendered the strike in favour of creating a close bargaining relationship with the coal owners. The electoral debacles of 1931 and 1935 saw the prospect of a Labour Government (and with it nationalisation) recede. The miners remained committed to the Party and nationalisation but they were forced to adopt a new short/medium term strategy in which the MFGB moved away from its role as a political coordinator to that of a national collective bargaining institution. The attempts to achieve this and national agreements meant changes in the organisation of the MFGB from a loose federation of district unions to a more 'national' body with the formation of the NUM.[9] After the 1920s the MFGB (and its successor) was dominated by an ethic of cooperation and conciliation. This was partly the result of the experience of 1926 and the Union's weakness in the early-1930s; and partly as a result of long term changes in the system of industrial relations and in the relationship between the State, the employers, and the unions which saw the acceptance of unions as legitimate participants in the political and industrial systems.[10]

Union leaders asserted that strikes were unnecessary as concessions could be negotiated in a nationalised industry. Traditionally, it was argued that after nationalisation a new era of industrial relations would dawn where there would be no need for strikes. This was opposed by those miners who felt that abandoning industrial action limited the ability of the NUM to defend its members' interests. This contributed to a high level of industrial conflict aimed in part at persuading the leaders of the NUM to use industrial action; when strikes were called in 1972 and 1974 the NUM had an enormous impact upon the political system. These strikes weakened the distinctions between 'trade union' and 'political' activity drawn in the inter-war period. To the

Introduction

constitutionalism of the miners' leaders was added
the Labour Party: a working class oriented party on
the threshold of power committed to the miners.
Naturally, union was subordinated to party, the
industrial to the political: the mining unions were
to provide money, personnel, organisation and votes
to the Labour Party to help it achieve majority
status to nationalise the mines. The 1920s were
the last era of the great set-piece industrial
battles in mining, these were to reappear in the
1970s but in between the miners placed their
political and industrial hopes in the Labour Party.
The miners were to be frustrated by their reliance
on the Labour Party (in and out of office) and
these frustrations were to contribute to the
resurgence of industrial militancy in the early-
1970s.

The Miners and Labour, 1945 - 1974
The problem confronting the miners and the NUM
throughout this period was: how can miners'
interests be best defended when the industry was
undergoing such massive shifts in market power?[11]
This brings us to our first concern: the nature and
extent of the Yorkshire miners' influence over
Labour Government and the Labour Party.
     The structure of the Party appears to give
effective power over policy to the trade unions, but
the unions have seldom asserted themselves.
Likewise, when in government Labour has secured the
deference of the unions to policies which ran
counter to the immediate interests of their
members.[12] The miners have been, perhaps, the
firmest supporters of the Labour Party, but has this
close relationship conferred great influence over
the Party? The evidence shows that the miners have
not enjoyed a high degree of influence largely
because of their acceptance of Labour's electoral
strategy and their unwillingness to take sanctions
against 'their' party or 'their' government.
     As a social democratic party seeking to
reform society by winning a majority of seats in
the House of Commons the Labour Party is motivated
by wider electoral and political considerations than
being either the parliamentary arm of the trade
unions, or even the party of the manual working
class. This supra-class electoral strategy has
enabled Labour Governments to ignore or reject
demands felt to be 'sectional' or inimical to the
electoral and political interests of Government or
Party. The deference of the miners to this

4

strategy was reinforced by the political history of
the coal industry which caused the MFGB and NUM to
seek government intervention as a solution to the
industry's problems.[13]   Conservative Governments
offered no hope and only a majority Labour
Government could provide the necessary security.
Yet, when a Labour Government savagely reduced the
industry the NUM felt unable, because of feelings
of powerlessness, loyalty and self-interest, to
take sanctions.   Thus, the influence of the miners
was limited by a refusal to challenge Labour in
deference to the Party's electoral strategy.
     Are the miners more willing to confront a
Conservative Government?   Labour is expected to
be more sympathetic, whereas the Conservatives are
seen as their traditional enemy, so few of the
inhibitions of the relationship with Labour apply.
However, the NUM has accepted that as mining is
nationalised it must cooperate with all
governments irrespective of the NUM's political
preferences.   The miners do, however, have a 'gut'
hostility to the Conservative Party and do not
expect to be treated fairly by a Conservative
Government;   equally, the miners have an
instinctive 'gut' loyalty to Labour and do expect
fair treatment from a Labour Government.

Party Political Influence
Miners have a long history of involvement in grass-
roots politics and were the first workers to
secure the election of their own number to
Parliament, but how influential are the Yorkshire
miners in the CLPs and in the recruitment of MPs?
What use is made of sponsored MPs and do the miners
have any control over them?
     There is a common assumption that because of
their history of political involvement, concentrated
numbers and union organisation the miners dominate
absolutely coalfield CLPs and the political process
therein.[14]   However, because of the decline of the
industry, changes in Party rules, problems of
participation by miners, defects in political
organisation and social change in the coalfield this
assumption is a myth.   Miners do constitute the
largest bloc of organised political influence in
these CLPs and there remains a potential for
considerable NUM influence.   In the post-war
period, however, the Yorkshire Area proved incapable
of mobilising and organising the miners' remaining
influence in CLP politics.
     Why does the Union sponsor MPs?   The Objects

of the Yorkshire Area call on the Union " To
promote legislative enactments for the efficient
management of the mines, whereby the health and
lives of miners may be protected."15   Parliamentary
representation is seen as a useful contribution to
collective bargaining.   The miners' MPs also have
a symbolic importance.   In an increasingly middle
class Parliamentary Labour Party (PLP) the Miners'
Group is composed solely of members of the manual
working class.   The Transport & General Workers
Union sponsors more MPs but occupationally the
Miners' Group remains the most homogenous in the
PLP.16
        Sponsorship makes it tempting to assume that
these MPs are under union control.   Again, myth
contrasts with reality.   These are not miners' MPs
in any proprietorial sense, and sponsorship cannot
be used as a means of political influence: he who
pays the piper does not call the tune.   Sponsored
MPs are expected to hold a 'watching brief' over the
industry, the miners and the mining communities,
but the Union rarely intervenes in their
Parliamentary activities.   The position of the
sponsored MP under the canons of parliamentary
privilege is complex, and sponsorship is accepted
as part of parliamentary democracy precisely
because it confers no power over the MP.   The
miners have made few demands on the MPs, but this
has its limits as, for example, in the 1975 EEC
Referendum controversy.

Internal Union Politics

The third area of concern is the political
transformation of the Yorkshire Area leading to the
emergence of a more militant Area leadership.
Traditionally, Yorkshire was regarded as a moderate
Area, yet in 1969 and 1970 the Yorkshire miners
were in the forefront of a massive unofficial
strike wave.   These strikes were as much against
NUM policies and leadership since 1947 as against
the National Coal Board (NCB).
        Union leaders had argued that nationalisation
would obviate the need for industrial action.
Between 1964 and 1970 the miners relied on
bargaining with the NCB and Government, but this
prevented neither pit closures nor the miners'
slide down the wages league.   After 1964 there was
growing disillusion with the policies of the Union
leadership and strong pressures emerged within the
Yorkshire Area with the aim of compelling Area and
National leaders to abandon their support of the

Introduction

Labour Government and their conciliatory attitude to
the NCB and defend militantly miners' interests.
Disappointment with the Labour Government and a
reaction to the post-war history of the industry
were not the sole cause of discontent: unrest over
wage restructuring under the National Power Loading
Agreement (NPLA) signed in 1966, over low pay for
underground workers, low pay and long hours for
surface workers combined with the uncertainty and
frustration generated by pit closures also
contributed to the explosion of unofficial strike
action in 1969.
     The strikes of 1969 and 1970 saw the emergence
of a new generation of leaders who rejected the
policies pursued after 1947, a rejection symbolised
by a willingness to use industrial action, against
government if necessary. Union orthodoxy argued
that strikes would only close more pits and that
the decline of the industry meant the evaporation of
the miners' power. Unofficial leaders countered
by arguing that 'moderation and reasonableness'
had failed and that the NUM should not rely on
untrustworthy governments to the exclusion of all
other methods. These policies were vindicated by
the 1972 strike, and by 1973 left-wingers were in
official positions in the Yorkshire Area.

The Politics of Industrial Action
Finally, we come to the role of the Yorkshire miners
in the national coal strikes of 1972 and 1974.
For the Yorkshire miners the 1972 strike was more
important than that of 1974: in 1972 they
recovered the self-confidence lost as a consequence
of 1926 and industrial decline. The 1972 strike
was organised and conducted by the membership and
their branch leaders and their contribution to
victory was considerable: they organised a wide
ranging intelligence network and contacts with
other unions whose help was essential in stopping
the movement of coal. Second, they perfected the
devastatingly effective tactic of the mass,
mobile picket which won the crucial battles before
the power stations.
     The 1974 strike was less spectacular, but far
more politically sensitive. The Heath Government's
response to the miners' challenge to their incomes
policy was the three day week and a General
Election, which the Government lost. These
victories created an aura of invincibility, but
victory was not guaranteed: both strikes were a
gamble. If, for example, the Conservatives had

won the 1974 election the miners would, perhaps, have
been blamed for giving Heath a renewed mandate, not
the credit for 'bringing down a government'.   Did
the miners bring down Heath?   The strike provided
the pretext for the election, but it was not fought
on the question of 'who governs?' but on the
government's record since 1970.
   The miners' victory was helped immeasurably by
the rise of OPEC.   The United Kingdom's dependence
upon increasingly costly and uncertain Arab oil
transformed the position of coal.   The rise of
OPEC was contemporaneous with the growth of miners'
militancy - a remarkable historical coincidence.
These strikes and the new market position of coal
returned the miners and their union to political
pre-eminence.   It became common to suggest that
events such as the coal strikes were rendering
Britain 'ungovernable'.   However, after
February 1974, with a Labour Government enjoying a
tiny majority, the NUM did all it could to smooth
the Government's path.   Thus, the traditional
deference to a Labour Government re-emerged.
Nevertheless, this support was far less secure
because of the political transformation of the
Yorkshire Area.   The Yorkshire miners' shift to
the left was crucial as it was the largest area in
the NUM.   The rise to power of a new, more militant
leadership in Yorkshire had a profound effect on
the politics of the NUM, creating a more solid bloc
of left-wing support on the National Executive of
the NUM.   This made it more difficult for the
leaders of the NUM to deliver the Union's support to
the government.

REFERENCES

1   The terms 'left' and 'right', although common
     in political analysis, are not authoritatively
     defined.   We propose the following.   For
     the bulk of the period covered by this
     dissertation the political and policy stance
     described as right wing is defined as
     believing in the disutility of industrial
     action and supporting negotiation and
     conciliation with management.   The right were
     firm believers in nationalisation and that it
     had, by and large, solved the basic problems of
     the miners and their industry.   Their
     reference point was the inter-war period.
     They were firmly committed to the Labour Party
     and Labour Governments, placing great emphasis

on party-political action. Their main policy aim was the preservation of the maximum number of jobs, even if the cost was low wages. The political and policy stance of the left wing is defined as believing in industrial action as essential for the defence of miners' interests and opposing too great a reliance on party-political action. Their reference point tended to be the period after 1947. Their main concern was the defence of the miners' standard of life as measured by his pay packet. Employment, they believed, should not, indeed could not, be guaranteed by low wages. By 1974 the left controlled formal union office in the Yorkshire Area. The majority of the membership cannot be placed in either category. They tended to support the official leadership, but this was slowly eroded, collapsing in the late-1960s. Memberships tend to be loyal to their leaders, no matter what the latters' ideology, if they are successful.

2   S & B Webb, History of Trade Unionism (London, Longmans 1894); p.1.

3   A J Taylor, Laisser-Faire and State Intervention in Nineteenth Century Britain (London, Macmillan 1972); p.58.

4   For a justification of the method of legal enactment see; YMA: Annual Report, 1884, pp.9-11 and Sheffield Independent, 16 and 25 April 1891. For a contempoaray critique see, S & B Webb, Industrial Democracy (rev.ed. London, Longmans 1913); pp. 223-234.

5   R Page Arnot, The Miners: A History of the Miners' Federation of Great Britain Vol. 1 (London, G Allen & Unwin 1949); pp.330-336, and, pp.342-348; H Pelling, The Origins of the Labour Party (2nd ed, Oxford, OUP 1962); pp.198-201 and pp.206-211, also his A History of British Trade Unionism (Harmondsworth, Penguin 1965); pp.109-114 and pp.123-127, F Bealey & H Pelling, Labour and Politics, 1900-1906 (London, Macmillan 1958); pp.223-234 and p.262; R Gregory, The Miners and British Politics, 1906-1914 (Oxford, Clarendon Press 1968); pp.104-106; and, J MacFarlane, British Miners and the Taff Vale Judgement: The 'Bag Muck' Strike at Denaby and Cadeby Collieries,

1902-1904 (unpublished ms).

6   R Miliband, Parliamentary Socialism (London,
Merlin Press 1972); pp.13-16, and, R Eldon-
Barry, Nationalisation and British Politics
(London, Cape 1966); p.235

7   G A Phillips, The General Strike (London,
Weidenfeld & Nicholson 1976) chapter xiii;
Labour Party Conference Report 1926 (hereafter
LPCR) 'The Mining Crisis'; p.162 and p.196;
The Miner, 15 October 1927; and, YMWA:
Annual Report, 1926-1927; p.10.

8   YMWA Mineworkers' Journal, Vol l(part iii)
30 September 1923; p.287 et seq.

9   G B Baldwin, 'Structural Reform in the British
Miners Union', in, Quarterly Journal of
Economics 67(1953); pp.576-597.

10.   K Burgess, The Challenge of Labour (London,
Croom Helm 1980); chapter 7, and,
K Middlemass, Politics in Industrial Society
(London, Deutsch 1979) chapters 7-10.

11   For an overview of trade unions as actors in
the British political system see, T C May,
Trade Unions and Pressure Group Politics
(Farnborough, Saxon House 1975) and R Taylor,
The Fifth Estate (Rev. ed., London, Pan Books
1980), chapter 5. For a survey of trade union
political power see, D Marsh & G Locksley,
'Trade Union Power in Britain: The Recent
Debate', in, West European Politics 4
(January) 1981; pp.19-37.

12   L Panitch, Social Democracy and Industrial
Militancy (Cambridge, Cambridge UP 1976);
pp.235-239. See also his, 'Ideology and
Integration: The Role of the Labour Party',
in, Political Studies xix(2) 1971; pp.184-200.

13   M W Kirby, The British Coalmining Industry,
1870-1946 (London, Macmillan 1977), and
I Berkovitch, Coal On The Switchback (London,
G Allen & Unwin 1977).

14   The CLPs with which we are concerned are
Barnsley, Don Valley, Dearne Valley, Rother
Valley, Hemsworth, Pontefract and Normanton.

15 <u>Yorkshire Area (NUM) Rules 1976</u>, Rule 3(a).

16 To qualify for sponsorship an NUM parliamentary
    candidate "must be a financial member .... of a
    Constituent Association of the NUM and is, or
    has been, for at least five years a worker in
    or about mines, or ancilliary undertakings, or
    a Union representative .... within an NUM
    Area."   <u>NUM Rules 1976</u>, Rule 84(4).
    NUM and TGWU MPs

	1945	1950	1951	1955	1959	1964	1966	1970	1974	1974
NUM	37	37	36	34	31	27	26	20	18	18
TGWU	17	16	14	14	14	21	27	19	23	21

The bulk of the TGWU's MPs come from occupations
not normally associated with membership of the
TGWU or manual working class.   They include
(1975), <u>inter alia,</u> 4 journalists, 3 lecturers,
3 solicitors and barristers, and a managing
director.
A Roth, <u>The Business Background of MPs</u> (London,
Parliamentary Profiles 1975).

Chapter One

THE YORKSHIRE MINERS AND THE LABOUR PARTY, 1945-1963

The Miners, Nationalisation and Coal Production

The mineworkers and their Union saw a Labour Victory
in the 1945 General Election as vital to their
future economic security. A Conservative
Government could not provide this security as it was
not committed to nationalisation and would repeat
the policies of the 1920s and 1930s.[1]   For the
NUM the General Election was about nationalisation;
"A vote for Labour is a vote for the public
ownership of the industry for the benefit of the
Nation".[2]   In his Presidential Address Will Lawther
warned Conference delegates that the Conservatives
"would use Churchill for all he was worth to
obscure the real issues" but insisted that the
electorate would see that the Conservatives offered
no hope, and, "for us as mineworkers ... the acid
test is the Government's policy for dealing with the
mining industry".   The only solution for the ills
of the industry was nationalisation;   the promised
reorganisation of private capitalism was not enough.[3]
Lawther warned that nationalisation would warrant a
reciprocal response from mineworkers: actively
co-operating with both Government and management in
the production of coal.
        Before the General Election the YMWA Council
issued a circular to all branches urging,

> ... our membership, whether having a vote
> or not, to support not only our mining
> candidates, but all who are pledged to
> the Labour Party's policy in the forth-
> coming General Election.   This election
> will prove to be the most vital and far
> reaching one in history, and dependent
> upon its result the future welfare of the
> working class community for generations
> to come will rest.[4]

The Labour Government immediately called upon the miners to help resolve the post-war economic crisis. The Government sought to promote an export-led economic recovery which depended on the level of industrial output which needed abundant cheap energy supplies. At all levels of the NUM the miners took the burden of an expanding demand for coal, and the level of coal production was made both an index of, and the test of loyalty to the Labour Government. This was coupled with warnings that a failure to produce sufficient coal might cause a postponement of nationalisation.[5]

A production drive was launched soon after the General Election. The YMWA passed a resolution attacking unofficial strikers for "sabotaging their own interests and those for which the present Government has been elected",[6] a good example of coal production being elevated to an index of political loyalty. In accepting joint responsibility for the level of coal output the Union saw itself as taking this responsibility to help keep the Labour Government in power - a task it readily accepted.[7]

The NUM willingly transformed itself into adjunct of the Ministry of Power to secure nationalisation and sustain a Labour Government. The result was a conviction that there was no distinction between the interests of the Government and the interests of the mineworkers and their Union. This may have carried weight with the NEC and at Area level, but many miners regarded this with increasing scepticism. The transformation of coal production into a political issue ensured that political conflict was introduced into every dispute in the industry; every stoppage affected the Labour Government and any failure to meet Government demands for coal helped the Conservatives. The mineworkers were constantly told of their duty and responsibility to help 'their' Government.

> We are no longer urged to do this in the
> interests of the coalowners ... the call
> is for the people of Britain to meet the
> needs of the Nation ... We must show the
> Nation whatever the difficulties there may
> have been in the past, there is now a
> disposition of full cooperation between
> the mineworkers, the Labour Government,
> and the ... Ministry of Fuel and Power,
> and that we will spare no effort to
> bring to a successful conclusion the

aims and purposes for which the Labour Government has been elected.[8]

Yorkshire reached its maximum output in the middle of December 1945 and after that date declined. The Yorkshire miners were exhorted to "Help the Nation" and maintain coal output.[9] The sentiments and attitudes of the era of private ownership continued amongst the mineworkers because of the persistence of the problems of the private coal industry: low investment, a chaotic wages system and an ageing workforce. The miners had high expectations of the post-war period, many of which were not met, the result being a crisis of expectations reflected in unofficial strike action.

The severe winter of 1947 saw a major fuel crisis. During the winter an Emergency Committee was established composed of cabinet members, TUC General Council members and the NEC of the NUM to consider ways of expanding the fuel supply. The NEC rejected any idea that the miners were responsible for the fuel crisis: "the roots of the present crisis are to be found in the policies that for years were carried out in the coal industry by those people who are attacking the Labour Government."[10]

Directing present discontent to past events was of great importance in explaining how the official leadership of the NUM could control what was, at times, a mutinous membership. Co-operation between the NUM and the Government was cemented not only by loyalty, but by a mutual antipathy to all things Conservative and an overwhelming desire to make a success of Labour's first majority government.

The year 1947 saw the mines nationalised heralding a new era for the industry. Will Lawther claimed: "We know that the NCB looks upon its employees in an entirely different light from those who employed miners in the past", and there could now be few grounds for industrial action.[11] However, the authority structures of private industry, pay systems, and methods of work remained unchanged, and the result was unofficial industrial conflict. There was a tendency to lay any dissent or unrest at the door of anyone who was politically unacceptable to the NUM leadership. Disputes were felt to be politically damaging to the Labour Government given Labour's dire need for coal, and the miners now had a duty to co-operate with the management: "There are now no opposing sides in the industry".[12] At

the 1947 NUM Conference Emmanuel Shinwell, the
Minister of Fuel and Power, praised the co-operation
of the NUM but emphasised that

> ... having sent to power a Labour
> Government, a Government of your own
> making, and having laboured long and
> hard throughout the period of the
> capitalist wilderness, clearly, it is
> the bounden duty as well as the high
> responsibility of those who returned a
> Labour Government to stand by that
> Government with the utmost loyalty.[13]

The Government and the NEC fell over each other
saluting each other's statesmanship and
responsibility, but this unity was not a feature of
the NUM as a whole.   Shinwell criticised those
branch leaders who refused to abandon the old
attitudes of private ownership and who were
reluctant to co-operate fully with the NCB,

> There seems to be in some parts of
> the country a lack of appreciation of
> the tremendous economic and social
> issues at stake ... the nation cannot
> afford monkey tricks ...[14]

Shinwell's oratory was greeted with applause:
there were strong feelings that miners owed a debt
of loyalty to Labour.
    This gratitude can be seen in the speech by
Joe Hall, the Yorkshire Area President, to the
Annual Demonstration of 1947.

> This day we demonstrate our thankfulness
> to those who fought for our cause, and
> we ourselves renew our faith and loyalty
> ... not only to the Trade Union Movement
> ...(but) to the Government ... for
> without this Government the realisation
> of our faith and hopes would have been
> vanquished.[15]

Yet, Shinwell noted the failure of the Yorkshire
Miners to keep their promises.   Speaking at the
same Demonstration he said,

> The Yorkshire Miners said to me, 'Give
> us the Five Day Week and if you do we'll
> give you the coal ...'   We have given

> (You) the Five Day Week: where is the
> coal? I do not want resolutions, I
> cannot burn resolutions, although some
> of them should be burnt ...[16]

Pressure for wage increases to compensate for
increases in the cost of living and constant
Government pressure for more coal at the cheapest
price, ensured that the NUM became subject to
increasing internal tension as union leaders sought
to reconcile their dilemma. Gaitskell's
appointment as Minister of Fuel and Power saw no
change in the Union-Government relationship:
Gaitskell declared to the Yorkshire Area Council,

> ... the pledge is continued support to
> the Labour Government ... in efforts to
> increase and then maintain a high
> standard of coal production(it is)only by a
> continuation of our efforts in this
> nationalised industry that the ultimate
> success of the Labour Government will
> be ensured and Labour's task make easier
> in the General Election.[17]

The narrow victory of the Labour Government in
the 1950 General Election was blamed by the NUM on
the failure of the working class and trade union
members to support 'their' government.[18] Critics
of Government policies within the trade unions were
attacked for eroding the workers' confidence in
'their' government.[19]
Internal union politics were dominated by
Labour's electoral decline and the prospect of a
Conservative Government in the near future. The
NUM leadership were determined to rally the
maximum amount of support to the Government and
prevent any behaviour detrimental to Labour's
electoral hopes.

> It is not playing the game to give
> expression of approval to the great
> achievements of your Labour Government
> and then to stop the pit on some paltry
> trivial matter ... if you have political
> views contrary to the Labour Government,
> and you think the sooner they are
> replaced by a ruthless, inhuman Tory
> Government the better, then I suppose
> such 'quisling' actions of unofficial
> stoppages can be understood ... the choice

> is between Labour, representing
> progress ... and the Tories who were
> responsible for the dark, dismal era
> between the two wars.[20]

Unofficial strikes and the collapse of the pay
policy in 1949-1950 were the inevitable product of
the internal tensions created by the vociferous
support of the Labour Government.   However, the
weakening of the members' support of their leaders
did not lead to a major cleavage between the NUM
and the Government; in fact, both leaderships
sought to combat factionalism and unofficial action
in both union and party.
    The miners remained committed to producing
the coal the Government wanted so as to avoid a
political crisis.[21]   A Special Conference of
January 1951 emphasised: "the day there ceases to
be the absolute minimum of coal necessary, that is
the day this Government will fall ..."[22]   The
Government's demand for coal, however, prompted the
NUM to seek and justify large pay increases on the
grounds of attracting labour into the pits and so
maintain output.   In this way the NUM was able to
reconcile their support for the Labour Government
with the demands of their members for wage
increases, but the NEC requested the Area Executives
to call special Branch Meetings to explain the
seriousness of the Government's position.[23]   The
mineworkers had heard this old and familiar message
before: coal, or the government will fall, but by
1951 this appeal was wearing very thin and had little
impact.   The miners were grateful to the Government
for nationalisation but were increasingly unwilling
to accept the trade-off accepted by the leaders of
moderate wage demands for the maximum effort.   This
can be seen in the evolution of the miners' attitudes
to incomes policy.

Miners and Pay Policy
The miners and their Union did all they could to
meet the Government's demand for coal.   However, the
burden of such demands on the workforce, coming after
the demands of war, naturally led to unrest and
disquiet.   The NUM was willing to urge its members
to greater and greater efforts but the Government,
" ... must work and strive in the interests of
working people who placed them at the helm to rid the
country of unemployment, poverty and want."[24]
    By 1946 exhortation was having, at best, a
marginal effect upon output, and other inducements,

notably financial, were called for, However, the Government was reluctant to see substantial increases in basic wage rates as this would effect the price of coal and the cost structure of the economy. This was serious as the Labour Government was seeking an export-led recovery and increases in the price of a basic commodity like coal would effect the competitiveness of British exports.

At the 1946 NUM Conference, J R A Machen from Yorkshire argued that fuel shortages were caused by a shortage of labour which could be remedied by an increase in wages. The 1944 Wage Agreement (due to expire in 1948) was a cause of much resentment.

> Our men in Yorkshire are, quite frankly,
> chaffing at the 1944 Agreement,
> particularly where there exists at many
> pits, bad price lists which were
> stabilised at that time ... there is
> a tremendous impetus in many pits to
> smash that and to get higher wages now.[25]

Given the Government's concern over domestic inflation, a major increase in the price of coal to finance increased miners' wages was unacceptable, but the NUM, striving to meet the Government's demand for coal, had to consider how they could satisfy their members' demands for increased rewards. In accepting the responsibility for increasing coal production and supporting the Government's economic policy, the NUM was in effect, trying to secure maximum amount of coal at the cheapest price which suggested the need for moderate pay claims. The relationship between coal production, government economic policy and miners' wages was, therefore, a major political problem.

In July 1947 the NEC met with Attlee and the Cabinet. Herbert Morrison emphasised that economic recovery was dependent upon coal production, and he suggested a thirty minute increase in the working day. This was rejected by the NUM. Ernest Bevin pointed out that the miners' pay had been increased and this had affected the price of coal, and output had not improved. The coal shortage was having an effect on domestic prices and the government did not want increasing inflation which might jeopardise full employment.[26] This is a clear indication that the Labour Cabinet saw a limit to the extent to which the costs of the industry could be born by the Government.

Several resolutions to the 1947 NUM Conference

demanded substantial increases in wages, but no
figures were included giving NEC negotiators the
widest room for manoeuvre.[27]   The NEC found it
difficult to resist demands for such increases as
the unpopular 1944 Wage Agreement was on the point
of ending, and there was a strong case for
increases for the lowest paid.   Unfortunately,
productivity continued to fall, (absenteeism and
unofficial strikes were blamed), and the culprits
were castigated for political disloyalty.[28]   Wage
militancy came to be the major factor in the
internal politics of the Yorkshire Area during 1948.
The branches sent in an increasing number of
resolutions about wages to the Area Executive: the
Dinnington branch demanded a minimum wage of 33/-
per shift, Houghton Main demanded a totally new
wages structure, and Dearne Valley demanded that the
NUM resist any attempt by Government to impose a
wage freeze or other type of incomes policy.[29]

     The demise of the 1944 Agreement was a major
factor in the rise of wage militancy, but another
factor was the endorsement by the General Council of
the TUC of the White Paper on price stabilisation.
The NEC examined the TUC proposals contained in the
document, A Statement on Personal Incomes, Costs and
Prices in February 1948.   At a subsequent NEC
meeting it was decided to accept TUC policy
providing that: first, free collective bargaining
was maintained;   second, productivity deals were
allowed;   third, justice was given to the low paid;
fourth, wages could be increased to attract labour;
and finally, differentials were safeguarded.[30]   A
TUC Conference of Executives held two weeks before
the 1948 Budget approved the TUC-Government pay
policy by 5,421,000 to 2,302,000.   This was
accepted by the NEC.   The unanimity of the NEC was
not matched by the membership, for example, the
Hickleton Main branch bitterly complained about the
level of company profits compared to the level of
food subsidies which the Budget pegged at £410m.[31]

     Within the Yorkshire coalfield conflict over
wages was slowly emerging articulated by an
alternative union structure based on the Area
Panels.   Area 1 Panel, for example, covering the
Rotherham pits was condemned by the Executive for
holding unofficial meetings which were critical of
official policy.   The Branch Secretary at
Brodsworth (Area 2 - Doncaster), G H Huckerby, was
called before the Executive Committee to explain
why he had called an unofficial Panel Meeting which
had been critical of official union policy.[32]   The

threat of an unofficial union structure was taken so
seriously that offenders were warned that they
risked expulsion from the Union.

At the 1948 Annual Conference there was
increased disquiet over pay in the industry.   A
number of delegates argued that piecemeal changes
were of limited value and that there should be a new
wages structure.   The main source of friction,
however, was the NEC's endorsement of the pay policy
in the light of the 1947 conference call for
substantial wage increases.   Discontent was
directed at the NEC and the Government, but as such
was inhibited and had little impact.   This did not
alter the fact that the NEC was caught in a dilemma
between support for Government policy and the
demands of the membership.[33]

The wage restraint that the Unions imposed
upon themselves was remarkable for its general
applicability as union leaders successfully
restrained their members.   This is not to deny that
there was considerable unrest over the pay policy,
but the authority of the leaders held and they,
including those in the NUM, acted as the
administrators of the policy.   The period 1945-
1948 was the period of maximum voluntary restraint
but during 1948-1949 this weakened as the
inevitable reaction began.   The Government was
forced to impose a statutory pay policy, again with
union help.   However, after 1948 union memberships
were unwilling to acquiesce in the pay policy and
union leaderships found themselves subject to
increasing pressure to abandon their support of pay
policy.

In the Autumn of 1948 the NEC received a
letter from the TUC General Council concerning a
meeting of the Special Economic Committee of the
TUC with Government Ministers to consider measures
needed to control inflation and maintain full
employment.   This letter urged all unions to
postpone current wage negotiations until the TUC
was able to issue a further statement on guidelines
for pay negotiations.   The NEC agreed to comply.[34]
This decision marks the beginning of the process
culminating in the breakdown of the NUM's support
for pay restraint.

There had been continuous support for pay
restraint from the official union leaders, but there
had also been significant hostility from the
grass-roots.   Nevertheless, strong traditions of
loyalty to established leadership and to the Labour
Government had secured compliance.   Compliance was

aided by the continued existence of wartime controls
which gave pay restraint the appearance of equity,
but the "Bonfire of Controls" in November 1948 left
only a shadow of price control, whilst pay restraint
remained very much a reality. The appearance of
wage militancy in 1947-1948 (fuelled by discontent
with some elements of nationalisation) forced the
National and Area executives to respond as they
risked losing the support of sections of their
memberships as a result of supporting the Labour
Government and ignoring grass-roots sentiment. The
NUM was subject to those strong internal tensions
which afflict any trade union which chooses to
support a political party at the expense of their
members' immediate demands. The NUM was committed
to making nationalisation a reality, but many miners
were coming to feel that this was at their expense.
The NUM's pursuit of moderate wage demands and
uncritical support for the Government forced the
Union leadership to make a choice: were they a
trade union seeking to defend their members'
interests, or were they an agent of government
policy?
        Support for the pay policy was originally
presented as in the miners' interests; it would
help the Labour Government and it would help
combat inflation, thus maintaining the value of the
miners' wage packet. However, as the policy
continued more and more miners came to feel that
restraint was not in their immediate interests.
The NEC sought to garner the maximum support for the
Government by appealing to the lowest common
political demoninator - opposition to the
Conservative Party - and by seeking wage resolutions
which avoided either specific figures or definite
instructions. In the short term this was
successful, but it was inevitable that the policy
would breakdown as internal opposition mounted.
        In September 1949 the Pound was devalued by
40% and this proved to be the immediate cause of the
breakdown of the pay policy. The TUC drew up
draconian proposals on pay (later modified after
pressure from union executives) and these proposals
were put to the trade unions in December 1949. The
NEC considered the policy (the alternative to which,
it was asserted, was massive deflation and an end to
full employment) which argued that inflation "must
be countered by vigorous restraint upon all
increases of wages, salaries and dividends", but
felt that restraint should be voluntary and "whilst
it is the responsibility of the Unions themselves to

operate the wages policy, Unions nevertheless must pay regard to the realities of the economic situation in framing their policy and act loyally in conformity with the policy". These proposals were discussed at length, and the NEC decided to recommend a Special Conference to accept the TUC policy.[35]

The Special Conference emphasised the voluntary aspect of the policy, that it was self policing and vital for the future of the Labour Government:

> ... whatever may be your decisions, we shall have to face a General Election. Either we stand up to this now, or we allow a breach within our ranks. Make no mistake, the choice is between what the Labour Government and the Trade Union Movement is able to do, or the opening of the floodgates of reaction.[36]

Adoption of the TUC policy would help the electoral prospects of the Labour Government, but to adopt that policy would force the NUM to abandon its present wage claim and risk internal conflict. The NEC resolution in favour of the TUC policy was moved by Arthur Horner who argued that sacrifices by the Unions were in the interests of the working class by helping sustain the Government.[37]

W E Jones, speaking for the Yorkshire Area, argued that the Government was trying to avoid the easy path of deflation and unemployment and prevent the return of a Conservative Government, and as such deserved the miners' support, "Because so much has been done for us..."[38] However, delegate after delegate warned that the miners would not accept pay restraint: J Conway, a delegate from Yorkshire stated,

> Mr Ernest Jones ... has mentioned that it is remarkable how external events have played havoc with the conditions of the workers, but it even more remarkable how the external events of the last four years have entirely failed to play havoc with the profits of the industrialists ... I cannot take (the report) back to Yorkshire

and expect the rank and file to act
upon it ...39

Although opposed to the NEC's report Conway was
forced to support the Yorkshire delegation which
accepted the report and it was approved by 406 to
173.
At the first Area Council Meeting of the New
Year the decision and recommendation of the Special
Conference was put and approved by 82 in favour to
26 against (see Table 1).40   Despite the
recommendation of the NEC, the Special Conference,
and Area Council the Branches voted to reject the
TUC policy proposals, by a majority of 483.
The NEC was therefore forced to oppose TUC policy.
Two other major unions, the NUR and the AEU, were
also opposed to the TUC policy, and their combined
opposition forced the TUC to relax its policy on
pay restraint.41

Table 1: Yorkshire Branch Vote on Wages Policy, 1950

Council Vote:	For	82
	Against	26
Branch Vote:	For	756
	Against	1,239

Source: YA (NUM): 9 January 1950.

On numerous occasions the TUC and individual
trade unions had emphasised that trade union
acquiescence in matters such as pay restraint was
crucial in helping the Labour Government remain in
power.   With the rejection of pay restraint,
however, the NUM did not abandon its political
support for the Labour Government; for example,
the Yorkshire Area began to prepare for the 1950
General Election as early as January 1949.42   In
the local government elections of May 1949 the NEC
issued a manifesto to all Areas urging the Branches
to do all they could in the Labour cause; "Every
miner and his wife ... must leave no stone unturned
to make sure that Labour's opponents, whether Tory
or Communist are defeated".   The elections were
regarded as a preliminary to the General Election in
which "one of our greatest tasks is to assist the
Labour Party to win .. and thus safeguard and
improve our standard of living".43   So, despite all
the disputes over pay, the basic loyalty of the
miners to a Labour Government was unimpaired.

The Costs of Political Support

Between 1945 and 1951 the Yorkshire Area was
motivated by a powerful desire to support the Labour
Government to which the leaders of the NUM felt
they owed a debt of gratitude for the
nationalisation of the mines. Redeeming this
involved a cost: securing the maximum output of
cheap coal meant the Union actively co-operating
with management in production and insisting that the
conciliation machinery be used to the full.
Naturally this gave the impression to many miners
that their Union had 'sold-out', and the result was
unofficial industrial action and internal conflict.
This internal conflict was exacerbated by NUM's
support of government pay policy, which meant
actively restraining what the membership saw as just
and legitimate wage demands. The NUM leaders were
able to restrain these demands in favour of their
political support for the Government until 1950
when they were forced to bow to the inevitable and
acquiesce to the pressure from the membership.
However, even with the collapse of formal pay policy
more informal methods remained in use.[44] In 1951,
for example, the Yorkshire Area Council urged that
"every effort be made to secure the carrying out of
the Wage Agreement", avoiding both unofficial
strikes and absenteeism.[45]

After 1945 coal production became an index of
political loyalty. The Government expected the
NUM to fulfil its obligations to itself and the
nation. The assumption was that, once the pits
were nationalised the miners would devote their
energies to coal production. However, the coal
situation was never as secure as the Government
wished and the miners showed themselves reluctant to
accept the moderation and responsibility of their
leaders in their support for the Government if the
price was to be the restraint of their wages. The
emphasis upon national politics is a reflection of
the political situation in the NUM at the time.
The period marks the most 'national' period in the
history of the NUM up to the late 1960s and early
1970s. The importance of the national perspective
was increased by the existence of a Labour
Government which urged all unions to increase output
and limit wage demands in the national interest.

The NUM's task of restraining national and
local demands was eased by the miner's close
historical relationship with Labour and their
gratitude for nationalisation of the mines. The
national aspect of the union's politics was also

influenced by the Government's commitment to
nationalise the industry and the NUM's concern to do
nothing to endanger nationalisation.   Supporting
the Government led to frustration amongst the
membership which exploded in the decisive rejection
of incomes policy in the ballot of 1949.
Nevertheless the miners wholeheartedly supported
the Labour Party in both the 1950 and 1951
elections, albeit with a subtle change of emphasis;
now the accent was on preserving socialism against
the depredations of a Conservative Government.[46]
The NUM proclaimed the disasters that would follow
the election of a Conservative Government.
Contrary to the prognostications of the NUM the
Conservatives did win in 1951, forcing the NUM to
reconsider its position.   Arthur Horner noted:
"Because we are dealing directly with the NCB, we
are in effect dealing indirectly, and sometimes
directly, with the Government of the day, whatever
its colour may be."[47]

1951-1964:   The Interregnum
Labour's defeat in 1951 posed a dilemma for the
miners;   because of nationalisation they had to
work with any government, but they were now forced
to work with their traditional enemy, the
Conservative Party, from which they expected
little.   The relationship between the miners and
the Government was not eased by the contraction of
the coal industry after 1956-1957.   The NUM tried
to persuade Government to adopt a fuel policy to
guarantee the position of coal and ensure the
future of the industry.   In this they failed.
      The miners were naturally apprehensive at the
return of a Tory Government ,

          If a reactionary Government is successful,
          then many of the improvements in the
          standard of living of the working class
          community brought about in the last six
          years will be affected.[48]

      However, after 1951 there was no confrontation
between the Government and the working class and
the general level of prosperity increased.   In
mining the potential for conflict remained in that
the Government (like its predecessor) pursued a
cheap coal policy as a hidden subsidy to industry
to keep production costs low so as to aid exports.
The inflation of the early 1950s caused both the
NEC and the Yorkshire Area to reiterate their

their determination to maintain the miners' standard of life.[49]

The generally conciliatory policy pursued towards the trade unions by the Government between 1951 and 1955 was accompanied by attempts to control inflation indirectly by fiscal and monetary means. Continued wage inflation and growing economic problems placed this policy in jeopardy. The Government, aware of the problems of 'fine tuning' the economy, increasingly used its authority over state employees to control inflation. As early as 1952 the NUM expressed a belief that the NCB was being prevented from engaging in free collective bargaining by the Government.[50] The rejection of an NUM claim by the National Reference Tribunal (NRT) confirmed government influence in wage bargaining.[51]

The Yorkshire Area leadership followed the moderate lead given at national level despite some discontent at branch level. The policy of the leadership was to channel unrest into politics, and away from industrial action: this opposition being expressed in militant resolutions attacking the Conservative Government. Opposition to the industrial and wage policies of the Conservative Government was linked with political support for the Labour Party.[52] The Yorkshire Area argued that only the election of a Labour Government could safeguard the industry and the miners.

Verbal animosity was not matched by a willingness to use the industrial power of the mineworkers, which the position of coal in the economy seemed to confer, to achieve either a fuel policy or satisfactory wages and conditions. For example,

> The Union did not want to talk "power-politics" but they thought it as well to make it clear that the Executive knew well enough the strength of the mineworkers which if exercised could do great damage. They looked to the Board to make possible the continuance of the avoidance of power politics by the Executive Committee.[53]

And

> The Union was well aware that the use of its industrial power might very well result in serious consequences

for the Nation as a whole and it was
essential that the negotiating
machinery worked efficiently.[54]

Up to 1956-1957 the dependence of industry on
coal gave the NUM enormous potential industrial power;
but after 1956-1957 the substitution of other fuels
for coal (and the concomitant decline of the
industry) caused this to evaporate. Consequently,
the NUM was compelled to rely upon the conciliation
machinery, direct contact and negotiation with
Government, and ultimately, the re-election of a
majority Labour Government. The Yorkshire Area
Council passed a long resolution in January 1957,
attacking Government policy over Suez, economic
policy, and rents which concluded by demanding an
immediate General Election.[55] The resolution was
designed to gather the maximum degree of support
from all shades of political opinion within the
Area, and so avoid any internal political cleavages.
The Union had committed itself to abiding by the
'rules of the game', hence the importance of
rhetoric as symbolic conflict. The Area Council
and the official leadership were attempting to draw
a clear distinction between industrial and
political activity. This distinction could be
encapsulated in Council resolutions ferociously
attacking the Conservative Government's policies,
whilst calling on the Labour Party "to organise a
campaign throughout the Country with the aim of
clearing out this dangerous Government".[56] The
problem was to maintain internal unity by attacking
the Government, whilst maintaining contact with
the Government in an attempt to influence policy.
The immediate economic and political aims of
the NUM were invalidated by its manifest inability
to influence the Government. The Yorkshire Area
and the NUM relied on the joint conciliation
machinery to maintain a facade of influence with
the NCB and the Government despite the all too
visible decline of the industry. However, whilst
the NUM tried to obtain the best possible wages and
conditions for their members, it was convinced that
the only long term solution for the industry and
their members was the election of a majority Labour
Government committed to a planned economy
encompassing an integrated fuel policy. The Area
Council, thus,

> ... call(ed) upon every member of this
> Union, along with their wives and
> families, to start an immediate campaign
> on behalf of the Labour Party to ensure
> that ... the Labour Party will achieve
> a huge majority (in the General Election).[57]

The "huge majority" was the sine qua non of
the NUM's strategy and the panacea for the ills not
only of mining, but also of the United Kingdom.
The defeat of the Labour Party in the General
Election of 1955 was a major set-back to this
policy.   As a result of the inability of the NUM to
influence the Conservative Government, and the
electoral failure of the Party in 1955 and then
1959, the NUM was reduced to ineffectual posturings
demanding the resignation of an impregnable
Conservative Government and the immediate adoption
of a fuel policy.[58]   In the context of a safe
Conservative Government and a working class which
refused to be mobilised in the Labour Party's
interest, the NUM was reduced to pointing to the
long-term prospect of some future Labour Government.
The reaction of the Yorkshire Area to the
problems facing the industry after 1956-1957 was to
sponsor a resolution to the 1958 NUM Annual
Conference seeking the amendment of clause ix of the
conciliation agreement.   Clause ix stipulated
that any deadlocked pay claim had to be submitted to
the NRT for a judgement, thus ruling out industrial
action.   Sam Bullough, the Area Vice-President,
moved the resolution to the Annual Conference, not
on the grounds that it would lead to a flowering of
industrial militancy but on the grounds that it
would enhance the ability of the NEC to bargain with
the NCB.[59]   Bullough argued that the NUM had
deprived itself of a basic trade union right - the
right to strike - and this self-denying ordinance
had unnecessarily limited the ability of the NUM to
defend its members' interests vis-a-vis the NCB,
and by implication with the Government.   Bullough
emphasised that the resolution was the product of a
deep seated feeling amongst the Yorkshire branches,
claiming that the branches believed the conciliation
and negotiation machinery was fraudulent because of
Government interference.   Bargaining was not
between equals and so, the balance had to be
redressed, by providing the possibility of strike
action.   This resolution was passed by Conference,
but the NEC ignored it as being impractical.
The Annual Council Meeting of the Yorkshire

Area of March 1958 was one of the most vociferous of the post-war period. Machen, the Area President, used the opportunity to deliver a vitriolic attack on the Conservative Government.

> It is a tribute to the power and
> application of the Trade Union and the
> Labour Movement that it has taken the
> Tories nearly seven years of constant
> endeavour to end full employment.
> Ever since they got back to power in
> 1951, the need for at least a million
> unemployed has been emphasised by the
> reactionaries as a means of disciplining
> the workers, and consequently keeping a
> high rate of profit.[60]

The address contained a number of references to the 1920s and 1930s, with all the powerful symbolism and emotion this period held for the miner. Emphasis was laid on the common factor of Conservative Governments and the argument that, " More than anything else we need a powerful Labour Government ..."[61] The key note of Machen's address was, significantly, unity in both Union and Party. Machen sought to unite the Yorkshire Area to avoid unofficial industrial action and to deploy the united strength of the mineworkers behind the Labour Party. Collective bargaining in the 1950s forced the Yorkshire Area, and the NUM, to accept that industrial and political questions were interlinked, but they went further: industrial problems could only be solved by political action, meaning the election of a Labour Government. Nevertheless, the Yorkshire Area was unwilling to abandon the joint procedures created by nationalisation despite government interference. Council passed a resolution of 'no confidence' in the-NRT as it "has been unduly influenced by Tory Government policy", but did not take the logical step of urging withdrawal.[62]

After 1957-1958 the NUM sought to persuade the Government to adopt a fuel policy: they failed. The NUM was impotent and totally dependent upon the election of a Labour Government.[63] Perhaps if an assault had been made on miners' wages the NUM might have reacted more militantly, but it was the productive capacity of the industry, not wages that were attacked. Capacity was very difficult to defend by strike action, particularly when the overall market for coal was contracting. Also the policy of the NUM had been to avoid industrial action at all costs; therefore, the only solution was political. There was,

> ... (a) great need for a Labour
> Government ...(as) modern society
> must be planned if it is to secure
> the interests of the majority of
> the people. We must end as quickly
> as possible this Tory foolishness ...
> At the present time we struggle like
> a boxer with one arm tied behind him.
> We must get the political arm of our
> movement free and powerful enough to
> strike blows against reaction, and
> with Labour as the Government of
> Britain to legislate socialist
> solutions to our problems ...[64]

Accepting that the NUM, as a trade union, was unable to influence Government policy in any significant way logically entailed seeking a political solution. The Area Executive recommended the branches to approve a grant of £1,000 to the Yorkshire Regional Council of Labour for use in marginal constituencies, and the membership of the Yorkshire Area were called upon to give all possible help to the Party in the 1959 General Election.[65] After Labour's defeat in 1959 the Yorkshire Area and the NUM abandoned any attempt to persuade the Government to adopt a fuel policy and re-directed its efforts,

> ...(we) are now proceeding to place
> (the fuel policy) before the TUC and
> the Labour Party in order to secure a
> fully agreed and co-ordinated policy
> on which to fight on the floor of the
> House of Commons, and, I hope, keep
> the Tories up in all-night sessions.[66]

The policy of the NUM was now reduced to making the Conservative Government and backbench physically tired. Industrial action was out of the question because of the decline of the industry, thus, the NUM placed emphasis upon political activity and upon trying "to soften the effects of this onslaught upon us".[67]

A Special Conference of 9 December 1960 marks the beginning of the process to secure a fuel policy

from a future Labour Government.   The recession in
mining continued and this crisis "exists solely as
a consequence of political impositions upon this
industry as a result of Government policy".68
This Conference committed the NUM to securing a
coal industry of 200m ton capacity by 1965,

> ... We have reason to be confident.
> We have secured the backing of the
> organised Labour and Trade Union
> Movement for the policy ... We now
> have to find the ways and means, not
> only at national level, but in the
> Areas and at Branch level also, of
> embracing all sections of the
> organised Labour and Trade Union
> Movement into activity with us, to
> retain this industry as the vital
> base of the economy ...69

The miners entered the 1960s in a deep crisis but
with a policy they believed would solve that
crisis.70   Thus, "our only hope of Government
assistance lies in the return of a Labour
Government" pledged to adopt a fuel policy.71   The
strategy of the NUM was to "...concentrate on
convincing the British electorate that the Labour
Party offers the only responsible and real
alternative to the already discredited and decrepit
Tory Government".72   Sam Bullough, the Yorkshire
Area President, noted, "We still have great
difficulty with the present Government ...   We must
all of us unite our efforts and be prepared when
the time comes to replace it by a Labour
Government."73   Thus, tremendous hope was invested
in the election of a Labour Government by the miners.

Internal Factionalism

During the 1940s and 1950s the miners formed the
core of the right-wing official support for the
policies of the Labour Party leadership, first
under Attlee and subsequently under Gaitskell.
Support for Gaitskell and the Revisionist wing of
the Labour Party was the product of the NUM's
long historical commitment to supporting the Party
and as part of the strategy to secure the election
of a majority Labour Government.   A majority
Labour Government could only be achieved by a
Labour Movement composed of a united Party and
united trade unions.   Pointing to 1945-1951
(albeit with a degree of selectivity) the NUM

emphasised the gains made by the Movement, secured
partly as a result of unity not only between the
Party and unions, but unity within Party and
unions.

Not surprisingly, electoral considerations
exercised a dominant influence over the leadership
of the NUM at all levels.   Internal political
conflict, in Party or Union, was detrimental to the
Labour Party.   First, it damaged the image of the
Party in the eyes of the electorate, implying that
the Party was not fit to govern.   Second, such
conflict ran counter to the belief of union leaders
in flexible, practical politics in that it sought
to place an ideological straitjacket on the Party.
Ironically, this stricture could also apply to
Gaitskell and his supporters in the struggle for
Clause 4.   The cumulative effect of factionalism
was that it restricted the electoral attractiveness
of the Party and weakened internal cohesion and
commitment;   on these grounds it was condemned by
the loyalist trade union leaders.[74]   The President
of the Yorkshire Area was in no doubt as to the
detrimental effects of factionalism: ascribing the
defeat of the Labour Party in 1955 to internal
party squabbles,

> It seems to me beyond question that
> thousands of workers and their wives
> did not vote for the Labour Party ...
> because they were alienated by the
> dissensions and divisions revealed in
> the speeches, writings and discussions
> of those who disregarded majority
> decisions, and on occasion attacked the
> Party's official policy and showed
> hostility to the leadership.   In the
> election campaign there was not one
> voice speaking for Labour, but many
> voices.[75]

The 1950s are conventionally described as the
classic period of factionalism in the Labour Party,
of Bevanism versus Revisionism, with these factions
offering different interpretations on the future
evolution of the Party.   Before 1955 these
interpretations and resulting disputes were largely
concerned with defence and foreign policy.[76]
Bevanism was an assemblage of inchoate elements
which placed a different emphasis upon party policy
to that of the leadership and cannot be regarded
as an attempt to restructure the Party in the same

sense as Gaitskell's attack on Clause 4. The Benavites were not a major organised force inside the trade unions, but the sentiments represented by Bevanism were important and Bevan was vital as a symbol.[77]

In June 1954, for example, Council voted to support Gaitskell for Party Treasurer in preference to Bevan by 71 votes to 28.[78] These 28 votes indicate a fairly considerable body of support for Bevan amongst the Branches. The main problem which faced Bevanism in the Yorkshire Area was not so much what it advocated, but the support it attracted from Communists and other left-wingers. Once a policy was identified as having substantial 'Communist' support it was immediately discredited in the eyes of the Area leadership as the Communists, often a vague and ill-defined group, were perceived as being totally opposed to the social democracy of the Labour Party and to legitimate authority in both Union and Party.

The effect of, and response to, Party factionalism can be seen in the 1955 General Election which took place in a period on in-fighting. Traditionally, general elections were used by the Yorkshire Area to promote internal political unity under the banner of electing a Labour Government. Thus, Council called "upon all our members to loyally and faithfully express their solidarity and support for the Labour Party programme and candidates".[79] Concurrently, Council was expressing concern at Communist influence within the Yorkshire Area, going so far as to examine the political allegiance of J T E Collins, the Area Compensation Agent. As a result of this enquiry Collins issued a statement in which he emphasised that he "was willing to conform at all times to the Constitution, programme, principles and policy of the Labour Party - of which he is an individual member ..." Collins also stated he owed no allegiance to the Communist Party.[80] This enquiry was the result of a letter from J T Anson (Secretary of the Yorkshire Regional Council of Labour) warning the NUM that any Labour Party member who attended a Daily Worker sponsored conference in September 1955 entitled, 'Labour - What Next?', would be in breach of the Party Constitution. Collins had attended.

Another example more closely related to the mineworkers' relationship with the Labour Party occurred at Thorne. The Thorne NUM branch enjoyed a reputation for political and industrial militancy, which appeared to be confirmed when the branch arranged a meeting at which Bevan was the guest speaker. The meeting was to be open to members of the NUM and the general public.[81] This was akin to waving a red rag before a bull and the Executive reacted angrily, referring the matter to Council.[82] In Council there was strong criticism of Thorne's actions but after hearing a recording of Bevan's speech, which had been made for educational purposes, Council decided that there were no grounds for proceeding against the branch.[83] Thorne escaped the wrath of the Council as it held the meeting in a private capacity and not as the Thorne NUM branch.

Although the Yorkshire Area was subject to the vicissitudes of Party factionalism, the Area and the NUM as a whole maintained its loyalty to the Labour Party. The NUM continued to emphasise its debt of gratitude to the Party for the nationalisation of the mines,

> The mineworkers know from experience
> that only a Labour Government can be
> expected to carry on the great work
> of social reform in our industry, and
> that this job cannot be entrusted to
> the Tories, the traditional enemies of
> the workers.[84]

The leadership of the NUM at Area and National level used political rhetoric as a means of channelling and controlling internal conflict and the lowest common denominator of this rhetoric was the election of a Labour Government.[85] Militant political rhetoric combined with moderate industrial postures was an attempt to encompass the maximum area of support within the union. Formal political opposition was based on the miners' traditional hostility to any Conservative Government , "The Tories, politically powerful, are leading the attacks on wage standards, on social services, and pressing forward with the iniquitous Rent Act ..."[86] The long-term hope of the NUM lay with the election of a Labour Government.

Nuclear Disarmament, 1958-1961
During the 1950s the NUM consistently supported the Party leadership on foreign and defence policy. This support for the Party leadership was produced as a result of the complex interplay of internal union politics based on the federal structure of the

NUM. In terms of internal Union politics the
Yorkshire Area was predominantly right-wing but
there was a significant left-wing minority. This
minority was not capable of changing Area policy
to oppose the policies of the Party leadership but
it was capable of vociferous opposition to Union
and Party policy.

As early as 1956 Wharncliffe Woodmoor 'A'
sent a resolution to Area Council for possible
adoption by the Area and inclusion in the 1956
Annual Conference agenda urging the NUM to call for
a four power summit to discuss the banning of
nuclear weapons and nuclear tests.[87] This
resolution attracted some discussion in Council but
it was decided not to adopt the resolution by 17 to
95.[88] This was repeated in 1957. The Armthorpe
branch submitted a resolution calling for the
Government to support international efforts to
abolish nuclear weapons and secure the
international control of disarmament. Wharncliffe
Woodmoor 'A' sponsored a similar multilateralist
resolution. Neither was accepted as Area
resolutions to the Annual Conference.[89] At the
Annual Demonstration of the Yorkshire Area a
resolution was passed supporting multilateral
disarmament. Council took the unusual step of
going on record to approve all the resolutions
passed and "particularly (Council) records its
support for banning by all Governments of Hydrogen
and Atom Bombs".[90] In December 1957 Council
officially endorsed Party policy, passing a
resolution endorsing a Labour Party protest at
American military aircraft carrying atomic weapons
over the UK. Council called upon the Government to
take the initiative in calling a summit of world
leaders to end all nuclear tests and begin
disarmament.[91]

In 1958 a resolution on multilateral nuclear
disarmament was adopted by the Yorkshire Area for
inclusion in the Annual Conference agenda. This
long resolution entitled Labour Party and World
Situation (sic) covered three areas: first, seeking
to mobilise the NUM in the interests of the Labour
Party in the forthcoming General Election; second,
support for Party policy on nuclear weapons and
opposition to the importation of missiles and
aircraft carrying nuclear weapons over the UK: and
finally, asserting that "world tension can only be
eased if countries adhere to the principles laid
down in the United Nations Charter, and (we urge)
all Governments of the world to make progress in

this direction."[92]   There were three other similar
resolutions: South Wales demanded the withdrawal
of all US nuclear weapons from the UK and the
cancelation of any agreements between the British
and American governments; the Kent Area announced
its complete opposition to any nuclear missile
sites; and Scotland supported a summit to ease
world tension, begin disarmament and end nuclear
tests.[93]   The decisions of the 1958 NUM Conference
demonstrate how a broad consensus was achieved by
adroit compositing: the right-wing were satisfied
by the formal acceptance of Labour Party policy in
the composite; and the left were satisfied by the
forthright condemnation of nuclear weapons in
general and US weapons in particular.[94]
     This unity was endangered at the 1959
Conference by a resolution from Derbyshire calling
for the unilateral renunciation of nuclear weapons
by the Labour Party. A Scottish amendment asked
for the deletion of the call for unilateral
disarmament in favour of the unilateral suspension
of nuclear tests as a step towards the international
agreement on disarmament.[95]   The resolution was
moved and seconded by Derbyshire and South Wales,
both of whom supported unilateralism.[96]
     Abe Moffat, from Scotland, in moving the
amendment urged Conference to support Party policy
as approved at the Scarborough Conference.[97]
Moffat was supported by Yorkshire. Yorkshire
denied that the amendment meant the rejection of the
principle of unilateralism but stressed that the
immediate and overriding task was to end nuclear
tests.[98]   The NEC urged Conference to reject the
Derbyshire resolution and adopt the amended
resolution. This was approved on a show of hands.
This resolution was accepted by the NEC "as
guidance of the Union's delegations to the Trades
Unions Annual Conference and Labour Party Annual
Conference".[99]   The Brierley and Armthorpe branches
proposed in Council that NUM should support the
unilateralists but this was rejected. Council
"having considered a proposal that we should support
the policy of the TGWU, hereby resolves that the
Union shall support the Labour Party Document -
'The Next Step'."[100]   This was approved by 69 votes
to33. The vote of 33 in Council in support of
unilateralism represents a considerably body of
opposition to Party and NUM policy.
     The Yorkshire Area's adherence to multi-
lateralism and Party policy was threatened by the
rumours that West Germany was to be armed with

nuclear weapons, an issue which united both left
and right. So concerned was Council it refused to
take a decision and the whole matter was referred
to the branches for delegates to be mandated.[101]
At the subsequent Council meeting the delegates, who
were prepared to oppose the rearmament of Germany
with nuclear weapons, were addressed by the
Yorkshire mining MPs who convinced them of the
Party's rejection of such a policy. Council voted
to support Party policy.[102]

At the Annual Conference Derbyshire again
moved a resolution similar to that of 1959 seeking
to commit the Party to unilateralism.[103] This
was supported by South Wales which had withdrawn its
own unilateralist resolution.[104] A major change
in internal politics was Scotland's support for
unilateralism.[105] This major shift in internal
power had a dramatic effect upon the Yorkshire
delegation. Sid Schofield announced Yorkshire's
opposition because "we in Yorkshire are of the
opinion that it is Communist inspired".[106] The
result was uproar. Schofield castigated the
resolution as an attack upon Gaitskell; "I think
that is what they intend to do - to seal the fate
of Mr Gaitskell, or whoever is the Leader of the
Labour Party. They intend to seal the fate of
the Leader, and then the Party."[107] Schofield
argued that if unilateralism became Party policy
the result would be a repeat of the 1959 General
Election. The NEC was opposed to the Derbyshire
resolution as it ran counter to the policy of
1958 and 1959. On a card vote there were 479
votes against the 201 for.[108] NUM policy remained
that of 1958 and 1959 even though the Communists
in the Union abandoned their advocacy of multi-
lateralism. Indeed the change in the Communist
position had the effect of increasing the
determination of the loyalists to resist any attack
upon the Party leadership.

Despite the unilateralist decision of the
1960 Party Conference the Yorkshire Area and the NUM
remained staunchly loyalist. Even so, feeling in
the Area was anti-American and anti-nuclear weapon.
Four resolutions demanded the immediate removal of
all American bases and missiles. These resolutions
were from Rossington, Aldwarke, Woodlesford, and
Bentley. One resolution, from Edlington, supported
this demand and was prefaced by an injunction that
"This Conference instructs MPs who are members of
the National Union of Mineworkers to abide loyally
by the Labour Party Annual Conference

decisions..."[109]   Not surprisingly none of these
resolutions were accepted by Council as an Area
resolution to Conference.[110]
    The sentiments expressed by the Edlington
branch were represented at the Conference by
Resolution 27 from South Wales which sought to place
the weight of the NUM behind the 1960 Party
Conference decision.   The South Wales resolution
was supported by Scotland.[111]   Sid Schofield spoke
in opposition to the Resolution on the grounds
that unity was essential.   This resolution and the
1960 Party resolution on unilateral disarmament was
interpreted as an attack on Gaitskell and the
Party.

> Confined in that resolution there is an
> attack upon Hugh Gaitskell, as there
> has been ever since he said that he
> would fight, fight and fight again,
> and in my opinion, my friends, I
> think that Hugh Gaitskell is the
> finest leader of this Labour Party
> we have had over a great number of
> years.[112]

Again the unilateralist resolution was defeated, by
417 to 199.

Clause 4
If the left was unable to deflect the NUM from its
loyalist stance over nuclear weapons it was far
more successful over Clause 4, though even on
nationalisation there were powerful inhibitions
against opposing the party leadership.   The miners
were, historically, fervent advocates of nationalisation and not surprisingly there was deep
hostility to any threat to the principle of
nationalisation.   The loyalty of the NUM can be
seen in the acceptance of the Revisionist policy
statement , Industry and Society (1957) but once
Revisionism took on more concrete ideological shape
(the attempt to remove Clause 4), the NUM
reluctantly opposed Gaitskell.
    In response to the rising tide of Revisionism
in the Party the Wombwell Main branch moved that the
Yorkshire Area amend Scotland's Resolution 25 at
the 1958 Conference.   This resolution called for
the next Labour Government to "extend
nationalisation to all big industries".   Wombwell's
proposed amendment sought to delete "all the big
industries" and add "to the following Industries

(i) Engineering, (ii) Building, (iii) Insurance.
Such industries should be taken over within the
duration of the next Labour Government". However,
only two delegates supported the amendment.[113] In
the 1958 Conference debates on the Resolution an
amendment suggesting a Labour Government take
measures against any financier or capitalist who
tried to thwart a future Labour Government was
defeated on the recommendation of the NEC by 82 to
53 votes.[114] Rejection was urged on the grounds
that Party and NUM policy rested on Industry and
Society which recommended incremental
nationalisation within a planned economy. The NEC
were concerned that the Party's chances of victory
would be jeopardised by a commitment to an
electorally unpopular programme of nationalisation.[115] A compromise was achieved: continued
support for the principle of nationalisation whilst
accepting the Party leadership's view that future
nationalisation should be on the merits of each
individual case not on ideological grounds.

This compromise was shattered by Gaitskell's
frontal assault on Clause 4. In March 1960 the
Party NEC approved a draft constitution with a
devalued commitment to public ownership, but from
the very beginning the big unions - so vital in
securing any victory for Revisionism - were
unwilling to give their support. Only USDAW and
the GMWU accepted the draft. The NEC decided
that it would take a decision on the draft and
then present this decision to Conference.[116] At
a subsequent meeting the NEC decided that it could
take no policy decision until after the NUM
conference had pronounced on Resolutions 30 and 31
which dealt with Clause 4. Further consideration
was therefore deferred "on the understanding that
any decisions taken on Resolutions 30 and 31 did
not commit the Union so far as its policy on the
Labour Party's Statement was concerned".[117]

If the NEC 'trimmed' on its reaction to the
draft and the amendment of Clause 4 the Yorkshire
branches were certain of their reaction. The
Bentley branch proposed "that Clause 4 ... remains
with the Constitution", similarly Askern urged,
"That this Conference repudiates the suggestion of
certain elements inside the Labour Party to remove
Clause 4 ... from the Labour Party Constitution and
reaffirms its belief in Socialist Nationalisation
of British basic industries." Edlington called,
"... upon this Conference ... to demand and campaign
for full support of Clause 4 of the Labour Party

Constitution...".   These were supported by the
Manton, Thurcroft, and Monk Bretton branches.   So
strong was the feeling amongst the branches one of
the Area's resolutions to Annual Conference was an
amalgam of the Rossington and Brierley resolutions,

> This Conference of the (NUM); arising
> from our own experience in connection
> with Nationalisation of the Mining
> Industry and our demand for the
> extension of Nationalisation in respect
> of the distribution of coal, reaffirms
> its belief in the common ownership of
> the means of production, distribution
> and exchange as set out in Clause 4 of
> the objects of the Labour Party
> Constitution.[118]

The first resolution on Clause 4 debated at
Conference was Kent's Resolution 30.   The NEC
opposed the last ten words ("that only a Socialist
Society can guarantee peace and prosperity") as
being "impracticable and impossible to implement".[119]
The NEC sought to maintain a facade of Union
support for the Party leadership by restating the
views of Industry and Society and giving the Party
leaders the maximum room for manoeuvre.   In
response to demands for a card vote, however, the
Kent resolution was passed by 354 to 326.
Resolution 31 from Yorkshire did not contain
any specific extension of nationalisation (except
for the distribution of coal) but it did reaffirm
the commitment to the principle and value of
nationalisation.   Frank Collindridge, who moved
the resolution, was adamant that "the wording
of Clause 4 cannot be altered or watered down, for
it would change the whole philosophy of the
Constitution".[120]   Clause 4 was identified as the
core of the Movement and to remove it would remove
the motivating spirit from the Labour Party.
Collindridge was supported by South Wales.
Yorkshire's resolution was passed unanimously.[121]
The opposition of unions like the NUM was decisive
in defeating the attack of the Revisionists on
Clause 4, but the philosophy of Revisionism was
not challenged by the NUM.

Loyalty: Investment for the Future
On two contentious issues the Area and the
National Union leaderships were able to maintain
NUM support for the Party leadership.   On nuclear

41

disarmament this was relatively easy as the unilateralists could be conveniently branded as Communists and schmismatics. Clause 4 was more difficult as the attack came from Gaitskell, but nowhere can one find a remark from the Yorkshire leadership critical of Gaitskell. Area leaders did feel that Gaitskell was mistaken and that Clause 4 was not important enough to risk splitting the Party and endangering the electoral prospects of the Party. During this period the policy of the Yorkshire Area was to have a united Party capable of winning a general election as a Labour Government was essential to protect the coal industry from the massive closure of pits by instituting a national fuel policy as part of a planned economy. Throughout the 1950s it is clear that the relationship between the Party and NUM was one of loyalty with the miners committed totally to the return of a Labour Government: "That is what we hope for, that is what we strive for".[122]

The Yorkshire Area's support for the Labour Party went beyond the ideological support of the Party Leadership and defending it from attack. The Executive Committee sponsored a grant of £1,000 to the YRCL and resolved "that we ask the Labour Party to ensure that the money is used in those marginal and rural areas in Yorkshire which can be so valuably won ... to the cause of Labour".[123]

After the third successive defeat of the Party in the 1959 General Election and in a situation where the Party was subject to severe internal strains Council held a long discussion on the means by which the unions could strengthen their links with the Labour Party. The first recommendation was to urge branch members to join the Party as individual members, by foregoing one branch fee per annum to the Party to pay their subscription. This was prompted by a letter from the Lofthouse branch urging greater participation in the Party by the miners. The letter pointed out that the Lofthouse branch committee enjoyed 100% Party membership and argued that any person elected to the branch ought to join the Party. The Executive agreed that a circular be sent to all the branches in the hope that this would encourage "a more keen, active and loyal participation within the Labour Movement". Council also felt that increased participation was essential as "miners were very badly represented on local authorities and ... on many matters such as the Clean Air Act, Education, Housing, Hospitals, etc., were not represented".

In response to the internal problems of the Party, Council called for "less public controversy by leading characters of the movement".[124]

The Union's concern at securing a more effective Labour Party continued into the 1960s. A Party NEC sub-committee planning the next General Election campaign felt that the unions had helped but concern was expressed "about the minor role played by some trade union branches in the affairs of some constituency parties". This was raised with the CLPs as they were regarded as having the major responsibility for recruiting union branches but the Labour Party did point out that unions could do a great deal to encourage their branches to affiliate and their members to participate.[125] Both the Party and the NUM sought the highest possible participation and commitment from the mineworker, the NUM responded by urging all its members to give the maximum help to the Party.[126] The Yorkshire Area felt that the miners had a major role to play in securing the return of a Labour Government.[127]

The NUM's response to the run-down of their industry was to invest tremendous hope on the election of a Labour Government. The NUM consistently urged that the future of the miners could be guaranteed by a Labour Government committed to a planned economy and a national fuel policy. The NUM was convinced that its steadfast loyalty to the Party would guarantee a 200m ton industry.[128] In this they were to be disappointed.

REFERENCES

1   NUM (EC): 28 April 1945
2   NUM: General Election Manifesto, 1945
3   NUM: Annual Conference Report, 1945; p17 and
        p21
4   YMWA; 11 June 1945
5   NUM: Special Conference Report, 10-12 October
        1945; p14
6   YMWA; 6 September 1945
7   As Circular 50/45 (31 August 1945)
8   See: Letter from Emmanuel Shinwell to all NUM
        Branch Secretaries, August 1945; and
     YMWA; 28 August 1945
9   YA (NUM); 7 May and 10 May 1946
     The YMWA became the Yorkshire Area (NUM) on
        1 January 1946
10 NUM (EC); 12 August 1947

11   NUM: Annual Conference Report, 1947; pp13-14
12   Annual Conference: p13
13   Annual Conference; p142
14   Annual Conference; p146
15   YA (NUM); Report of the Annual Demonstration,
         21 June 1947; p4
16   Report; p31 and p36
17   YA (NUM); 14 September 1948
18   NUM; Annual Conference Report, 1950; pp17-18
19   Annual Conference; pp17-18
20   NUM; Annual Conference Report, 1949; p20
21   NUM (EC); 3 January 1951
22   NUM: Special Conference Report, 17 January
         1951; p9
23   BS Circular 66/50 (20 December 1950); and
         YA (NUM): 19 January 1951
24   NUM (EC); 13 February 1946
25   NUM: Annual Conference Report, 1946; p59
         See also:
         NUM (EC): 18 March and 2 April, 1945
         (Appendix)
26   NUM (EC); 8 August 1947 (Report of a Meeting
         with the Cabinet)
27   NUM: Annual Conference Report, 1947; p181
28   BS Circular 11/48 (9 February 1948)
29   YA (NUM); Branch Resolutions for Annual
         Conference (Full List); March 1948
30   NUM (EC); 11-12 February; and
         20 February 1948
31   YA (NUM): 26 July 1948
32   YA (NUM): 22 March, 30 August 1948; and,
         BS Circular 6/48 (18 February 1948)
33   NUM: Annual Report of the NEC, May 1949;
         p201
34   NUM (EC); 16 November 1948
35   NUM (EC): 28 December 1949
36   NUM: Special Conference Report,
         29 December 1949; p10
37   Special Conference; pp19-22, For Horner's
         justifications of the policy
38   Special Conference; p22
39   Special Conference; p32
40   YA (NUM); 3 January 1950
41   NUM (EC); 11 January 1950
42   YA (NUM); 22 January 1949 (Finance Committee).
         On the 28 February, £1,200 was allocated
         for distribution amongst nine CLPs in the
         Yorkshire coalfield
43   YA (NUM): 21 March 1949
44   BS Circular 5/51 (2 January 1951)

45   YA (NUM);   19 March, 9 April, and 23 April
          1951
      The quote is from the 19 March
46   NUM: General Election Manifesto, 1951
47   NUM: Special Conference Report, 7 December
          1951;   p4
48   YA (NUM);   27 September 1951
49   AS Circular 58/52 (14 March 1952);   and
      YA (NUM):   22 March 1952
50   JNNC;   22 July 1952
51   National Reference Tribunal (NRT);
          30 October 1952;   and,
      JNNC;   30 October 1952
52   YA (NUM);   President's Address to Council,
          13 December 1953
53   NUM (EC);   7 January 1954
54   NUM (EC);   10 November 1955
55   YA (NUM);   27 January 1957
56   YA (NUM);   27 January 1957
57   YA (NUM);   3 March 1958
58   For example: NUM: Special Conference Report,
          11 April 1958, p3-4
59   NUM: Annual Conference Report 1958;
          pp132-133
60   YA (NUM);   22 March 1958 (Presidents' Address
          to Council)
61   President's Address
62   YA (NUM); 2-3 June 1958
63   As Circular 53/59 (27 February 1959)
64   The Yorkshire Miner, No 1 (May 1959).
          Publication was discontinued after the
          second issue
65   YA (NUM); 23 September 1959
66   J R A Machen in response to the NCB's Plan for
          1960, in
      YA (NUM):   7 December 1959
67   YA (NUM);   Annual Reports (General Secretary's
          Report for 1959);   p5
68   NUM: Special Conference Report, 9 December
          1960;   p8 (my emphasis)
69   Special Conference;   p13
70   See for example: NUM (EC);   Report of a
          Meeting with the Cabinet;   9 February 1961;
          and
      Report of the NEC (May 1961); especially p4
71   NUM: Annual Conference Report, 1962
          President's Address);   p126
72   President's Address;   p131
73   YA (NUM);   22-24 March 1962 (President's
          Address to Council)

74   S Haseler, The Gaitskellites (London,
        Macmillan 1969);   pp29-31
75   YA (NUM); Annual Reports, 1955; p22
76   See: D Howell,British Social Democracy
        (London, Croom Helm 1976); pp186-190
77   YA (NUM): 10 April 1954, for example
78   YA (NUM); 28 June 1954
     Two years later the Area agreed to support
        Bevin for Party Treasurer see: YA (NUM);
        27 February 1956
79   YA (NUM); 23 May 1955
     Council also donated £200 to the Regional
        Council of Labour for use in marginal seats
80   YA (NUM); 22 October 1955
     Collins had been a member of the CPGB at the
        time of its formation. He left soon after
        "but I had told them that they'd no need
        to worry: they could always rely on me
        supporting anything that was in the workers'
        interests", in,
     J MacFarlane, 'J T E Collins - Socialist and
        Miners' Leader' in Bull Soc Study of Labour
        History 26 (1973); p46
     Collins lost a parliamentary nomination because
        of his support of the Peace Movement,
        a CP front organisation
81   Minute book of the Thorne NUM Branch (June 1954
        - March 1955); 7 March 1955. Bevin also
        spoke at Hull, Doncaster and Sheffield
82   YA (NUM): 7 March 1955
83   YA (NUM): 22 March 1955
84   NUM (EC); Annual Report, May 1955; p15
85   See for example: YA (NUM); 22 January 1957
86   YA (NUM); President's Address; 26 March 1955
87   YA (NUM); 18 February 1956
88   YA (NUM); 27 February 1956
89   YA (NUM); 11 February 1957
90   YA (NUM); 25-26 June 1957
91   YA (NUM); 23 December 1957
92   YA (NUM); 3 March 1958. See also:
     President's Address to Council, 26 March 1958,
        which restated the Area's support for
        Party policy
93   NUM: Annual Conference Agenda, 1958;
        Resolutions 29, 30 and 31
94   NUM: Annual Conference Report 1958; pp213-215
95   NUM: Annual Conference Agenda. 1959; pxiv
96   NUM: Annual Conference Report 1955; pp269-
        279
97   Annual Conference: pp273-274
98   Annual Conference; pp274-275

99 NUM (EC);   20 August 1959.   My emphasis
100 YA (NUM):   31 August 1959;   and,
     BS Circular 71/59 (5 September 1959)
101 YA (NUM);   25 January 1960
102 YA (NUM);   29 February 1960
103 NUM: Annual Conference Report 1960;
        pp291-293
104 Annual Conference;   pp293-294
105 Annual Conference;   pp295-296
106 Annual Conference;   p296
107 Annual Conference;   p297
108 Annual Conference;   p306
109 BS Circular 9/61 (2 February 1961)
110 YA (NUM);   27 February 1961
111 NUM: Annual Conference Report 1961;   pp304-
        306
112 Annual Conference: p311
113 YA (NUM);   21 April 1958
114 NUM: Annual Conference Report 1958;   pp151-
        158
115 Annual Conference;   pp157-158
116 NUM (EC);   13 April 1960
117 NUM (EC);   1 July 1960
118 BS Circular 17/60 (18 February 1960P;   and
     NUM: Annual Conference Agenda, 1960;   pxliv
        (Resolution 31)
119 NUM: Annual Conference Report 1960;   p197
120 Annual Conference;   p199
121 Annual Conference;   p200
122 LPCR 1960;   pp203-204
     Speech by B G Goddard, a miner from
        Houghton Main in Yorkshire and secretary-
        agent of Dearne Valley CLP
123 YA (NUM):   22 September 1959
     This was a complete change from the confident
        attitude of the Area in the 1950s.   In
        the General Election, for example, Council
        refused to make grants to non-mining CLPs
        in the area of the coalfield "as it would
        open a very wide door"
     (YA (NUM):   4 February 1950)
124 YA (NUM);   28 September 1960
     BS Circular 84/60 (30 September 1960);   and,
     BS Circular 31/59 (21 April 1959)
     At a Council Meeting in 1958 the Darfield and
        Lofthouse branches had urged that the NUM
        take a major role in a Labour Party
        recruiting drive
     (YA (NUM):   17 February 1958)
125 BS Circular 8/63 (11 January 1963)
126 YA (NUM);   18-20 March 1963

127 BS Circular 6/64   (15 January 1964)
128 NUM: Report of the NEC, May 1964;
     Report of the Miners' Parliamentary Group;
        p67, and
     NUM: Annual Conference Report, 1964; p102
        (President's Address)

Chapter Two

THE YORKSHIRE MINERS AND THE LABOUR GOVERNMENT, 1964-1970

The Potential for Conflict

Between 1964 and 1970 the miners' relationship with the Labour Government was dominated by the NUM's desire for a fuel policy as the only guarantee for job security, as well as by incomes policy. The miners' leaders were convinced that a Labour Government would regard the coal industry as a special case, warranting favoured treatment. The problem was that the Government consistently refused to adhere to what the Union regarded as a joint, agreed fuel policy designed to maintain employment in the coal industry. Government sought an efficient, economic coal industry by closing high cost pits and holding down costs, of which the largest was wages. The Labour Government set the basic parameters of coal policy, but the NCB was responsible for implementation, this allowed the Government to claim that it was the NCB which was responsible for closing pits and devastating numerous mining communities.

Many at branch leadership level, rejected the search for a fuel policy arguing that fuel policy was a chimera in the pursuit of which the NUM was actually participating in the rundown of the industry and ignoring their members' immediate economic interests. They sought to defend the immediate interests of the miners, particularly his wages, arguing that if the price of maintaining the coal industry was low wages, then this was too high a price to pay. This entailed opposition to the Labour Government's incomes policy which the NUM had agreed to support.

By the mid-1960s the NUM leadership was 'shell-shocked' by the decline of the industry and their inability to stop that decline. NUM policies had not saved the industry, but there seemed to be no option other than to acquiesce in the run-down of the industry. Wage restraint was an attempt by

The Miners and the Labour Government, 1964-1970

the NUM leadership to 'buy' the maximum
number of jobs and so maintain the level of
union membership by holding down costs in the coal
industry. High wages meant increased costs,
threatening marginal, uneconomic pits and coalfields
causing a fall in mining employment. The National
Power Loading Agreement (NPLA) implemented between
1966 and 1971, was designed partly to keep the NUM
together by slowing the rate of pit closures in
the coalfields of the periphery and the 'Celtic
fringe' by subsidising their wages from those of
the Central Coalfields. It was also intended to
help the NUM to avoid coming into open conflict
with incomes policy as wage rates in the various
coalfields were equalised. Faced with a continued
decline in the industry the Union leadership opted
for a policy of wage restraint for everyone in
the industry. Therefore, the policy of the
planned growth of incomes was attractive to a union
like the NUM in a declining industry, but still
with a substantial role in the economy as it
promised steady improvements in pay as productivity
improved. As the NUM was a committed supporter
of the Labour Government it was unwilling to
challenge incomes policy until forced to do so by
the Union membership. Thus, from 1964 onwards
there built up within the NUM a tremendous fund of
discontent over the policies of both the NUM and the
Labour Government.

The General Election of 1964
The Address of the Area President delivered in
March 1963 devoted more space than usual to politics
reflecting the optimism of the Labour Movement as
the Conservative Government foundered and as a
General Election approached. The Address was
particularly concerned to maintain the political
unity of the Labour Party created by Gaitskell.

> ... in the last two years of his life
> Gaitskell united our Labour Party into
> something like a movement, to the
> greatest stage of unity I ever remember
> ... I hope that our Party members ...
> will preserve and consolidate this
> monument by their actions in the future.
> If this is done, not only will the
> Yorkshire miners benefit, but the
> millions of ordinary working class
> people whose future and destiny is in
> the hands of the Labour Party.

50

The Miners and the Labour Government, 1964-1970

When the General Election was called for October
1964 the miners were, urged to do all they could
to secure the election of a Labour Government as,

> ... increased pit closures, social
> dislocation and unemployment would
> effect all sections of people ...
> where coal mining operates ... (a)
> Labour Government is pledged to
> planned economic growth which means
> a constant growth in energy demand
> which is the best guarantee of security
> for the coal mining industry.[2]

The appeal was more mining oriented than even the
1945 NUM manifesto: the NUM was staking all on
the election of a Labour Government.
   In January 1965 the Yorkshire Area issued a
press statement emphasising the need for
government aid for the miners,

> The few paltry shillings increase our
> men receive from time to time cannot
> be tolerated much longer, their
> loyalties have been stretched almost
> to breaking point and they can see
> that the present fiscal policy under
> which the NCB has to operate spells
> gloom for any hope of realistic wages
> being earned by them. It is therefore
> absolutely necessary that our present
> Government initiates a National Fuel
> Policy as quickly as possible ... before
> it is too late.[3]

   The Yorkshire Area was expecting immediate
succour from the Government, whilst hinting that
the alternative to a fuel policy was wages
militancy. The reference to pay is important as
the TUC and the Labour Government were formulating
an agreed incomes policy between December 1964
(Joint Statement of Intent) and the publication of
a White Paper (Prices and Incomes Policy) on the
8th April 1965. The press statement suggested that
the miners' docility might not be relied upon.
The Yorkshire Area made the Labour Government's
attitude to the coal industry an index of the
miners' loyalty to the Government, an interesting
reversal of the position of 1945-1951 when the
Government made coal output a matter of political
loyalty.

Dissatisfaction with wages can be seen in the wages resolutions submitted by the Branches of the Yorkshire Area for possible inclusion in the Annual Conference agenda of the NUM. Four were concerned with payments for shift-work, two with changes in the system of wage payment, but four were concerned with more substantial wage demands. One expressed opposition to the proposed pay policy; Wharncliffe Woodmoor 'A' proposed, " This Conference opposes any form of Incomes Policy which would imply wage restraint". The Resolution from the Bullcroft Branch implied opposition to pay policy,"(Conference) respectfully urges the (NEC) to procced immediately ... and before the statement of intent on productivity, prices and incomes becomes a reality ... with a demand for a minimum rate of £3-10s-0d per week for all colliery workers." The Hatfield Branch requested an immediate increase of £3 per week for all mineworkers and Rossington sought a levelling up of all wage rates.[4]   None of these resolutions made any reference to any action by the NUM to realise these demands. Wharncliffe Woodmoor, for example, did not suggest how wage restraint might be opposed whilst the 'respectful urging' of the Bullcroft Branch suggests a lack of confidence as a result of the battering the industry had suffered. The interesting part of the Bullcroft resolution was the assumption that the future incomes policy would, in effect, be wage restraint. Thus, whilst there was dissatisfaction over wages in the coalfield, a lack of confidence and feelings of powerlessness meant that these resolutions had no teeth and remained expressions of discontent.

The Miners and Fuel Policy
Immediately Labour took office the NEC sought the implementation of the Party's commitment to the mining industry. At their first meeting with the new Minister of Power, Fred Lee (a Cabinet member), the NUM was disabused of any notion that they would obtain a speedy settlement. The NEC 'won' a vague commitment that coal would remain the basic fuel in the economy but Lee refused absolutely to commit himself a 200m ton industry. Consequently, the NEC decided to continue to press for a full declaration by the Government that it will "honour the pledge given by the Labour Party in Opposition ..."[5] The Government was unwilling to abandon a cheap fuel policy and subsidise massively the coal industry to secure a 200m ton capacity.

Lee had Cabinet support and government policy was
merely that of declaring it was 'pro-coal' as part
of a planned economy.[6]
      The Labour Government, far from entering office
with a clear fuel policy as the NUM believed, was
engaged in <u>formulating</u> a policy and its commitment
to the miners was only one element in the process.
Of the NUM's immediate demands, an end to pit
closures and a write down of the NCB's capital debt,
the second was accepted by the Government but the
Minister informed the NUM that he had no power to
stop individual closures which meant that the
closures would continue.   However, the NEC remained
confident that a fuel policy would soon be
implemented given the support of both TUC and Party
despite the lack of an immediate response.[7]
      Sidney Ford, the NUM President, who was
'plus royaliste que le Roi' in his support of the
Labour Government, expressed the grave
disappointment of the NUM over the inaction of the
Government.   At the same time he emphasised that
the miners understood the Government's difficulties
in solving the nation's economic problems.   Face
was saved by blaming the problems of the government
and the shortcomings of government policy on the
legacy of thirteen years of Tory mis-rule.   Unity
was maintained by the narrowness of Labour's
majority in Parliament and out of a fear of endangering the Labour Government.   The well-being
of the mineworkers was seen as conditional on the
survival of a Labour Government.   In a trade union
with a powerful tradition of loyalty to the Party
there was a willingness to postpone 'sectional'
claims to smooth the path of the Labour Government
in which so much hope had been invested.   Thus,

> We shall make clear where our own interests
> lie ... we have a right to do this.   On
> the other hand, we shall win no support
> ... if the pursuit of our own interests
> reaches a point at which it endangers
> the success of the Government itself.
> There can be no rocking the boat ...
> there will be no forgiveness for any-
> one ... who willingly helps to bring
> the Government down.   We shall sometimes
> have to subordinate our own interests to
> those of the great majority.[8]

In his address to the NUM Conference, Fred Lee, the
Minister of Power, assured the delegates that, "coal

has a future, there is no occasion for alarm and
despondency about this industry, but efficiency,
costs, and the resulting prices are absolutely
paramount."[9]
     Coal would remain but as a smaller industry:
uneconomic pits, not just exhausted pits, would be
closed and the remainder would be modernised and
then employ fewer miners.   The Labour Government
was to continue the strategy of the previous
Conservative Government.   Lee emphasised that the
1965 Coal Industry Act and the cancellation of
£415m of £960m of the NCB's capital debt were both
designed to create a modern and efficient industry,
denying this was a prelude to reducing the industry
to a capacity of 170-180m tons.[10]
     Lee's speech did little to dampen the
suspicions of some delegates that the Government was
holding back something unpleasant, but there was
little public criticism of the Government.   The
debate on Resolution 39, dealing with Government
economic policy, was couched in the same terms as
Resolution 38 on fuel policy, blaming "financiers,
bankers, industrialists and their Tory Party" for
forcing the Government to abandon socialist policies
and Conference pledged support for any effective
measures to restrict prices, profits and dividends.
Conference did administer a gentle rebuke to the
Labour Government in that it warned that without
effective price restraint there could be no wage
restraint.[11]
     At this Conference an emergency resolution
sponsored by the NEC was passed in response to a
ministerial statement of the 1st July announcing a
substantial programme of capital investment in the
industry.   The NUM welcomed this but was
"disquieted at the suggestion of a speed up in the
closure of uneconomic collieries".   Fred Lee
denied there was a speed-up, but he did admit that
closures would continue.[12]
     In September 1965 the Government published
The National Plan.   The Plan laid down that coal
was to produce 170-180m tons by 1970, but the
industry was to be further rationalised and
employment in the industry would continue to fall.
Overall policy was to abandon high-cost units
irrespective of their coal reserves.[13]   The worst
fears of the NUM were confirmed; the 200m tons
capacity was abandoned by the Government and
extensive pit closures and social dislocation of
mining communities were guaranteed.[14]
     A second blow was delivered by the White Paper,

Fuel Policy, which noted coal's problems in
competing with oil and gas.   The White Paper
emphasised that this decline would continue, but
"indigenous coal will remain a primary fuel."[15]
Production was to be concentrated on those
coalfields which had covered their costs since
1947, mainly Yorkshire and the East Midlands.
Overall costs in the industry, particularly wages,
had been rising, which coupled with the costs of
raw materials meant that productivity increases
were essential if the industry was to stay at the
170-180m ton size.   An industry above this
figure was ruled out on the grounds of cost.[16]
These two statements of policy meant that Labour
would shut pits on a scale comparable to that of
a Conservative Government.   The White Paper made
the important point that " The size of the
industry within the framework set by the general
fuel policy will depend significantly on its
success in reducing costs."[17]   This meant that
wage restraint was increasingly likely in the
mining industry as labour costs were the largest
single cost.
        The NEC was convinced that it enjoyed the
full support of the TUC for a 200m ton industry.
In January 1965 it informed the General Council
that it was seeking the implementation of the
joint TUC-Labour Party statements on the coal
industry made in the early 1960s.   The General
Council informed the NEC that it believed the
Government "had gone as far as could be reasonably
expected in existing circumstances to meet the
1961 statement ... it would be unreasonable to hold
the Minister to every detail and figure ..."[18]
        The reaction of the Yorkshire miners to the
National Plan and the White Paper was swift and
bitter.   Letters from Wombwell Main, Edlington,
Hickleton Main, Goldthorpe and Hadfield Main were
sent to the Area Executive attacking the policy.
The letter from the Edlington Branch pointed out
that Branch members "were very perturbed at the
further contraction which it is envisaged will
take place ... it being obvious that Yorkshire
will most certainly be affected ..."[19]   The
Yorkshire coalfield had escaped relatively
unscathed from the first round of pit closures as
previous plans called for the concentration of
production on the most productive coalfields, the
new policy called for the concentration upon the
most productive pits within those coalfields.   The
Goldthorpe Branch rejected the National Plan and

asked sardonically what had become of the fuel
policy?   This Branch then demanded a conference of
Area Officials, MPs and Branch Officials to examine
Government policy as, "our long and faithful
support of the Labour Party over the years should
be enough to secure the consideration which is our
right".[20]   The Yorkshire miners were to learn the
lesson that loyalty counts for little in politics.
        Council spent considerable time considering
the implications of the policy for the industry.
The consensus was that the NUM must at least
persuade the Government to take adequate measures
to ease the social impact of closures.   There was
little overt criticism of Government policy, the
general reaction of the Area being one of resignation and fatalistic acceptance, revealing the
quiescence characteristic of the official leaderships in this period when faced by a crisis in the
industry.   In these crises the NUM sought to
ameliorate the impact of the policy;   union leaders
felt this to be the only realistic policy open to
the NUM but it had the effect of conveying the
impression that the leadership was 'kow-towing' to
the NCB and Government and, at worst
cooperating in the run-down.   The rhetoric of the
leaderships at Area and National level was regarded
with a suspicion often bordering on cynicism by
sections of the membership.   The only overt
criticism debated in Council was a resolution from
the Manton Branch which demanded that the Yorkshire
Area resist any attempt at a statutory incomes
policy or any attempt to interfere with free
collective bargaining.[21]   This policy was accepted
by Council by 103 votes to 2, suggesting that
Council felt that if the NUM was unable to deflect
the Labour Government from closures then it would
defend free collective bargaining.   The NUM's
quiescence over pit closures thus fuelled a latent
wages dissatisfaction.
        In November 1965 the Yorkshire NCB determined
that 75 pits in the coalfield were category 'A'
(long life), 10 were category 'B' (in some danger
of closure), and 18 were category 'C' (pits with a
life of less than three years).   Of these 18 pits,
14 were to the north and south of Barnsley.[22]
Council considered these projections at some
length and concluded,

> This Council Meeting ... is of the
> opinion that, whilst there may be
> little we can do to oppose closures
> on the grounds of exhaustion ... (we)
> can and (will) strenuously oppose
> closures for solely economic grounds.
> We are convinced that the Government's
> planning under the White Paper
> cannot justify closing pits on uneconomic
> grounds.[23]

This discontent was mirrored at national level,
where the NEC expressed dismay over the proposed
closures,

> The Committee was reminded of the
> statements contained in the General
> Election Manifesto that the Labour
> Government accepted that the Coal
> Industry should have an annual output
> of 200m tons ... it was suggested that
> the present Government policy was
> wrong ...[24]

This unanimity of condemnation did not extend
to the methods to resolve the crisis; indeed, no
response was put forward. As a result the
statements of the NEC lacked credibility. After
the reconciliation within the Labour Party in
1962-1963 a consensus governed the relationship
between the Unions and the Party, a consensus
dominated by the belief in the planned economy of
which the fuel policy was a part. After 1965,
so far as the NUM was concerned, this consensus was
under strain. The National Plan and the Fuel
Policy White Paper mark a watershed in the miners'
relationship with the Labour Government.
By January 1966 there was open acrimony over
the fuel policy between the NUM and the Government.
Meetings were held with the Minister in the hope
that persistence coupled with the threat of wage
militancy would induce a change of heart. The
NUM accused the Government and the Minister of
betraying the mineworkers, a charge hotly disputed
by the Minister who argued that the industry had a
secure future and that £400m had been wiped from
the NCB's accumulated debt. Unfortunately neither
did anything to ease the miners' immediate sense of
insecurity. Some members of the NEC made no
attempt to disguise their bitterness.

> The policy ... (of) the NCB was
> influenced by Cabinet decisions ...
> it was suggested that the Government
> had no national fuel policy, but in the
> main was simply projecting the policies
> which had been in existence under the
> previous Government ... (but) ... There
> was no point in arguing with the Minister
> as to whether or not the present
> Government had broken faith with the
> miners ...   The Government was either ...
> guilty of political chicanery or had been
> hopelessly incompetent in the assumptions
> they had made before the election.
> Government policy accepted free-for-all
> competition ...[25]

In response the NEC called a Special
Conference.   This was welcomed by the Yorkshire
Area which also agreed to lobby their MPs on the
17th February, the day before the Special
Conference.[26]   Despite bitter criticism of both
NEC and Government the Special Conference
confirmed the NEC's existing policy of attempting
to persuade the Government to change its policy by
verbal pressure not out of conviction, but because
of the belief that no other response was available.
The extensive lobbying conducted by the miners had
no visible impact on Government policy which was
committed to creating a modern, efficient coal
industry by closing uneconomic pits.
     The rapid development and exploitation of
North Sea Gas meant major changes in fuel use and
the NUM felt that this offered an opportunity for
the Government to reduce further the role of coal
in the economy.   Despite protestations to the
contrary, the NUM lamented,

> ... it has been our unfortunate
> experience in the last year or so,
> that speculations which we discounted ...
> because of our faith in the policies and
> the attitudes to which we believed the
> Labour Movement was firmly committed,
> were later found to be well founded in
> that they conformed fairly accurately to
> subsequent Government pronouncements.[27]

By 1967 there was a growing distrust in the
NUM of the Wilson Government and the beginning of
questioning of the traditional unstinting

loyalty to Labour Governments.   By 1967 it was
clear that there would be no fuel policy on the
lines advocated by the NUM and suggestions were
made that perhaps it would be better if the NUM
was to concentrate on pay increases.   Such a policy
invited a clash with the Labour Government.
     All government pronouncements emphasised that
the mining industry must be more efficient and cost-
effective, therefore wage increases had to be
matched by increased productivity.   This was
balanced by an increased rejection of long term
solutions   the problems of the coal industry on
the part of the mineworkers in favour of immediate
gains.   Ford's position, together with much of the
NEC, was that such a change in Union policy was not
in the real interests of the membership.   The
NEC remained committed to the idea of a fuel policy
and to persuading the Government to bear the social
costs of the run-down.   Accepting that pits could
be closed on grounds other than seam exhaustion was
a major concession which lead to increased
criticism of the NEC, which in turn attacked these
critics for promoting feuding which did nothing to
solve the industry's problems.   The NEC was still
attempting to win support for a policy no longer
seriously entertained by the Government after
July 1966 - that of a planned economy. Nevertheless,
political considerations were central in policy
making within the NUM, as the NEC argued that the
Government had not betrayed the mineworkers as it
was pursuing policies that were in the 'national
interest'.
     On the 5th July Richard Marsh, the Minister of
Fuel and Power, told the miners in his Conference
speech that they must accept that the patterns of
fuel use were not amenable to control;   " You
cannot reverse them, because they are prisoners of
history".   The Government was halting the rapid,
unplanned contraction of the industry, it had
considered, and rejected as too low, a capacity of
140m tons, but Marsh reiterated that coal could
only be competitive if costs were reduced.[28]   The
debate on the situation in the industry was, in
fact, a debate of the NUM's attitude to the Labour
Government.   Will Paynter, the General Secretary of
the NUM, summed up the feelings of many delegates
when he declared his first loyalty was to the men
in the pits;   "my loyalty to ... government is
influenced and determined by the treatment (of) the
people to who my primary loyalty lies."[29]   Many
delegates felt that the NUM should demand further

Government action to reduce the impact of and
social costs of the pit closures Government felt to
be necessary to slim the industry down to a size
of 155m tons, a figure accepted by the NUM as being
the Government's target.
     At a special NEC meeting on the 4th July an
emergency resolution was tabled demanding a
guaranteed size for the coal industry.   This was
debated on 6th July.   M W Rowe, speaking for the
NEC, warned,

> I want this Government to recognise that
> the social and political costs (of massive
> pit closures) could be disastrous to a
> Labour Government.
> The red light is on!
> ... at the last County and Municipal
> elections (the miners) voted with their
> backsides.   They did not vote Tory,
> but they stayed at home ...[30]

     Arthur Scargill, a delegate from Yorkshire
stated,

> I can honestly say that I never heard
> flannel like we got from the Minister ...
> he said that we have nuclear power
> stations with us, whether we like it
> or not.   I suggest to this Conference
> that we have coal mines with us ... but
> they did something about this problem:
> they closed them down.   This was a
> complete reversal of the policy ... that
> was promised by the Labour Government
> before it was put into office ... this
> represents a betrayal of the mining
> industry.[31]

The emergency resolution was passed unanimously.

     Despite such bitterness little could be
decided until the Government published its revised
White Paper on Fuel Policy in November 1967.   In a
parliamentary speech on the 18th July, Marsh
recognised the NCB could not bear the full social
costs of pit closures.   He therefore proposed to
extend the availability of government money in
easing the burden of these costs and £133m was
made available.   The NEC welcomed these measures
but it also urged an immediate slow down in the
rate of pit closures.[32]   The Government had been

shocked by the results of the 1967 municipal
elections.   They feared that if the loyalty of
the miners was shifting (and the attitudes of the
Annual Conference suggested this), then no pool
of Labour support was secure.   At a meeting of the
NEC on the 21st September, Harold Wilson announced
the postponement of the closure of 16 pits to
alleviate winter unemployment.   The NEC greeted
this with suspicion bordering on hostility
commenting that "these people expect something
better from a Labour Government."[33]   A few days
later the NEC commented," the measures proposed for
the winter were a political measure designed to
meet criticism about unemployment rather than
alleviate (the) position (in mining communities)."[34]
    The NEC remained far from satisfied.   Sidney
Ford, moving composite Resolution 22 at the 1967
Labour Party Conference, attacked the lack of a
fuel policy,

> I seek the support of this
> Conference not as some reward for the
> mineworkers' loyalty in the past, but
> because of the deep rooted fear that
> the Government, in reviewing their fuel
> policy, might well find themselves
> committed to a plan in total disregard
> of the successive annual Conference
> decisions of this Party for a national
> fuel policy ...[35]

This was supported by the unions associated with
the fuel and power industries and was passed
unanimously.
    Marsh restated the policy of the Government but
with one difference.   He revealed that Government
had been considering an industry of 150m tons by
1970, but this had been rejected in favour of 155m
tons.[36]   Earlier in the year the NEC of the NUM
had discussed a rumour emanating from Whitehall
that 140m tons was the size of the industry, and
"it was suggested that the apparent disregard by
the Government of the views of the Union stemmed
from a belief that the NUM would cooperate in any
measures the Government adopted".[37] On the eve of
the publication of the White Paper the NUM believed
it knew what to expect.   The National Plan target
of 170-180m tons by 1970 had been dropped and that
envisaged in Cmnd 2798 was reduced to 155m tons.
Even the figure of 155m tons was provisional on the
NCB increasing productivity.[38]

After the 1967 Annual Conference of the NUM
there was a growing correlation between wages
dissatisfaction and the uncertainties and frustrations generated by the Government's policy towards
the coal industry. In response to Marsh's speech
of the 18th July the Yorkshire Area Executive
called a Special Council Meeting to discuss the
implications of the policy. Council concluded,
" The Government's policy represents a challenge
to use to fight for our futures."[39]

By late 1967 fuel policy was firmly based on
Cmnd 3438. However, in November 1967, the
Government withdrew the White Paper in circumstances
that derived from considerations other than the
mining industry. On the 6th November the NUM
organised a conference in the Central Hall,
Westminster made up of delegates from the NUM, the
TUC and the mining MPs which was bitterly critical
of the White Paper. This did not lead to the
withdrawal of the White Paper but mining and other
interested MPs arranged a meeting with the Leader
of the House and the Chief Whip where they asked
for its withdrawal.[40] During the intervening
weekend the devaluation crisis broke and in the
following week the Miners' Group met the Prime
Minister, the Chief Whip and the Minister of Fuel.

> We stated that almost all of the Miners'
> Group would refuse to vote for the
> White Paper whilst a number stated that
> they would go so far as to vote against.
> We pointed out that other members with
> mining interests would in all probability
> do the same.[41]

The PM agreed to withdraw the White Paper to
allow for a re-examination in the light of
devaluation, in face of a revolt from some 80
members of the PLP. A joint conference of the
Yorkshire Area Executive Committee and the
Yorkshire Mining MPs was "pleased to note the
deferment of the White Paper", the result of the
solidarity of the mining MPs.[42]

The NUM welcomed devaluation as an opportunity
to create prosperity but it also called on the
Government to establish price control. The NUM
pledged itself to a policy of "economic stability,
sustained expansion and full employment."[43] The
devaluation crisis, which helped the NUM to secure
the deferment of the closure policy, was used by
the NUM as an excuse to rally to the Government and

avoid open conflict.

The deferment of Cmnd 3438 did not end concern over the future in the Yorkshire coalfield. The Brodsworth Branch wrote to the Executive urging that the NUM seek the re-call of the Party Conference as the fuel and economic policies of the Government had precipitated,

> ... an unprecedented crisis of confidence ... between the miners, the working class, the Party and the electorate on one hand and the Government on the other, the White Paper is not a special, parochial concern for the miners alone: with large pools of unemployment throughout our country and the broken promises of Government ... makes it the concern of the whole Labour Movement.[44]

This branch saw Cmnd 3438 as symptomatic of Labour's bankruptcy: the Government could only be saved by full-blooded socialism. The branch,

> ... remind(ed) the (NEC) of the Labour Party that it was the miners who put this Party on the map and gave it some of its greatest leaders ... We have a special claim upon the loyalty of all organisations affiliated to the Party, but we ask for nothing for ourselves only that the pledges made by the Government be honoured: full employment, planned growth of the economy including ... a fuel plan.[45]

The purpose of a re-called Conference was to force the Government to implement the policies on which it had been elected. The Area Executive took the unusual step of printing the letter in full in the minutes and it was approved by Area Council. This was not the only protest at the Council; letters were received from the North Gawber and Woolley Branches complaining about the behaviour of Roy Mason, the MP for Barnsley. North Gawber asked Council to censure Mason "for his lack of interest and assistance in the mining situation as a whole". The Area Executive were reluctant to accept this as Mason was a rising star, but he had accepted appointment as Minister of Fuel and Power: an NUM sponsored MP in overall charge of the closure programme. The Branch insisted that the letter go on the minutes, but it fell in Council due to a lack of support. The Woolley Branch proposed the withdrawal of financial support from Mason, but this was rejected by 96 votes to 8. At the same meeting Bullcroft asked for a clarification of the Area's views on pit closures. From the reply of the Executive it is clear that it was at a loss as the NCB continued to shut pits no matter what the NUM said or did. The NUM was in the position of being able to offer no effective response to the NCB.[46]

As a result of concentration on the most productive pits an increased burden was placed on the Yorkshire coalfield by the siting of a large number of major coal burning power stations in the vicinity of the Yorkshire coalfield (one of the few fruits of the ill starred National Plan). The rundown of the industry in Yorkshire was exacerbated by the lack of alternative sources of employment for redundant miners, and this served to increase the miners' sense of insecurity and uncertainty.[47] The importance of the dispute in 1967 over fuel policy was that it demonstrated the depth of feeling not only amongst the miners, but also amongst the mining MPs, the most loyal element in the PLP. In the July debate Edwin Wainwright, the MP for Dearne Valley, warned Marsh, "he must not take it for granted the ... mining constituency members will always allow him an easy time ... we are sometimes a little doubtful about his conduct in regard to the mining fraternity".[48] Despite the bitter sentiments this also reveals the tremendous inhibitions against taking action against the Labour Government.

Throughout 1968 the policy of the NUM was to persuade the Government to implement Composite Resolution 22 passed at the 1967 Party Conference. With the publication of the White Paper in November it became clear in Yorkshire the Labour Government had no intention of implementing the Conference Resolution. The Brodsworth Branch had demanded the re-call of the Party Conference to bring the Labour Government to heel and this had been passed by the Yorkshire Area Executive to the National Executive for action. In reply Will Paynter wrote that there was no reason to take action as both the NUM and Party Conference had decided policy and the NEC was seeking to "ensure that the Labour Party brings pressure on the Government to act in accordance ... with composite Resolution 22."[49]

The NUM was trying to pressure a Government

which had repudiated both Party and Union policy
and which had shown itself to be willing and able
to ignore Conference. Formal pressure from
mining MPs enjoyed a limited success because of a
number of special factors which were unlikely to
re-occur. With the failure of conventional
attempts at political influence some branches in
the Yorkshire coalfield saw industrial action as the
only remaining response. Houghton Main, for
example, proposed that "in protest against the
Labour Government's policy of pit closures ... the
NUM Yorkshire Area shall withdraw its labour."[50]
Council rejected this by 61 votes to 30. The large
number in favour is significant: in the past such
a resolution might have attracted ten votes but an
increasing number of branches were willing to
contemplate industrial action to pressure a
Government.
    Similar sentiments were expressed at national
level. On the 15th December the Economic Sub-
committee of the NEC of the NUM met the Minister
to discuss the state of the industry. The Sub-
committee came away from the meeting empty handed
and promptly called a Special Conference to consider
the state of the industry.[51] On the day before the
Special Conference the NEC met and decided that it
should be frank about the bleak future of the
industry, and, in view of this it was suggested
that if the NEC was to continue with its campaign
some form of industrial action would have to be
resorted to.[52] A majority of the NEC were opposed
to this, proposing" ... the concentration of Union
pressure ... on the social consequences of
contraction (with every prospect of wide support
in the Labour and Trade Union Movement) ..."[53]
Contraction was inevitable and the NEC saw its job
as softening the blow whilst doing "everything
possible to ensure the competitiveness of coal
prices." The NEC, thus, abandoned the fuel policy
in favour of the planned contraction of the industry,
urging Conference not to vote in favour of
industrial action.
    Officially the Special Conference was called to
decide how the NUM could ensure that the social
costs of contraction would be met by Government.
In fact, Conference was to decide whether or not
the NUM would use industrial action against a Labour
Government. Paynter for the NEC argued that the
6th November meeting at Westminster Hall and
subsequent events showed the utility of party-
political action. Concessions were won because,

> "... of the agitation and the pressure
> that we and the Miners' MPs have been
> able to exercise upon the Government ...
> Would industrial action ... improve
> what is the main problem for us?
> How do we maintain the coalburn in
> the economy of Britain? (The
> Resolution) means that we ... will
> continue our efforts with the Government,
> through our (MPs), through all the
> allies that we can get in the Trade
> Union and Labour Movement in and out
> of Parliament, to continue to exercise
> the maximum pressure we can on the
> Government ...[54]

A J Pratt of the NEC argued that the NUM was
no longer capable of effective industrial action
because of the decline: noting the empty rows of
seats he declared: " We should have filled this
damned place at one time. We are insignificant
now." Pratt doubted that the membership would
obey a strike call and that it would be a farce
as it would have no effect on the economy.[55]
Jock Kane, the Yorkshire Area Financial
Secretary, rejected angrily Pratt's arguments.
Pointing to the empty hall Kane declared, "they are
not empty as a result of industrial action", blaming
instead the moderation of the NUM which had given
the miners influence with no-one.

> We are arguing for action that will not
> only put a stop to the number of pit
> closures but will also lead to this
> Government introducing (socialism)...
> it is necessary now to introduce some
> form of action that will sharply bring
> to the notice of the powers that be the
> fact that the miners are no longer
> prepared to go along the road they
> have ...[56]

Kane was opposed by Tommy Burke, a Yorkshire NEC
member. Burke argued that the Area Council
Meeting of the 2nd February had rejected
industrial action. The core of his argument was
an embourgeoisement thesis - that the miners of
1968 were different from those of 1926 because,

> Today our lads have set on things
> like £800 cars and £3,000 bungalows,

all that kind of thing and it all
has its effect.   It is a different
system of life and I do not think
that for one moment that they would
jeopardise all those things for the
sake of a strike which ... could have
no impact whatsoever.[57]

Tommy Mullany, the next Yorkshire delegate, adopted
a similar line to Kane, arguing that the main
problem was leadership.

We have two kinds of leaders ... the
first kind has a policy and he
imagines the world or rather the
Government in this case to suit that
particularly policy.   We have a
Labour Government.   That is his policy.
So everything will be all right.   Now
you have another kind of leader who
when he sees the actions of the Labour
Government, says, "This is indeed a
queer kind of world we live in.   It is
a world that has got neither father or
mother ..." and he makes his policy to
suit that world ... after talk, talk,
talk, the policy that you have got to
come to is a policy of some kind of
industrial action . [58]

The last delegate from Yorkshire, Mick Welsh,
argued that the bulk of the membership were ready
to take industrial action, "... after conferring
with my workmates at snaptimes and other times ...
there is no other choice ... than strike action ...
but after serious thought the only thing opposite
to strike action is your ... mates unemployed."[59]
Conference voted by a show of hands to reject
the use of industrial action.   The decision of the
Conference was put to a branch vote which approved
it by 1671 votes to 210.[60]   The idea of
industrial action had not yet been assimilated
by the bulk of the membership.   Council, for
example, approved a decision to continue to oppose
the closure of Shawcross colliery.   However, at
this Council Meeting Sam Bullough, the Area
President, ruled out of order a move by the Branch
for industrial action, an idea which had won
support from some delegates.[61] In its Annual
Report the NEC was aware that the Special
Conference had marked a significant

point in the evolution of the NUM's relationship
with the Labour Government.[62]
    The NEC was arguing that there was no alter-
native to accepting the continuing decline of the
industry.   The first fruits of continuing the
traditional policy was a meeting with Roy Mason,
MP for Barnsley and also the Minister of Fuel and
Power.   After the meeting it was announced that
the Government was engaged on a 'retrospective'
examination of the November 1967 White Paper.
From this the NEC argued that their strategy had
been justified and successful.[63]
    In an attempt to damp down discontent in the
coalfields, Mason and Tom Urwin, a junior minister
in Mason's department, addressed the Yorkshire Area
Council in December on the Government's fuel policy
and the state of the coal industry.   Mason
emphasised his links with the industry, that the
impact of closures in Yorkshire had not been as
great as in other areas, and there were to be fewer
closures in 1969-1970.   Urwin argued:

> We are tackling the problems of
> adjustment to change in the coal
> industry on a systematic and
> sympathetic basis for the first time
> in history and I am convinced that
> we are tackling them on the right
> lines.[64]

Many members of Council remained unconvinced.
    By the end of 1968 a fund of mistrust and
anger had built up in many branches in the Yorkshire
Area over the Labour Government's policy towards
the coal industry.   Quite simply many miners felt
betrayed.   Despite this, the official leaderships
of the NUM acquiesced in government policy in the
sincere belief that they had no other choice: they
had to accept government policy to ensure that the
social costs of the run-down were met and to resist
would be futile both politically (fratricidal
strife would damage the government) and economically
(it would speed up the closure of marginal pits).
Other elements in the NUM rejected this and
advocated resistance to government policy by
industrial action.   This was a truly radical
alternative;   first, it meant the NUM sanctioning
industrial action, something foresworn since 1944-
1947;   and second, it meant industrial action for
political purposes, something which had been
rejected ever since 1926.   However, such action

was uncongenial because it would have been taken
against a Labour Government.   The absence of mass
support for a policy of resistance ensured that
the policy of acquiescence would continue but there
was a distinct groundswell in Yorkshire for a
change of policy by the NUM.   For the moment, fuel
policy was not enough to mobilise the mass of
mineworkers.

REFERENCES

1   YA (NUM);   Annual Reports (President's Report
          for 1962);   March 1963
2   NUM: General Election Manifesto, 1964
3   YA (NUM);   5 January 1965
4   BS Circular   11/65 (5 February 1965)
     For notification of the emerging incomes policy
     see:
     AS Circular   26/65   (16 January 1965);   and
     TUC Circular   44 (64-65) of the same date
5   NUM (EC);   Report of a Meeting with the
          Minister of Power;   7 January 1965
6   NUM (EC);   14 January;   and 4 February 1965
7   NUM: Annual Conference Report, 1965;   p71
8   Annual Conference, 1965;   p84
9   Annual Conference, 1965;   p185
10   Annual Conference, 1965;   p187
11   Annual Conference, 1965;   p192
12   NUM(EC);   8 July 1965
13   The National Plan (Cmnd 2764);   chapter 11
14   NUM (EC);   Economic Sub-Committee;
          15 September 1965
15   Fuel Policy (Cmnd 2798);   paras 5, 16 and
          38
16   Fuel Policy;   para 47
17   Fuel Policy;   para 54
18   TUC Report 1965;   p265;   and   pp499-501
          (my emphasis)
19   YA (NUM);   18-19 October 1965
20   YA (NUM);   18-19 October 1965
21   YA (NUM);   18-19 October 1965
22   W H Sales, The Question of Pit Closures in the
          Next Five Years (Yorkshire NCB 1965);
          speech to Council;   18 November 1965
23   YA(NUM);   23-24 November 1965
24   NUM (EC);   25 November 1965
25   NUM (EC);   12 January 1966
26   YA (NUM);   24 January 1966
     This Special Conference was called to consider
          the situation in the industry.   Although
          dealing with pit closures and fuel policy

the Conference was far more important with
regard to wages policy. As such it will be
examined at length in the next chapter.
Nevertheless, the Conference does show the
depth of bitterness and unrest amongst the
mineworkers.

27   NUM: Annual Conference Report, 1967; p74
         (my emphasis)
28   Annual Conference, 1967; pp178-186
29   Annual Conference, 1967; p227
30   Annual Conference, 1967; pp239-240; and
         NUM (EC); 4 July 1967
31   Annual Conference, 1967; p249
32   NUM (EC); 20 July 1967
         5s HC Debs 750 (18 July 1967) contains the
         statement
33   NUM (EC); 21 September 1967
34   NUM (EC); 29 September 1967
35   Labour Party Conference Report, 1967;
         pp201-202 (LPCR)
36   LPCR; p207
37   NUM (EC); 8 June 1967 (my emphasis); and
         NUM (EC); 11 May 1967; and 1 June 1967
38   Fuel Policy (Cmnd 3438); chapter 5
39   YA (NUM): 25 September 1967
40   NUM: Report of the NEC, May 1967; pp67-69
         See Chapter 5 for further detail
41   NEC Report; pp67-68
42   YA (NUM); 25 November 1967
43   AS Circular 218/67 (29 November 1967); and
         TUC: Statement on Devaluation, in above
44   YA (NUM);   18 December 1967
45   YA (NUM);   18 December 1967
46   YA (NUM);   18 December 1967
47   See:
     M Barrat Brown, 'The Concept of Employment
         Opportunities with Specific Reference to
         Yorkshire and Humberside; Yorkshire Bulletin
         of Economic and Social Research 22 (1970);
         pp65-100; and 'What Will the Miners Do
         Now?', in
     New Society: 23 November 1970
     Also,
     Yorkshire and Humberside Planning Council,
         Regional Strategy, (London, HMSO/MHLG 1970);
         paras 126-141
48   5s HC Debs 750 (18 July 1967); col 1892
49   W Paynter to S Schofield: 12 January 1968;
         and
     YA (NUM); 19 February 1968
50   YA (NUM); 29 February 1968

70

51   NUM (EC);   Economic Sub-Committee;   4 January
        1968;   and
      Report of a Meeting with the Minister of Power,
        4 January 1968
52   NUM (EC);   14 March 1968
53   NUM (EC);   14 March 1968
54   NUM: Special Conference Report;   15 March
        1968;   pp15-17
55   Special Conference;   p21
56   Special Conference;   p28
57   Special Conference;   p28
      Kane corrected Burke by pointing out that
        Council had rejected the proposition that
        Yorkshire strike alone.
58   Special Conference;   p31
59   Special Conference;   p37
60   YA (NUM);   29 April 1968
61   YA (NUM);   21 June 1968
62   NUM: Report of the NEC, May 1968;   p10

63   NUM (EC);   25 July 1968.   The meeting was
        held on the 12 July
64   YA (NUM);   23 December 1968

Chapter Three

THE YORKSHIRE MINERS AND THE LABOUR GOVERNMENT,
1964-1970: PAY, POLITICS AND PROTEST

The Miners and Incomes Policy

The trade unions' historic connection with the
Labour Party made it much more likely that they
would co-operate with a Labour Government in
securing 'the planned growth of incomes'. The
NUM believed that it would benefit from the policy
as productivity in the industry improved.
Co-operation with the Labour Government was not out
of the question as long as the NUM and other unions
were able to offer their members compensation for
wage restraint. If this was not available,
however, the result was likely to be growing
opposition to pay policy. In the case of the
leaders of the NUM a planned fuel policy and long
term security for the industry was the price of
co-operation. However, some sections of the NUM
felt that wage restraint was too high a price to
be paid for a non-existent security. Nevertheless,
at the outset in 1964 the NUM was willing to give
the Government the benefit of the doubt and
acquiesce on incomes policy.
      The NUM was well aware of the political
sensitivity of wage increases; the Yorkshire Area
considered a number of wage resolutions in
February 1965, two of which implied opposition to
wage restraint.[1] So great was the concern about
the possible shape of government pay policy that
the NEC decided to call a Special Conference. The
1964 Conference passed a resolution demanding
substantial increases for the lowest paid grades
in the coal industry and for a general increase in
the minimum national wage rates. Negotiations had
begun with the NCB but the October General Election
and the Government's intention to institute an
incomes policy had led to the NUM and NCB suspending
wage negotiations until the proposed government
policy was made clear.
      At the Special Conference it was announced

that

> ... wages ...have become the subject
> and an issue of national politics.
> As you very well know there are
> discussions proceeding now between
> the Labour Government, the Employers'
> Association, and the TUC in the
> direction of establishing certain basic
> principles that will govern future incomes
> policy. I am not suggesting ... that
> this is a factor which ought to determine
> the wages claim we make, but it obviously
> is a factor that has to be taken into
> account when we are examining the
> general political and economic climate ...[2]

The implication was that the NUM had to recognise
that Government policy might be inimical to the
immediate economic interests of the mineworker.
It was also clear that the fuel policy was closely
tied to discontent over wages as satisfactory
wages could only be guaranteed by a viable
industry.   The NEC recommended Conference accept
their policy of urging a fuel policy and adopting
a 'wait and see' policy over wages.   This was
criticised by some of the delegates.   Tommy Ryan,
for example, the Branch Secretary at Cadeby Main,
cautioned the NEC on the feelings of the miners in
the coalfields warning that, "the dissatisfaction
is general throughout Yorkshire."[3]   Conference
did accept the NEC policy, but in Yorkshire there
was eloquent testimony to support Ryan's appraisal
of the general mood as Area Council "expressed its
deep disappointment with the proceedings (of the
Conference) in all its aspects."[4]   This
dissatisfaction prompted the NEC to appease unrest
by a change in its attitude towards collective
bargaining, by seeking a second wage increase in
the Autumn.[5]
     At a time of wage restraint the NUM was
deliberately seeking to breach the twelve month
convention as part of an attempt to pressure
Government into adopting a fuel policy.   The first
wage increase was negotiated in July 1965 and was
put before the branches with a recommendation to
accept.   The Area Council "having taken into
account the state of the economy and industry" voted
by 93 to 8 to accept, and the branches accepted by
1966 votes to 389.[6]
     The Annual Council Meeting of 1965 was used as

an opportunity for the Yorkshire Area to define its
attitude to the Labour Government.   The main
concern of the President's Address was the state of
the economy which had forced the Government into
restricting pay increases.   The implementation of
the manifesto depended on economic expansion and
a socialist incomes policy which sought to promote
economic stability and social justice.[7]   The
miners were asked to accept an incomes. policy as
part of a planned economy to replace deflation and
stop-go which had led to the decline of their
industry.   The central concern of the NUM was still
a Government guarantee of the industry, something
that the Government was unwilling to give, but it
was only with such a guarantee that the NUM was
likely to secure compliance over incomes policy.
The Yorkshire Area was in a difficult position:
it was committed to supporting TUC policy on wages,
to supporting a Labour Government, but at the same
time the Union was disquieted over the unresponsi-
veness of 'their' Government to the request for a
fuel policy and there was clear pressure for
substantial wage increases.   The tension between
these contradictory demands was to have a major
effect upon internal Area and NUM politics;   for
example, the TUC convened a Conference of Executives
in early April to discuss the document,
Productivity, Prices and Incomes.   The NEC was
decided to attend with a predisposition to support
TUC policy, but at the same meeting it was decided
to submit a claim for a substantial increase in the
rates for daywagemen in the industry.[8]
     The result was ambiguous.   The NEC accepted
the need for the planned growth of incomes but
argued that the time was not yet ripe for such a
policy.   This was largely due to the fact that
wage settlements in the mining industry were
already above the 3.4% norm suggested by the TUC.
The NEC felt that "unions were going to be in
difficulties with their members" if 3.5% was the
pay limit and to adhere to the norm and to pay
policy in general would seriously disrupt their pay
talks which were about to start with the NCB.   As
the NUM's wage claim was in excess of 3.5% the
Executive were forced to reject the specific
recommendation of the TUC, but they did accept the
general principle behind the policy of the TUC.[9]
The NUM was emotionally and politically committed to
the Government but it was unwilling to surrender
its rights to free collective bargaining, arguing
the Government should be given a chance in spite of

the miners dislike of pay policy.   The **Government**
was urged to take draconian powers to control
prices, and price rises were blamed on the sinister
machinations of the enemies of Labour. Thus, the
specific policies of the Government were not
attacked; generalities were politically safe.[10]
    In defiance of the TUC the NEC informed the
General Council that it intended to submit a wage
claim in excess of the pay norm and the TUC Incomes
Policy Committee requested a meeting with the NUM.
The NEC quoted the DEA's statement of the 30th April
allowing increases beyond the norm that were
necessary to maintain manning levels in vital
industries.   The TUC objected strongly as it was the
second claim in six months; a 5% increase had been
conceded in June, now the NUM was seeking a further
5-6%.   This would mean an annual increase of 10-11%
or roughly three times the agreed norm.   The TUC
argued that other workers would try to repeat the
action of the NUM fuelling inflation to the
detriment of all workers.   The NUM stuck to the
claim.   The TUC then "suggested a sacrifice on the
part of the miners", which meant at least postponing
the claim until March.   The NUM rejected this as
the claim was in the "national interest" as it would
sustain the domestic fuel industry.   Faced with
such intransigence the TUC gave up and the claim
went ahead.[11]   The wage claim made in defiance of
the TUC and the Government was submitted to the NCB
in December 1965 and rejected out of hand.[12]   This
angered the NEC (although it was not unexpected)
and "very strong resentment was expressed."   The
NEC concluded that some demonstration was called
for and it voted to impose an overtime ban from 28th
March, the first official industrial action
proposed by the NEC since the creation of the NUM.[13]
This reflected feeling at branch level; of the
resolutions submitted by Yorkshire branches for
possible inclusion in the Annual Conference eight
demanded wage increases and four sought to prevent
any interference in free collective bargaining.[14]
    This advocacy of industrial action cannot
be accounted for entirely by discontent over pay.
During this period the NUM was fighting a losing
battle over fuel policy and the call for industrial
action was influenced by this battle.   In showing
the Government that the NUM was willing to fight
over wages and act against a key Government policy
it seems that the NUM was encouraging a deal on the
lines of 'give us a fuel policy and we will restrain
our wage demands'.   However, there was a second

argument: that the NUM should ignore long term
benefits which could not be guaranteed and should
instead seek the highest possible immediate benefits
in wages. A Special Conference called by the
NEC was used to define the NUM's position vis-a-vis
the Labour Government. As to the overtime ban, the
NEC felt it had to "do something dramatic, something
salutary, to compel the NCB, and, if necessary, the
Government to face the situation in the industry".[15]
Sidney Ford, who was opposed to the decision, was
forced to accept it but pointed out that industrial
action would put pits and jobs at risk. He saw
the decision as a major change in the direction of
NUM policy: "in relation to our history as a
miners' organisation since 1926, rather a drastic
and dramatic action." For leaders such as Ford
the decision to hold an overtime ban was contrary to
all that they had advocated and believed about the
role of the NUM in the nationalised industry. The
miners had benefited from nationalisation but by the
late 1960s increasing numbers of miners were willing
to challenge these assumptions and use industrial
action. Such calls for industrial action were
remarkable in that they proposed to use industrial
action as a political weapon, something which the
entire movement had fought shy of since 1926. In
reality, of course, an overtime ban was not a major
industrial event but for the NUM it was a major
innovation as it was aimed at pressuring both the
NCB and Government. So great a departure from
the past was it that Jack Leigh, the Yorkshire Area
Vice President, was concerned that the ban should
not be a stunt. If the overtime ban was meant
seriously, Leigh suggested that the NUM had been
too reasonable and moderate in the past and cast
doubt on the NEC's sincerity.[16]
    A second Yorkshire delegate, Arthur Scargill,
noted that the Yorkshire miners had lobbied their
MPs on the day before the meeting of the Special
Conference for the re-adoption of the 200m ton
capacity coal industry. Scargill contrasted the
wishes of the Yorkshire miners with the policy of
the Government whose policy was,

> ... completely in contradiction of
> the policy ... that the Yorkshire
> Area had, and ... (the NEC report)
> seems ... to be an acceptance of this
> policy provided we can get it brought
> about with a little harm as possible to
> the people who are going to be affected.[17]

In spite of the apparently new leaf turned by the NEC, both Leigh and Scargill remained suspicious of the real extent of the NEC's commitment to industrial action.

The special Conference closed with Ford warning that up to September 1965 they believed they enjoyed the full support of the trade union movement; now they were without allies, either political or industrial, and the delegates were asked to bear this in mind when judging the policy of the NEC. NEC policy was accepted, with some dissent.[18]

As the mineworkers awaited the outcome of the negotiations, there was a strike of craftsmen in the Yorkshire coalfield over the anomalies of the earlier award. Negotiations were being conducted at the national level, but they were proceeding very slowly and the craftsmen struck out of impatience. The striking craftsmen began to picket other branches and the Area Executive ordered all branches to do all they could to stop the spreading of the strike.[19] This unofficial activity continued unbated and began to spread. As a consequence certain branch officials from Area Panels 2, 4, 6 and 8 together with officials from the Area Workshops were called before the Executive and charged with organising and promoting unofficial activity in opposition to official union policy.[20] None of the accused denied the charges. They were asked to sign a document abjuring their actions and promising not to repeat them. Eight signed, four refused and were suspended under Rule 42 (b), but these signed on the 24th April.

At the end of March the NEC decided that the NCB was giving their wage claim serious consideration; therefore the proposed overtime ban was called off having served its purpose.[21] The rapidity with which the ban was cancelled was interpreted by many miners as proof of the NEC's 'cold-feet'. The NUM's claim had been for a two shilling per shift increase for surface workers and two shilling and ten pence per shift for underground mineworkers. The NCB refused the ten pence differential, offering an increase of twelve shillings per week on both surface and underground rates. The NEC recommended acceptance by an Area vote, the result of which was 435 in favour and 39 against.[22]

The events of February-March suggested that more could be gained by rattling the sabre than by acting moderately. The Executive of the Yorkshire Area accepted a resolution calling for an

increase of £3 for all mineworkers and at the same
Council Meeting the delegates approved the
commencement of the overtime ban (on the 28th March)
with only 8 delegates opposed.[23]   On the 26th March
the NEC cancelled the ban.   The decision of the
NEC on the 10th February to call the overtime ban to
begin one month ahead, at the time of the year when
winter demand for coal was tailing off does suggest
that the ban was not meant as a serious proposal
for industrial action (which is why, perhaps,
Council supported it so heavily) but as a bargaining
factor, and to forestall unofficial industrial
action.   The wages dissatisfaction received no
catharsis and the unrest of some sections of the
Area was expressed in other ways.   For example, the
Bentley and Thurcroft Branches moved that the
Yorkshire Area donate £200 to the Seamen's Union
strike fund to demonstrate solidarity with another
union in a wages battle, but a counter-resolution
not to give support to a union in conflict with
a Labour Government was passed by 80 votes to 17.[24]
     On the 4th July the Prices and Incomes Bill
was introduced into the House of Commons.   The
Bill had the effect of sharpening internal conflict
over the wages issue and the cost of support for the
Labour Government within the NUM.   At the NUM
Annual Conference a delegate from Yorkshire, W Carr,
insisted that the ordinary member could be ignored
no longer, that the Yorkshire miners opposed
Government interference in free collective
bargaining and that, "in a society where it is
openly stated that expansion of profit is necessary
for the provision of national economic growth, it
behoves us as a trade union to sustain and assert
our right to obtain from the wealth created
whatever free negotiations can extract.   That is
our job ..."[25]
     Carr and other delegates doubted that incomes
policy would make adequate provision for the low
paid in the industry, and that the social justice
promised by Wilson's speech to the 1964 TUC had not
applied to the seamen who were on strike against low
pay.   The NEC countered with a powerful plea for
loyalty to the Labour Government and acceptance
of the incomes policy.   In the vote on the
Government's incomes policy Conference decided by
243,000 to 241,000 (a majority of 2,000) against
support for Government policy.[26]
     Significantly as a General Election became
a distinct possibility the NEC modified its critical
attitudes to the Labour Government and its policies.

The NUM urged all miners to vote Labour, but this advice did not rest easily with the Union's earlier opposition to aspects of Government policy, "You may well ask how we reconcile this advice with our attitude over recent months when we have felt impelled to criticise the present Government on various aspects of their fuel and power policies."[27]

This reconciliation was carried out as follows: after 1945 the miners received more consideration from Labour than Conservative governments, but a Labour Government "must of necessity have ... regard to its total responsibilities."[28] A Labour Government had to act as a national government and so the NUM could commit itself (and its members) to supporting a Labour Government without committing itself to supporting specific policies, additionally, the thirteen years of 'Tory misrule' must not be allowed to happen again: things might be bad under Labour, but they would be a whole lot worse under the Conservatives. Thus,

> It would be the greatest folly to permit feelings of dismay and any strained sense of loyalty to distort our judgement of the political issues involved at this General Election.[29]

This appeal was aided by the general, un-programmatic appeal of the Labour Government in the General Election of March 1966 and the need of the Government to increase its tiny majority. The appeal of the NUM added conviction to the view that the problems of the industry could not be settled in isolation from the general malaise of the economy. The rejection of incomes policy in July demonstrated an increased willingness to question the NUM's loyalty to a Labour Government when the interests of the mineworkers were threatened by that Government, even though the NUM leaders felt the mineworker would benefit from incomes policy as a whole.

The policy of the Yorkshire Area had a strong unilinear aspect; it was largely oriented around the fuel policy as a panacea for the industry. The relationship of the NUM with the Government was influenced by the NCB's attempts to rationalise the industry by pit closures. Such a policy placed a severe strain upon the normally loyal NUM, which had felt it had a joint fuel policy with the Labour Government. This strain was eased by seeking improvements in pay. However, this impeded by

80

the incomes policy of the Government and the NUM's general desire to support Government incomes policy. Initially the bulk of this opposition came from sections of the NUM that were politically to the left of both the Union leaderships and the Labour Government.

The initial approval of the incomes policy in April 1965 in indicative of the amount of support from the Union movement for such a policy. The NUM approved this policy but by July 1966 the NUM had moved against such support. The NUM, the GMWU and the AEU had been committed to opposing a statutory incomes policy and there was a distinct possibility of a repeat of the rejection of incomes policy in 1949-1950. This was prevented by the willingness of a number of union leaderships to overturn, or disregard, official union policy and support the statutory incomes policy. Amongst these leaderships was that of the NUM, particularly Sidney Ford, the President.

To explain this we must return to the NUM Annual Conference of 1966. Ford had pleaded with the delegates to give the Labour Government time and to be loyal to that Government,

> ... we must not ask too much of it too quickly ... Rome was not built in a day ... We must not assume that, governing in the interests of the whole country, the Government's decisions will always please us. We must not forget that fundamental loyalty to the Labour Party ... [30]

Ford was our of step with Conference. This can be seen in Composite Resolution III which sought "substantial increases" in all day-wage rates which although couched in militant language included no cash amounts included (Yorkshire sought to include a figure of £3). On this W Carr stated,

> We in Yorkshire are resolved that no longer should we be compelled by one circumstance after another to be fobbed off with pittances that are substitutes for wage increases that do not even measure up to the rise in the cost of living.[31]

Conference committed the NUM to substantial increases in wages and to opposing the statutory incomes policy of the Labour Government. However,

as soon as the Conference ended elements within the
NEC tried to close the breach with the Labour
Government.   Resolution 30, for example, was deemed
by the NEC to be subsumed within the NUM resolution
to the 1966 TUC, and as such it was decided not to
procede until after the TUC had met.   Action on
the Prices and Incomes Bill was deferred until after
a Special Meeting of the NEC at Blackpool at the end
of September during the Labour Party Conference.[32]
These decisions provided the NEC with a breathing
space of two months to attempt to reverse, or
nullify, the decisions of the NUM Conference.   The
fact that the Conference had rejected Government
policy by the tiny majority of 2,000 votes was used
to argue that the vote did not represent the true
feelings of the Union membership and was a freak.
This was taken up by the Yorkshire Area Council
which endorsed the TUC-Government policy on Prices
and Incomes by calling for a standstill on wage
increases.[33]

At the Special Meeting of the NEC on the
2nd September, certain members of the NEC gave
prominence to the Prime Minister's statement of the
20th July and the fact that Parliament had already
approved the Prices and Incomes Bill.   The NEC
expressed its disappointment at the Government's
failure to consult the trade unions, but the NEC
decided, in defiance of the Conference resolution,
to support Government incomes policy.   This was on
the grounds that the vote had been taken in early
July before the 20th July economic crisis measures,
therefore circumstances had changed, and that the
adverse resolution had been formed around the
undesirability of a statutory incomes policy and not
incomes policy per se.   Two viewpoints emerged in
the NEC: first, over a compulsory incomes policy;
and second, upon the powers of the NEC vis-a-vis
Conference.   The supporters of Government policy
argued that the Conference decision had been taken
before the July economic crisis and the NEC should
express "misgivings" over compulsion, but that
"the Union should support the General Council in
their acquiescence to the Government's proposals
for a prices and incomes standstill."[34]

The word 'acquiescence' is of critical
importance, implying neither support nor opposition.
This was countered by the argument that Union policy
had been laid down by the Annual Conference.[35]
Ford resolved this dispute by ruling that Resolution
30, "did not preclude the NEC from discussing and
dealing with the situation which had developed as a

consequence of the Prime Minister's statement on
the 20th July".[36]
    Ford and his supporters on the NEC successfully
overturned the Conference decision, but the NUM was
still left with its critical TUC resolution on pay
policy.   This had been referred to the TUC grouping
committee but the NUM resolution remained the basis
of the composite, therefore the NUM had to move.
Some members felt that their decision over Resolution
30 would be open them to ridicule as the Union was
opposed to a compulsory policy but committed to
supporting an incomes policy of which compulsion was
a part.   The NEC resolved this by recognising
the gravity of the economic situation, whilst
emphasising its disquiet over pay compulsion.[37]
    Ford overturned Rule 23 which enunciates the
sovereignty of the Annual Conference in favour of
Rule 8 which states that between the Conference the
Union will be governed by the NEC.   Rule 8 also
states that the NEC "shall perform all duties laid
down for and by resolution of Conference, and it
shall not at any time act contrary to, or in
defiance of, any resolution of Conference."[38]
Ford over-ruled the Conference in order to give
political support to a Labour Government, an act he
was to admit was unconstitutional.[39]
    Composite Resolution VII at the 1966 TUC, of
which the NUM resolution was the core, expressed
opposition to the statutory pay policy.[40]   Will
Paynter, the NUM General Secretary, moved the
resolution arguing that the NUM was solely
concerned about the right to free collective
bargaining.   Paynter prophesied that a statutory
pay policy would mean that strikes "are more likely
to be emotional, far more elemental, far more
forceful in their character than those which arise
from the normal frustrations of collective bargaining."[41]   The TUC approved Composite Resolution VII
by 4,209,000 to 4,683,000 a majority of 474,000.
    On the 28th July the NCB informed the NEC that
the White Paper on pay policy required that pay
commitments entered into on or before the 20th July
but not yet implemented must be deferred for six
months.[42]   By the end of 1966 the NUM was committed
to and enmeshed in a statutory wages policy.   This
commitment did not have formal sanction and
according to the NUM Rules this support was
unconstitutional.   Both the AEU and the GMWU had
similarly decided not to oppose Government policy at
the TUC.   These unions and their supporters were
able to defeat a TGWU-NALGO resolution critical of

Government pay policy.
        Branch anger was inevitable result of the NEC's
behaviour.   In the Yorkshire Area four resolutions
were submitted (from Edlington, Bentley, Brierley,
and Brodsworth) bitterly attacking the Government
pay policy and NEC support for that policy.
Sixteen resolutions were submitted complaining of
the anomalies created by the implementation of
NPLA, low daywages, and the failure to implement
wage increases.   The standstill on pay talks was
made worse by the delay in publishing the TUC
guidelines on pay until March.   The NEC could not
begin negotiations until it knew the parameters of
these negotiations.[43]
        In response to this frustration the TUC called
a Conference of Executives for the 2nd March to
consider the future of pay policy as Part IV of the
Prices and Incomes Act was due to lapse in August
1967.   The NUM Executive felt that there was little
chance of agreeing to a renewal of compulsion, and
emphasis was placed on voluntarism.   The Government, however, sought to strengthen Part II of the
Act and increase its delaying power from four to
twelve months.   This presented the NEC with an
opportunity to abandon a policy which was promoting
internal conflict.   The NEC grasped at this opening
by arguing that legal compulsion was purely
temporary, but the NUM was unwilling to further
impede the implementation of NPLA and the daywage
structure.   The NUM did agree to support the TUC
for the present.[44]
        The TUC policy - Incomes Policy in the Period
of Transition - was issued against a background of
rising unrest over pay restraint, and demands for
justice for the low paid.   This allowed the NUM
to revert to the pre-July 1966 practice of sub-
mitting above the norm pay demands, whilst
protesting their loyalty to the Labour Government,
arguing that the miners were 'a special case'.[45]
In its Annual Report the NEC announced that it
proposed to adhere to the 1966 Conference decisions
on pay, but warned the membership that they would
have to take into account pay policy and the NCB
finances.   The NEC argued that the easing of pay
restraint would allow the NUM to concentrate upon
low pay and the problems of NPLA.[46]
        During the debates at the 1967 Annual
Conference the General Secretary of the Yorkshire
Area, Sidney Schofield, demanded the creation of
an "equitable wages structure" to redistribute
wealth inside the industry in favour of the low

paid. Schofield's speech demonstrated a desire
within the Yorkshire Area for a wage offensive, that
moderation and reasonableness had won little for
the miners and should be abandoned.

Schofield argued that if the future of the
industry was dependent upon cheap coal and that if
wages had to be financed by production when moderation was the correct policy, but events of the
recent past had destroyed confidence in the ability
of the NUM to secure the interests of their members
(particularly the low paid) and if employment could
only be secured by low pay then the Union must
reject this policy. Schofield argued that the job
of the NUM was to fight for the low paid: "this
union must support their arguments", and, "we expect
something more than glowing tributes from
Ministers."[48]

The dilemma of the NEC was to reconcile this
rising discontent with their political support of the
Labour Government. The NEC had two aims, first, an
immediate increase for the low paid so as to divert
demands for a general wage increase; second, maintain
the NUM's general support for the Government. The
plight of the low paid can be seen from the speech
of A Beecham, a Yorkshire delegate.

> ... as recently as Friday I had £9-16-0
> on my (pay) note. Take stoppages off,
> incomes tax, what have you? I had
> £6-10-0 to take up that pit lane ...
> I do not know where we are going at
> all ... (but) you can understand my
> feelings and (those of) a hell of a
> lot more.[49]

The National Power Loading Agreement

NPLA was signed in 1966 and marked the creation of
a national daywage structure, a long-standing aim
of the NUM. NPLA meant the progressive end of
piece work which, in effect, meant a wage cut for
many miners. This was the case in Yorkshire
which had been one of the best paid coalfields,
and indeed Yorkshire voted against the implementation of NPLA. The first review of NPLA had been
due in January 1967 but this had been postponed
by Government pay policy. The review took place
after the lapse of Part IV of the Prices and Incomes
Act (1966) and by the Autumn of 1967 considerable
frustration had emerged over the anomalies generated
by NPLA. The NUM's 1967 wage claim had been for
"substantial" pay increases for the low paid and for

increased uniformity in NPLA rates.   The NCB's
offer amounted to an average increase of two
shillings and threepence per week on NPLA rates.
The NEC were dissatisfied with the offer, but felt
"this was the best settlement which could be
obtained in the present circumstances" and that the
offer was "the best pay offer since 1961."   The
Areas were recommended to accept by an Area vote.
The effect in Yorkshire was a one shilling and
fourpence increase in NPLA rates, a weekly increase
from £24-15-0 to £25-3-0.   Yorkshire voted by 145
with no votes against, to accept.[50]
    Miners' wages had been restrained by Government
pay policy, but the implementation of NPLA was
important as it provided for a standstill in wage
rates in well paid coalfields so as to allow low
payed coalfields to catch up. This caused much
resentment.   NPLA was the culmination of the NUM's
(and MFGB's) attempts to abolish piece work and
create a truly national wage system, it was
therefore greeted as a major achievement by the
NUM.[51]
    NPLA had a number of attractions for the NUM.
First, it ended the interminable wrangling at pit
and Area level over piece rates by substituting a
set of common national task rates.   Second, in
ending piece work NPLA would secure the equalisation
of wages throughout the coal industry so that, for
example, the mineworker in South Wales would be
paid the same rate for the same job as the mineworker in Yorkshire.   Third, NPLA took power away
from the Areas to national level as after 1966
collective wage bargaining became a totally national
activity.   The coalfield unions - the traditional
power houses of the Union - lost their wage
bargaining functions to the NEC.   Fourth, NPLA was
a means of subsidising high-cost pits in the Celtic
fringe and the small coalfields (with the exception
of Kent) from the more economically viable , low
cost pits of the Central Coalfields.   This subsidy
was intended to maintain pits in existence,
preserve mining communities and maintain the membership of the NUM.   Finally, as NPLA was a
productivity agreement, wages could be increased
without there being an open challenge to Government
incomes policy.
    The Agreement was important to the NCB for
two major reasons.   First, the Board was given
increased control over the production process and
the deployment of manpower because of the need to
use machinery in the most efficient manner.

Second, under NPLA the Board was given greater
control over wage costs. NPLA ended the steady
escalation of wage costs due to the wage drift
inherent in the piece work system. The end of
piece work also increased the NCB's ability to plan
production as it did away with the need to re-
negotiate frequently price lists and ended the
disputes which resulted from these negotiations.
The Board obtained greater control over manpower as
under NPLA all mineworkers became 'taskworkers' with
a far less closely defined job, working to a pre-
determined production plan to achieve the most
efficient use of mining technology. This greater
flexibility of labour had disciplinary overtones as
it could be used to move mineworkers on to a less
favourable task rate should management deem such a
move necessary to production. Management obtained
greater control over the production process and the
deployment of labour; for the mineworker NPLA was
inherently unsettling, involving greater and closer
supervision, the loss of immediate job control and
the disruption of longstanding habits and practices.
     For the leaders of the NUM, NPLA seemed to
offer the answer to their immediate industrial and
political problems. The price to be paid for this
solution was wage restraint in the better paid
coalfields such as Yorkshire. With increased use
of power loading and mining technology productivity
became less dependent on physical effort from the
mineworker. Piece rates were replaced by a series
of task rates determined by time and motion studies.
The actual amount of money available for wages was
largely the responsibility of the NCB, and in wage
negotiations the basic role of the NUM was not in
influencing the size of the 'wages cake', but in
deciding how that 'cake' was to be divided amongst
the various task rates. The NUM was aware that to
press for an increase in the amount of money
available for distribution as wages would jeopardise
high cost pits by increasing their wages costs.
Under NPLA the NUM sought to achieve long term
wage and cost equilibrium (wages increasing in line
with productivity) and therefore long term security
of employment for the NUM's members.
     The equalisation of wage rates could have been
accomplished at once. Immediate equalisation,
however, needed money which the NCB did not have,
hence the gradual implementation of NPLA between
1966 and 1971. The cost of immediate implementation and equalisation could have been met by a
massive government subsidy, or by further pit

closures. The former was ruled out by the
Government, and the latter would be contrary to one
of the NUM's main objectives. The alternative
method was to restrain wages in the highest paid
coalfields to provide the surplus needed to finance
equalisation and to maintain the level of employment
in mining.

The impact of NPLA proved to be more proble-
matic than was ever envisaged by the NUM. As the
NCB closed high cost pits, national productivity
increased and there was a slowdown in the rate of
closures. However, the slowdown did not represent
an increase in job security. In a falling market
for coal the extension of mechanisation inevitably
meant the further contraction of the industry. As
collieries closed, production was concentrated on
low cost pits and coalfields whose efficiency was
used to equalise wages on low wage coalfields.
Therefore, as equalisation progressed costs in these
coalfields increased, making more pits vulnerable to
closure. The industry and the NUM seemed caught in
a vicious circle; as high cost pits closed, output
was concentrated on low cost pits and productivity
increased, thus threatening more pits. To avoid
a situation where equalisation meant pit closures
the NUM sought a balance between wages and employment. The balance was provided by low wages for
everyone in the industry so as to maintain the
maximum number of jobs.

The effect of NPLA was to equalise pay, but in
doing so, low pay was 'nationalised' and the unfore-
seen effect of NPLA was to 'nationalise'
dissatisfaction over wages throughout the NUM.
Before 1966 the extent of low pay was disguised by
the adding of local piece rates to the national
minimum wage rates. Between 1966 and 1971
dissatisfaction with wages progressively achieved a
common national standard. NPLA was to prove vital
for the relationship between the NUM, the mineworker
and politics.

As mineworkers' pay stabilised and as an
increased burden of production was placed upon the
Central Coalfields, men left the industry for better
paid jobs. As pay stabilised as a consequence of
NPLA and pay policy, the miners continued their
slide down the wages ladder. In the NPLA period
1966-1968 the NUM was officially committed to
stabilising wages and to increasing productivity.
In theory NPLA was to redistribute wealth amongst
the mineworkers but the problem was that the total
available for redistribution was being produced by a

declining number of mineworkers increasingly
demoralised by pit closures and stagnating wages in
an overall context of falling living standards.
The problems of the industry were not blamed on NPLA
but on the failure of the Labour Government to
institute and operate a fuel policy, and this was
reflected in the attitudes of the Yorkshire Area
branches. So great was the hostility to the
Government's coal policy that a National Demonstration was organised to bring over their "opposition
to the Government's fuel policy and our conviction
that they and further contraction will be contrary
to the National Interest". A resolution was
passed attacking Government fuel policy.[52]

Wages, Hours and Unrest
At the 1967 NUM Conference a joint Yorkshire-
Derbyshire resolution demanded that hours of work
for surfacemen should be reduced to 7½ hours per
day. The figure was proposed by Yorkshire but the
original Yorkshire resolution instructed the NEC to
secure the reduction, whereas the Derbyshire
resolution requested that the NEC "give immediate
priority" to the claim. This was adopted in the
Composite, F Glover, a Yorkshire delegate, stated
that the surface hours issue had been debated many
times at Conference but no progress had been made,
and as a result, the surfacemen were losing patience
and confidence in the NUM. The NEC had asked for
remission of this resolution as negotiations were
underway with the NCB for a reduction in surface
hours.[53] This was agreed by Conference.
    Yorkshire also supported Composite I, demanding
an end to "paltry increases" in wages. Moving the
Composite, Sid Schofield argued that NPLA was not
meeting the expectations of the miners as the NCB
was refusing to make the money available for
equalisation; likewise daywagemen were increasingly
dissatisfied with low wages.[54] Despite years of
co-operation some 30,000 mineworkers received less
than £13 per week take home pay. The resolution
was passed unanimously.
    By mid-1968 negotiations were in progress on
the 1967 NUM Conference resolution calling for
substantial increases on NPLA and daywage rates.
This claim had to be settled before the 1968 claim
could be negotiated. The NUM was keen to secure a
speedy settlement, and they also sought to move the
date of implementation from the 1st January to the
1st November. Under the negotiating procedure no
claim could be implemented until after November 1968

and increases had to be within the limits of pay
policy.   The decision to try to change the date of
implementation was an attempt to make any industrial
action more effective.   Any dispute called after
November meant that industrial action would take
place further into the winter, thus increasing the
chance that coal stocks might last out.   The NUM
also sought to narrow the differential between
daywagemen and those on the NPLA rates, a policy
accepted by the 1967 NUM Conference.   Negotiations
had been extremely slow and frustration was clearly
building up in some areas of the NUM.
       By 1967-1968 every section of the Yorkshire
Area NUM's membership had some reason to complain
at the effects of NUM policies; in addition to the
everyday hazards of underground work, equalisation
had antagonised the faceworker, his wages having
been held back; those employed underground but
away from the coalface were increasingly hostile to
low pay; and finally, surface workers endured low
pay, relatively longer hours and, in many cases,
dreadful working conditions.   The immediate aim of
the NUM was to secure a minimum wage of £15 for
surfacemen and £16 for underground workers not
conditioned to NPLA.   These modest aims were
complicated by the NCB's finances and incomes policy
policy.   The TUC Economic Review of 1968 supported
claims of 3½-5% plus 1% for productivity. This had
been accepted by the NEC of the NUM.[55]   The NCB
argued that it was unable to meet the NUM's demands
under the incomes policy and that they would have to
consult the Government on the proposed increases.
The NEC accused the NCB of prevarication and
expressed annoyance that a third party had been
brought into the bargaining process.[56]   The NCB
made an offer of a 15s per week increase for
daywagemen and 12s for NPLA rates which was all
their accountants and the Government would allow.
The NEC decided to seek further concessions.   They
were annoyed that their sacrifices in the 1950s and
1960s had not led to better wages.   They "wondered
what more the men had to do to earn the gratitude
of Board and warrant better treatment."[57]   The
NCB pleaded the constraints of the pay policy, but
on the 24th October the NCB submitted an increased
offer, (after consulting with the Government),
conceding the £15/16 minimum and the 1st November
starting date.   The NEC formally recommended
acceptance and that the offer "was the maximum which
could be obtained by negotiations in the present
circumstances."[58]   Some NEC members had suggested

that industrial action would secure a greater
increase but this had been rejected.   The offer was
to be put to the membership with a recommendation
for acceptance.   It was made clear that not to
accept risked referral of the claim to the Prices
and Incomes Board and that the government had no
intention of subsidising wage increase made outside
the NCB's finances (any excess would be paid for by
pit closures).[59]   The NUM argued,

> The issue in the ballot is not as to
> whether the offer is adequate, (but)
> as to whether more money could be
> obtained and what needs to be done
> to get it ... The suggestion by
> those who oppose acceptance is that
> the Union should organise some form
> of industrial action.   It is claimed
> that this represents leadership ...
> Any form of action must be judged
> against the situation in a particular
> industry.   In the coal mining industry
> it involves the serious risk of increasing
> the number of pit closures ...   The test
> of leadership is its ability to assess
> factors operating inside the industry and
> the effects of external forces and to
> obtain the maximum result with a minimum of
> hardship to the Union members.[60]

In the Yorkshire area during this period a letter was
received by the Executive Committee from the
Kellingley Branch demanding a series of one day
stoppages and demonstrations until all unemployed
or redundant miners were found jobs, and urging
that the NUM should end all financial support of
MPs who refused to oppose Government policy.   The
Executive stated there could be no official support
of attacks of this type upon the Government.[61]
    As in the case of the fuel policy and pit
closures a deep resentment over the level of wages
in mining had built up in Yorkshire by the end of
1968.   Again, the main cause was Government policy.
However, the miners were in the unique position of
having their wages held back twice: once by prices
and incomes policy and by the implementation of
NPLA after 1966.   As in the case of fuel policy
there was an alternative to acquiescence, that of
resistance via industrial action, but the same
constraints applied.   Support for industrial
action remained localised and confined.   Clearly

there was a great deal of diffuse unrest in the
coalfield but what was lacking was an eruptive
factor which would generate conflict in the
coalfield.   After 1968 there was a growth of
militancy in the coalfield and the Area leadership
found it increasingly difficult to control or
manage this unrest.

During the summer of 1968 the tensions in the
coalfield welled to the surface.   There was an
acrimonious dispute at Wheldale over the marketmen
which led to an unofficial strike in North Yorkshire
and a stiff fight between left and right.   This
dispute also revealed the considerable hostility to
the policies of both the Labour Government and the
NUM.[62]   However, of greater importance was the
continuing problem of miners' pay.

Council had already protested at the slowness
of the wage negotiations.   In October, after a
report on pay negotiations by Tommy Burke, Council
went,

> ... on record as being against the wages
> offer of the Board, and demands that any
> wages settlement shall include the
> principle of a guaranteed minimum of
> £16 per week underground and £15 for
> surfacemen.[63]

Next business was moved and defeated by 53 votes to
41.   Sam Bullough ruled that he could not accept
this resolution under the constitution, but he was
voted down and the resolution deemed accepted
by 75 to 17.

The Area leadership faced two sources of
unrest: first, that of pay;   and second, a general
feeling of frustration at the state of the
industry.   An important element was the feelings
of impatience, disappointment and hostility to
the Labour Government and the NEC's support of that
Government.   Within Yorkshire there was a growing
willingness to contemplate strike action;   for
example, Wombwell Main, a pit threatened with
closure asked the Area Executive to sanction a
branch ballot on resistance to the closure.   Under
Union rules such a resolution was inadmissible, but
15 delegates expressed vociferous support for
Wombwell.[64]   The Executive responded by stating
that they would attend the Labour Party Conference
with a view to lobbying and influencing the
Government and Delegates on the Government's fuel
policy.   Mick Welsh, an Executive member suggested

that twenty delegates be sent in addition. The
Executive agreed but warned, that the delegation
should be orderly.[65]
     The NUM was scheduled to move the reference
back of the section of the Labour Party NEC Report
on fuel policy on the grounds that no action had
been taken to implement Composite Resolution 22.[66]
     Caught between deep loyalty to the Labour
Government and the unrest of the members, the Union
emphasised the gratitude of the miners to the
Government for cushioning the impact of the run-
down of the industry on the miners, but was equally
critical of the failure to act on the Conference
Resolution. Roy Mason, the Minister of Fuel and
Power, emphasised the positive aspects of Government
policy (to considerable barracking from Yorkshire
miners who had forced their way into the Hall) and
contrasted it with that pursued by the previous
Conservative Government. Mason argued that the
speed of the decline was negotiable, and on these
grounds the Conference was urged to accept the NEC
Report.[67] In spite of formidable opposition from
the NEC and the Government, the Conference voted
to accept the reference back by 3,400,000 votes.[68]
This appeared to be a victory for the policy
advocated by the NUM Special Conference. However
the 1968 Party Conference was notable for the
number of defeats sustained by the Government, there
being no less than six. All proved to be hollow
victories as the Government ignored the defeats and
did not alter its policies.

The Yorkshire Miners, the Union and Politics
Between 1964-1970 there built up considerable
tension in the relationship between the NUM and the
Labour Government. By 1969-1970 there was a
willingness on the part of some NUM branches in
Yorkshire to consider industrial action in an
attempt to persuade the Labour Government to modify
its policies towards the industry. There were
other manifestations of this feeling: for example,
the Area Executive Committee decided to seek
official permission to hold a ballot on industrial
action unless the NCB increased a pay offer.[69] A
number of branches exhibited considerable animosity
to the Labour Government's attempts to reform
industrial relations.[70] These tensions exploded
in the unofficial strikes of 1969 and 1970.
     Despite animosity to the policies of the
Labour Government the leaders of the Yorkshire Area
were concerned to prevent a breach appearing

between the Union and the Government.   Shafton
Workshops, for example, urged total opposition to
the proposals contained in In Place of Strife.
Total opposition implied the use of industrial
action.   Shafton was persuaded from moving this
resolution by the Executive on the grounds that NUM
policy would be decided at the Annual Conference.[71]
The Government was also aware of the tensions in
their relationship with the miners.   This recognition can be seen in the passage of the Coal Industry
Act (1967), the Coal Industry Bill (1970) which
boosted aid to the industry, and the postponement of
pit closures.   These sentiments represent a joint
NUM-Government attempt to repair their damaged
relationship.   The weight of sentiment, history,
and political calculation were major factors in
recreating this relationship, as was the possibility
of a return of a Conservative Government in the
General Election due in 1970 or 1971.   This
reconciliation was helped by the Conservative
Party's strident espousal of industrial relations
legislation after the defeat of the Labour Government's own proposals.[72]

The announcement of the General Election ended
all criticism of the Government.   The Yorkshire
Area Council immediately and unreservedly pledged
its full support: "We are convinced that the
return of a Labour Government is in our best
interests as only a Labour Government is conscious
of and sympathetic to our aims, aspirations and
needs."[73]   The NUM urged the miners to vote Labour
on three grounds: first, hostility to the Tories;
second, "the Labour Government ... have to their
credit introduced many measures of social reform
designed to remove the fears and worries created by
old age, injury, sickness and redundancy"; and
finally, because of their aid to the coal industry

> The fact that the Coal Industry Bill of
> 1970 which would have continued aid to the
> industry was already before Parliament,
> highlights the need for the re-election
> of the Labour Government.   Experience has
> shown that we shall obtain a more reasonable
> solution from Labour than from a Tory
> administration.[74]

The NUM concluded, " The   record shows there will be
more progress under a Labour Government ..."   These
statements are remarkable given the attitude of the
Government to the industry and to the NUM: the NUM

was unwilling to push criticism to the point at
which they felt they might damage the electoral
chances of the Labour Government.
     The dilemma of the NUM leadership is June 1970
can be seen from the General Secretary's Annual
Report.   Sidney Schofield urged the Yorkshire
miners to support Labour,

> Notwithstanding the disappointment we
> may have endured from time to time,
> because our own Government has not
> always acted in the way we thought
> they should, do we really believe it
> possible that the Conservative Government
> would have given more financial support
> to our industry than our own Government?[75]

Miners were being urged to vote Labour not
because of Labour's achievements, but out of a
belief that the Conservatives would have done less.
Labour had savaged the coal industry, but even this
was turned into a virtue,

> ... one would think it fair to assume
> that even the critics would accept
> that the Labour Government has gone a
> long way to try to minimise any
> hardship on our members ... I
> honestly believe that had we a
> Conservative Government ... the
> contraction of our industry would have
> been much more savage, and the victims -
> our members - would not have received
> the same assistance to help cushion the
> effects of unemployment.[76]

Unemployment under a Labour Government was different
to unemployment under a Conservative Government:
the aid offered by the Government to unemployed
miners "should be sufficient to persuade our members
... to turn out (and vote Labour)."[77]   If there had
been a Conservative Government, and if that
Government had carried out the same policies as
Labour Between 1964-1970, then Schofield would have
been full of indignant outrage.
     This same reasoning was applied to the
position of the working class as a whole.   Labour
did not govern in the interest of one section of
the community or even of one class;   "the majority
of our members do appreciate that ... our Government
has not satisfied our every wish ... to have done

so would have brought opposition from other sections
of the working class ..."[78]   However,

> There may be those ... who believe that
> the road taken by the Government caused
> unnecessary hardship to many people
> (but) the Government maintain that had
> they taken any other road more of our
> people would have suffered for a much
> longer period ... it would be prudent
> for the Government to say now that it
> was unfortunate that the road taken
> resulted in many people having to suffer
> hardship to achieve the good, but just as
> quickly as circumstances will allow we
> intend to take action that will alleviate
> and remove the hardship.[79]

The Report concluded with a strident appeal for
unity,

> ... there is only one party which is
> worthy of the support of those who believe
> in the Brotherhood of Man ... By all means
> let us criticise when criticism is
> necessary, but when the decks are cleared
> in preparation for the next fight let us
> go into the battle united ...[80]

The possibility, and then reality, of a Conservative
Government exerted an influence over NUM policy -
instinctive hostility to, and suspicion of, a
Conservative Government.   This was tempered by the
appreciation that the NUM had to work with all
Governments.
     At the NUM Annual Conference of 1970, the
Vice-President (and acting Conference Chairman),
Sidney Schofield, warned the delegates that the NUM
should not automatically attack the new Government.

> We are conscious of the fact that the new
> Government may have a different approach to
> our industry, but at this stage I respect-
> fully submit that no useful purpose could
> be served in crying "stinking fish". We
> are fortunate to be citizens of a country
> that believes in democracy. Just as we
> have opposed and criticised the Labour
> Government, on issues that in our view
> interfered with the well-being of our
> members, similar action will be

taken if the new Government attempts
to bring in measures or cause hardship
to the miners. We must wait and see what
the future holds in store for us and we
must co-operate with the Government of
the day, if we are satisfied that by doing
so we are acting in the best interests of
our members.[81]

The NUM and the Yorkshire Area were committed
to the TUC's proposals on resistance to the
Industrial Relations Bill.[82] However, these
proposals and the existence of a Conservative
Government made it easier for the Yorkshire Area
to consider industrial action. A Special Executive
Committee meeting, for example, proposed that "the
Yorkshire Area would be prepared to recommend its
members to support any industrial action proposed
and agreed by the TUC."[83] During this period the
Yorkshire Area became much more familiar with
industrial action; there being massive unofficial
stoppages in the Autumn of 1969, and in the
Autumn of 1970 - the latter was an 'official'
unofficial strike.

The Paradox of the Miners' Political Strategy
The period 1945 to 1969 was a period of changing
perceptions about the role of the NUM in the
political system. During this period the official
leaders of the NUM were dominated by, first, the
memory of the inter-war years (and especially of
1926) which gave them a strong antipathy to strike
action; and second, a belief that the nationalisation of the mines offered the only chance of a
secure future. The common factor was the role of
the Labour Party and a Labour Government.

Nationalisation could only be achieved by a
majority Labour Government, and the miners' leaders
felt that both nationalisation and a sympathetic
Labour Government would ensure that miners'
interests would be served. Thus, the miners'
leaders had an almost blind faith in the Labour
Party, so that when a Labour Government nationalised
the mines, their gratitude knew no bounds.

The relationship between the NUM and Labour
Governments involved a paradox; miners' interests
could only be secured by a Labour Government and
to be effective such a Government had to have
control of the House of Commons. The Labour Party
could achieve this by the widest possible electoral
appeal and by appearing to be supra-class national

party.   This meant first, that the NUM's strong
loyalty to Labour became a deference to the Party's
political and electoral strategy;   and second, that
despite this loyalty and deference the national
supra-class strategy of the Labour Party enabled it,
when in Government, to resist 'sectional' demands
from groups such as the NUM.   The NUM tended to
orient its activities as a trade union around what
were seen as the overriding political-electoral
interests of the Labour Party and Labour Government.
Thus, a Labour Government and political action
were seen as the only viable protection for the
interests of the miners.
    Unfortunately, the Governments of 1945-1951
and particularly that of 1964-1970, felt themselves
able and willing to resist sectional demands made
by the NUM and by other trade unions.   The primary
vehicle of working class political influence showed
itself to be primarily concerned with governing in
the 'national interest' which compelled the
organised working class to turn in on itself and
rely on class specific organisations - notably,
the trade unions.   The trade unions became
involved not only in conflict with their employers
but also in political conflict with the Government
as Government tried to restrict the activities
of trade unions.
    At the same time the bulk of mineworkers were
unwilling to abandon their historic relationship
with 'their' Party.   The persistence of the
feeling that in some vague and mystical way the
Labour Party in Government remained the party of
the working class was a crucial factor in
preventing and abiding cleavage developing between
Union and Party.   The dilemma of supporting a
Government seeking to restrain a union's ability
to satisfy the immediate demands of its members
caused an increase in the level of internal conflict
as groups of miners came to challenge the hitherto
dominant perspective of the official leaderships.
The bulk of this challenge was not ideological in
any structured sense although much of this
challenge was politically and industrially left.
The miners who supported these unofficial leaders
were motivated by poor pay, bad working conditions,
long hours, inflation, rent increases, together with
the feeling that the official leaderships were
doing nothing to meet their demands.   In a
situation where trade unionists are thrown back on
their own resources and organisations, industrial
action is looked upon as an increasingly attractive

and rational method of applying pressure.   This
feeling can be seen in the Houghton Main resolution,
the Kellingley resolution and latterly in the
Executive Committee's request for permission to
ballot.   These requests are important as they
sought to apply direct industrial pressure on a
Labour Government, and the effect was to help to
familiarise the Yorkshire Area with the idea of
industrial action.
        By the late 1960s there was a change in the
attitude of many miners.   In an interview Will
Paynter was asked if the miner of 1968 was different
to that of 1926;   he replied,

> In mining the militancy is directed
> today against the insecurity of
> employment which exists because there
> has been a run-down of the industry.
> There had been a change in the
> relationship of forces over the years
> and there is a change in the character
> of militancy.[84]

Paynter argued that the run-down freed the miners
of their defensiveness and that the miners could
now be expected to move onto the offensive over
wages.
        By 1970 there were tremendous pressures
building up in the Yorkshire coalfield as a
consequence of NPLA, the run-down of the industry,
and pay policy.   The basic aim of Wilson was to
complete the work of Ramsay Macdonald and Clement
Attlee in establishing the Labour Party as the
'natural' party of Government.   By 1970 it appeared
that this had been accomplished but at the cost
of severe internal tensions inside many trade
unions and a 'crise de conscience' within the
Party.   In the case of the NUM, the butchery of
the industry and the impact of NPLA and pay policy
did not lead to a deep split, indeed conscious
attempts were made to cement the relationship
between the Union and Party at the official level.
At the unofficial level there was an increased
emphasis upon industrial action.
        The defeat of the Labour Government in 1970
and its replacement by a Conservative Government
pledged to industrial relations policies obnoxious
to the trade unions helped the incipient unofficial
militancy to ultimately flower into official
militancy in 1971-1972.   The outburst of unofficial
militancy in Yorkshire in 1969-1970 was the product

of the mineworkers' experiences in the post-war period and particularly under the 1964-1970 Labour Government. The effect of this was to push the NUM as a whole further to the left.

REFERENCES

1   YA (NUM);   5 February 1965;   and
      BS Circular 11/65 (5 February 1965)
2   NUM: Special Conference Report;   12 March 1965
      1965;   p2
3   Special Conference;   p18
4   YA (NUM):   22-24 March 1965
5   NUM (EC);   25 June 1965
6   YA (NUM);   12 July;   and   16 August 1965
7   YA (NUM);   Annual Report of the President for
      1964 (March 1965)
8   NUM (EC);   1 April 1965
9   NUM (EC);   29 April 1965
10   NUM: Annual Conference Report, 1965;   pp182-
      183
11   NUM (EC):   9 December 1965
12   JNNC;   15 December 1965
13   NUM (EC);   10 February 1966
14   BS Circular 15/66 (9 February 1966)
15   NUM: Special Conference Report, 18 February
      1966;   pp4-6
16   Special Conference;   p11
17   Special Conference;   p21
18   Special Conference;   p28
19   BS Circular 10/66 (26 January 1966)
20   YA (NUM);   14 March;   and   13 April 1966
21   NUM (EC);   25 March 1966
22   NUM (EC);   12 May 1966;
      JNNC;   11 May 1966;   and,
      NUM (EC);   9 June 1966
      See also,
      YA (NUM):   23 March 1966;   and
      BS Circular   71/66 (9 June 1966)
      An Area Vote is one where the attitude of the
         Areas is decided by the Area Executive on
         behalf of the Area members
23   YA (NUM);   28 February;   and 1 March 1966
24   YA (NUM);   27 June 1966
25   NUM: Annual Conference Report 1966;
      pp205-206;   and   p209
      My emphasis
26   Annual Conference;   p215
27   NUM: General Election Manifesto, 1966
28   NUM: Manifesto (my emphasis)
29   NUM: Manifesto

30   NUM: Annual Conference Report 1966; pp96-97
      (my emphasis)
31   Annual Conference; p143
32   NUM (EC); 28 July 1966
33   YA (NUM); 30-31 July 1966
34   NUM (EC); 2 September 1966
35   NUM (EC); 2 September 1966
36   NUM (EC); 2 September 1966
37   NUM (EC); 2 September 1966
38   NUM Rules 1974; Rule 8; and Rule 23
39   The Guardian; 5 September 1966
40   TUC Report 1966; p568
41   TUC Report; pp466-467
42   NUM (EC); 2 September 1966
43   BS Circular 17/67 (16 February 1967); and
      NUM (EC); 9 February 1967
44   NUM (EC); 1 March 1967
45   AS Circular 94/67 (4 May 1967); and
      TUC Circular 83 (66-67); 27 April 1967
46   NUM: Report of the NEC, May 1967; p13
47   NUM: Annual Conference Report, 1967; p123
48   Annual Conference, 1967; p124
49   Annual Conference, 1967; p131
50   NUM (EC): 21 September 1967;
      JNNC; 20 September 1967; and,
      NUM (EC); 12 October 1967
      See also,
      BS Circular 85/76 (26 September 1967)
51   The National Power Loading Agreement (NPLA),
      November 1966; p4
52   YA (NUM): 23 October 1967; and
      BS Circular 88/67 (16 October 1967);
      YA (NUM): 13 November 1967
53   NUM: Annual Conference Report 1968; pp150-
      154
54   Annual Conference, 1968; p123
55   NUM (EC); 27 February 1968
56   NUM (EC); 12 September 1968; and
      10 October 1968
57   JNNC; 23-24 October 1968
58   NUM (EC); 14 November 1968 (my emphasis)
59   BS Circular 118/68 (20 November 1968)
60   As Circular 218/68 (20 November 1968)
61   YA (NUM); 15 December 1968
62   The Wheldale Dispute will be examined in more
      detail in Chapter 6
63   YA (NUM); 28 October 1968
64   YA (NUM); 26 August 1968
65   YA (NUM); 16 September 1968; and;
      BS Circular 96/68 (25 September 1968)

66   Labour Party Conference Report 1968; pp278-
        279; and,
      Labour Party NEC Report 1968; pp98-100
67   LPCR; pp279-280
68   LPCR; p281
69   YA (NUM); 10 February 1969.   The NEC later
        rejected this request
70   BS Circular 21/69 (21 February 1969)
71   YA (NUM); 21 April 1969
72   YA (NUM); 22 April 1970
73   YA (NUM); 28 May 1970
74   NUM: General Election Manifesto, 1970
75   YA (NUM); Annual Reports for 1969 (March 1970)
        (March 1970); p91
76   Annual Reports; p91
77   Annual Reports; p92
78   Annual Reports; p92
79   Annual Reports; p93
80   Annual Reports; p93 (my emphasis)
81   NUM: Annual Conference Report, 1970; pp89-90
82   YA (NUM); 26 October 1970
83   YA (NUM); 30 December 1970
84   Tribune; 29 November 1970

Chapter Four

THE SPECIAL RELATIONSHIP: THE MINERS AND THE LABOUR PARTY

The Foundations

Although the MFGB affiliated to the Labour Party
in 1909 many Yorkshire miners were unwilling to
abandon their traditional Liberal political
loyalties.   Consequently, Labour organisation was
initially rudimentary and electoral support for the
Labour Party was small but vociferous.[1]   By 1914
the Yorkshire miners had come to terms with the
Labour Party as the future of party-political action
lay with Labour as nationalisation of the mines
was now the MFGB's prime aim.   The Party was drawn
to the MFGB as it offered an organisational base,
union funds and the support of their members.[2]
However, the NEC of the Labour Party wanted local
political organisation to conform to the national
requirements of the Party, not those of the miners.
The Party's dependence upon the YMA forced a
pragmatic acceptance of a compromise in which the
YMA ran local political organisation and candidate
selection.[3]   Theoretically, affiliation to the
Party subordinated the miners' political activity to
the Party Conference, but the local dominance of the
miners led some Party leaders to fear that the
Party would become the tool of the unions.   This
did not happen because the miners accepted the
leading role of the Party in politics and because
the miners' MPs rapidly assimilated the Party's
role as a national integrative party as opposed
to a trade union or working class party.   The
mining MPs did represent the Yorkshire miners, but
first and foremost they represented the constituency
for which they sat in the interests of the Labour
Party, not the YMA or the MFGB.   These factors led
to the deference of union to Party.

The Yorkshire Miners and Party Organisation

In August 1914, Arthur Henderson, General Secretary
of the Labour Party wrote to the MFGB Executive

asking about their plans for local organisation.
The Executive discussed this at some length, then
passed the letter to the Districts recommending
they organise "Political Labour Committees".[4]   A
committee had already been appointed by the YMA to
consider party-union relations in the coalfield.
This committee's report recommended creating a
sophisticated electoral organisation in which the
miners and YMA would play a pre-eminent, though not
dominant role in the selection and election of
Labour MPs.[5]   These grandiose plans were frustrated
by the war, parliamentary politics only resuming
in 1917.

A second committee established in July 1917
enquired into the state of political organisation
in the coalfield so as to recommend to Council which
of the new constituencies under consideration should
be contested by the YMA on behalf of the Labour
Party.[6]   The committee recommended the YMA contest
Normanton, Rothwell, Wentworth, Rother Valley, Don
Valley and Hemsworth, begin the selection of
candidates and create the necessary electoral
organisation.[7]   At the next Council meeting the
delegates approved this report, with only seven
delegates opposed.[8]   It must be emphasised that, as
in 1914, the Yorkshire miners acted as the
instigators of constituency organisation, and made
efforts to involve other trade unions.   However,
because of their physical presence it was inevitable
that the miners would dominate both constituency
organisation and candidate selection.[9]   By
December 1917 the candidates selection process was
well underway.[10]   Whilst these organisational
matters were attended to the miners completed their
connection to the Party: on 21 December Council
approved an MFGB Executive resolution accepting the
draft of the new Party Constitution containing the
all-important Clause 4.[11]   In January 1918, four
of the YMA's six constituencies had selected
candidates and all were miners: Fred Hall
(Normanton), John Guest (Hemsworth), William Lunn
(Rothwell), and Thomas Grundy (Rother Valley).
These candidates and their supporting organisations
were then instructed "to take the necessary steps to
consult other Trade Unions and Labour Representation
Committees in the Divisions and report to these
offices (those of the YMA) as to the confirmation
of our candidates or otherwise."[12]   The YMA Council
appointed a second committee to examine the extent
of political finance needed "and also as to what
finance shall be paid to constituencies where it is

intended to run Labour candidates for Parliament."
Adequate finance was essential for electoral success
and the committee recommended the distribution of
£1,000: Don Valley £200, Rother Valley £175,
Rothwell £175, Wentworth £150, Hemsworth £150,
Normanton £100, and Wakefield £500. As the MPs'
salaries would be paid centrally by the MFGB these
sums were for organisational purposes.[13]

The Establishment of Labour's Dominance

By November 1918 the YMA was ready to fight seven
seats on behalf of the Labour Party. In the 1918
General Election all these seats, with the
exception of Don Valley and Pontefract, were won by
Labour.[14]   1918 is a watershed in the miners'
relationship with the Labour Party: miners' MPs
were the core of the PLP and their constituencies
the bedrock of Labour's electorate. The miners'
connection to Labour was complete.[15] During 1919
the YMA took an active role in establishing Party
organisation and in propagating the Party's
message, organising a series of mass meetings on
behalf of the Party in all the constituencies fought
by the YMA. To pay for this Council voted £100
to its seven seats.[16] The YMA's support was vital
in securing Labour's dominance in the coalfield, it
provided this support in accord with MFGB policy,
because of its traditional commitment to electoral
politics, but the main reason was to increase
working class representation to help achieve
nationalisation of the mines.
     The Party was not yet an independent organisa-
tional force in the coalfield. The Party was
anxious to establish an independent existence to
avoid organisational overdependence upon the YMA,
there being a fear that such dominance would be
used for sectional ends. The Party was often
ignorant of the state of organisation because of
the reorganisation necessitated by the 1918
Constitution, the expansion in grass-roots political
organisation since 1917, and because in many Labour
seats, including those on the Yorkshire coalfield,
no independent organisation existed. In Barnsley,
for example, there was an embryonic organisation
but it shared its electoral functions with
Barnsley Trades and Labour Council until 1949 when
a conventional CLP was created.[17]
     The main tasks of CLP organisation (apart from
candidate selection) were electoral mobilisation
and political education, but these were undertaken
by the YMA. In all of the YMA's constituencies there

was not one full time agent, but in all of them there was some electoral organisation and miners were prominent in this: in Doncaster the secretary-agent was W Paling a miner from Armthorpe; in Hemsworth, G A Griffiths, a miner form Royston; in Wentworth, T Phipps a miner from Dodworth; in Normanton, A Smith, a miner from Castleford; and in Rother Valley, T Smith a miner from the Nunnery YMA branch.[18] Of these five men, Paling, Griffiths and T Smith were to be miners' MPs. In the 1918 election the local press had been surprised at the Labour Party's strength in the coalfield, attributing this to an organisation built around the YMA branches.[19]

The Hemsworth constituency provides a good example of this linkage. The Labour candidate John Guest, MP since 1918, was a miner from Hemsworth enjoying wide support not only from the miners but from other trade unionists.[20] Guest made few claims based on Party ideology, appealing to the electorate as a miner and a trade unionist (the same grounds as the pre-1914 Lib-Labs), emphasising his local origins, and his experience as a working class representatives on the Board of Guardians. His party label was important, but it was part of a wider appeal based on work and community, party ideology was woven into the mining electorate's everyday experience at work and in the pit villages. Guest was a good constituency man, deeply concerned at improving the conditions of his own people. His agent, G A Griffiths, the branch delegate at Monckton Main, coupled his union office with his political activities, synthesising both party and union. Hemsworth enjoyed the reputation of being the best organised of all Yorkshire mining seats.

The sheer physical weight of the Labour vote in the coalfield intimidated the Liberal and Conservative parties from challenging the miners and the YMA. By the 1923 General Election the truism that miners vote Labour was established: in Doncaster, for example, Labour organisation was based on the YMA branches everyone of which was a "potential committee room"; in Wentworth no Liberal candidate could be found to challenge the miners; in Don Valley a Conservative Association was established for the first time to take over the functions of the moribund Liberal and National Labour parties; in Barnsley no Liberal would challenge John Potts, the Conservative withdrawing on "health grounds"; in Doncaster (in 1924) the

Liberals were urged to join the Conservatives in an anti-Labour alliance.[21]
    The political activity of the Yorkshire miners between 1918 and 1924 is comparable to that of 1883-1885. New voters were entering the electorate and transforming coalfield politics, as in the 1880s the YMA branches were unaffected by redistribution and provided a surrogate political organisation of crucial importance to the Labour Party. After 1918 a new and higher degree of political organisation was introduced into coalfield politics, which despite its shortcomings, was superior to that of its opponents.[22] The miners' dominance was, however, short-lived. During the 1920s the Party established a clearly separate organisational structure from that of the Union codified in the 1933 Hastings Agreement. Miners did indeed remain prominent in the CLPs, but there was a tacit agreement between the two that the 'industrial' wing of the Labour Movement should not seek to dominate the 'political'. The two should cooperate for mutual benefit, but neither should interfere for its own ends in the other's affairs.

The Politics of One-Party Dominance
The British party system is traditionally described as competitive, but a number of geographical areas are characterised by one-party dominance. The Labour Party's electoral dominance in the Yorkshire coalfield, established between 1918 and 1924, ensures that the Party has no incentive to maintain an efficient vote mobilising machine. The prime CLP function (once it has an MP) is as a recruitment channel to the local political establishment. Electoral security is the determining influence in CLP politics.
    Labour voting in mining constituencies is a complex mixture of class consciousness, rational calculation, and habit. Turnout levels above the national average (between 1945 and October 1974 average turnout was 78.2% compared to a national average of 77.6%) indicates that voting is an act of collective affirmation which has a symbolic import beyond that of merely endorsing a political party.[23] The political ecology of mining constituencies - the occupational dominance of mining, social homogeneity, shared historical experiences, intergrated communities - has created a locally dominant party system in which the reinforcing link between mining trade unionism and the Labour Party was, and remains, of pivotal

importance.[24]   Labour dominance in the Yorkshire
coalfield, however, as in other coalfields, "is
due largely to the social homogeneity and one-class
character of the area, not to the efficiency of the
Labour Party machine."[25]   Massive Labour majorities
and consequent electoral security in these CLPs has
spawned weak organisation and a closed oligarchical
style of politics.[26]
    The Labour Party has criticised local
organisation in the Yorkshire coalfield.   The
Wilson Report (1955) attacked the misconception that
union branches provided a ready made CLP and
bemoaned the lack of cooperation between union and
party in safe seats.   These seats were criticised
for their inactivity, their reluctance to divert
resources to the politically vital marginals and for
failing to maintain an efficient party organisation.
The CLPs with the greatest electoral strength made
the smallest contributions in membership fees:
Dearne Valley £15, Hemsworth £23, and Barnsley £9
were quoted as examples.[27]   The Report, though
accurate, was unfair: individual commitment was as
high in these CLPs as in the most crucial marginal,
and the miners' contributions to central party
coffers were considerable.   The point ignored by
the report was that the political development of
mining CLPs made mass organisation unnecessary given
the mass partisan support of an electorate dominated
by miners and other working class voters.
    A large individual membership with a high
ratio of activists is held to be a prerequisite of
mass democratic politics, and particularly for
electoral mobilisation.   Once the tradition of
Labour partisanship was established, however,
mobilisational politics were unnecessary given the
reinforcing cycle of work - community - politics.
Ultimately this had a politically enervating effect
as without the spur of adversarial competitive
electoral politics party organisation tends to
ossify, becoming the domain of relatively few
ideologically homogenous activists concerned
primarily with the allocation of the spoils of
office.   CLPs of this type, then, tend to become
caucus parties, dominated by a clique whose
position depends on the absence of organised
opposition to retain control.   Despite the
accusations of political rhetoric, this dominance
was not predicated on a right wing political
machine.[28]   Grassroots politics in the coalfields
are the product of electoral security.   This then

directs our attention to internal CLP politics, and to candidate selection in particular. Oral and documentary evidence from party and union sources emphasises the inadequacies of the miners as a political force in these CLPs, stressing that, historically, miners have been reluctant to join the Party as individual members in large numbers. Even in the hey-day of miners' influence, individual membership tended to be low relative to their numbers and political commitment.

Miners, as an occupational community, have been frequently noted for a high propensity for industrial and political activism generated by mining as a job and the miners' social and geographical isolation. [29] However, despite powerful ties of sentiment, history and organisation the number of miners who join the Party as individual members is small, and further, the close organisational relationship described earlier no longer exists. The generally accepted image of the miners' political influence is that it is a product of their political finance as well as their presence.

The Labour Party at all levels depends on union money: does he who pays the piper call the tune? The Yorkshire Area annually pays affiliation fees to the CLPs on a per capita basis, calculated according to how many miners from each branch live in which CLP. It is on these sums that delegate entitlement and therefore voting strength is calculated. Election expenses are precisely calculated under the Representation of the People Act and the Hastings Agreement, each CLP having its own separate agreement with the Yorkshire Area, and sponsorship is not the responsibility of the Areas but is paid from NUM funds. So, if political finance is to confer influence it must stem from affiliation fees. Conventionally, money is held to confer influence by either bidding for seats, or withdrawing union funds. Harrison suggests that a succession of trade union sponsored MPs indicates venality and that unions are thought to have bid for seats, Ranney notes rumours of unions buying seats and making contributions to CLP funds as 'sweetners', whilst McKitterick claims that Labour's selection procedures "leads to the virtual sale of certain seats to the Unions" but offers no evidence.[30] There is no evidence of such behaviour in the Yorkshire coalfield. In seats with a more differentiated occupational structure a number of potential sponsors or unions may be in competition, but in the coalfield CLPs there is, in

effect, only one sponsor, (though if the miners lose
a nomination, because these are safe seats a
replacement sponsor is soon found), as long as a
CLP choses a miner as its candidate, sponsorship
will follow.   Selecting a miner guarantees sponsorship but the existence of sponsorship does not
guarantee the selection of a miner as prospective
parliamentary candidate (ppc).

Affiliation fees are far more important for
political influence as they determine the number of
miners' delegates at a GMC, which in turn
influences the composition of the Executive.   Both
are crucial in candidate selection.   In Yorkshire
these fees are paid by the Area directly to the
CLPs, but the branches are responsible for providing
the delegates.   Attempts have been made to use
affiliation fees as a means of influence.   In
1968, for example, the NUM branch secretary at
Houghton Main (who was also a member of the Barnsley
Labour Party executive) urged the Area to 'contract
out' as a sign of its displeasure at pit closures
and other policies.[31]   A suggestion that the
area end its financial commitment to the Rother
Valley CLP when a non-miner was selected as ppc in
1967 was likewise rejected.   These attempts to
use money as a tool of political influence sought
the withdrawal of funds but this would have been
self-defeating as union influence would have
evaporated as it would no longer have been entitled
to any delegates.   Whilst accepting that the Party
relies on union money the evidence from the
Yorkshire coalfield suggests that the political
importance of money as an instrument of influence
is exaggerated and misunderstood.   Mining CLPs,
enjoying massive majorities and copious supplies of
union money, do seem somnolent and sluggish, but
this is a consequence of electoral security not
union money.

Membership Participation and Delegate Mobilisation
In the 1950s Harrison claimed "Many of these mining
constituencies are run almost completely by
miners ..... In some areas the function of the
(GMC) are effectively exercised by the miners'
lodges."[32]   This is not so in the Yorkshire
coalfield and is part of the myth of the miners'
role.

Since 1918 the individual member has been
regarded as the authentic Party member, whilst the
affiliated member has the status of a 'second class
citizen'.   The individual member is held to be

personally committed to the success of the Party,
whereas the affiliate is held to be committed
solely by a 'cash nexus'.   The individual member
has a direct relationship with the Party, and
because of this is accorded greater weight by the
Party.   However, what the affiliate lacks in
personal commitment, his organisation compensates
with resources, and in the coalfields with a rich
history.
     The Yorkshire Area (NUM) was well aware that
mineworkers were not mass joiners.   To be a
committed Party supporter was not dependent on
individual membership: this failure to join and
participate was criticised frequently by the Area
Executive.   In 1952, for example, it "consider(ed)
that an individual membership representing a
negligible percentage of those who voted Labour at
the last General Election is most unsatisfactory ..
.."33   Similarly, at the end of 1961 the Labour
Party NEC appointed a campaign committee to plan for
the next General Election and the first phase was
a drive for 150,000 new members.   The NEC was
impressed by the commitment of the Party's organisation at all levels but "some concern was expressed
about the minor role played by some trade union
branches in the affairs of some constituency
parties."   The Yorkshire Area Executive
urged all NUM branches to respond to this criticism
and promote individual membership.34   Some branches
were also critical of their comrades.
     The Lofthouse NUM branch secretary wrote to
the Area Executive to announce that every member of
the branch committee were individual members of
the Party, commenting that the Union should inform
newly elected branch officials that they ought to
join the Party.   This letter was enshrined in a
circular and sent to all branches in the hope that
it would promote "a more keen, active ... participation within the Labour Movement."35   When the
Northumberland miners lost the parliamentary
nomination at Morpeth, a seat held by miners since
1874, the NUM issued a report on the loss emphasising the weakness of the union at the grassroots
and hinting that the miners could expect to lose
further nominations to non-miners.   This report
was considered at some length by the Yorkshire Area
Executive and was forwarded in toto to the branches
with a recommendation that they "take all possible
steps to safeguard the Union's interests."36   These
appeals had little effect.
     The political influence of the miners can best

be charted by the number of delegates able to attend
Party GMCs, selection conferences and so on.
Simply because a branch is <u>entitled</u> to delegates
does not mean that it will <u>be able</u> to provide its
full delegate contingent.   The Yorkshire Area (NUM)
has long recognised the deficiencies of delegate
mobilisation.   As early as 1948 Area Officials
consulted the Yorkshire Regional Council of Labour
(YRCL) in an attempt to improve its position.[37]
In the candidate selection process in Barnsley in
1951 the Union found to its horror that it had
lost delegate representation because of the non-
payment of affiliation fees.   When the seat became
vacant again in 1953 the Yorkshire Area made a
determined effort to increase its delegate
strength.[38]   This same problem reappeared in 1959
when the Yorkshire Area's candidate failed to be
selected as ppc in the Dewsbury constituency.[39]   The
reasons for the loss are significant,

> ... our own candidate ... did not make
> much ground in securing other votes
> following the elimination of other
> candidates.   We understand that he
> obtained about 19 miners' votes out
> of a possible 25 and that thereafter,
> when other candidates were eliminated he
> failed to improve on this figure.[40]

The loss revealed two weaknesses in the NUM's
political influence: first, the NUM candidate
failed to appeal to non-NUM delegates.   This was
crucial as their numbers and political importance
had increased.   Second, the NUM was unable to
secure the full turnout of its delegates.   The
Area Executive urged "our members everywhere, when
opportunities such as this arise, to show unity to
an ever greater extent to ensure the return of
miners' candidates."[41]   In 1959 the Area experienced similar problems in Don Valley and Dearne
Valley, although here the miners retained the
nominations.   The Area Executive admonished the
branches, "we deplore the non-attendance of a few
branches at these Conferences."[42]
As a response to these shortcomings the Area
Executive appointed a Parliamentary Divisions Sub-
Committee to examine the miners' relationship with
the CLPs.   Up to 1959 there was an unspoken belief
that these seats would remain miners' seats in
perpetuity.   The loss of Dewsbury and seats in
other coalfields shocked the Union as they

demonstrated the weakness of the NUM: that their
position was based on tradition and an absence
of competition, not organised influence. The
major recommendation was that the branches must
mobilise their full delegate entitlement "so that
the interests of the Miners can be fully
represented and protected whenever the need may
arise." Branches were urged to become involved
in the day-to-day work of the CLPs as the sudden
appearance of large numbers of new or unfamiliar
faces (for example, Barnsley in 1953) at major
political events caused bad blood in the CLPs.
The Report criticised the failure of NUM branch
committee members to join the Party as individual
members and participate in CLP affairs. Finally,
the Report suggested that the secretary-agent of a
CLP inform the Area Executive when, in his opinion,
a branch was not participating fully. The Report
concluded with the now familiar exhortation that
the miners should be full participants in Party
affairs. The Area Executive accepted the Report,
passing it to the branches for their action.
However, the impact of the Report was minimal.[43]
     Effective participation was made more difficult
by the decision of the 1965 Labour Party Conference
to make individual membership of the Party a
condition for appointment to CLP committees and
for service as a delegate.[44] Aware of the
implications, the Yorkshire Area Executive
instructed its secretary to write to Bill Paynter
(NUM General Secretary) urging a national inquiry
into the effect of this change. The Area also
wrote to A L Williams (Labour Party General
Secretary) stating that the Yorkshire Area was
dismayed at the effects this change would have on
their local influence.[45] In reply it was pointed
out that this was an extension of the 1962
decision that annual Conference delegates be
individual members and that the NUM could do
nothing.[46] The Area Executive retreated into
trying to motivate the branches to remedy the
defects in the NUM's political influence, thus "to
have any effective part in the administration of
the Party, but especially in voting, miners, as
individuals, or their Representatives and delegates
at any level must be individual members ... "[47]
     This change, coupled with the miners'
unwillingness to join the Party and the decline of
the industry had a major effect on the influence of
the Union in these CLPs.
     In 1967 the candidate of the Yorkshire Area

(NUM) failed to be selected as ppc in Rother Valley, a seat represented by a miner since 1918. The reasons for the loss are complex but the Area Executive ascribed them to problems of membership and participation,

> .... we had delegates missing who might
> have swung the vote to our own candidate.
> Some branches were entitled to send delegates
> but could find none to appoint. Some
> delegates did not even attend. At all
> levels of the Labour Party individual
> membership is a requirement of nomination
> or representation ... (we) think this is
> right and that industrial affiliation is
> not sufficient .. Please get down to
> the job immediately. Find your
> delegates; submit their names; see that
> they attend. Use your influence with
> them. Times are working against us.
> Our representation is reducing, (but)
> in most places we are still by far the
> biggest single voice in the Labour
> Movement.[48]

The Yorkshire Area's response to this decline was exhortation: they had no power to compel the branches to remedy these deficiencies. The colliery branch plays a key role in the political influence of the union and the branch secretary is expected to be the linkage between the NUM and the CLP; recruiting individual members, mobilising delegates and transmitting the party's message. The branch secretary is therefore crucial in maintaining the NUM's influence, yet nowhere is there mention of his political functions in the Rulebook. The job of branch secretary is de facto full time. Branch officials and committee members are seldom the opinion or community leaders they once were. Previously, they were often party officials and they were expected to be politically active. The level of political awareness in a branch is, therefore, generally dependent upon the personal commitment and interest in politics displayed by branch officials and the prominence they chose to give to Party matters. Branch officials do not have enough time to carry out all their NUM duties, let alone see to Party matters. A branch secretary who was also a Party agent remarked that, in his experience, branch secretaries rarely dealt with Party matters at branch meetings.

The political role of the branch has been made
more difficult by the increased mobility of mining
labour.   Before the rundown of the industry a
branch secretary could be reasonably certain that
the bulk of his members lived in one constituency.
The link between pit, community and Party was
stronger and relations with the CLP were relatively
simple.   Pit closures and labour transfers have
meant increased labour mobility which has destroyed
this simple relationship.   The workforce at a pit
might be drawn from as many as five constituencies
and this makes the task of political co-ordination
far more difficult.   Not surprisingly under the
pressure of union work, party politics are
neglected.
       Whilst few branch officials hold major CLP
posts, branch officials are often participants.
Of the twenty branch officials (president, delegate,
treasurer and secretary) of the five major NUM
branches in the Dearne Valley CLP, for example, 16
were individual members of the Labour Party.   Of
these, 8 were branch delegates of a CLP (6 to Dearne
Valley CLP, 2 to Barnsley CLP).   The Houghton
Main branch delegate to the Yorkshire Area (NUM)
Council was chairman of the Dearne Valley CLP, a
member of the Regional Conference Arrangements
Committee,[50] and was selected as ppc for Dearne
Valley.[50]

The Distribution of Political Influence, 1964-1974

Political influence is a function of the miners'
concentrated numbers and trade union organisation.
Mass union membership and their Union's organisation
gave the miners a dominent role in mining CLPs
where they were, for a time, unchallenged.   This
dominance was eroded by post-war social change in
parts of the coalfield, changing perceptions of the
criteria necessary for an MP and the failure of
the NUM to organise its strength.
       From Table 1 we can see the overall decline
in the NUM's delegate strength.   This decline was
the consequence of the contraction of the industry
in Yorkshire: in 1964 there were 100 pits employing
111,900 miners;   by 1970 this had fallen to 75 pits
and 73,200 miners.   Again, it is worth making
the point that the figures in Table 1 represent
delegate entitlement, not delegate attendance, and
given the difficulties of collecting accurate data,
these constitute estimates.   If these constituencies are ranked according to delegate strength we
can see where NUM influence was maintained (see,

Table 2). Between 1964 and 1970 the political presence of the miners slipped most in the traditional core areas of the coalfields: Barnsley, Dearne Valley and Normanton. Between 1970 and 1974 there was a marginal recovery in these constituencies as the rate of closures and job losses slowed. The overall decline can be accounted for by the contraction of the industry, compounded by the problems described in the last section, but how can we account for the variations in Table 2?

Mining constituencies are a distinct 'family' characterised by socio-economic stability and stable patterns of working class political behaviour. Where these patterns have been eroded (as with pit closures) then the socio-economic factors which underpin political behaviour are disturbed and a more complex pattern of politics emerges.[51] As the occupational structure of the coalfields differentiated as a consequence of pit closures and the emergence of new industries a more complex pattern of politics emerged in which miners are only one element, albeit an important one: "We realise it is no longer easy to gain seats in communities where the pattern of employment by virtue of pit closures in changing. It is no longer a passport to selection to claim that the candidate is a mineworker ..."[52] If a CLP is overwhelmingly manual-working class in composition and is dominated occupationally by mining, there is little to be explained if a miner is selected as ppc. The decline of mining and a less solidly manual working class CLP has led to resistance to the 'cloth cap' style of political representation symbolised by the miners' MP. Many individual members, whilst holding white collar employment (teachers, office workers, local government officers, health service employees, supervisory jobs, technicians etc) may well be the children of miners. Education and a degree of social mobility and affluence have not eroded Labour partisanship, but they have sometimes affected the perception of the qualities necessary for an MP: impeccable working class credentials are no longer sufficient in themselves. However, there also exists in these CLPs distrust of the outsider (often described as carpetbaggers), and the ideal ppc and MP is often seen as someone who has got on in the world but who remains in touch with his roots.

The position of the Yorkshire Area has never been challenged by other trade unions. They

The Special Relationship

Table 1:   Estimated NUM Delegate Strength, 1964-1970

Constituency	1964	1970	1974
Barnsley	65	38	41
Dearne Valley	65	42	41
Pontefract	57	43	38
Normanton	44	32	23
Rother Valley	61	47	41
Hemsworth	92	66	55
Don Valley	65	58	44

Table 2:   Ranking of Constituencies by Delegate
           Strength, 1964-1974

Rank	1964	1970	1974
1	Hemsworth	Hemsworth	Hemsworth
2	Barnsley/ Dearne Valley/ Don Valley	Don Valley	Don Valley
3	Pontefract	Rother Valley	Barnsley/ Dearne Valley/ Rother Valley
4	Rother Valley	Pontefract	Pontefract
5	Normanton	Dearne Valley	Normanton
6		Barnsley	
7		Normanton	

Calculated from figures provided by the Yorkshire
Area (NUM) Finance Department.

recognise the pre-eminent historical role of the miners and, anyway, a challenge to the miners would need several unions to co-operate and achieve a very high level of activism to hope to oust the NUM.   The Yorkshire Area is aware that its size and sometimes proprietorial attitude (the very idea of a miners' seat annoys some unions) may antagonise and it has restrained branches who seemed to be threatening inter-union rivalry for parliamentary nominations.   The Pontefract and Kellingley branches, for example, asked (in 1971) for permission to promote an NUM candidature in the Goole constituency.   The Executive rejected the request, "it is our opinion that, for this Union to contest Goole, in opposition to the TGWU who regard this constituency as being theirs, would be a mistake which would re-bound against us."[53]   Some Unions do have significant delegations, for example, the GMWU were, in 1974, entitled to 22 delegates to the Dearne Valley GMC.   The evidence suggests, however, that they suffer from the same problem of delegate mobilisation as the NUM.

Post war socio-economic change has not destroyed the position of the NUM, but it has made it more complex.   The presence of hidden, or secondary, miners' influence should be noted: many individual members are, of course, miners, many women members will be miners' wives, miners' children (even if not employed in the pit) and ex-miners remain sympathetic to the Union.   Similarly, other unions tend to accept the pre-eminence of the miners as a result of an agreement, because of their own organisational problems or because of tradition. In these ways the influence of the miners is but-tressed.   In identifying a close relationship between socio-economic composition and political behaviour there is the danger of falling into an ecological fallacy.   Socio-economic patterns must be related to the history of each CLP.   If the miners have traditionally been active participants in a CLP there is a distinct tendency for their political influence to be maintained.   Hemsworth and Don Valley have always been miners seats (with the partial exception of Don Valley between 1918 and 1922) and remain safe political fiefs for the NUM.   Hemsworth and Don Valley are very much one industry areas, dominated by mining and the pits have a tradition of political activism: Hemsworth, for example, was the cradle of the Independent Labour Party in the coalfield, and the isolated pit

villages around Doncaster have long been noted
for their political and industrial activism. These
two seats most closely correspond to the 'ideal
type' of mining constituency in the Yorkshire
coalfield.

The weakness of the Yorkshire miners' political
influence can best been seen in the candidate
selection process. This is perhaps the most
important function of a CLP, and it has long been
recognised that the selection of parliamentary
candidates is dominated by relatively small numbers
of activists.[54] Students of party dynamics have
noted that the distribution of power within a party
can be examined most easily during the nomination
and selection of candidates. Ranney, for example,
argues, "Who controls selection controls the
Party."[55] The belief that locally dominant groups
of workers such as the miners dominate the
political process of these CLPs in a manner akin
to that of the pre-1832 landed grandees has led to
allegations that they constitute "The Modern
Boroughmongers".[56] The 'selectorate thesis'
appears both damning and easily provable, a matter
of common sense. In reality it is harder to
substantiate. This will be examined in the next
chapter.

The image we have of the selection process
in mining seats is that the NUM branches select
their candidate and then, if necessary, impose him
on a reluctant CLP. The implication being that
the miners can secure the nomination by sheer
weight of numbers against the wishes of the party.
However, we have already presented evidence to
show that the miners do not have that sort of
presence and that there is a powerful historically
based reluctance within the Union to be seen to be
dominating a CLP. Additionally, this view implies
a distinction between a union candidate and a
party candidate, that the two are distinct species,
and politically incompatible. It also fails to
consider how NUM candidates are selected by their
Union, the type of men that have been selected and
how they have reacted to the decline in the NUM's
presence in the coalfield's politics. Thus, an
essential preliminary is to consider the NUM's
political recruitment process.

Political Recruitment, 1904-1975

The means whereby the Yorkshire miners selected
their potential parliamentary candidates was by the
election of a Parliamentary List. This was

governed by Rule 67 and the last was elected in
1975, Rule 67 being amended considerably in 1979.
The changes increased the influence of the Area
Executive in the selection of ppcs, section e was
abolished empowering Council to select a candidate
should a vacancy occur.[57]   In considering the List,
four points must be borne in mind.   First, the
List was a functional institution which recruited
potential MPs from amongst working miners.   Second,
it was 'non political' in that it sought to secure
the election of miners to Parliament, and no
difficulty was experienced in adapting it to the
needs of the Labour Party.[58]   Third, membership of
the List was confined to union members of at least
five years standing.   Finally, membership of the
List was not tantamount to election to Parliament
or selection as ppc.   A List member had to be
selected as NUM candidate by the branches in a CLP,
and then by the CLP as candidate.

Any branch official, ordinary member, or
permanent official could stand for election, all
candidates had to be individual members of the
Labour Party, and no permanent official could
become an MP and retain his union post.[59]   This
was not always so, before 1918 it was acceptable
that officials be MPs as the work of the MP and
official was not as heavy as today, and many felt
that the two could be advantageously combined.
This was a source of conflict within the YMA: one
side argued that duality was inefficient (the MP
could not devote his whole attention to either
political or industrial matters, so failing in
both) but opponents believed it essential that the
unions have a top voice in Parliament.[60] Before
1918 when the Yorkshire miners had only two MPs
duality was not a major problem.   After 1918 the
Yorkshire miners never had less than 7 MPs and it
was obviously impossible for top officials to be
absent for long periods of time, particularly at a
time of constant crisis in the industry.   Also,
after 1918 the Party imposed a stricter discipline
on its MPs, and the MFGB accepted that officials
should not be MPs.[61]   This widened the zone of
recruitment within the Union and as the membership
tended to vote for well-known candidates, obviously,
officials enjoyed a clear advantage.

In 1901 the MFGB Conference adopted a general
scheme to finance parliamentary candidates.   This
was the brainchild of Ben Pickard of Yorkshire.
Although adopted by the MFGB in 1901 the YMA did not
implement it until 1904 as it was only then that the

YMA experienced hostility from local Liberal
associations unwilling to concede safe seats to the
miners.[62]   The scheme proposed a one shilling per
member per year contribution from the YMA to
finance political activity.   The scheme laid down
no method of <u>selecting</u> candidates, leaving this to
the constituent areas who enjoyed differing
political traditions.[63]
     In March 1904 the Executive of the YMA
recommended that the branches "appoint five men as
Labour Representatives in case of any emergency
that may arise at the next General Election."[64]
This was the first List, and the process remained
basically the same: after each election the
branches were asked to nominate men for election to
the List and the whole District voted on these
names.   The number elected being in the proportion
of one candidature for every 10,000 union members.[65]

Factors in Election
     The key to election was to get one's name known
around the coalfield and amongst the branches.   It
is argued that there is a <u>Cursus honorum</u>, or
promotion ladder, to becoming a miners' MP.   There
were three ways of securing election to the List:
first, the aspirant could be a permanent official,
though as we have seen, this method is redundant.
It was far more important to make a name in local
politics.   Every miners' MP has had local
government experience; this gives a man a wide
reputation in local Party circles as an approved
Party councillor.   Activity in the Union was the
only certain way to be elected to the List.   The
vast majority of men on the List served as branch
officials whose connections helped to promote a
coalfield wide reputation.   A major effect of
this process, however, was that because the men
elected to the List were elected because they were
known, this took time.   Consequently, members of
the List tended to be older men, although there are
exceptions.   There is a tendency to see miners'
MPs as a stereotype -- old, solid, unimaginative
and with little talent, forming the ballast of the
PLP.   The List did not provide an adequate
political cross-section of the political views of
the membership.   Indeed, in the 1950s the Area
Union leadership went to great pains to prevent
anyone of unorthodox political views securing
election to the List.   All the members of the List
were orthodox right wing supporters of the Union
and Party leadership, with the exception of Dick

Kelley who enjoyed the support of the Doncaster pits whose independent power base enabled him to gain election to the List. Because the miners were predominant in Don Valley, they were able to secure his selection as ppc. Kelley was elected in 1959 and retired in 1979, the only Yorkshire mining MP with a left-wing reputation.

Does a cursus honorum exist? The answer must be yes. Although it is incorrect to argue that all follow a common path, there are a number of relevant factors: union service, local government activity, local party activity, which form the basis of selection process. These were the 'power bases' which a man had to utilise to secure election to the List. The average time spent on the List between 1945-1970 for those elected to Parliament was 4.3 years. Turnover was dependent on the frequency of elections and the retirement of existing MPs, there was no 'buggins turn' on the List. Simply because a man was on the List for a long time did not necessarily guarantee selection as a ppc.

CLPs are not monolithic. As we shall see in the next chapter post-war social change has rendered the balance of political forces in these CLPs far more complex. The actual balance of power within the CLPs has been accurately described thus,

> Although the miners are slowly, but
> steadily losing ground they are still
> a powerful force in the selection of
> candidates. But their power, once
> based of numerical superiority or
> equality, now often depends on being
> the largest organised minority.66

The result is that the NUM has been able to retain a substantial number of seats, but it has also lost many. The very concept of a 'miners seat' arouses a great deal of opposition within some CLPs.

The changes in the style, ideology and personnel of the leadership of the Yorkshire Area in the early-1970s did not, initially lead to any major change in the political participation of influence of the miners in the CLPs. At the time of the creation of the new District Labour Parties (DLPs) in 1975 to correspond with the new local government boundaries, there was an attempt to increase miners' influence in the new Barnsley DLP by securing the election of miners to influential posts. Arthur Scargill, the Area President, acting

as the delegate of the Worsborough Labour Party,
said,

> We think the miners have a vital part
> to play in the local Labour Party.
> Obviously we hope that the NUM delegates
> at the meeting will support NUM members
> nominated for any position.[67]

This 'offensive' was unsuccessful. The
challenge from the NUM originated within the Barrow
NUM branch,which is of major importance in the
Barnsley CLP, from left-wing local councillors and
from Arthur Scargill but not from the NUM as an
organisation. Branch participation, the key to an
NUM revival was low: only Barrow, Elsecar and
Shafton Workshops sent delegates, a total of six and
the 'challenge' was easily beat off.[68] As this
new party organisation would coordinate party
activity in the new county council area and would
cover many mining constituencies in South Yorkshire,
it might have been expected that the NUM would have
made every effort to mobilise its strength.
This political style underwent considerable
change after 1979 when the Yorkshire Area, as part
of the effort to democratise and radicalise the
Labour Party, organised its remaining influence into
a faction of NUM delegates (in company with allies
from other unions and the wards). The mobilisation
of the Yorkshire Area cannot be divorced from the
motives of the then Area President, Arthur Scargill
and the Area had two motives: to revive the role of
the NUM in local politics. In 1945 there were
eight miners' MPs from the coalfield,in 1980 there
were five.[69] The second motive led on from this,
but was of far wider significance: contributing to
the transformation of the Labour Party by securing
the selection and the election of a bloc of left-
wing miners MPs.[70] Despite this new level of
factional organisation the uncertainties generated
by the redistribution of constituency boundaries
and resistance from right-wing elements in these
CLPs prevented the extension of this new political
style, thus limiting the miners' influence.[71]

The Structure of Influence
The decline of the NUM's political influence as
described in this chapter can be accounted for by
the contraction of the coal industry, particularly
between 1964 and 1970. The rationalisation of
Labour led to a fall in numbers employed and

therefore in the number of NUM delegates.
Consequently, the political influence enjoyed by
the miners was drastically reduced, and this was
amplified by weaknesses in the miners' political
organisation, but a potential for considerable
NUM influence remained.

The miners' political influence depended,
originally, upon physical concentration and
superior trade union organisation. Mining depends
on a concentrated labour force: this still applies
albeit to a lesser extent because of the rundown of
the industry, but the miners still constitute the
most significant single occupational group and the
union is aware of its historical role. Previously
the occupational structure of these CLPs was
relatively simple and undifferentiated, being
dominated by mining. As the mining industry
declined the occupational structure of these
constituencies became far more pluralistic and the
inevitable concomitant of a more differentiated
occupational structure is a more differentiated and
complex pattern of political behaviour. The NUM
constitutes only one element in the political
process, albeit an important one. The political
presence and influence of the miners largely depends
on the socio-economic profile and occupational
structure of each constituency -- the more 'simple'
the occupational structure, the more likely is the
political influence of the miners to be maintained.
One important factor which must be taken into
account is the role traditionally played by the
miners in the constituency. The miners' political
influence is determined by the number of NUM
delegates, the existence of competitors, and the
tradition of NUM involvement. The two constituencies which most closely match the 'ideal-type' of
mining seat suggested by these variables were
Hemsworth and Don Valley. In these seats the
presence of the miners had declined, but because of
an absence of political competitors the NUM's
political influence was maintained. Even where
the physical presence of the miners has declined,
the absence of rivals suggests that the presence of
a tradition of political involvement enables the
NUM to maintain its influence.

REFERENCES

1   R I McKibbin, The Evolution of the Labour
     Party, 1910-1924 (London, Oxford University
     Press 1974); pp24-29 and pp56-62;
     R Gregory, The Miners and British Politics,
     1906-1914(London, Oxford University Press,
     1968); pp104-119; and, R Douglas, 'Labour
     In Decline', in, K D Brown(ed), Essays in
     Anti-Labour History (London, Macmillan 1974);
     pp105-125
2   Even before formal affiliation there was co-
     operation, for example MFGB(EC); 27 March
     1907.   This was a joint meeting of the TUC
     Parliamentary Committee, the Labour Party
     and the MFGB to coordinate the MFGB's
     legislative programme.   Cooperation can
     also be seen in the Minimum Wage Act(1912)
     strike,   "The Labour Party was being asked
     all kinds of questions regarding the miners'
     strike and questions are being asked in the
     House of Commons and (we) desire to get in
     closer touch with the Federation so that (we)
     understand the whole matter."   MFGB(EC);
     5 - 8 March 1912.   The MFGB kept control of
     the industrial aspects of its affairs whilst
     looking to the Party to secure its interests
     in Parliament.   When a Minimum Wage Bill
     was presented to the House of Commons the
     MFGB surrendered control ot the Party.   See,
     R Page Arnot, The Miners, Vol.2(London, Allen
     & Unwin 1953); pp132 et seq.
3   Labour Party, National Executive Committee
     Minutes: Memorandum on Electoral
     Performance, March 1910, hereafter LPEC, and
     also LPCR p78.   Party control over
     constituency organisation in strong trade
     union areas was only to become a reality when
     a higher source of loyalty was created as
     the Labour Party neared office in the 1920s
     and 1930s.   This led to a further subordina-
     tion of union to party.   This relationship
     was codified in the Hastings Agreement (1933).
     See, LPCR 1933, Parliamentary Candidates and
     Constituency Finance.
4   MFGB(EC); 14 August 1914
5   YMA; 17 August 1914
6   YMA; 9 July 1917
7   Report of the Parliamentary Committee,
     16 October 1917; in, YMA; 22 October 1917.
     The Yorkshire miners did not contest Barnsley

in 1918.   After the YMA selected its seats
in 1917, John Potts (the YMA's
candidate in Barnsley) resigned.   The YMA
appeared unwilling to challenge James Walton,
the sitting MP since 1897.   Nevertheless,
Herbert Smith instructed the YMA branches to
oppose the Coalition, urging Labour "to stand
on its own feet".   Walton stood as a Coalition Liberal, enjoying the support of both
Conservatives and Patriotic Labour.   Splits
in the Labour forces in Barnsley led to
the decision not to challenge Walton.   The
YMA fought and won the seat in 1922.   YMA;
20 December 1917; and, Sheffield Daily
Telegraph, 5 November, 27 November and
28 November 1918.

8   YMA; 19 November 1917
9   YMA; 20 December 1917.   At this meeting it
     was   announced that the could, under MFGB
     rules, contest a seventh seat.   The
     Parliamentary Committee was instructed to
     make recommendation.
10   YMA; 20 December 1917
11   YMA; 21 December 1917
12   YMA; 14 January 1918.   Hall had been MP for
     Normanton since 1905.   The Parliamentary
     Committee recommended the YMA contest
     Wakefield as the seventh constituency.   See,
     Parliamentary Committee to J Wadsworth,
     27 December 1917; in, YMA; 14 January 1918.
     This was approved, see, YMA; 4 February and
     19 February 1918.   The remaining candidates:
     E Hough (Don Valley), G Hirst (Wentworth),
     and I Burns (Pontefract) were selected in
     early 1918.
13   YMA: 19 February and 18 March 1918, and,
     Report of the Parliamentary Committee,
     9 April 1918.   In 1918 the YMA did not
     contest Wakefield in September 1918 the YMA
     decided to transfer Burns' candidacy to
     Pontefract at the behest of the YMA branches
     in the Pontefract constituency.   W Smith to
     YMA Executive, 4 September 1918.
14   YMA; 18 November 1918.   The candidates were:
     F Hall (Normanton), J Guest (Hemsworth),
     W Lun (Rothwell), G Hirst (Wentworth),
     T Grundy (Rother Valley), E Hough(Don Valley)
     and I Burns (Pontefract).
15   MFGB(EC); 15 November 1918.
16   YMA; 10 February, 24 May and 13 October 1919.

17   T Lindley, 'The Barnsley Labour Party, 1918-
     1945', in, Bulletin of the Society for the
     Study of Labour History 39(Autumn 1979);
     pp10-11, and interview with participants.
18   The Labour Year Book, 1919. The YMA council
     voted by 103 to 27 to contest Doncaster
     at the next election. The YMA also agreed
     to provide the necessary finance. The
     branches approved by 1,441 to 387 votes.
     YMA; 13 October and 25 October 1918. One
     month later Council recommended that the
     YMA contest Barnsley by 95 votes to 55.
     YMA; 10 November and 21 November 1919.
19   Sheffield Daily Telegraph, 5 December 1918.
20   Sheffield Daily Telegraph, 21 October 1922
21   Sheffield Independent, 14 November 1923;
     Sheffield Independent, 19, 21 and
     23 November and 3 December 1923; and,
     Sheffield Daily Telegraph, 26 November 1924.
22   Sheffield Independent, 8 November 1923
23   H G Nicholas, The British General Election of
     1950 (London, Macmillan 1950); p.318.
     Similarly, "the traditional identification
     with the party (by the miners) who have
     strong historical grounds for a sense of
     working class solidarity ... for the voters,
     being Labour supporters is just one of the
     aspects of identifying with their locality
     or community".   G C Moodie & G. Studdert-
     Kennedy, Opinions, Publics and Pressure
     Groups (London, G Allen & Unwin 1970);
     p.56.   Though, note, Labour has lost mining
     seats, Bosworth & Cannock (1970) and Ashfield
     in the 1977 by-election, are examples.
24   D Butler & D Stokes, Political Change in
     Britain (Harmonsworth Penguin 1969);
     pp190-215.   For the locally dominant party
     system see, A Arian & S H Barnes, 'The
     Dominant Party System: A Neglected Model of
     Democratic Stability', in, Journal of
     Politics 36(1976) pp592-614, and,
     M Duverger, Political Parties(London,
     Methuen 1959); p308 et seq.
25   M I Bulmer, 'The Character of Local Politics',
     in, Bulmer(ed), Mining and Social Change
     (London, Croom Helm 1978); p139
26   For other examples of this type of politics
     see: T Brennan (et al),'Party Politics and
     Local Government in Western South Wales',
     in, Political Quarterly, xxxix(1954),
     pp76-83; R Butterworth, 'Islington Borough

Council: Some Characterists of One Party
Rule' in, Politics I(1966); pp21-31;
I McAllister, 'The Labour Party in Wales',
Llafur 2(ii) Spring 1981; pp78-79;
A Morgan, 'The 1970 Parliamentary Election
in Merthyr Tydfil', In, Morgannwg (1978);
pp61-81; and C Cockburn, The Local State
(London, Pluto Press 1977); pp87-94. For
the Yorkshire coalfield see, The Sheffield
Star, 9 October 1975, 4 February 1976, and,
10 October 1979.

27 Labour Party Conference Report, 1955: Interim
    Report of the Sub-Committee on Organisation,
    p79(para 69) and p82 (para 111-112)

28 Caucus is used in the more descriptive American
    sense of a private or preliminary meeting of
    party members to select a candidate for
    office or to concert measures for the
    furthering of its interests. British
    usage is more pejorative: an organisation
    seeking to manage or manipulate elections,
    or dictate to the constituency. Also,
    "The machine took a clearly hierarchical
    form, with a boss as the head of an
    organisation of workers held together by the
    spoils of politics and capable of determining
    the party's nomination and exerting a mighty
    influence at elections as well. In its most
    developed form the urban machine became the
    government in that many major decisions ...
    were decided by the party functionaries who
    managed their puppets in public office."
    V O Key jr, Politics, Parties and Pressure
    Groups (5th ed. New York, T Crowell 1965);
    p337.

29 For a discussion of this occupational community
    see the Introduction to R Harrison(ed)
    Independent Collier (Hassocks, Harvester
    Press 1978); pp 1-16. The locus classicus
    of the isolated mass thesis is, C Kerr &
    M Siegel, 'The Inter-Industry Propensity to
    Strike: An International Comparison', in,
    A Kornhauser et al(eds) Industrial Conflict
    (New York, Holt 1964); pp189-212, and for
    a critical view G V Rimlinger, 'International
    Differences in the Strike Propensity of
    Coal Miners: Experience in Four Countries',
    in Industrial and Labour Relations Review 12
    (1959); pp389-405, and M Bulmer, 'Sociological
    Models of the Mining Community', in,
    Sociological Review 23(1975); pp61-92

30   M Harrison, Trade Unions and the Labour Party
        Since 1945 (London, G Allen & Unwin 1960);
        p81, p273 and p278; A Ranney, Pathways to
        Parliament (London, Macmillan 1965), p11,
        and T McKitterick, 'The Labour Party', in,
        Political Quarterly xxx(July-September)
        1955, pp219-220 and p223.
31   'Miners May End Labour's Union Levy Cash', in,
        The Sheffield Star, 8 March 1968.
32   Harrison, Trade Unions ..., p114
33   YA(NUM); 3 July 1952
34   BS Circular 8/63 (11 January 1963)
35   YA(NUM); 28 September 1960 and BS Circular
        84/60 (30 September 1960)
36   YA(NUM); 8 November 1954.   The loss of
        Morpeth and its wider implications were
        considered by the NEC in October 1954.   The
        loss was ascribed to the non-attendance of
        NUM delegates at the selection conference
        despite the fact that the miners paid 80%
        of the trade union affiliation fees to the
        CLP.   NUM(EC); 14 October 1954.

37   YA(NUM); 14 June 1948
38   BS Circular 5/52 (14 January 1952), and
        W E Jones to all NUM Branches Affiliated
        to Barnsley Labour Party, 30 January 1953.
39   C J James, MP For Dewsbury (C J James,
        Brighouse 1970); p246, and pp252-3
40   YA(NUM); 16-20 March 1959
41   YA (NUM); 16-20 March 1959
42   YA (NUM); 31 August 1959
43   Report of the Parliamentary Divisions Sub-
        Committee, in, YA(NUM); 31 August 1959.
        The non-impact of this report and the
        policy of exhortation can be seen in the
        Hemsworth candidate selection process of
        1972: ".... a lot of our Branches may be
        below strength in appointing delegates ...
        they must be individual members and they
        must reside within the ... Constituency.
        Appointing qualified delegates is your
        responsibility and if Branches do this,
        there ought not to be any fear of Hemsworth
        being lost as a miners' seat -- but check
        now!"   S Schofield to all Branches
        Affiliated to the Hemsworth CLP, 21 August
        1972.
44   Labour Party Circular, 6 October 1966
45   YA(NUM); 1 November 1965, and, S Schofield to
        W Paynter, and, S Schofield to AL Williams,

            2 November 1965.
46   W Paynter to S Schofield, 19 November 1965
47   BS Circular 90/65 (24 November 1965)
48   BS Circular 2/68 (2 January 1968)
49   YA(NUM) Rulebook 1976; Rules 25 a - d
50   This refers to November 1981 and was the result
        of a determined effort by the Area to
        increase its influence.
51   R Webber, Parliamentary Constituencies: A
        Socio-Economic Profile (London, Centre for
        Environmental Studies/Office of Population
        Censuses and Surveys,Occasional Paper 1,
        1978); pp25-28.   See also the article by
        Bulmer cited in note 29, D Lockwood,
        'Sources of Variation in Working Class
        Images of Society' , in, Sociological
        Review, xiv(1966); pp249-267;
        J Goldthorpe (et al).   The Affluent Worker:
        Political Attitudes and Behaviour
        (Cambridge, Cambridge UP 1968), and N Dennis
        (et al), Coal Is Our Life (London,Methuen
        1966).   In his critique of Goldthorpe,
        Crewe confirms the existence of solid
        Labour voting in 'Traditional Worker' (TW)
        seats, and of his sample of 17 TW seats, 7
        are in the Yorkshire coalfield.   See,
        I Crewe, 'The Politics of 'Affluent' and
        Traditional' Worker in Britain: An
        Aggregate Data Analysis', in, British
        Journal of Political Science 3(1973);
        pp29-52.   For a historical exploration of
        these themes, see, D J Rossiter, The Miners'
        Sphere for Influence.   An Attempt to
        Quantify Electoral Behaviour in Mining
        Areas Between The Wars (unpublished Ph.D.
        thesis, University of Sheffield 1980).
52   NUM: Annual Conference Report, 1967; p291
53   YA(NUM), 19 January 1971.   In 1951 The TGWU
        refused to sanction a T & G candidate in
        Barnsley.   The T & G Area Organiser
        commented, "Barnsley is regarded as a
        miners' seat.   There is an agreement
        between the Unions that the (TGWU) would
        support the miners in their nomination."
        Barnsley Chronicle, 5 November 1951
54   J Rasmussen, 'The Implications of Safe Seats
        for British Democracy'in, Western Political
        Quarterly, 1966, p257. Also, Ranney,
        Pathways ...., pp6-7, M Rush, The Selection
        of Parliamentary Candidates (London, Nelson
        1969); pp6-7, and P Paterson, The

Selectorate (London, MacGibbon & Kee 1967).

55   Ranney, Pathways .... p10, and see also
     .   E E Schattschneider, Party Government (New
         York, Holt 1942);   p64

56   This is the title of chapter 5 of Paterson's
     book.

57   YA(NUM) Rule 1976, Rule 67 as amended.   See,
         YA(NUM);   19-21 March 1979.   The change was
         proposed by the Executive and accepted
         unanimously by Council.

58   No ppc can be sponsored by the NUM unless he
         stands solely as the Labour candidate and
         signs the Party Constitution.

59   Under the Rules the permanent officials are:
         the President, Compensation Agent, General
         Secretary, Vice President, Financial
         Secretary and the four Area Agents.

60   A bitter critic of the then YMA's electoral
         policy, John Potts, wrote on duality,
         "There is a strong and growing feeling
         against Messrs Wadsworth and Hall standing
         for parliamentary honours whilst still
         holding the important positions of General
         Secretary and Agent of the YMA, as should
         they be returned, such would be a calamity
         to the cause (and) the miners' interests ...
         the officials are nearly always away from
         home whilst they ought to be in the office
         and attending meetings of the men ...
         Wadsworth and Hall know perfectly well that
         in the event of their return to Parliament,
         their work must be done by a deputy ... No
         deputy under a superior would undertake
         authority, responsibility and action in
         the absence of his chief.   Thus chaos and
         disorganisation must ensue".   Sheffield
         Daily Telegraph, 16 January 1906.

61   MFGB: Special Conference Report, 20-22 August
         1918; p23.   As late as 1943 the Labour
         Party suggested that the PLP suffered
         because union chief executives were not MPs
         and unions were asked to consider allowing
         such men to enter Parliament.   LCPR 1943,
         Appendix III; p232.   The MFGB refused.
         MFGB(EC); 17 March 1943.

62   R Page Arnot, The Miners, Vol 1 (London,
         G Allen & Unwin 1949); pp352-369

63   Pickard's intention can be seen from his
         declaration that "the Scheme is not
         established for the purpose of wrecking
         any political party."   Its aim was simply

to boost miners' parliamentary representation.

64   YMA;   22 February 1904, and, Gregory, The
       Miners ...., p24 et seq.

65   YA(NUM) Rules 1976, Rule 67.

66   Rush, The Selection of Parliamentary
       Candidates, p173 my emphasis.   It is
       important not to give the impression that
       CLPs are marked by mass membership either
       now or in the past.   The Houghton Committee
       found "the vast majority of (CLPs) have a
       membership of less than 1,000 ... (whilst)
       an eigth of Labour (CLPs) claim membership
       of over 1,000 none claims membership of
       more than 2,000."   Report of the Committee
       on Financial Aid to Political Parties
       Cmnd 6601 (August 1976);   para 1.1.6,
       pp162-163.

67   Morning Telegraph, 19 February 1976.

68   Interview with participants.

69   Morning Telegraph, 4 March 1980.

70   A Scargill, 'The New Unionism', in, New Left
       Review 92 (July-August) 1975;   p31.

71   This political style, its consequences and
       limits is considered in greater detail in
       my paper, The Modern Boroughmongers?   The
       Yorkshire Area (NUM) and Grassroots
       Politics, presented to the Annual Conference
       of the Political Studies Association at the
       University of Kent, April 1982.

Chapter Five

THE YORKSHIRE MINERS AND PARLIAMENTARY POLITICS

The Politics of Selection: Barnsley

The Barnsley District Labour Party (DLP) came into
being in March 1949.[1]   Before 1949 the electoral
tasks of a conventional CLP were exercised by the
Trades & Labour Council and the local Labour
parties in the surrounding districts of the Borough.
The leading political figure in the DLP was
Alderman A E McVie, the local organiser of the shop
workers union.   McVie's political importance can be
seen in his reputation as the 'town boss', enjoying
the epithet "Mr Barnsley".   Although the DLP was
created by, and run by McVie and his union the
mineworkers were the numerically dominant political
force on the Executive and General Management
Committee of the DLP.[2]   At the first meeting of
the DLP executive the NUM was the largest single
bloc of trade union votes: of 12 union delegates,
five were miners, two shopworkers, three TGWU, one
NUR and one from the plumbers.   The NUM was not
absolutely dominant, but constituted the largest
bloc of trade union political influence, neither was
the DLP run by them.[3]
        Barnsley had been a Labour seat from 1922 to
1931 and again from 1935, and was by now one of the
safest Labour seats in the country.   The post-war
incumbent, Frank Collindridge, had been elected in
the 1938 by-election caused by the death of John
Potts, a miner who had won the seat in 1922.
Collindridge came from the pit town of Wombwell just
outside Barnsley.   Born in 1891, he received an
elementary education at Barnsley Road School and at
the age of ten began work as a newsboy.   He began
work at Houghton Main three years later, then moved
to Wombwell Main.   In his youth he left for Canada
where he worked on farms, the railways and in the
mines where he became a branch secretary of the
Socialist Party.   Collindridge returned to England
in 1918, joined the Labour Party and in 1926 toured

the North in a Clarion Van.   He was elected check-
weighman at Wombwell Main and later, branch
president and delegate being a union official for
twenty years.   For 22 years he was a member of
Wombwell UDC, being twice chairman of the council,
additionally he was a member of the YMA and MFGB
executives between 1935 and 1938.   For fourteen
years he was the president of the Wentworth CLP.
After his election in 1938 he became a right-wing
member of the PLP.   Under the wartime coalition he
was PPS to the Minister of Mines, in 1945 a
government whip, and in 1946 Comptroller General of
the Royal Household.   He was a traditional miners'
MP: solid, practical but a good constituency man.[4]

Collindridge was popular with the other unions
in Barnsley.   When readopted in 1950 as candidate
he was seconded by "a large number of delegates
representing the various trade union branches..."[5]
He was motivated by a desire to improve the lot of
the miners and the working class in general, but
his socialism was similar to that of George Lansbury
in rejecting class hatred.   In 1951 Collindridge
was unanimously re-adopted and the campaign was
proceeding as expected when on 16 October
Collindridge suddenly collapsed and died after
addressing a factory meeting of glassworkers.   This
naturally halted the campaign and polling was re-
scheduled for 8 November.[8]

Barnsley DLP moved quickly to select another
candidate.   McVie contacted Transport House who
sent the National Agent, Morgan Phillips, to
Barnsley to supervise the selection.   A special
GMC was held on 20 October and at the meeting
J T Anson (Secretary of the YRCL) assumed the task
of secretary agent from McVie who was a candidate
for selection nominated were, Alderman A E McVie
(Secretary of DLP/NUDAW), Councillor H Dancer
(DLP Executive/TGWU), Mr P Morriss (Chairman Darton
LP), Mr S Schofield (Glasshoughton NUM), and
Mr. Wainwright (Mitchell's Main NUM).   Rumour had
it that the speed with which Phillips had come to
Barnsley indicated he had come "with the name of a
prospective candidate in his pocket".   He denied
this, but admitted that the Party was ready to
suggest a name if the DLP could not agree on a
candidate.[9]   Of the two NUM names proposed only
Schofield was a member of the NUM Parliamentary
List.   Wainwright was proposed by number of NUM
branches who wanted a local man (there being no
Barnsley man of the List):   he came from Wombwell
and was also secretary-agent of the Dearne Valley

CLP.   However, as Schofield was at the top of the
List only he could be the <u>official</u> NUM candidate
and Wainwright withdrew.   The following were then
nominated: A E McVie (aged 50, secretary agent and
NUDAW organiser), Harry Dancer (42, TGWU and
Secretary of Barnsley Fabian Society), Peter Morris
(25, a graduate and Collindridge's nephew), and
Sidney Schofield (40, faceworker at Glasshoughton).
Some 150 delegates from 50 affiliated organisations
could have attended the selection conference.
Naturally, Schofield was expected to win the NUM
votes (16 branches with 77 votes), McVie the bulk
of the DLP delegates, Dancer was believed to have 42
delegates pledged, whilst Morris was an unknown
quantity.   Barnsley Trades & Labour had 20 votes,
Darton LP 10, Worsborough 10, the GMWU 11, and the
NUR 3.   The remaining 45 were distributed amongst
19 other affiliated organisations.   The miners
could not automatically secure the nomination.
The results were,[10]

Table 1:   Barnsley DLP Selection Conference Voting,
           1951

First Ballot		Second Ballot		
Morris	13	McVie	85	(+22)
McVie	63	Schofield	109	(+17)
Schofield	92			
Dancer	30			
Votes to be Distributed	43	Spoilt Paper	1	
Total	198		195	

        Of the votes to be distributed, McVie won over
50%.   There was, therefore a strong swing to
McVie from Schofield who, nevertheless, on the
basis of his massive first ballot was selected as
ppc.   This swing was explained by Schofield not
being a Barnsley man, but although from West
Yorkshire he was suitable in all other respects:
he was chairman of the local NUM panel representing
3,000 miners, chairman of the Castleford Labour
Party, Vice-chairman of Pontefract CLP, a magistrate
and, from 1946, a member of Pontefract UDC.   The
NUM retained the nomination with the aid of other
unions.   Mr Heale, the area organiser of the TGWU,

stated that his union did not put forward Harry
Dancer "as this seat is regarded as a miners'
seat.   There is an affiliation agreement between
the unions that the T & GWU would support the
miners in their nomination."[11]   Schofield was thus
selected (and elected) as Barnsley's MP.

In January 1953 it was announced that
Schofield, MP for only fifteen months, intended to
resign for personal reasons.   McVie rejected
suggestions that this was due to conflicts with
the constituency party, a rejection supported by
Schofield.[12]   At a special meeting of the DLP,
attended by Sarah Barker the assistant national
agent, and J T Anson, Schofield explained his
reasons for resignation, reasons of a "domestic and
personal nature", rejecting all attempts to
dissuade him.[13]   Some in the DLP had felt that
Schofield's selection had been hurried but now there
was ample time to find a local man, and not
necessarily a miner.[14]   The Yorkshire Area
immediately invoked Rule 67, calling a conference of
branches in the Barnsley constituency to select
their man.[15]   Roy Mason, a 28 year old mineworker,
was tipped as the NUM's choice.

The NUM delegation deployed about 83 votes, but
this was insufficient to guarantee their victory,
there being a possible 230 delegates.   The miners
had the largest single bloc of votes and enjoyed
either agreements with, or the tacit support of,
other unions and it was expected that after the
close contest of 1951 the NUM would do all it could
to mobilise its full strength.   A major factor in
the selection was the DLP's determination to have
a Barnsley man, and it was believed that the miners
would have to respect this desire if they were to
retain the nomination.

There was some opposition to another miners' MP.
A letter to the Barnsley Chronicle, for example,
urged the DLP to choose its own candidate and tell
all outside organisations to "mind their own
business".   The writer, complaining about the
"Tammany Hall on Huddersfield Road" (the address of
the Yorkshire Area NUM), advocated that the union
branches should keep out of the selection process.[16]
The miners disagreed: their selection conference
chose Roy Mason.[17]   Support for Mason was
immediate. A miner from Cudworth argued it was
essential that a miner represent Barnsley, and that
he be a local man: Mason met both criteria.[18]

The close fight of 1951 prompted the Yorkshire
Area to redouble its efforts to mobilise its

delegates. The Area emphasised that branches must
send their full entitlement as "The failure of
any one delegate to attend the Conference may
jeopardise the selection of our candidate" and the
branches were urged "to take all possible steps to
win support from other organisations for our
candidate." The Yorkshire Area felt powerless in
the selection process "owing to the fact that it is
the branches and not the Yorkshire Area which are
affiliated to the Barnsley (DLP)".[19]
There were only two candidates for the nomination: McVie and Mason. Again McVie relinquished
the secretary-agent's post to J T Anson, and both
candidates were proposed and seconded.[20] The
general belief was that Mason's selection was a
foregone conclusion as whilst McVie was well known
and popular, his support was confined to his union
and his supporters in the DLP. Mason's chances of
selection were increased further when Harry
Wilkinson, a bus driver from Wombwell, refused to
accept a local TGWU nomination after receiving a
letter from the TGWU national executive reminding him
of the agreement with the NUM.[21] The selection conference took place on 16 February, there was only one
ballot which Mason won by 139 to McVie's 111.[22]
McVie won the support of his union and the
DLP, whilst Mason won the bulk of the trade union
votes. Again the gap between the contestants was
fairly narrow and was all the more significant
because 30 delegate votes were not used.[23]
Nevertheless, Mason enjoyed considerable support
amongst non trade-union delegates. He was 28
years old, employed as a fitter as Wharncliffe
Woodmoor, but he was also a leading activist in the
DLP. He was, in short, an active able young man.
McVie had a strong claim to the nomination and
ran the NUM close on both occasions but Mason has
been described as "a young man in a hurry" who spent
a considerable amount of time "learning his stuff"
in both party and union thus entering the selection
process very well prepared.[24]
In Barnsley the miners won the nomination with
relative ease. Nevertheless, it is clear that
their victories were not walkovers: the NUM was
unable to mobilise its full delegate entitlement;
and second, a powerful challenge was mounted from
within the DLP against the NUM candidates.

The Politics of Selection: Rother Valley, 1967
Many factors which influenced the events of 1967
originated in the type of parliamentary

representation the seat enjoyed after 1918. The
major industrial and political force in the area
were the mineworkers and the first two MPs, T W
Grundy (1918-1935) and Edward Dunn (1935-1945)
were both pillars of the local community: Alderman
and JPs, and both owed their nomination and
election to the YMWA branches. In 1918 the local
press was adamant that the mining communities were
the dominant political factor in the new
constituency.[25] The press was keen to expose any
"bolshevist" tendencies in Labour candidates but
regarded Grundy as the epitome of the "safe" Labour
man: as Mayor of Rotherham in 1915 and throughout
the war he had done a great deal of recruiting, he
had been convinced of the moral rightness of the
war never doubting labour's duty to help win the
war.[26] Grundy was a typical miners' MP of the
period -- solid steady, to the right of his party,
loyal, and above all, a constituency MP popular with
his constituents. Grundy's successor came from
the same mould, but Dunn was a far more charismatic
figure. The pit village of Maltby, just outside
Rotherham, was Dunn's personal fief, but he was
popular with miners throughout the constituency.
He arrived in Yorkshire from Shropshire in 1911
starting work at the newly opened Maltby Main. In
1923 he was elected to Maltby Parish Council,
which in 1924 became an Urban District as a result
of a campaign orchestrated by Dunn. He remained
UDC chairman until elected to Parliament. In
1918 he was elected to the WRCC where he was noted
for his progressive views, becoming leader of the
WRCC Labour Group. In 1926 he became Grundy's
secretary agent. The two men were personally and
politically very close and when Grundy announced
his intention of retiring Dunn was seen as his
natural successor, not only by the mineworkers but
by the CLP ward parties. There was a consensus in
Rother Valley on the type of man they wanted as
their MP. Both Grundy and Dunn were local men who
saw their task as MPs as representing the interests
of Rother Valley at Westminster. Dunn spent six
years on the MFGB Executive and was Maltby branch
secretary for 24 years.[27] He was, therefore, a key
figure in local party and union circles.

Thus, when Dunn suddenly died before the 1945
General Election, not only was the constituency
shocked at the loss, but it was clear there would
be a fierce battle for the succession as there was
no 'favourite son' as in 1935. As soon as
Dunn's death was announced the YMWA began to select

their candidate.   Council instructed the Officials
to call a Conference of all the YMWA branches in
the constituency to select their candidate.[28]
Unfortunately, the Parliamentary List elected in
1942 contained no-one from the pits in the
constituency, there was no-one as 'local' as Grundy
or Dunn.   All, with three exceptions, were West
and North Yorkshiremen and thought unlikely to
appeal to the South Yorkshire miners.   Of the
three exceptions, two were from Doncaster and the
only South Yorkshireman was not known in Rother
Valley.   The problem was resolved when J J Frain,
a List member, died and under the Rules Council
could appoint a replacement.   David Griffiths,
the delegate of Hickleton Main, was that replacement.   He was not well known and his pit was not in
the constituency (though it was on the borders),
but as a branch delegate he was well known at
Barnsley and to the YMWA delegates from the Rother
Valley pits.
      At the YMA selection conference at the
Cooperative Cafe in Rotherham on 28 April 1945
delegates attended from Silverwood, Treeton,
Orgreave, Kiveton Park, Maltby Main, Beighton,
Nunnery, Thrybergh Hall, Manvers Main and Wath
Main.   Invitations to attend were accepted by
T E Dawson, H E Holmes, E Keen, A Roberts and David
Griffiths.   Each was allowed ten minutes to
address the delegates and "to give a record of
his activities and public service, and his
qualifications for carrying out the duties of
Parliamentary Representative if elected."   Some
delegates were clearly unhappy with the candidates
but the chairman ruled that a candidate must be
selected from the List, and that there could be
no outsiders.   This was approved by 16 votes to
7.   The result was:

Table 2: Rother Valley Selection Conference Voting,
          1945

T E Dawson	Withdrew
H E Holmes	7
J Hibbert	0
E Keen	0
A Roberts	1
D Griffiths	13

However, a number of branches declared "that they had no mandate, and that they could not guarantee their branches standing by the decision of the Selection Conference."29 This was unprecedented and the YMWA General Secretary, W E Jones, warned the delegates that the decision was final and that the branches had a duty to support Griffiths.30 The opposition to Griffiths may have come from the Maltby, Silverwood, Dinnington, Kiveton Park and Beighton Branches who wanted a local candidate.

That the YMA candidate did not have the full backing of the Rother Valley miners was clear, but the extent of the opposition to Griffiths in the CLP was also apparent. Keen competition for the nomination was expected and confirmed. The nominees were: D Griffiths (YMWA), J Jones (Thurcroft Labour Party), T J Curtis (Handsworth Labour Party), L Hinchcliffe (Thrybergh Labour Party), and A Sawyer (Maltby Labour Party and YMWA branch). No less than three had intimate connections with mining and the YMWA. Griffiths we have discussed, Jones had been General Secretary of the YMWA (1924-1938) when he left the union to join the Coal Commission. In 1931 he had been elected president of the MFGB and had an active career in local politics in association with the Dinnington branch and Thurcroft Labour Party. Clearly, the Maltby branch and miners were unwilling to allow 'their' seat to go to an outsider, hence their support for their own branch secretary. In Maltby he was seen as Dunn's successor: he was a councillor, branch secretary, a Labour activist and so on, but he had been over-shadowed by Dunn and his power base was confined to Maltby. The Maltby YMWA branch were challenging the decision of the delegate Council and selection conference who subjected them to strong pressure to abandon Sawyer. Other YMWA branches were also anxious to avoid a split in the miners' vote.31 Sawyer was abandoned and the YMWA united behind Griffiths.

What sort of man was Griffiths? He was 49 years of age, had worked in the pits since the age of 13, had been a member of Bolton-on-Dearne UDC from 1924 and chairman three times and was a branch official at Hickleton Main for over 20 years.32 Griffiths was not unique when considering the qualifications of miners' MPs. However, in the context of Rother Valley politics he was a second-rater. As an MP he corresponded closely to the stereotype miners' MP: he also had

a reputation for inactivity, of being colourless to
the point of transparency and many felt him to be
too closely identified with the 'cloth cap' Labour
Party of the 1920s and 1930s. This image was
disliked intensely by some sections of the CLP and
when he announced his intention of not seeking re-
election there was a feeling that the new MP should
be of a different type.

In July 1967 Griffiths made his announcement
and the Yorkshire Area thanked him for his service.
Council immediately authorised the conventing of a
selection conference to select a miners'
candidate.[33]   The CLP had already begun this
process and time was short: nominations had to be
presented to the Party by 14 October. Griffiths
was, on his retirement, aged 71 and personally
felt fit enough to carry on but wished to give a
"younger man a chance". Responding to his critics
he commented, "I have been very active and I have
served the district very well. I think the
results of my enquiries into grievances in the area
are a pretty good record."[34] Griffiths was not
ill and as he felt capable of continuing as MP it
might be concluded that 'suggestions' were made
he should retire. If such hints were made, they
did not come from the Yorkshire Area. His
resignation caught the miners unprepared and this
was compounded because of the difficulties in
convening a selection conference as many pits
were taking their summer holidays. From the
outset the NUM selection process did not procede
smoothly.[35]

The battle for a successor would be lively,
and it was clear that some miners were unwilling to
accept uncritically the decision of the selection
conference if it produced a candidate of whom they
disapproved. A letter from "Realistic Miner"
condemned the type of MP symbolised by Griffiths,
arguing that Richard Marsh and Brian O'Malley (MP
for Rotherham) were a new breed of Labour MP more
attuned to the needs of the modern world. They
were "young men looking to the future unlike so
many of the miners' MPs, who are old men living
in the nostalgic days of King Coal" and it was no
longer essential for miners to be represented by a
miner.[36] It has also been claimed that a number of
active branch and CLP officials were anxious for a
change and were working to avoid a second
Griffiths.[37] The initiative for change came from
the ward parties, but they were unwilling to
challenge the NUM openly, as it was still regarded

by all factions as the arbiter of the selection process. The Thrybergh ward party actually issued a press statement justifying its nomination of a 34 year old lawyer, Barrington-Black, in which they denied any attempt to "break the hold of the NUM on the parliamentary nomination" arguing it was the aim of the process to obtain the best MP for Rother Valley. The statement claimed that Rother Valley was no longer a mining constituency to the same extent as in the past and so a miners' MP was not a necessity.[38]

Thrybergh was not the only ward to raise a pretender to the vacant throne. The Wickersley party announced the candidature of P F Johnson, a 24 year old water-works chemist. He was treasurer of his ward party and of Rother Valley Young Socialists.[39] Despite their manifest strengths, one was (literally) an outsider, the other only 24. The selection process remained wide open.

The leading NUM candidates were Fred Jerram and Jack Layden. Jerram was a County Councillor, a member of Maltby UDC, chairman of the housing committee, and secretary of the Maltby NUM branch. Layden, also from Maltby, was a JP, a member of the UDC, chairman of the finance committee, president of the CLP and delegate of the Maltby NUM branch. However, the NUM's choice was complicated by the presence of Friend Cooper on the Parliamentary List. Cooper's advantage was that he was secretary-agent of the CLP and had come first in the election for the List; his major disadvantage was that he had lost his branch office in 1965. The initial contest would, then, be between Layden and Jerram who were competing for the same branch votes, raising the possibility of a split. Opinion in the CLP gave Layden the advantage. A branch ballot was held at Maltby to decide between Layden and Jerram. The branch split 31-31 and the branch president refused to give a casting vote; a pit vote was held, Layden winning by 711 to Jerram's 450. This contest was watched with great interest by the local press who concluded that the winner would most likely be the next MP, but it also warned of the mounting hostility to the NUM.[40] Council then resolved,"That we call upon all Branches to support Mr Layden in every way and urge affiliate branches to make sure that their support and vote is forthcoming at all stages of selection."[41] Layden was immediately identified as the favourite to win the Party nomination. Layden was selected by the NUM after a two-hour meeting, defeating his nearest

rival, Cooper, by a "substantial majority."[42]
     In this period the anti-NUM forces in the CLP
were gaining more ground. The Brinsworth ward,
for example, announced its support for Barrington
Black. A second letter from Realistic Miner"
repeated his original themes: noting the decline
of the industry he asked what miners' MPs had done
to stop the decline? The letter argued that
Griffiths ought to have retired at 65, and that at
41 Layden was too old in comparison to the non-NUM
candidates.[43] Layden's selection had manifestly
failed to unite the NUM, or to quieten the discontent in the CLP. Commenting on this questionning
of the NUM's traditional place in local politics
The Advertiser commented,

> In dozens of communities in the rural and
> urban districts around Rotherham, prosperity
> depends on the state of the mining industry
> and will continue to do so long after
> Mr David Griffiths' successor at Westminster
> has been decided ... from the Labour
> standpoint the choice of Councillor Jack
> Layden ... would therefore be an admirable
> one.[44]

Despited the difficulties of his candidacy, Layden
was accepted as Griffiths' successor. Nevertheless, his candidacy was damaged by rivalries
between some NUM branches affiliated to Rother
Valley, rivalries which affected the unity of the
NUM delegation.[45] Further challenges to the miners
appeared. In late September Rotherham Rural
Labour Party announced the candidature of Tom
Wheaton, a 34 year old headmaster, president of the
lcoal NUT branch and ward secretary. Wheaton was
regarded as the main challenger to Layden.[46] By
now the Yorkshire Area in Barnsley appreciated that
Layden was faced with formidable problems, and there
was criticism of personal rivalries within the NUM
which were affecting Layden's chances. Council
"urged all Branches to do all in their power to
support ... Mr Layden."[47]
     The most serious rival to Layden was not
Wheaton, however, but Peter Hardy who was nominated
by the Wath Labour Party. In 1967 Hardy was 36
and had spent all his political life in the area.
He was a graduate of Sheffield University, a party
member for 20 years, chairman of his ward party,
a local councillor of ten years standing and had
fought Scarborough and Whitby in the 1964 election

143

and Sheffield Hallam in 1966. In a mining CLP
a candidate's social origins can be a crucial
consideration, and in this Hardy was fortunate: his
father and grandfather were both miners and as a
school teacher he had worked in a mining area. He
was, therefore, intimately acquainted with the
mining communities of South Yorkshire.

The CLP's short-list had five names: P Hardy
(school teacher, nominated by Wath Labour Party
and NUPE), Barrington Black (Solicitor, Thrybergh
Labour Party), R Truman (TGWU), J Layden (miner,
NUM), and T Wheaton (headmaster, Rotherham Rural
Labour Party). Only two of the candidates held
manual working class jobs; three held middle class
jobs and were, significantly, nominated by the ward
parties. As the selection conference approached
the NUM became increasingly doubtful of Layden's
chances. The main problem was the mobilisation
of the branch delegation, Council resolved "to once
more bring to the notice of the affected branches
the necessity to ensure that they have names of
delegates who can attend the Constituency meetings,
especially the Selection Conference ..."; delegates
had to live in the constituency and be individual
members of the Party; finally Council noted,
"Branches have been told this time and time again."
The Darfield and Edlington branches, for example,
were not untypical in finding no-one to serve as
delegates. The Area commented on this, "The only
consolation about this -- if it is a consolation --
is that we have heard that other unions are
similarly affected. It is most unlikely, however,
that the Constituency Local Labour Parties will be
so affected."48

The selection conference confirmed the worst
fears of the NUM. Hardy defeated Layden and the
Yorkshire miners lost a seat held since 1918.
Layden's defeat was the product of a concurrence
of three factors; personal rivalry between Layden
and Cooper; structural changes in the mining
industry; and changing expectations in the CLP.

Two strong NUM candidates, Layden and Cooper
both had claims to the NUM nomination, but the
formal selection process went against Cooper. It
has been suggested that in response to this Cooper
did not "exert himself unduly" in the NUM cause
and as secretary-agent he searched for another
candidate. Cooper was asked to stand by both
individual members and members of the NUM, but he
apparently felt he had most chance of influencing
the selection process as secretary-agent.

Table 3:   Selection Conference Voting in Rother
           Valley, 1967

	First Ballot	Second Ballot
Layden	58	65(+7)
Hardy	50	85(+35)
Black	18	
Wheaton	13	
Truman	10	
	149	150
Abstentions	1	
Total Vote	150	150

In the CLPs Cooper could have garnered sufficient
votes to fight Layden but he refused out of loyalty
to the NUM and to avoid bitterness within the CLP.[49]
Naturally, the loss of the nomination came as a
blow to Layden: "I played the game cleanly and by
the rules", the implication being someone did not.
Indeed, there were elements in the CLP and NUM
who did their best to ensure he did not win.[50]   The
imputation is that the Cooper faction actively
blocked Layden and encouraged a third.   Anonymous
sources have claimed that Cooper as Secretary-agent
canvassed non-NUM votes on Hardy's behalf, whilst
others claim he did little to help him whilst not
actively working against Layden.[51]
     Did the decline of the coal industry have any
effect?   Rother Valley did not suffer from
extensive pit closures, but the total labour force
did fall by 27.3% between 1950 and 1966.   Thus,
the NUM had a smaller pool of activists from which
to recruit its delegates, and in the previous chapter
we saw the difficulties faced by the union in
mobilising its political influence.   Evidence from
the Rother Valley selection suggests that 32 NUM
delegate votes were not taken up as no-one could be
found to use them.[52]   The changes in party
standing orders in 1965 are of crucial importance
in that only individual members could serve as
delegates, but the vast bulk of miners -- even
politically interested miners were affiliated
members.
     The Rother Valley selection shows the important

role of the wards, demonstrating a shift away from
the unions to the individual members who had a
different conception of the role of the MP. This
was connected to the changing social and occupational composition of the CLP. This can be seen by
comparing the 1945 short list (working class in
composition) with that of 1967. By 1967 the wards
were 'middle class' dominated wanting more from
their MP, and, note, so did many miners.[53] Hindess
identified "The Decline of Working Class Politics"
as the key feature of post-war Labour Party
politics, claiming that at all levels the Party was
moving away from the working class.[54] This thesis
has been criticised, but retains a general validity
and the example quoted here shows its
applicability.[55] Evidence presented in the
previous chapter demonstrates that post-war social
change has not led to the destruction of the
miners' influence, but has made CLP politics far
more complex. This, in turn, led to changing
conceptions of the qualities necessary for an MP,
qualities not found in the traditional miners'
nominee.

Factors in Labour Party Selection
The Parliamentary List procedure inevitably
encouraged the election of middle aged men. Age
was of little relevance when the miners dominated
these CLPs, but with their decline and with changing
expectations there emerged a demand for younger,
more vigorous parliamentary candidates.[56]
     Similarly, the relevance of social class was
not important but changes in social composition had
made it relevant.[57] If the social composition has
become more cosmopolitan, making it less mining
dominated and less solidly manual working class,
then there may well be resistance to the 'cloth
cap' image presented by the traditional mining MP.
This was certainly so in Rother Valley.[58] Social
origins, when coupled with age, level of education,
the perception of the CLP's character by its members
may result in the rejection of the image of a
'miners' seat. This is not to suggest that the
political process is explicable by social class:
conflict between a middle and working class party.
Even when the dominance of the miners has been
reduced these constituencies retain their Labour
partisanship. Despite higher levels of education
and occupational diversification these people
remain Labour supporters; what has changed is
the perception of what constitutes a good MP. The

Yorkshire Area could not isolate itself from these changes. Yet, there also exists in these CLPs a distrust of the outsider: these CLPs do not like to be made to feel intellectually or socially inferior by a potential candidate; thus, the ideal MP is "the local lad made good".

Political views are rarely a factor in selection. The seats were traditionally represented by orthodox right-wing members of the PLP, and any miner with suspect political views was weeded out by the NUM selection process. The one exception to this was Dick Kelley (MP, Don Valley 1959-1979) whose left-wing views were supported by the left-wing pits who control the Don Valley CLP. The Area was particularly vigilant for signs of infiltration by communists or fellow-travellers. In 1950 for example, the Area General Secretary warned branches when nominating for the List only bona fide members of the Labour Party could be nominated and it was the duty of the branch secretary to establish this.[59] In 1955 there was considerable debate as to whether a man could remain on the List if he was subsequently found to have dubious political loyalties.[60] This was not of major importance as the left was rarely interested in Parliamentary politics.

Finally, it is worth emphasising once more that union political finance is not a factor in selection. If the NUM withdrew finance a replacement sponsor would quickly be found. Likewise, to cease paying affiliation fees would cause NUM influence to collapse as it would not be entitled to any delegates.

Sponsorship and Parliamentary Politics
The miners have, since 1874, been at the forefront of working class parliamentary politics.[61] Parliamentary politics were used to avoid the limitations imposed by the unions' organisational and numerical weakness. Formal political equality offered the prospect of miners electing MPs to press for legislation, thus circumventing the owners' economic power.[62] A belief in Parliament's neutrality and responsiveness and the efficacy of legislation grounded on Parliamentary sovereignty determined the evolution of working class electoral politics.

Affiliation to the Labour Party did not, therefore, represent a new strategy. Political change in the coalfields and the redundancy of Lib-Labism, were coterminous with the emergence of

nationalisation as the miners' key demand and their
commitment to Labour was sealed by Clause 4. The
sponsored MP enapsulated both the traditional direct
representation of miners in the House of Commons and
the miners' contribution to the Party's advance
towards government.
  Massive majorities and the YMWA's local
dominance aroused a fear that the CLPs and MPs
might be used for 'sectional' purposes.[63] However,
the miners' MPs were never union delegates; they
did accept that the miners formed the largest single
interest in their constituencies to which they
felt a deep loyalty. Signing the Party Constitution
meant accepting a higher political loyalty: the
Labour Party and Labour Movement.[64] In any case,
the miners did not rely upon the MPs and made few
demands upon them. Although financed by the Union
the MPs were not the Union's in any proprietorial
sense: they represented the miners within the
combined political and industrial forces of the
Labour Movement. Thus, the Party had little to
fear: neither the MPs nor the constituencies were,
or were about to become, the creatures of the
miners. Circumstance compelled the Party to accept
the numerical and financial dominance of the
Union, but it insisted (and the Union accepted)
that the Party was above any single interest and
enjoyed a political destiny wider than that of the
unions or any single union. Party supremacy was
codified in the 1933 Hastings Agreement.

The Subordinate Role of the MP
Ramsay Macdonald described the PLP of 1918-1922
as a party of checkweighmen, yet the links between
the Yorkshire miners and their MPs are traditionally weak. In July 1919 the Yorkshire miners
struck, officially over piece rates, (in reality,
an attempt to force the Coalition Government to
accept nationalisation). Speaking for the
Yorkshire MPs, William Lunn (MP for Rothwell)
complained at the lack of contact with the union.[65]
Despite attempts to improve the Union-MP relationship, little has changed since 1919.
  The MP was important historically because of
the centrality of Parliament to the miners as a
counterweight to the coalowners. The miner and
coalowner were formally equal ('one man, one vote');
their inequality as collectivities in the social
whole tended to be ignored by the Union which
argued that increased parliamentary representation
could counter socio-economic power. The sponsored

MP is a product of the **conviction** that if the State
was captured from within by a Labour majority in the
Commons then real social change would follow.[66]
Nevertheless, many in the Labour Movement remained
sceptical of the utility of trade union MPs.[67]

The emergence of the Labour Party and the
affiliation of the MFGB changed the MP's role.
However, because of the Party's dependence on the
unions in these early years the changes were not
readily apparent.   The PLP remained dominated by
trade union MPs, a dependence which was criticised
frequently.[68]   Ironically, the growing separation
of union and party in the 1920s and 1930s led to
fears of a rupture.   These fears were voiced at the
end of the second world war at a time when the
political influence of the unions independent of the
Party was increasing.   In response to a plea from
the Party the MFGB Executive proposed that two
members of the Executive sit with the Miners' Group
of MPs "whenever matters affecting the industry
are under consideration", and that two MPs sit with
the Executive "when matters of political importance
are being discussed."[69] After 1945 attempts were
made to involve the MPs in industrial matters when
they affected the Labour Government.   When the coal
shortage threatened the existence of the Government
the MPs became frequent visitors to Council
and to the Branches to urge greater and greater
efforts.[70]

The Yorkshire Area has urged frequently the
virtues of increased participation in CLP politics,
but it has paid remarkably little attention to
the end product of such political and electoral
activity.   What is the role of the MP and what is
the Area's view of them?

In his Presidential Address for 1964, Sam
Bullough, emphasised the traditional importance of
party-political activity and the sponsored MP to
the miners.   His experience as a trade union
leader "brings to me more strongly the importance
of their work and how they use their own personal
knowledge in debate and in contributions in the
House of Commons when the Coal Mining Industry is
being considered."[71]   During this period the
Yorkshire miners were urged to recognise the value
of MPs, to support their work and that of the
Party of which they were both a part.[72]

Between 1964 and 1970 the Yorkshire Area
became increasingly ambivalent towards the Labour
Government.   This embivalence affected the
position of the MPs, some miners questioning the

value of 'representatives' who remained loyal to a
government which was closing pits. The official
attitude recognised the problems being faced by
the government and the MPs and that the MPs were
still useful. Critics were enjoined to remember
that they were Labour Party MPs primarily:

> We must ... realise the problems which
> face our mining MPs ... They are always
> alive to the situation in the industry,
> and the valuable work they perform in
> committees and on the floor of the House
> often occurs without the publicity which
> attaches to more sensational aspects of
> their work ... we urge them to continue
> in the struggle to win for coal, an ever
> increasing share for solid fuel in the
> Power Stations of this Country ...[73]

Coexisting with the traditional 'arms length' union-
MP relationship there is a second attitude which
seeks a relationship where the MP is more responsive
to union wishes.

At a meeting of the Barnsley Miners Forum
called to consider how the NUM might achieve retirement at 55 the then Area President, Arthur Scargill,
sought a coordinated campaign of industrial and
political action to force the Labour Government to
concede.[74]   Sympathy was not enough ("there was
enough sympathy to float the NUM headquarters");
Scargill wanted the MPs to play an active role
in securing early retirement. When the NUM had
decided in favour of industrial action (if necessary
necessary) to achieve early retirement, some 80 MPs
signed a motion urging the Government to concede.
Amongst the signatures were those of Michael Foot
and Wedgewood-Benn, but one notable absentee was
Roy Mason, MP for Barnsley. Scargill was annoyed
at Mason's failure and that of the other Yorkshire
MPs to do anything concrete to help. The one
exception was Dick Kelley (MP for Don Valley).
Scargill went so far as to claim that "the miners'
MPs should lead the campaign" and adopt an attitude
similar to that of Dennis Skinner (MP for Bolsover)
and Dick Kelley who were vocal supporters of the
union's case. Connected was a strong plea for
internal party democracy, particularly the
mandatory re-selection of MPs and adherence to
Conference decisions.

Scargill argued that the MPs had no excuse
for not making their position clear as they were

well aware of NUM policy.   The Area had made sure
by sending them details of union decisions "by first
class mail."   The value of sponsorship and the
notion of "our MPs" was constantly reiterated but no
threats of retaliation against recalcitrant MPs were
made.   It seems that the Area would have been
satisfied with a letter of support from the MPs but
none was forthcoming except from Dick Kelley.
       The attitude of Arthur Scargill to the
sponsored MP is clearly a departure from the
generally 'laisser-faire' line of his predecessors.
There is always a tendency on the part of some
members to see the MP as a union delegate, whereas
the traditional view sees him as a representative
who was expected to 'bear in mind' the interests of
the mining communities.   Scargill's interpretation
seems to lie between these interpretations.   Party
politics and parliamentary democracy prevent an MP
from being a delegate.   However, these MPs are
elected with miners' votes and supported by miners'
money, and as such the Union has a right to expect
the MP to support Union policy.   Scargill wanted
a much more integrated relationship in which the
Union takes the initiative.   Should an MP actively
oppose Union policy, then the NUM must have the
right to end its support.   This naturally leads
to a commitment to increased NUM activity in CLPs
and the promotion of intra-party democracy.

Union-MP Conflict
There are two types of Union-MP conflict: an MP
in conflict with the union for criticising union
policy;   or, the union, or some part of the union,
criticising an MP.   Two examples of the first
are Lunn's complaints in 1919 and an article written
by Roy Mason in 1959 which voiced remarkably similar
sentiments.   This difference was that the latter
was published by The Sunday People.
       Mason claimed that as a member of the trade
union group he was elected to be the unions' "voice
in Parliament".   However, the MPs were "by passed
by their own unions.   No longer do they use their
own MPs to ventilate grievances on the floor of the
House.   They prefer to go round by the back
door ..."   Mason complained further that the MPs
were excluded from industrial matters such as
unofficial strikes "even though (they are) doing
untold harm to both the trade union movement, and
the Labour Party", whereas the unions felt competent
to make statements on contentious issues such as
nuclear disarmament "that are the greatest

embarassment to the Labour Party." Mason called for an end to this "lopsided" arrangement.[75] This article sparked off a furore in the NUM, it being rumoured that action might be taken against him. The Miners' Group sent a strongly worded resolution to the NUM declaring Mason's statement to be unjustified and praising the NUM-Miners' Group relationship.[76] The article and the controversy were quickly and quietly forgotten, being ascribed to the exuberancy of youth.

Union criticism of MP behaviour has had remarkably little effect. In 1960 the Party Conference passed a resolution supporting unilateral nuclear disarmament. The NUM was multilateralist and supported Gaitskell, but within the Yorkshire Area there was a powerful minority composed of the Labour Left and Communist Party which advocated unilateralism and which seemed strong enough to change the Yorkshire Area's stance.[77] This group was bitterly critical of the MPs who, in Division 22 of 13 December 1960 supported the Opposition resolution condemning Government defence policy but which ignored the Conference decision. Of the five Yorkshire MPs only Alan Beaney and Dick Kelley did not vote for the resolution, and Beaney abstained.[78] Several branches demanded that the MPs vote in accordance with Party policy as determined by Conference. 'Next Business' was moved, seconded, and approved by 85 votes to 13.[79]

When Minister of Power, Roy Mason was responsible for implementing a fuel policy which resulted in pit closures. Mason was bound to carry out Government policy but as a miners' MP he was bitterly attacked. Despite the Government's fuel policy and the hostility of a number of branches the Area Executive refused to accept any censure motion and secured the defeat of all criticism in Council.[80] A proposal that the NUM withdraw sponsorship from Albert Roberts (MP for Normanton) because of his support for the Franco regime enjoyed more success. The Kellingley branch refused to withdraw the resolution and in order to extricate itself from a difficult position Council agreed to note the resolution by 56 votes to 19.[81]

What is notable from these instances of Union-MP conflict is the reluctance of the Union as an organisation to legitimise branch hostility towards MPs. Traditionally, the NEC of the NUM, which actually sponsors the MPs, refuses to intervene in a dispute between an MP and his Area.[82] Such conflict is regarded as an Area matter and one for it to reconcile, and complaints tend to be quietly forgotten.[83]   A further reason for this is that for the Union to interfere with an MP's behaviour risks the wrath of Parliament.   This, and the limited influence of the Area over the MPs was demonstrated in 1975.

The Limits of Sponsorship: The EEC Dispute

The 1971 NUM Conference voted unanimously to oppose Britain's application to join the EEC.   After entry, the Yorkshire Area remained implacably opposed not only to membership but also to having any relationship with any EEC or EEC related body.[84] When returned to office in 1974 the Party was committed to re-negotiate Britain's terms of membership and submit the results for approval in a Referendum.   The NUM was divided on this: at the 1974 NUM Conference delegates approved a resolution reaffirming the union's opposition to membership and calling for the NUM to break off all links with the Community.   Yorkshire supported this, demanding a clear instruction that Labour withdraw and "dispense (with) this charade of renegotiation of terms.[85]   On a card vote the resolution was approved by 180 to 92 and the NUM was compelled to sever all links with the EEC.   Official union policy, determined by Conference, was crystal clear.

The NUM's opposition contrasted with the favourable attitude of the sponsored MPs.   In June 1975 Area Council considered two resolutions from the Barrow and Kellingley branches and a letter from the Cadeby branch which proposed action be taken against those sponsored MPs who openly flouted union policy and campaigned for a 'yes' vote in the referendum.   The Kellingley branch proposed that the Area "cannot, and will not, continue to give financial or political support to the (MPs) who do not support the policy of this Union." The letter stated, "we feel the time has come, even passed, when these people should be brought to heel and told they must toe the NUM line or have their sponsorship withdrawn."[86]

Area Officials were, despite their sympathy, reluctant to accept these resolutions and it was, proposed that Council should not seek immediate withdrawal of sponsorship, but should censure the MPs and set out guidelines for the future.   Barrow and Kellingley agreed to withdraw their resolutions, a compromise was put, voted upon and approved by 73 votes to three.   It read,

> That we can no longer tolerate the
> position where a 'sponsored' MP can
> oppose his Union's policy on major
> issues.
> Therefore, it is agreed that the following
> guide-lines shall apply to MPs sponsored
> by the Yorkshire Area:
>
> (1) No Miners' MP shall actively
> campaign or work against the Union's
> policy on any issue which affects the
> coal mining industry.
> (2) No Miners' MP shall actively campaign
> or work against the Union's policy on
> any other major issue.
>
> (3) If any Miners' MP refuses to agree to
> the 'guide-lines', the Area Council
> shall withdraw sponsorship from the
> MP.
>
> We wish to make it clear that the
> Yorkshire Area will no longer tolerate a
> situation where a Miners' MP accepts the
> 'privilege' of sponsorship and then
> demands the 'luxury' of independence
> from Union policy.[87]

The hostility came from the branches: the Area
Officials were aware of the dangers inherent in such
powerful opinions and attempted to 'water-down'
the branch resolutions.[88]
    This resolution was referred to the Committee
of Privileges of the House of Common as a prima
facie breach of privilege. Several newspapers
reported a statement by Scargill to the effect that
"Miners are entitled by virtue of their sponsorship
to tell their Members of Parliament which way to
vote."[89] The Select Committee found the Yorkshire
Area guilty of a breach of privilege as the
resolution sought to use a financial relationship
to exert pressure on MPs.[90]
    The definitive statement on an MP's relation-
ship with an extra-parliamentary organisation is
that of W J Brown (MP for Rugby) and the Civil
Service Clerical Association (CSCA) put to the
Committee in 1947. The judgement revealed the
complexity of the sponsoring relationship: any
attempt to threaten, or to take action, calculated
to affect an MP's parliamentary behaviour was
interpreted as a breach of privilege. However, it
was quite legitimate for extra-parliamentary bodies

to try and influence an MP's opinion by, for
example, passing a resolution. The crucial
factor lay in the nature of the relationship between
the MP and his sponsor. If there was a financial
relationship under which the MP 'represented'
that extra-parliamentary interest in the Commons
any threat to use that relationship to influence
an MP was a breach of privilege. Sponsorship has
been accepted as a legitimate aspect of parliamentary life, but should not be used as a tool of
political influence.[91] What Scargill in fact
claimed was: "The miners who sponsor a candidate
are entitled to claim the right to tell him he
must not act or vote against Union policy on issues
which affect the coalmining industry".[92] His
reported statements in the press were, under
the 1947 judgement, a breach of privilege, but
Scargill's actual statement implied that the Union
was entitled to tell MPs what NUM policy was and to
expect them not to actively oppose it. It implied
that should an MP refuse, the Union could argue
that the relationship was no longer in the interests
of the Union and terminate it. Thus, the Area's
resolution can be seen as a legitimate response to
MPs who took union money and then in full knowledge,
acted against union policy. It was not an attempt
to convert the MP into a union delegate. No
further action was taken by the Committee as the
NEC repudiated the Yorkshire Area resolution.[93]

The MPs' Dilemma: The 1967 Fuel Policy Crisis

The MPs' duality (representing both Union and Party)
causes problems when a Labour Government is
pusuing policies detrimental to the interests of the
miners. In their 1969 Parliamentary Report, for
example, the MPs expressed great concern at the
decline of the industry but they could not oppose
the Government. They emphasised their uneasy
acquiescence in the policy whilst welcoming the
measures taken to limit the social impact of pit
closures.[94]

Sponsored MPs give direct access to the
legislative process, but access does not guarantee
influence. Between 1964 and 1970 the Labour
Government progressively ran down the industry. A
key policy statement was the White Paper, Fuel
Policy (Cmnd. 3438, November 1967) which was
preceded by a ministerial statement on 18 July 1967
predicting further contraction. This placed
the miners' MPs in a delicate position, divided as
they were between their occupational and communal

loyalties and their political loyalties to a
Government, passing through one of its many crises.
However, they felt a protest should be made.
Richard Crossman described the result,

> After ten o'clock we had an all night
> sitting specially arranged for the
> miners' group of MPs.   It was their
> idea that Dick Marsh's long Statement
> on pit closures should be made after
> ten o'clock so that they could debate
> it for as long as they liked throughout
> the night.   I thought it was a perverse
> idea, but I discovered that they were
> right because by the end of the night
> there were two or three Tories present
> and the miners' MPs were able to have
> the whole House of Commons to themselves
> for the protest which they wanted to make
> before accepting their fate ... It was a
> cosy occasion but pathetic because it was
> clear that provided they could make their
> protest these miners felt that they were
> bound to support the Government in an
> action which really meant the destruction
> of the mining industry.   What the
> miners' MPs showed was not a very edifying
> loyalty, because people should not be as
> loyal to a Government which is causing the
> total ruin of their industry ... I was ...
> shocked by their pathetic lack of fight.[95]

By November 1967 the Government was facing a
number of serious problems notably over unemployment
and a general economic crisis.   When Marsh
expanded his July statement into the November White
Paper, the crisis broke,

> Dick Kelley has already denounced the
> Minister ... and our friend Joe Gormley,
> who is a miners' member of the NEC and
> chairman of the Org(anisation) Sub-
> (Committee), has stated that he's
> prepared to start a new Miners' Party
> because the Labour Party is betraying
> them.[96]

To defuse the crisis the White Paper's opponents
were given two days of debate, delayed for one
week.   Crossman, "thinking everything was easy I had
announced ... a debate on the White Paper and

assumed we would put down a motion of approval.
But ... found that the Miners' Group were raging
around saying they bloody well weren't going to
approve ..."[97]   Crossman reported to Cabinet that
as many as 60-70 MPs were prepared to defy the
Government, and this prompted Wilson to reach a
compromise.   However, the White Paper remained
the basis of government policy but the MPs had made
their protest, and thanks to a number of fortuitous
events (notably, the devaluation crisis) were able
to secure concessions.

The Nature of Sponsorship

The development of the Union-Government relationship
and achievement of stable collective bargaining
in the coal industry means that the need for
specifically party-political representation has
declined.   Originally the MPs were both defensive
(protecting their constituents) and initiative
(promoting incremental reform), but the creation
of the Labour Party which aimed at national
political power caused the separation of the MP
from his union.   He represented his constituents
(as he had always done) but no longer 'represented'
the miners in any meaningful sense.   He was elected
under the banner of the Labour Party to help
realise a Party programme and support Labour
Governments.
    The unions and the Party had different
functions within the political system despite the
unions' links with the Party, and sponsorship is
not a mainstream union activity.   The TUC has
acknowledged that when in government, the interests
of union and party will diverge despite these
loyalties.[98]   Sponsored MPs can be useful, but
parliamentary democracy and representative government compells the MP to expand his field of
interest.   After his election in 1922, for example,
Tom Williams commented, "The return to Westminster
reminded us that there were other things in the
world to bother about besides the needs of the
coalfields ..."[99]   The evolution of sponsorship
means that no trade union can legitimately claim
the type of authority sought by the branches in
1974-1975.   The conventions of parliamentary
democracy enable an MP to resist these pressures
and sponsorship is accepted precisely because it
conveys no power over the MP.   The idea that 'he
who pays the piper calls the tune' remains
influential in left wing circles but overt attempts
at influence via sponsorship risks the intervention

of the Committee of Privileges.100   Sponsorship
has been questioned on the grounds that these MPs
rapidly lose that intimate contact with the
industry but these are constituency MPs who retain
a close relationship with local political culture
and they remain an authentically working class
element in an increasingly middle class parliament.
It has been alleged that "the sponsorship system
provides the unions with an anomalous and disproportionate weight within both the Labour Party and
Parliament."101   Clearly, this is not so.   Given
the importance of the NUM and the miners to the
Party, it is remarkable that they have been content
to play so inactive a role.

REFERENCES

1   Barnsley District Labour Party Minutes:
        19 March 1949.   Hereafter, BDLP
2   BDLP: 15 April 1949

3   Occupation Composition of Barnsley, 1951

Mining	5,348	Transport	2,420
Glass	2,429	Distribution	5,052
Engineering	2,505	Public Administration	1,448
Clothing	1,395	Services	2,097
Building	1,425		

Census of 1951 (County Tables), and, interview with
participants

4   This information came from a variety of sources
        sources
5   BDLP;   Executive Committee, 14 January 1950.
6   BDLP;   Special GMC;   28 September 1951
7   Barnsley Chronicle;   20 October 1951;   and,
        Interviews with participants
8   BDLP;   Special GMC;   28 October 1951
9   Barnsley Chronicle;   27 October 1951
10   BDLP;   Special GMC;   23 October 1951
11   Barnsley Chronicle;   5 November 1951
12   Barnsley Chronicle;   10 January 1953
13   BDLP;   Special EC;   11 January 1953
14   Barnsley Chronicle;   17 January 1953
15   YA(NUM);   17 January 1953
16   Barnsley Chronicle;   24 January 1953
17   YA(NUM);   29 January 1953
18   Barnsley Chronicle;   31 January 1953

19   Letter from W E Jones, the Yorkshire Area
     General Secretary, to all NUM Branches
     affiliated to the Barnsley DLP;
     30 January 1951.
20   BDLP; Special EC; 9 February 1953.
21   Barnsley Chronicle; 14 February 1953.
22   BDLP;   Management Committee; 16 February 1953.
23   Barnsley Chronicle; 23 February 1953.
24   Interview with participants.
25   Sheffield Daily Telegraph; 5 December 1918.
26   Sheffield Daily Telegraph; 5 December 1918.
27   South Yorkshire and Rotherham Advertiser;
     14 June 1945.
28   YMWA; 23 April 1945.
29   YMWA; 11 June 1945.
30   YMWA; 17 September 1945.
31   Interview with participants.
32   Details from The Times House of Commons.
33   YA(NUM); 10 July 1967.
34   South Yorkshire and Rotherham Advertiser;
     15 July 1967.
35   Interview with participants.
36   South Yorkshire and Rotherham Advertiser;
     5 August 1967.
37   Interview with participants.
38   South Yorkshire and Rotherham Advertiser;
     12 August 1967. Barrington-Black was
     certainly different to Griffiths; he was an
     ex-President of the NUS, an ex-member of
     Harrogate Trades Council, and had fought
     Harrogate in 1964.   The key point about his
     nomination is that the ward "looked around"
     specifically for such a candidate outside
     the Rother Valley.   This suggests that
     they felt that their perception of a good
     MP could not be satisfied from the
     resources available to them.
39   South Yorkshire and Rotherham Advertiser;
     12 August 1967.
40   South Yorkshire and Rotherham Advertiser;
     26 August 1967, and personal information.
41   YA(NUM); 30 August 1967.
42   South Yorkshire and Rotherham Advertiser;
     2 September 1967.
43   South Yorkshire and Rotherham Advertiser;
     2 September 1967.
44   South Yorkshire and Rotherham Advertiser;
     2 September 1967.
45   Information from participants.
46   South Yorkshire and Rotherham Advertiser;
     23 September 1967.

47   YA(NUM); 9 October 1967.
48   YA(NUM); 9 October 1967, My emphasis.
49   Information from participants.
50   Information from participants.
51   Oral evidence from many sources lays great
          emphasis upon the personal antagonism
          between the two leading NUM protagonists,
          and one is forced to conclude that such
          antagonisms played a major role in the
          selection process.
52   Information from participants.
53   Information from participants.
54   B Hindess, The Decline of Working Class
          Politics (London, MacGibbon & Kee 1971).
55   For example, R Baxter, 'The Working Class and
          Electoral Politics' in, Political Studies,
          xx(1972); pp93-107.   See also Hindess'
          auto-critique in B Pimlott & C Cook(eds),
          Trade Unions in British Politics (London,
          Longmans 1982); pp237-257.
56   For examples of complaints about the calibre of
          mining candidates see:
          Barnsley Chronicle; 14 February 1953; and
          South Yorkshire and Rotherham Advertiser;
          15 July 1967.
57   M Rush, The Selection of Parliamentary Candida
          Candidates (London, Nelson 1969);   pp206-207.
          A Ranney, Pathways to Parliament (London,
          Macmillan 1965); p175.
          J Blondel, Voters, Parties and Leaders
          (Harmondsworth, Penguin 1976) pp100-102
          All emphasise that changes on the social
          composition of a CLP from an overwhelmingly
          working class to a more middle class seat
          changes expectations about the MP.
58   Information from participants.
59   YA(NUM); 6 March 1950.
          For a similar statement see: 5 November and
          3 December 1950.
60   YA(NUM); 12 September 1955.
61   The first working-men elected to Parliament
          were miners: Thomas Burt (Morpeth) and
          Alexander Macdonald (Stafford) both in
          1874.
62   See, G Potter, 'The Workingman in Parliament',
          in Contemporary Review xvi (1870); and
          S & B Webb, Industrial Democracy (London,
          Longmans 1913); pp233-234 for a discussion
          of trade union parliamentary activity.
63   R I McKibbin, The Evolution of the Labour
          Party, 1910-1924 (London, OUP 1974);

pp236-237; and, R Moore, <u>The Emergence of
the Labour Party</u> (London, Hodder & Stoughton
1978); pp186-193.

64   W D Muller, <u>The Kept Men?</u> (Hassocks, Harvester
     Press 1977); pp34-35.

65   W Lunn to YMA Executive, 20 August 1919,
     in <u>YMA</u>; 3 September 1919.

66   R Miliband, <u>Parliamentary Socialism</u> (London,
     Merlin Press 1972); pp13-14.

67   Muller, <u>The Kept Men?</u>; pp12-26. Ben Pickard
     (MP for Normanton, 1885-1904) was regarded
     as a poor MP: "His interests were narrow,
     his speeches rare, bad and sometimes
     muddled". H Clegg, A Fox & A Thomson,
     <u>A History of British Trade Unionism since
     1889, Vol.1 1889-1910</u> (Oxford, Clarendon
     Press 1964); p.285.

68   B Barker(ed), <u>Ramsay Macdonalds Political
     Writings</u> (London, Allen Lane 1972); p224.

69   <u>MFGB(EC)</u>; 7 March 1944. The MPs were to be
     supplied with relevant papers. The
     Secretary of the Miners' Parliamentary
     Group was to supervise the relationship.
     This liaison remains in force.

70   <u>YA(NUM)</u>; 19 August 1950, <u>AS Circular</u> 87/50
     (12 September 1950), and,
     <u>BS Circular</u> 59/50 (12 September 1950).

71   <u>YA(NUM)</u>: Annual Report, 1964; p10.

72   <u>YA(NUM)</u>; 23 September 1964, and, <u>BS Circular</u>
     93/64 (28 September 1964)

73   <u>YA(NUM)</u>, Annual Reports for 1968; p8. See
     also the Report for 1969, p7, and <u>The Miner</u>
     (February 1969), article by Alex Eadie, MP
     for Midlothian.

74   This account is based on notes made at the
     meeting held on 6 December 1976.

75   R Mason, 'I Speak for 100 Gagged Men!', in
     <u>The Sunday People</u>, 22 November 1959.

76   <u>NUM(EC)</u>; 17 December 1959.

77   A Fox, 'Trade Unions and Defence', in,
     <u>Socialist Commentary</u> xxv (February 1961);
     p5.

78   W D Muller, 'The Trade Union Sponsored MPs and
     the Defence Dispute, 1960-1961', in,
     <u>Parliamentary Affairs</u> xxiii(3) 1970;
     p264 table 1.

79   <u>YA(NUM)</u>; 28 November 1960, and, <u>BS Circular</u>
     9/61 (27 February 1961).

80   <u>YA(NUM)</u>; 18 December 1967, T Coleman,
     'Interview with Roy Mason' in <u>The Guardian</u>,
     6 August 1977, and information from

        participants.
81 YA(NUM); 10 June, and, 22-23 July 1974.
82 Muller, The Kept Men, pp143-154 for a general
        survey of union-MP conflict.
83 NUM(EC); 31 March 1955.
84 NUM: Annual Conference Report, 1971; pp222-
        227.
85 For example, YA(NUM): Annual Reports, 1973;
        p15; and, NUM, Annual Conference Report,
        1974; pp250-259.
86 YA(NUM); 25 June 1975
87 YA(NUM); 25 June 1975.   This censure did not
        include Dick Kelley.
88 O Briscoe (General Secretary, Yorkshire Area)
        to the Clerk of the Committee of Privileges,
        30 June 1975, in, HC 643 Second Report from
        the Committee of Privileges (1974-1975),
        14 October 1975: 'Complaint Concerning a
        Resolution of the Yorkshire Area Council of
        the National Union of Mineworkers'.
        Hereafter, HC 643.
89 HC Debs, 26 June 1975; col. 667-669.
90 HC 643; p.iv and p.viii.
91 HC 118 (1946-1947), in, HC 643, p.ix.
92 A Scargill to the Clerk of the Committee,
        30 June 1975; in, HC 643; p.xiii.
93 HC 643; para 4 (p.vi); J Gormley to the Clerk
        of the Committee,18 July 1975, in, HC 643;
        para 5, p.v; and, NUM(EC); 11 September
        1975.
94 NUM: Report of the NEC (Miners' Parliamentary
        Group), May 1969; pp63-64.
95 R H S Crossman, Diaries of a Cabinet Minister,
        Vol 2 (London, Cape 1976), pp431-432 (entry
        for 18 July 1967).
96 Crossman, Diaries ....; p571 and 573-574
        (14 and 15 November 1967).
97 Crossman, Diaries...; pp583-584 (21 November
        1967).   Crossman's account has been
        corroborated by oral evidence and the Miners
        Miners' Parliamentary Group report.
98 Trade Unionism (London, TUC 1966); para 152.
99 Lord Williams of Barnburgh, Digging For Britain
        (London, Hutchinson 1965); pp60-61.
100 'Remove the Five Right Wing NUM Sponsored MPs':
        All Trades Union Alliance handbill for a
        meeting at the Devonshire Hotel, Barnsley
        24 July 1975.
101 J Ellis & R W Johnson, Members From the Unions
        Series 316, 1974); p1.

Chapter Six

THE INTERNAL POLITICS OF THE YORKSHIRE AREA(NUM), 1947-1968

This chapter explores the shift of the Yorkshire
miners from the right to the left.   It is not
concerned with the detail of industrial relations,
but with how they influenced power and politics
within the Area.   Changes in the miners' industrial
attitudes were to have a profound effect on the
miners' political influence.[1]

The Nature of Internal Politics
Union politics have been concerned with two areas:
disagreement over the methods (industrial,
political or collective bargaining) to be used to
achieve the miners' demands.   Disagreement led to
unofficial action caused by union leaders' concern
to settle disputes via the joint conciliation
procedures, whose slowness generated considerable
frustration amongst the mineworkers.   The second
source of conflict has been concerned with defining
the membership's best interests, particularly with
conflict over the immediate demands of the members
for wage increases and the long-term strategy of
the Union leadership which often involved pay
restraint.
     Nationalisation introduced a new dimension into
industrial politics.   The NUM accepted a commitment
to ensure the success of 'their' industry.
However,

> Nationalisation ended the unambiguous and
> simple position of branch officials and
> substituted for it one which is far more
> complex.   While the possibilities of
> achieving the branches' aims are increased
> .... so are the occasions for ...
> misunderstandings between the men and their
> leaders.   Simple opposition is easily

>understood ... Cooperation is more
>complicated and it is not easy to
>reconcile the miner to the idea of
>cooperation with the management.[2]

Such conflict made the Yorkshire coalfield the most
strike prone in the industry, with many being the
product of differences between leaders and led.

The responsibility of the union leader is to
obtain the best possible reward for the labour
power of his members.   This depends on his
perception of many factors, the economic environment (not merely the whole, but the place of coal
in the economy) is vital.   However, market
economics are not the sole factor, for example,
when coal was in a strong market position union
leaders have restrained their members demands for
political reasons, or out of regard for 'the
national interest'.   When the industry contracted
the weakening of coal's market power was interpreted by union leaders as preventing industrial
action.   This was a refinement of a policy pursued
since the War and the creation of the NUM in 1944
after which the union relied upon collective
bargaining with the NCB and upon the election of a
Labour Government to defend its interests.[3]   This
decline continued in the 1960s under a Labour
Government whom the NUM believed was committed to a
fuel policy favourable to coal.   The result was an
enormous fund of bitterness in the coalfields
directed three ways: at the NCB, at the Government,
and at the union leadership.

Conflict arose over how the Union was to defend
the miners in these changing circumstances.   Union
leaders, socialised by their experiences in the
1930s accepted the inevitability of decline and of
ensuring that those who remained in mining enjoyed
job security and that the run-down was implemented
as humanely as possible.   Opponents rejected the
assumptions upon which the run-down was based, and
moreover, advocated industrial action to change
Government policy.   In Yorkshire the opposition,
initially, came from the relatively well paid
Doncaster and South Yorkshire pits who had suffered
less than most from closures.   The leadership
opposed industrial action as it violated the entire
ethos which had permeated the mining union after
1926, because it offended against the spirit of
nationalisation, and because it was believed it
would close pits.   A successful union leadership
seeks to protect its members' interests by "the

realistic calculation of tactical possibilities
and bargaining strengths ... within a fixed framework of industrial relations."[4]   Leadership skill
lies in identifying when these possibilities have
moved in the union's favour.   The two sides in
the NUM arrived at different results from their
calculations.   The quiescence of the 1960s and
what came to be regarded as the abject failure of
the leadership's policies led to increasingly
vocal demands from some sections of the NUM for
more militant policies.   The immense task
confronting the opposition was to win over the
membership.   This they did between 1969 and 1972.
      The political environment is a crucial influence
on internal politics.   Much internal conflict has
been over wages and frequent incomes policies have
therefore contributed to this unrest.   This was
particularly so under Labour administrations.
Accepting restrictions on wages in the political
interests of a Labour Government generated great
frustration amongst the members.   Flanders argued
that too great a level of political support for a
party or government by a union means, inevitably,
devaluation of the members interests in favour of
those of the political party.   This increases the
likelihood of internal conflict with the aim of
forcing the leadership to act in a 'trade union'
manner.[5]   Between 1948-1949 and 1964-1969 the
leadership's belief that the interests of the mineworkers could be best met by support of a Labour
Government committed to incomes policy conflicted
with the membership's belief that their interests
could best be met by pay claims above a government
approved level.   Ultimately, the leaders were
forced to accept this.   With the rise of a left-
wing leadership in Yorkshire, conflict arose after
1974 between the Area and the NEC over the value
of the social contract.   Again, confronted by
internal opposition, national leaders moderated
their support of the social contract.
      The system of collective bargaining is a third
factor in internal politics.   Unofficial strikes
were often the result of the piecework and allowance
system added to basic national minimum rates.   The
NUM was committed to replacing this byzantine system
by a centralised and nationalised daywage system.
This process began in 1955 and culminated in the
National Power Loading Agreement (NPLA) implemented
between 1966 and 1971.   NPLA contributed to the
upsurge in unrest in the Yorkshire coalfield by
imposing a wage freeze, and in some cases, a wage

cut while the poorer paid Areas caught up.   NPLA
also had the effect of nationalising pay grievances
and creating a new national solidarity by placing
all mineworkers on a comparable wages scale.   NPLA
was, then, vital for the success of 1972 and 1974.
This also helps to explain why militant areas were
so opposed to productivity or incentive deals, as
these weakened solidarity.

The Official Structure of Authority
The basis of the Yorkshire Area, of any union, is
the membership, but the supreme government is the
Area Council (Rule 4).   Council is composed of
the Area President/Compensation Agent (the posts
have been combined since 1973), Vice-President,
General Secretary, the four Area Agents, and one
delegate from each NUM branch.   Council decides
Area policy, subject, of course, to national policy.
At each Council a report on the National Executive's
work is made to the delegates (Rule 5).   When
Council votes the branches are bound by that
decision and are expected to implement loyally that
policy.   Area policy must accord with national
policy as determined by Annual Conference and the
NEC.   The supremacy of the National Union is a
constant factor in the Area's authority structure.
        No branch can send more than one delegate
to Council (Rule 6).   Branches with less than 50
financial members have one vote; for every 50
extra members one extra vote is allowed.   There is
one branch per pit or workshop, and there is also
a branch for winders.   Voting in Council is by a
show of hands or by a card vote after a decision of
the Chairman (the President).   All delegates must
vote and no-one can abstain or remain neutral.
Should a branch wish to bring any matter before
Council there must be a branch meeting where a
formal resolution is moved, seconded, debated and
voted upon.   If approved it is sent to the
General Secretary who, in conjunction with the Area
Officials, is responsible for preparing the agenda.
Officials and the Executive Committee discuss
the agenda and decide upon the 'official' line
before the final agendas are sent to the branches
two full days before the Council meeting.
        The Area Officials are full-time and are
elected by a pit-head ballot by the Transferable
Vote method (Rule 12).   They are not subject to
re-election.   The Area President is essentially a
chairman and his main task is ensuring the smooth
running of Council and the Area Executive Committee

Table 1

THE FORMAL STRUCTURE OF AUTHORITY IN THE YORKSHIRE AREA

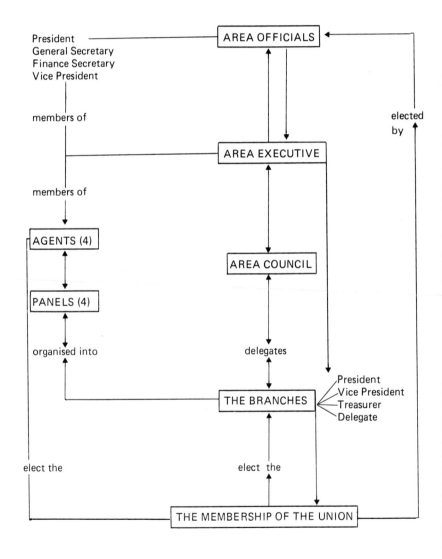

President
General Secretary
Finance Secretary
Vice President

AREA OFFICIALS

members of

elected by

AREA EXECUTIVE

members of

AGENTS (4)

AREA COUNCIL

PANELS (4)

organised into

delegates

President
Vice President
Treasurer
Delegate

THE BRANCHES

elect the

elect the

THE MEMBERSHIP OF THE UNION

meetings, and by implication, the smooth running of
the Area. The President's task is far more complex
than this, however, and his role depends very much
on his personality. Sam Bullough, for example,
Area President from 1960 to 1973, was a colourless
figure who kept very much in the background as a
'ceremonial' figure. He was relegated to the
background by two assertive General Secretaries,
Fred Collindridge (1954-1964) and Sid Schofield
(1964-1973). Arthur Scargill (1974-1981) was
clearly much more than a chairman, being regarded
as the authentic voice of the Yorkshire miners. In
this, he continued the style of his predecessors
Herbert Smith (1906-1938), Joe Hall (1938-1952) and
J R A Machen (1952-1960). The President is
responsible for calling together the Executive "for
the purpose of formulating a common policy for the
general guidance of the Area" (Rule 15a).

It has been suggested that he who prepares the
agenda controls the decision making process in any
organisation; is the General Secretary the 'power
behind the throne'? Under Rule 17 his function is
simply that of recording the decisions of the
Executive and Council, of preparing agenda
and so on. However, some have exerted considered
influence over the union; for example, Benjamin
Pickard (1881-1904) was a crucial figure not only in
the YMA but also in the MFGB; W E Jones (1939-1954)
introduced many administrative innovations, and
Sidney Schofield (1964-1973) presided over the
transition of the Area from moderation to militancy.
Clearly, the General Secretary's functions extend
beyond those in the Rule Book.

In 1950 the Area created four Area Agents
(North Yorkshire, South Yorkshire, Doncaster and
Barnsley) whose function was to oversee the
operation of the conciliation machinery (Rule 19)
and act as local 'troubleshooters' for the
Executive. They are an extension of the Area
Officials in that they act as assistants to the
General Secretary carrying out any task set by him.

The Area Executive Committee is composed of
the permanent officials and not less than 17 lay
members; four from each NCB Area plus one craftsmen (Rule 23a). The Executive is not responsible
for the day-to-day running of the Area (the task of
the officials). It has four main tasks: it
oversees the organisational and financial arrangements of the union; it establishes new branches;
it deals with industrial relations matters relevant
solely to Yorkshire; and it prepares and submits

monthly reports on Area activities to the NEC (Rule 23b). The Executive Committee acts, in effect, as an inner Cabinet (Rule 15a), though its decisions must be approved by Council. Its composition allows the Executive to formulate proposals on the basis of branch opinion. When a policy is adopted and approved by the Executive, it is its task to ensure branch compliance (Rule 23a). It is also the direct representative of the NEC and the NEC can approve or forbid any decision taken by the Area Executive. Finally, the Area Executive is the disciplinary body, with the accused having a right of appeal to Council (Rule 10 a-e).

During the 1960s the Area lost a number of functions as a result of NPLA and the reorganisation of the Yorkshire NCB in 1967. NPLA took wage negotiations to the national level, whilst NCB reorganisation into four areas left the Area NUM without an NCB equivalent. This increased the importance of the Area Panels.

The Area Panels are barely mentioned in the Rule Book, but they have an enormous significance in internal politics. At times they have acted as alternative union structures. Under the Rule Book the branches in each of the four area NCBs must organise a Panel of representatives to be convened after every executive Committee to receive a report (Rule 23f). This implies they are <u>receivers</u> of information; communication is not, however, one way as the Panels naturally pass comment on these reports and it is only a short step for a 'panel viewpoint' to emerge. These views are then communicated to the Executive and/or Council formally or informally. Their importance, then, is belied by Rule 23f. Far from being passive recipients they have often been active as foci of opposition and dissent amongst the branches. The official channels of communication between the branch is the delegate in Council, or direct communication by the branch secretary. There is no other formal opportunity for branch representatives to meet and discuss common problems, indeed the Rule Book frowns on such factionalism. The branch is supposed to decide in isolation how it will vote in Council, or on its attitudes to the Executive's actions. Thus the Area Panels provide an excellent opportunity for the branches to meet and formulate a common response. The best example is the Doncaster Panel, which between 1949 and 1973 was an articulate counter-force leading unofficial strikes in 1955, 1961, 1969 and 1970 against Area

and National policies.   In 1972 and 1974 the Panels
were the organisational basis of the strike effort
and they acted as springboards for a number of
union officials.   The Doncaster Panel was the
power base of Jock Kane (Financial Secretary 1966-
1972) and the present General Secretary, Owen
Briscoe.
         The Area Union has always been aware of the
dangers of the panel system.   Under Rule 23k a
meeting cannot be called other than by the Area
Officials, or the Executive Committee (with the
exception of the four Area Agents).   The Area
Agents are not panel leaders; the panels elect
their own officers.
         The Yorkshire Area is not sovereign.   Rule 90
states that should there be a clash between an
Area and a National Rule, the national predominates.
National supremacy is enshrined clearly in both
Rule Books and is a product of the nationalisation
of the MFGB in 1944.   Previously, the district
unions were virtually independent but in 1944 they
were brought under a common legal framework.
National Rules 36 and 37, for example, set out
clearly the functions of the Areas, and Rule 34
makes Area organisation subject to national
approval.
         The government of the entire union is the
Annual Conference (National Rules 8 and 23).
Conference votes on resolutions submitted by the
Areas (each is allowed three and two amendments)
and if approved these are union policy.   Between
Conferences the NUM is managed by the NEC, and
Rule 8 states categorically that the NEC shall
not act in defiance of Conference, though this has
not prevented NECs from doing exactly this.   NEC
membership is not based on the numbers in each
Area but on fixed proportions (Rule 12):   less than
22,500 - 1 member; 22,500-55,000 - 2 members; and,
55,000+ - 3 members.   The smaller and generally
less militant areas form a semi-permanent majority
on the NEC.   NEC members are elected by the Areas,
and so they are rather like American Congressmen --
aware of the reaction of 'the folks back home'.
Thus, no matter what the national rules lay down,
it is Area opinion, the Areas being the real power-
houses of the NUM, which really counts.
         The reorganisation of the MFGB in 1944 marks
the modification of the MFGB into a national
collective bargaining body.   In 1944 it was clear
that the industry would be subject to a thorough
reorganisation whichever party won the General

Table 2:   NUM MEMBERSHIP BY AREA, 1947 and 1974

	1947	1974
Cokemen	3,214	4,959
Cumberland	4,710	1,253
Derbyshire	28,239	11,261
Durham	71,073	18,420
Kent	4,953	2,471
Lancashire	31,359	9,309
Leicester	4,285	2,656
Midlands	40,190	14,063
Northumberland	27,707	8,842
North Wales	6,691	1,766
Nottingham	31,078	30,300
Scotland	48,424	21,577
Somerset	2,194	---
South Derbyshire	4,112	2,617
South Wales	96,299	28,460
Yorkshire	85,816	62,124
Group No 1	16,727	11,033
Group No 2	15,895	4,767
Group No 3	10,399	18,306 (COSA)
Power Group	12,602	4,900
Power Group No 2		2,087
	547,567	261,171

Election, and so a more centralised collective
bargaining body was essential. The war saw the
extension of national collective bargaining for which
the MFGB had long fought, and which they were determined to preserve. The reorganisation of 1944 meant
that the Areas had to surrender some autonomy to
the national level, and the branches lost their
autonomy in many spheres to the Area leaderships.
This loss was compensated by the branches challenging management prerogatives of job control and
asserting the branches' rights in production. The
1944 reorganisation, however, seriously impaired the
ability of the NUM to contain unrest amongst the
membership.
       Strike action was covered by Rule 41. Any
industrial dispute arising at branch level which is
"likely to lead to a stoppage" must be referred
immediately to the Area Officials and, if necessary,
to the NEC. Under no circumstances was strike
action to take place "without the previous sanction
of the NEC." In every case an internal area
dispute had to be sanctioned at national level.
National strike action is covered by Rule 43.
Strike action has to be proposed by the NEC and
approved by a pit head ballot sanctioned by a
Conference or Special Conference decision. A
national strike could only be called if there was
a two-third majority in favour as "it is considered
essential that on an issue of this kind there should
be a substantial majority in support of such
action."[6] The 1944 Reorganisation Conference,
then, saw in Will Lawther's words the "nationalisation of your organisation."[7] Strike action, as
the most serious decision ever taken by a union
should only be entered into after the most careful
consideration.[8] All amendments to this procedure
were lost.[9]

The Ethos of Nationalisation
The creation of a national system of collective
bargaining, together with nationalisation was seen
by the leaders of the NUM as a new beginning, a
chance to defend miners wages and conditions
without the bitter industrial relations of the
past:

       ... the industry can only be so re-organised
       as to offer satisfactory conditions and
       employment providing there is the fullest
       cooperation on the part of all employed
       therein. We, therefore, urge all members

172

> of the Union to recognise the
> necessity of breaking with the past
> and accepting their responsibilities
> with a view to ensuring the reorganisation
> of the industry and the success of the new
> system of ownership.[10]

Any threat to this long sought goal was to be
bitterly resisted.   There was no place for the old
ways and attitudes in the new coal industry.
The distinction between the official and
unofficial sides within the Yorkshire Area in the
1950s were described thus:

> the rank and file interpret militancy
> in terms of dealing with day to day
> grievances to their own benefit ...
> The Union   interpret it in terms of
> the operation of a public utility directed
> towards strengthening the economy of the
> country for the benefit of the community
> as well as of the miners.[11]

The NUM was created to achieve, <u>inter alia</u>, national
collective bargaining.   Moderation was reinforced
by powerful sentiments of loyalty and solidarity,
not only towards union leaders but also towards
'their' industry by the miners whose occupational
consciousness has two components.   First, of
seeing the employers' interest as contrary to his
own;   and second, a 'cooperative' aspect born of
actual experience at the point of production and
a belief that the worker and his union have a
legitimate role in running the industry.   The
membership have tended to emphasise the former, the
leadership the latter.   Nationalisation sought to
reform the opposition-confrontation model of
industrial relations into consensus-cooperation
relations, indeed, industrial relations was
identified in 1945 as the industry's most pressing
problem.[12]   The loss of Area initiative and the
effects of this loss only clearly emerged when the
industry settled down into the post-war patterns
of industrial relations and the new nationalisation
ethos.[13]

Left-Right Union Politics in Yorkshire
Between 1947 and 1973 the Yorkshire Area's political
process was dominated by the political and
industrial right wing.[14]   The right was dominant
throughout the NUM and this hegemony was maintained

by strict control of the political process via the
1944 Rule Book. This constituted a major resource
in the hands of the leadership, limiting the area
of initiative open to opposition groups whilst
maintaining democratic procedures. This was
compounded the sovereignty of the National Union
and the composition of the NEC with its right-wing
majority.

In Yorkshire the right's dominance was but-
tressed by a number of procedural devices; for
example, a three months rule was used by the Area
Executive to keep unpalatable matters off the
agenda. The Executive Committee also maintained a
strict supervision over all matters submitted for
inclusion on the Council agenda. Anything proposed
by a branch of which the Executive disapproved was
the subject of a letter sent to the branch and which
appeared to constitute an official reply. If the
branch insisted on raising the matter further, the
Executive could then claim the matter had already
been dealt with. Should the branch insist on a
vote in Council, the Executive could rely on a
loyal Council to defeat the resolution. A
favourite procedural device of the right was for a
friendly branch to move 'next business', again
Council secured the defeat of the offending
resolution.

These formal (and informal) processes have been
described as 'machine politics'. The right
dominated union politics until the late-1960s when
this hegemony collapsed under pressure from the
membership aroused by its cumulative failure.
Nevertheless, a major resource of union leaders
was loyalty to established leaders, a crucial
element in all trade union politics. If the NEC
or Area Executive recommended a course of action
many were willing to abide by the recommendations of
their leaders. They were not afraid of smearing
opponents to discredit their policies, branding them
as anti-union, anti-Labour and inspired by
'communism'.

Between 1947 and 1970 voting in Council on
left-wing issues followed two patterns: first, a
resolution sponsored by members of the Communist
Party and supported by the Labour left would garner
in the region of 17 votes; second, a resolution
sponsored by the Labour left (supported covertly
by the CP) would gather 30 - 38 votes. Thus, a
well organised broad-left faction was the only
tactic likely to overcome the hostility of the
leadership. It is this tactic of the broad-left

and the 30-38 vote base that enabled the left to
capture the leadership of the Area.

The Panel system was of tremendous importance
in this transformation.   Before the reorganisation
of the Yorkshire NCB in 1967 there were eight
panels, and of these only Doncaster was politically
and industrially left, though there were left
elements in the others.   The Doncaster Panel's
militancy was not securely based, it was not
monolithically left-wing but the left was better
organised and more highly motivated than else-
where.[15]   Combined, however, the other Panels
orchestrated by the Executive, were able to limit
its influence.

An important figure on the left was Frank
Watters, the Communist Party Industrial Organiser
in the coalfield in the 1950s and 1960s.   Watters
helped to organise the election of Sammy Taylor and
Jock Kane to Area office despite their Party
membership.   Whilst the CP provided vital cadres
and organising experience, its influence would
have been considerably less without the Labour
left in the Panels.   By the mid-1960s the CP
gave up on the miners and in 1967 Watters was
transferred to the Midlands car plants.

The seeds planted since 1947 bloomed in 1973.
In the early-1970s the left had no clear candidate
to replace either Sam Bullough, who was ill, or
Sammy Taylor, who was about to retire.   The only
available left candidate was Arthur Scargill, an
ex-member of the Young Communist League [16] but
never a Party member, who was elected both President
and Compensation Agent.   Left organisation had
gradually moved westwards from Doncaster by the
emergence of the broad-left in 1969 around the
Barnsley Miners' Forum, a study group of members
drawn from all four Panels.   The victory of the
left in 1972 and 1973 saw the fusion of a new
loyalty to a left-wing Area leadership dominated
by the charismatic figure of Arthur Scargill.   This
broad-left has been criticised for not being as
politically 'pure' as the old left, but its
effectiveness cannot be doubted.

Before 1972-1973 the right had no need for
clandestine organisation as they controlled the
machine.   After the left's victory an attempt was
made to organise the outsted right.   In 1972-1973
the Labour Councillors' Association, later re-named
the Labour Miners Association, was formed.   Its
object was to organise Labour Party members in the
NUM against a 'communist' takeover.   It sought to

turn the left's tactics and weapons against the left but it was a failure.   No NUM branches were affiliated, for to do so would have brought down the wrath of the Area.   There were about 80 active individual members drawn (mainly) from North Yorkshire pits, though it had some support in the South Yorkshire panel.   The bulk of the Association's meetings were in the Castleford area and its influence was confined to the North Yorkshire Panel which remains dominated by a right wing group. The Association lacked two essential attributes for underground opposition: it lacked a secure and committed mass base;   and second, it lacked the motivation and organising talents of the CP and Labour left.   It faded rapidly into obscurity.

The Panel System

A major justification for nationalisation was that industrial relations would improve and past bitterness would be exorcised.   However, soon after nationalisation the traditional pattern of poor industrial relations re-asserted itself.[17]   The transfer of legal ownership did not transform power relations in mining and many aspects of nationalisation failed to meet the expectations of many mineworkers, but the hostility of the official union leaders prompted some mineworkers to look for an alternative.   They found it in the Panel system.
     The Panels' functions were expanded in 1949 there was one for every 10-12 pits),[18]   but even so their official role within the Area was lowly, a situation changed by the Panels themselves. Initially, only No2 Panel (Doncaster) took on an autonomous existence, largely as a consequence of the special nature of mining development in this area.[19]   As early as 1951 this Panel angered Area Officials by holding unofficial meetings to formulate a common policy on price list revision. The Area Executive forbad such a role absolutely and in response the Panel wrote to the Daily Herald complaining at the authoritarianism not only of the NCB but also of the NUM.[20]   The Area Executive censured the Panel and warned that a repitition would result in suspension from the Union.[21] Despite this clear hostility the Doncaster Panel continued to play an important role in union politics.
     The Panel's legitimacy in the eyes of the Doncaster miners can be seen in their massive response to the strike call of May 1955.[22]   The strike was concerned with inadequate price lists and

and the slowness of revision.   The strike began at
Markham Main (Armthorpe) whose branch appealed for
Panel support.   The Panel decided that if there
was no satisfactory agreement by the evening of
3 May, the Doncaster pits would strike.   The Panel
was ordered to withdraw the strike call and told
that negotiations would only begin when work
resumed.[23]

The threat of a major unofficial strike led to
the calling of a special Council Meeting, which
was attended by three members of the NEC.   By 80
votes to 19 Council called on the strikers to
return so that negotiations could start and to
abide by NUM-NCB conciliation procedures.[24]   The
Panel not only disobeyed these instructions but
tried to spread the strike by the sophisticated
use of flying pickets.

On 4 May 44,660 miners were on strike (not all
from Doncaster) and the Panel was rumoured to be
seeking a national unofficial stoppage to force a
change in NUM wage policy.   The Panel Chairman,
G H Huckerby, stated, "(T)he Panel is desirous of
getting the Division, and if possible, the Country
to support them on this issue."[25]   The Doncaster
pits refused all appeals to go back as "the matter
was out of their hands, and was now something in the
hands of the No 2 Panel".[26]   The Panel, seeking a
role in collective bargaining, posed a threat to
the organisational coherence of the Yorkshire Area
which was compelled to meet with the NCB to settle
the strike.   The Panel officially ended the strike
on 13 April 1955.

The Panel was again involved in a major
unofficial dispute in 1961.   Though the dispute
originated in North Yorkshire, the Brodsworth
branch called on Doncaster Panel to call a strike
over piece rates.   The Panel actively fomented
opposition to official Area policy and Council,
again by 80 votes to 19, empowered the Executive
"to take such steps as they think necessary to
counteract picketing and unofficial activity."[27]
The Panel's aim was explicit: "The men are aiming
to force the hand of both the Union and Coal
Board ...".   Panel leaders believed that the Area
had been cooperative to the point of submission
with the NEC.[28]   Bill Kellher, Brodsworth branch
secretary, and Jock Kane, the panel chairman, were,
nonetheless, sensitive to charges of irresponsi-
bility and disloyalty:

> There has never been any intention to
> negotiate through any other channel than
> the legitimate one. We are not seeking
> to start a war inside the Union. We
> say we have a fair claim, but up to now
> there has been a reluctance on the part
> of the Board to concede the fairness of
> the claim.[29]

On 26 February the Panel struck but the strike
largely failed to spread despite the efforts of the
flying pickets. Kellher was adamant that the
strike's purpose was to change union policy: "We
are not trying to overthrow our County officials
(but) we say they have been too modest in their
demands"; Kane declared, "It is not our job to
negotiate."[30]   Doncaster stayed out until the
middle of May, when the Panel ordered a return.
    In his Presidential Address Sam Bullough warned
of "certain alarming aspects" which had appeared
in the Area:

> ....(the) Council Meeting, after considering
> and debating and deciding policy, has always
> been, and must be the supreme power of our
> Yorkshire Area. If that power is weakened
> or removed by certain activities, it is
> the beginning of the collapse of the Trade
> Union Movement. We must see that this
> never happens. We must see to it that
> the breaking and violation of the Rules
> is stopped. We must remember all the
> sufferings and the work that our prede-
> cessors did in fighting for the establish-
> ment of trade union acknowledgement.[31]

During the 1961 strike Council postponed the
Area Vice-Presidential election as both Kellher and
Kane were candidates (naturally, their role was
seen by some as an election 'stunt'). The result
was important, as although J Leigh with 29,797
votes defeated Kane with 23,030 (Kellher withdrew
to avoid splitting the left vote) the result
illustrated the balance of political forces in the
Yorkshire Area.[32]   The Yorkshire Area was right-
wing dominated, but with a substantial left-wing
minority. This can also be seen in the 1960
ballot for national President. This was won by
Yorkshire's Alwin Machen, but Machen died before
taking office. The re-run was won by Sidney Ford,
the leader of the NUM's clerical section. Partly

because of this Yorkshire nominated Alex Moffat,
the brother of Abe Moffat who was also an official
of the Scottish NUM and an active communist. This
was despite virulently anti-communist attitudes in
some Yorkshire branches.[33] In the ballot for Area
President in 1960 the two leading candidates were
Bullough and Kane. Bullough won by 1,037 votes to
Kane's 566.[34] Finally, in the voting for the
national Vice-President, Council voted by 82 to 16
to support Fred Collindridge (their own Area
Secretary), but 16 delegates supported Alex
Moffat.[35] These instances demonstrate considerable
support for left-wing candidates, support which made
it impossible for the Area leadership to discipline
the leaders of internal opposition as severely as
some in the Area wished.[36] The close balance of
political forces preserved an organised opposition
to the policies and perspectives of the leadership
which, in turn, provided a solid foundation for
the outburst of unrest considered in the next
chapter.

Sources of Unrest and Change

During the early and middle 1960s the Yorkshire
Area was quiescent largely as a consequence of
the rundown of the industry. The miners were a
beaten army in retreat, lacking the confidence
necessary to try and take charge of their destinies.
This was to change in 1969-1970 and this change was
the product of a number of factors.

In 1958 the NUM adopted a national fuel policy
plan to secure the industry's future. This was
urged upon government, but to no avail. Consequently, the NUM relied on the election of a Labour
Government to implement that policy: "we realise
that only a Labour Government will give us an
adequate and satisfactory national fuel policy."[37]
In the early-1960s the NUM argued consistently that
a Conservative government would not help the
miners; for coal to prosper there had to be an
expanding economy which would only come from
Labour's national planning.[38] Until Labour was
elected, then, what was the NUM to do? Sidney
Ford, the NUM President, asked, "Are we to stand
aloof from the problems facing the industry, leaving
the Board to shoulder the burden of maintaining
this industry at a level which enable it to offer
security and fair conditions of employment ...?"[39]
Cooperation with the NCB meant, however, cooperating
in the rundown of the industry but militant resistance was of no use,

> We cannot solve the problems facing us
> in 1962 by adopting the slogans of the
> '20s; neither are we likely to advance
> the interests of the members by
> renouncing the policies which we helped
> to pattern and to which we are indelibly
> committed.[40]

The national leadership was motivated by a desire to maintain employment which involved a trade-off over wages. Ford and other NUM leaders were willing to pay this price because of their experience during, and fear of, the mass unemployment of the 1930s. They sought to use the mechanisms of nationalisation to at least soften the blows of industrial decline, whereas many miners were coming to feel that 'security' of employment achieved with low wages was not worth having and security often meant frequent moves as pits closed.

After the election of the Labour Government in 1964 (which was to both continue the rundown and restrain wages) the NUM continued to cooperate because of loyalty and because of its belief that a policy of cooperation and acquiescence was their only viable option whilst trying to reconcile this political passivity with the growing unrest of the members. The conviction that the miners could not engage in industrial action, coupled with a commitment to a government which closed pits against all expectations, contributed to the enormous fund of unrest in the coalfields which exploded in 1969 and 1970.

Sections of the Yorkshire Area's membership became increasingly restive over closures and the labour transfers they entailed, contributing to an atmosphere of uncertainty in the coalfield. Anger and uncertainty there was, directed at the policies of Union and Government, but there also existed powerful support for the Union. Yet between 1969 and 1971 the official attitudes of the Area leadership were first challenged and then replaced by more militant attitudes and policies.

There were in Yorkshire 1,350 mineworkers known as marketmen. These were fully trained face workers who did not have a regular job on a coalface and formed a reserve available for deployment throughout the pit. It was accepted that any marketman transferred to a job with a lower NPLA rate than the one for which he was trained would be paid the rate for his own job. This practice was increasingly called into question by managements

anxious to cut costs.   This led to an acrimonious
dispute at Wheldale colliery in North Yorkshire,
which, while not important in itself, illustrates
the strains and tensions within the Yorkshire Area
at this time.
     On 8 April 1968 the Area Executive received
a letter from the Wheldale branch written by the
son of the branch secretary (who was also a branch
committee member).   This letter complained at
the treatment of the marketmen and at the policies
of the NUM.   The Executive viewed this letter with
alarm, first, because only the branch secretary
could communicate with the Area;   and second, it
noted the author "is reputed to be a Trotskyist" and
was thus fomenting unrest.   Wheldale had been
annoyed for some time by the marketmen and other
problems but had been persuaded by the Area Agent
to wait on negotiations.   However, at a branch
meeting on 2 March 1968 a motion of 'no confidence'
was passed in both the Area and National leaderships
and sent to the Executive.   On 5 March a second
letter from the branch complained at the inaction of
the Area over pit closures, doing   nothing
until November 1967 "and then all they could do was
organise a futile demonstration in London."
Wheldale argued that the advice of the NEC not to
contest the closure of pits on economic grounds
demonstrated conclusively the Union was more
concerned with supporting the Wilson government
than defending its members.   The letter demanded
the recall of the Party Conference, concluding
angrily that union leaders were not interested in
the men who were not "paying them to further the
aims of a political party."   The Executive ignored
the first letter as unconstitutional and refused
to put the second on the agenda.[41]   Wheldale
objected and it was placed on the agenda to die a
public death: it found no seconder and was passed
over.[42]   Subsequently, an unofficial strike began
at Wheldale.
     The Sharlston branch secretary, Charles Churm,
a well known 'hammer of the left', wrote to the
Executive complaining that he had pickets from
Wheldale ejected from the pit yard who were trying
to persuade Sharlston miners to support them.
Council and the Executive censured the pickets.[43]
Wheldale appealed and it was decided that Schofield
try to settle the dispute quietly and both sides
were ordered to attend the next Council meeting.[44]
The branch admitted picketing Sharlston and other
pits in the vicinity and the censure was affirmed.[45]

Wheldale again appealed and threats were made of
legal action.
    The strike over the NPLA rate for marketmen
was due to Wheldale seeking a higher local rate.
It was claimed that an Area Executive member from
Doncaster actively supported Wheldale and stated
publicly at a meeting in Castleford Park Field
that Wheldale had the support of the Doncaster
Panel and their allies, a total of 22 pits.[46]   It
was also revealed that Area Officials had called an
unofficial panel meeting at the Carlton Hotel in
Castleford to stop the strike, and Wheldale branch
members accused the Union of victimisation.[47]   The
issue was clearly in danger of getting out of
control: there existed a joint strike committee of
Wheldale and three other pits, there was a danger
of the Doncaster Panel intervening, and there were
expressions of personal support for Wheldale from
some branches, for example, Houghton Main.   This
dispute ended when the Wheldale branch was promised
that the marketmen problem would be settled in the
next NPLA review.
    A further cause of unrest was the slowness of
wage negotiations.   In October, after a report by
Tommy Burke council went "on record as being against
the wages offer of the Board, and demands that any
wages settlement shall include the principle of a
guaranteed minimum of £16 per week underground and
£15 for surfacemen."   Next business was moved and
defeated by 53 votes to 41.   Sam Bullough ruled
that he could not accept this resolution under
union rules, but he was voted down and the
resolution deemed accepted by 75 to 17.   'This
unprecedented militancy carried over to the
marketmen problem with Council insisting that the
problem be resolved quickly.[48]
    The NEC was aware of this unrest and attempted
to assuage it.   For example, it made clear that
the problem of the marketmen was subject to
negotiations in the NPLA review.   However, in
implementing NPLA the NUM-NCB agreed to a six month
standstill on wage rate changes to provide a period
of cost stability whilst implementing changes
in the daywage structure.   The standstill began in
February 1969.[49]
    Feelings remained high in the coalfield and
some members of the Area Executive felt that a
display of anger was called for, suggesting that
the Yorkshire Area seek permission under Rule 41 to
ballot the members on a strike to force a settlement
of the Area's problems.   This was rejected in

favour of further negotiations with the four Area
NCBs.[50]   An Area agreement on NPLA anomalies was,
however, impossible because of the February
agreement and the NEC forbad any industrial action
action.[51]   Ford insisted that the Yorkshire miners'
problems could be settled by the joint conciliation
machinery.[52]   Thus, the nationalisation of
collective bargaining prevented the Area from taking
any action to ease the immediate tensions and
dissatisfaction revealed itself in branch resolutions
demanding the periodic re-election of permanent
officials at Area and National level.[53]
    Surface workers' hours were a further problem.
In March 1969 the Nostell branch submitted a
resolution to Council demanding a 7¼ hour day
inclusive of mealtimes.[54]   Ten branches submitted
resolutions on wages and five were opposed to any
attempt at trade union reform: these resolutions
(submitted for Council's consideration for inclusion
in the Annual Conference agenda) show the depth of
unrest amongst the branches.[55]   Council determined,
also, that despite the NEC's decisions of
26 February over the marketmen, that permission be
sought to take industrial action.   In fact, the
Cortonwood branch was already on unofficial strike.
This was approved by 45 to 26.[56]   The NEC's
position was extensively discussed and criticised by
Council, and members of the Executive urged the
delegates to postpone any decision until after the
July Conference.   Council accepted this, but forty
delegates walked out in protest threatening that
their branches would join Cortonwood.   This
caused the adjournment of Council until 1.30pm so
that Officials could contact the Area NCBs who agreed
to meet and report to Council on 22 March.[57]
    On 20 March the Cortonwood and other branches
began to picket pits in an attempt to spread the
dispute.   Cortonwood's actions and the demand for
a strike caused uproar in the Council chamber.
Schofield attacked those who were trying to force
changes in policy by striking.   He admitted that
closures (nine in one year) had "inevitably created
a feeling of resentment against the leadership,
(who) notwithstanding their opposition to the rate
of closures, were not prepared to encourage their
members to take industrial action."[58]   Schofield
argued that militancy would only close pits and
that the bulk of the Yorkshire miners were opposed
to strike action concluding sardonically, "I must
be careful not to antagonise the warriors who
thought it was time we had a 'show-down' with the

Board ...."[59]   After the disruption of Council,
the Area Officials met with the four NCB Area
Directors who refused to accept a coalfield
settlement of outstanding problems.   This, and
the slowness of wage negotiations, fuelled the
demands for action.   The Officials went to great
lengths to emphasise to Council that the Area NCBs
would not agree to a coalfield settlement of the
marketmen dispute and were immediately inundated by
demands for a strike.   A resolution was put and
seconded, but ruled out of order:

> There can be no official strike.   The
> Chair cannot accept such a motion.   If
> branches agree to strike is it likely
> any more will be granted or forced ...
> are you fully satisfied the men will follow
> the call to strike ...?[60]

Bullough was bound by the Rule Book and
delegates agreed to abide by his ruling, but their
anger was plain.   The Area and NUM leaders were
being seen by an increasing number of branches
as incapable of taking effective action to
safeguard their members.   The potential for an
unofficial strike was, therefore, very high
and increasing.
In May 1969 a claim for a 40 hour week for
surfacemen, plus a night shift allowance for
low paid grades, was submitted to the NCB.   The
NCB agreed to the hours claim but only if the
allowance was abandoned.[61]   This offer split the
NEC and further talks were requested.   The NCB
argued that the cost of both could only be met
by closing pits and government pay policy prevented
a full settlement in any case.   Subject to
government approval, the hours claim would be met
if the allowance was dropped.[62]   The NEC were in
a dilemma: to press the full claim would shut
pits, but to go solely for the hours meant that
the low paid would suffer.
At the 1969 Annual Conference a Composite
Resolution demanded a 7¾ hour day inclusive of
mealtimes for surface workers.   The Nostell
resolution was the basis, and it was moved by Mick
Welsh.   He claimed that the NUM had betrayed the
surfaceworker: "There is a feeling of shame and
frustration when you think you belong to a union
which allows this minority group to be exploited
as they are ..."[63]   Surfacemen suffered low pay,
and endured long hours and bad conditions.   Welsh

claimed he represented these men as he was subject
to re-election as a branch official unlike "those
sort of officials who get on for life and can sit
back if they desire ...."[64] Welsh insisted that
many mineworkers, not just surfacemen, were
alienated from the Union because of the inactivity
and ineffectiveness of the NEC. Welsh rejected
the excuse that their hands were tied by
government policy and warned,

> ...on several occasions the Yorkshire
> Area has called for 7¾ day for all surface
> workers inclusive of mealtimes, but they
> have called in vain. Our patience is
> fast running out, and we insist that
> immediate negotiations be entered into
> with the Board on our claim.[65]

Sammy Taylor, a Yorkshire delegate, and member
of the NEC, accepted that Welsh's criticisms were
totally justified. He suggested that certain
members of the NEC might care to work on the pit
top for a fortnight and they would forget about
reasonableness and moderation: "The question of
statesmanship and constitutionalism is all right but
when we are faced with an issue so burning as this,
a just cause, we have to tell the Board that we do
not intend allowing it to continue any longer."[66]
Summing up the debate and replying for the NEC,
Lawrence Daly appreciated the depth of feeling
amongst the delegates, but pointed out that all
negotiations had been conducted on the basis of an
8 hour day inclusive of mealtimes for the surfaceworker. It was, therefore; foolish to abandon
present negotiations which were so close to success
for 15 minutes. The NEC was rebuffed and the
7¾ hour day became NUM policy.
    The transformation of branch attitudes between
1947 and 1968 was remarkable. Disappointment
with nationalisation, frustration generated by
NPLA, the uncertainty caused by pit closures and
the conviction that they had been betrayed by
'their' government created a deep well of bitterness
amongst the Yorkshire miners. By March 1968 the
pressure for industrial action was considerable.
All that was needed was an eruptive factor to begin
the final stage in the political transformation of
the Yorkshire Area.

REFERENCES

1   B J McKormick, Industrial Relations in the
    British Coalmining Industry (London
    Macmillan 1979); and his 'Strikes in the
    Yorkshire Coalfield', in Economic Journal
    (1965); pp171-197. See also
    T Chester, 'Industrial Conflict in the
    British Nationalised Industries, in,
    A Kornhauser, R Dubin and A M Ross (eds),
    Industrial Conflict (New York, John Wiley
    1954); pp454-466; and,
    C E Jencks, 'British Coal: Labour Relations
    Since Nationalisation' Industrial Relations
    vi(1966); pp95-110.
2   N Dennis, F Henriques & C Slaughter, Coal is
    Our Life (London, Tavistock 1967 2nd ed);
    p 97.
    For a general discussion of the problems of
    democracy and government in trade unions
    see;
    J Hemingway, Conflict and Democracy (Oxford,
    Clarendon Press 1978), ch. 1.
3   V A Allen, Militant Trade Unionism (London,
    Merlin Press 1966); p19.
4   E J Hobsbawm, 'Trade Union History', in
    Economic History Review (2s) (1967); p360.
5   A Flanders, Management and Unions (London,
    Faber 1970); pp30-31.
6   MFGB(EC): Executive Report on the Draft Rules,
    February 1944; p15.
7   MFGB; Special Conference on Reorganisation;
    16 August 1944; p2
8   Special Conference; pp214-217
9   R Page Arnot, The Miners, Vol. III (London,
    George Allen & Unwin 1961); pp420-423.
10 NUM(EC); 22 August 1946
11 J A Banks, Marxist Sociology in Action (London,
    Faber 1970); p420.
12 Coal Mining: Report of a Technical Committee
    (Reid Report) Cmd. 6610 (March 1945).
13 G B Baldwin, 'Structural Reform in the British
    Miners Union', in, Quarterly Journal of
    Economics 67 (1953); p582 and p589.
14 For a definition of left and right see the
    Introduction.

15   The general distribution of political support
      from 1947 was as follows:

The Doncaster Panel

Left Pits	Right Pits
Edlington	Rossington
Armthorpe	Askern
Hatfield	Highgate
Bentley	Bullcroft
Hickleton	Frickley
Goldthorpe (?)	Brodsworth

      Geography was politically important as
          Hickleton, Frickley, Goldthorpe and
          Highgate tended to move together and support
          each other. Any weakening of the Left
          tended to come from Hickleton and the
          others would follow. The question mark
          against Goldthorpe indicates that it was a
          'left' pit but with a reputation for
          immoderation and poor discipline, and has
          been described as 'anarchistic'.
16   For details of Arthur Scargill early political
          and industrial experience see his, 'The New
          Unionism' in New Left Review 92 (July 1975).
17   District Consultative Committee; 1 November
          1949.
18   BS Circular 6/49 (8 February 1949); and,
      YA(NUM): 9 December 1949.
19   For a contemporary description of, and reasons
          for the importance of the Doncaster Panel
          see;
          'The Doncaster Miners', in, The Manchester
          Guardian: 12 September 1957.
20   Letter from Matt Thompson (Panel Secretary)
          and G H Huckerby (Panel Chairman) in,
          Daily Herald, 3 September 1951.
21   YA(NUM); 10 September 1951
22   C Slaughter, 'The Strike of Yorkshire Mine-
          workers in May 1955', in Sociological Review
          6(ii) 1955; pp241-259.
23   Sheffield Daily Telegraph; 2 May 1955.
24   YA(NUM); 4 May 1955.
25   Sheffield Daily Telegraph; 4 May 1955
26   BS Circular 33/55 (5 May 1955)
27   YA(NUM); 25 February 1961.
28   Sheffield Daily Telegraph; 24 February 1961.
29   Sheffield Daily Telegraph; 25 February 1961.
30   Sheffield Daily Telegraph; 30 March 1961.
31   YA(NUM): President's Address; 22 March 1961,

p1.
32 YA(NUM); 14 August 1961.
33 The significance of this is reduced by the
       fact that Arthur Horner (South Wales and a
       member of the CPGB) was a moderate trade
       union leader who never led the NUM in
       any official industrial action, or expressed
       approval for unofficial action.
       See also:
       YA(NUM): 9 April 1960.   The voting was:
       Moffat: 1,293, Ford: 857.
34 YA(NUM); 12 July 1960.
35 YA(NUM); 22-24 March 1961.
36 For example: the letter from the Wooley NUM
       Branch which demanded the expulsion of all
       communists from the NUM.
       YA(NUM); 22 March 1961.
37 NUM: Annual Conference Report, 1961; p347.
       See also;
       NEC Report 1961; p13
38 NEC Report 1962; p11
39 NUM: Annual Conference Report; p26
40 Annual Conference; pp126-127.
41 YA(NUM); 8 April 1968.
42 YA(NUM); 6 May 1968.
43 YA(NUM); 15 July 1968.
44 YA(NUM); 10 August 1968.
45 YA(NUM); 16 September 1968.
46 YA(NUM); 23 September 1968.
47 YA(NUM); 6 October 1968.
48 YA(NUM); 28 August, 28 October and
       23 September 1968.
49 JNNC: 28 February 1968. See also;
       NUM(EC); 28 June, and 12 December 1968.
50 YA(NUM); 10 February 1969.
51 NUM(EC); 26 February 1969.
52 The Miner 3(March 1969).
53 BS Circular 13/69 (30 January 1969).
54 YA(NUM); 3 March 1969.
55 BS Circular 21/69 (12 February 1969).
       Resolutions for Annual Conference.
56 YA(NUM); 3 March 1969.
57 YA(NUM); 17-19 March 1969.
58 YA(NUM): Annual Reports (General Secretary)
       for 1968 (March 1969) p87.
59 Annual Report; p88
60 YA(NUM); 21 April 1969. Sam Bullough (Area
       President).
       Schofield warned the Panels about unofficial
       meetings but "Inspite of this it would
       seem that there has been behind the scenes

contact between the Areas.
61   JNNC   30 May 1969.
62   G C Shepeard to L Daly;   28 May 1969.
63   NUM: Annual Conference Report, 1969;   p130.
64   Welsh was reproofed by Ford for his comments
        see;   p130
65   Annual Conference;   p131
        J C Robinson speaking for the NEC rejected
        charges for incompetence "We have failed
        because we have not got the bargaining
        power we hand in the past." (p137).
66   Annual conference;   p138

Chapter Seven

THE UNOFFICIAL STRIKES AND THE RISE OF THE LEFT, 1969-1973

The Strike of 1969

On 9 October the NUM submitted the hours claim approved at the July Conference, warning the NCB of the rising tide of hostility in the coalfields. The union emphasised that this was not a short-term discontent but the product of a longstanding resentment "and the men were saying that if the matter could not be settled at the negotiating table it would be necessary to take industrial action."[1]   After consulting the Government, the NCB conceded the minimum wage of £15 (surface) and £16 (underground), plus 10% on all NPLA rates. The hours claim was rejected.[2]   Jock Kane had warned " The present situation demands rapid action and a better deal for the surface workers.   The men's mood indicates that they are ready to show they mean what they say, but the fact that talks are likely could result the men staying at work."[3]

On 9 October the Doncaster, Barnsley and South Yorkshire Panels issued a strike call to force the NCB to reduce the surfacemen's hours.[4]   In response the NCB placed full page advertisements in the local press urging the miners to reject the call as a strike would do untold harm.[5]   The South Yorkshire Panel resisted the strike call.   A strike at Cadeby Main (in South Yorkshire) had begun on 15 September but the Panel refused support, urging the branch to wait on negotiations.[6]   Despite this Panel's opposition the South Yorkshire pits began to drift out on strike at the end of September.

By the first week in October it was apparent that the Doncaster Panel would determine whether or not there would be a strike.   The JNNC meeting called for 9 October led Owen Briscoe, the Panel Secretary, to announce that the strike call had been postponed but if an acceptable offer was not made the strike would be called.[7]   A Special Council Meeting called for 6 October allowed the Officials

191

to gauge the coalfield's mood and attempts were
made to stem the strike wave.[8]   However,

> The bitterness of a decade has welled
> up ... grievances are now knitting
> together to threaten the industrial
> peace of the coalfield ... the
> campaign in favour of the lower hours
> is now so firmly rooted among the rank
> and file miners that it now appears that
> little short of an NCB climb down will
> satisfy them.[9]

On Saturday 11 October a Special Council
Meeting, held at the insistence of a number of
branches, heard a report on the negotiations over
surface hours.   At its conclusion Council
expressed "deep regret that our claim .... has not
yet been conceded", and, "because of this, the
Yorkshire coalfield will be at a standstill on
Monday morning.   This unofficial action will have
been taken because the patience of our men has
come to an end."[10]   Bullough objected, but was
over-ruled by the delegates, and he then officially
dissociated the Yorkshire Area from the resolution
commenting, "I've never known a more angrier or
bitter meeting in my sixteen years as a miners'
official."[11]   The other Officials, Jack Leigh
(Vice President), Sammy Taylor (Compensation Agent)
and Jock Kane (Financial Secretary) supported the
delegates.   Schofield was absent through illness.
This support gave the Panels' strike call an added
legitimacy, and both the North Yorkshire and
Doncaster Panels welcomed Council's decision.
The strike's expansion was rapid, testifying to
the mood in the coalfield.   Hostility was directed
not only at the NCB and the national Officials, but
at the Labour Government.   One branch secretary
claimed it was the direct result of the government's
disdain for the miners.[12]   In response the NEC
vainly pleaded for the dispute to be pursued
through the conciliation machinery before contemplating strike action.[13]   After the JNNC meetings
of 9 and 17 October, the Yorkshire Area circularised
all branches emphasising that the wages demand had
been conceded, but there was no concession on hours.[14]
The NEC insisted "that there was no possibility at
this stage of obtaining any improvement in the
Board's offer on hours, and therefore, the (NEC)
felt no purpose would be served in going back to
the Board before the present offer was cleared."[15]

The NEC called a Special Conference for 30 October,
recommending the acceptance of the wages offer,
followed by a membership ballot.   Outside this
meeting were 200 picketing Yorkshire miners sent by
the Doncaster Panel.   When the NEC's decision was
announced Sammy Taylor commented, "This is hardly
likely to satisfy the Yorkshire coalfield", and
Bill O'Brien, chairman of the North Yorkshire Panel,
claimed, "The support we have in other coalfields is
not reflected in the representation on the (NEC).
These men here today are frightened.   The lads at
the pits are not."[16]
     By 24 October, however, a settlement seemed
increasingly likely due to the intervention of Vic
Feather at the request of the Yorkshire Strike
Committee (formed of representatives from the
Panels).   An eight man deputation met Feather and
the NEC on 24 October, and a compromise was thrashed
out involving a return to work followed by talks.[18]
However, on 22 October, Council had rejected the
NCB's offer by 80 votes to 3, so the recommendation
to return to work was greeted with some puzzlement.[19]
Several delegates were reluctant to accept the
call, but a widespread return became likely when the
Barnsley Panel voted to end the strike.   By
25 October the 1969 strike was effectively over.[20]
     Opening the Special Conference, Ford made a
plea for calm, otherwise "you take the first step
towards chaos and disorder and the break-up of
the Union as we have known it ...."[21]   The NEC's
policy was acceptance of the pay offer without the
hours question being settled, followed by further
talks.   The Yorkshire delegates, already angry
with the NEC, saw this as a thinly disguised attempt
by the NCB to split the membership.   Yorkshire
accepted that the wages offer was acceptable, but
agreed that it should have been won long ago and the
bitterest anger was reserved for the surfacemen's
hours: "As far as the hours are concerned, (this)
is an abject failure.   Don't hide, ...(the NCB)
has rejected this.   They have treated us again
with contempt."[22]   The pit head ballot was a
swindle as the men would obviously vote for the
cash, so Yorkshire argued that pay and hours should
be separately voted upon by proxy at the Special
Conference.
     Conference ended in disorder.   Delegates
forced a card vote and the NEC recommendation to
accept was lost by 165 to 174.   The Cokemen's
Area had abstained, but Ford counted them against.
When this was rectified the margin was 165 for the

NEC recommendation and 168 against.   Under Rule 23
Conference could then have voted by proxy which
would have meant defeat and the prospect of strike
action.   However, the NEC moved for a pit head
ballot and this was accepted by 66 to 40.
        Yorkshire Area Council urged the rejection of
the NCB's offer as their strike "was on hours not
wages ... Your Area Council wants hours kept
separate from wages and urges you to reject the
Coal Board offer."[23]   This was accepted by 70 to
9.   Nationally, the offer was accepted by 193,985
(81.6%) to 4,322 (11.4%).   In Yorkshire the result
 was, for 37,597 (72.3%) to 14,373 (27.6%) against.
The failure over surfacemen's hours led to warnings
from the Doncaster Panel about further action, and
Jim Millar, branch secretary at Kellingley in
North Yorkshire, warned that the ballot had settled
nothing: "We feel we have been betrayed.   The
Board has had sufficient time to make a settlement.
I have had great difficulty in keeping some of my
surfacemen working because the feeling in growing
that unless something is done there will be another
strike."[24]

The Wage Claim of 1970

In June 1970 the Labour Government was defeated
and replaced by a Conservative Government pledged
to free-market capitalism.   The advent of the
Heath Administration caused trepidation in the
union movement: the commitment to sell profitable
sections of the nationalised industries public
sector wage restraint, industrial relations reform
and a free rein for market forces boded ill for
the NUM.[25]   The election removed the inhibition
provided by a Labour Government to the use of
industrial action.   The leadership's perception of
the Conservative Government as anti-union made them
more amenable to contemplating industrial action
to defend their members.   Thus, 1970 is important
as it saw the Yorkshire Area leadership officially
adopt industrial action as a legitimate means of
defending miners' interests.   The Yorkshire Area
expressed disquiet at the new Government's coal
policy: "It seems that it would not be a sympathetic policy ...."[26]   Before the election
several branches called for the NUM to resist any
further closures on economic grounds with
industrial action.[27]   To this was added concern
over wages.
        At the beginning of March Council met to
decide which three branch resolutions would be

submitted by Yorkshire to the NUM Conference.
Fourteen wage resolutions were submitted. Only
six mentioned amounts and of these the Woolley
resolution sought a basic NPLA rate of £30, £21
underground, and £50 for surface grades. The
Executive recommended the adoption of
resolution. This Council did.[28]
There were eleven wage resolutions on the
Conference agenda, but only five referred to
specific increases. These were: from the
Cokemen's Area, a general increase of £1.50;
Yorkshire Area, £30/£21/£20; South Wales, a
general increase of £5; Scotland, £20 minimum
surface wage with appropriate differentials; and,
Derbyshire Area, an underground minimum of £22 and
a £20 minimum for surface workers. The South
Wales resolution concluded: "Should the Board
refuse to concede this demand then the British
miners take strike action until the claim is met."[29]
Conference could not debate all eleven, so the
General Purposes Committee met to composite them
into a generally acceptable resolution.
Yorkshire's resolution formed the basis, but South
Wales refused to allow their resolution to be
composited as they considered the demand for strike
action to be the key part. At the end of this
process Conference had three wage resolutions:
Composite III seeking £30 NPLA Grade A, £22 minimum
underground, and £20 for surfacemen (supported by
the Cokemen, Yorkshire, Scotland, the Power Group,
Durham, Kent and Northumberland). Resolution 12
demanding £20/£22 minima plus a demand for strike
action from South Wales; and, Resolution 16 from
Nottingham in support of local incentive schemes.
The latter was rejected by Conference: only
composite III and Resolution 12 were of importance.

Composite III was moved by Arthur Scargill who
welcomed it as a "realistic wage demand" and he
urged the NEC and Conference to adopt the resolution
and vigorously pursue it. Failure to do so,

> ...will release an anger that will make
> last October look like a Sunday school
> picnic. No longer will our membership
> accept that a small increase is better
> than none. They are fed up with being
> asked not to rock the boat. They have
> been told to remain passive since 1956
> and what has it got us? Half the coal
> mining industry has been obliterated ....[30]

Scargill warned Conference that unity could only be maintained by the successful pursuit of a major wage claim,

> Let the Coal Board be warned.   The miners last October showed that (we) have been passive long enough and I suggest to this Conference that if we have people in this industry in splinter groups who are going on adventurous paths .... then I am proud to associate myself with them.   I am confident that a call from the NEC to the membership of this Union would mean a positive reply.[31]

This was a less than veiled reference to Schofield's comments opening Conference ,

> We must not allow the minority who are already holding unofficial meetings (to make union policy).   I am quite satisfied that the minorities in our Union, who are arranging unofficial meetings, printing and issuing pamphlets, ignoring the policies agreed upon at Annual Conference, have a purpose in mind to try to undermine the status of Area and National Officials of our Union, and incite our members into taking unconstitutional action .....[32]

The Composite, supported by the NEC was passed by Conference.

In the debate on Resolution 12,   South Wales emphasised their acceptance of the aim of Composite III but disagreed with the means.[33]   Industrial action had the support of the Yorkshire Area. Henry Daley, the Nostell branch delegate and secretary of the North Yorkshire Panel, argued that the NEC were out of touch with the membership and these men were willing to follow their local leaders.[34]   The NEC naturally opposed Resolution 12 and were supported by Nottingham, Durham and the North-West Area.   Lawrence Daly, replying for the NEC, claimed it was illogical to have two pay resolutions, particularly one with lower figures than the other, and he urged rejection.   However, it was passed by 169 to 160.[35]

The miners' pay claim, based on both Composite III and Resolution 12, was put to the NCB in early 1970.   The NEC specifically reminded the NCB of

the latter's implications and that they were bound
to act upon it.[36]   The Board considered the claim
and rejected it despite the strike threat, informing
the NUM there could be no further offer.[37]   Next
day the NEC unanimously agreed to ballot the
membership on industrial action.[38]

The 1970 Unofficial Strike in Yorkshire

The Yorkshire Area Council supported fully the NEC,
recommending "with all its power and influence that
the membership ... support the NEC in the forthcoming national ballot by voting in support of a
national strike to achieve our just demands."[39]
Council agreed to convene strike rallies in the
four Panels to organise and mobilise the 'no'
vote.[40]   This campaign was a massive success in
Yorkshire: 36,291(62%) voted for strike action
and 22,307 (38%) against; nationally, the result
was more equivocal: 143,666 voted for a strike
and 115,052 against, a majority of 55% which under
Rule 43 was insufficient.   The NEC was therefore
compelled to re-open negotiations.
        The 1970 strike campaign sees the change in
the Yorkshire miners' mood.   A mass meeting of
1,500 miners in Barnsley ABC Cinema heard Schofield
"issue a clarion call for a strike vote" and at
the pits the left worked tirelessly for a strike
vote.   Sammy Taylor saw the result of the ballot
as vital not only for the miners, but also for the
rest of the union movement and Schofield declared
"we cannot afford to lose."[41]   In response to the
NUM's unprecedented threat, Alfred Robens,
chairman of the NCB, offered to settle the NUM
claim in full, albeit over two years.   This,
and other offers, termed by Robens "thinking aloud"
were rejected by the NEC as "gimmicks".[42]   The
Board hoped that such offers, coupled with the
two-thirds barrier, would split the NUM, isolating
the militants in unofficial strikes.   NCB counter-
propaganda in the pits seems to have exactly the
opposite of its intended effect.[43]   The
Yorkshire Area's campaign included mass meetings at
Doncaster, Goldthorpe and Maltby which drew huge
audiences.   The chief speaker was Lawrence Daly.
As such they represented a reconciliation between
Daly and the Yorkshire miners after the acrimony of
October.   Many felt Daly had betrayed his militant
reputation, which had helped win him the general
secretaryship.[44]   Yorkshire was naturally disappointed at the result and five areas (South Wales,
Scotland, Kent, Cumberland and the Scottish

Enginemen) polled larger yes votes than Yorkshire.
Many Council delegates argued that the coalfield had
been brought to the verge of action, and as a 55%
majority had been won, the NEC had a moral
obligation to take some industrial action.

Rule 43 was, however, categorical, and Council
ratified the result. However, Council warned that
"dissatisfaction has been so strongly expressed at
this Council Meeting that a failure to get a
satisfactory conclusion to negotiations ... could
well lead to a complete stoppage of work in the
coalfield ...."[45] Before the ballot and during
the campaign the branches displayed formidable
forebearance, which was all the more impressive as
Yorkshire was "rapidly becoming the militant nerve
centre of the union."[46] After the declaration
many mineworkers were "angry and confused"; they
were "near boiling point and there is a real danger
of an unofficial strike."[47]

Much, then, rode on the NEC's negotiations. On
27 October the NCB improved its previous offer
by 50p, this was rejected initially but after a
further 11 hours of talks the NEC accepted by 16
votes to 8.[48] They were confident that the
membership would accept. The NEC could have called
a Special Conference, but this was rejected
because it might throw out the offer and in the
intervening time unofficial strikes might begin.[49]
The decision to accept or reject would be taken by
the Area delegate meetings. The Yorkshire Council
recommended rejection and criticised the NEC.[50]
At this Council unofficial strike action became
certain. The Goldthorpe branch was already on
strike and appealing for support, and several
others were operating an overtime ban (Cadeby, and
Maltby in South Yorkshire, and Kellingley in North
Yorkshire). At the end of the 29 October Council
delegates from the Doncaster panel appealed for
support, and they agreed to take this appeal back to
their branches. By 30 October 20,000 mineworkers
were on strike in the Yorkshire coalfield.

The NEC's meek acceptance of the NCB's offer
after so much 'fighting talk' and preparation for
industrial action created frustration and threatened
a severe bout of internal conflict between left
and right. Nothing had been done to ease the
tensions in the coalfield and some on the left
advocated selective, or 'guerilla' strikes, legitimised by the 55% majority irrespective of Rule 43.
The NEC rejected this as unrealistic, declaring
that the ballot ended all chance of official

industrial action.   Whilst Council was meeting
on 29 October miners were already striking and
delegates demanded that they be supported and the
full claim be fought for.   Bullough refused to
accept any resolutions contrary to national policy,
as he was bound to do, and faced by a plethora of
demands he "summarily ended the meeting and walked
out."[51]   The strike call was taken up in other
Panels, aided by flying pickets from Doncaster,
which had become the focal point of unrest.   The
Panel Secretary, Owen Briscoe, declared their
intention to stay out until the full claim was
met.[52]   The 20,000 miners represented by the
Barnsley Panel were considering an overtime ban,
but Don Baines, the Panel Secretary, announced they
would not join Doncaster until the branches so
decided.   The Panel was, then, not officially
recommending action, but a number of branch
officials were known to be lobbying their men for
a strike.   This strike was defined as a rank-and-
file strike prompted by the lack of national leadership: if national leaders could not lead then the
branch officials would.[53]   The pickets concentrated
on the North and South Yorkshire Panels who had,
as yet, made no decision.   The Barnsley pits were
beginning to come out, and the North Yorkshire Panel
expressed its support but only Wheldale and
Kellingley had struck.   The South Yorkshire Panel
was split: some pits were out but others, perhaps
a few hundred yards away continued working.   The
situation was very confused, with rumour chasing
rumour.   It was suggested that, for example,
military convoys would be used to move fuel which
"with the present mood of the men, particularly
in Doncaster, ...would lead to something near civil
war...."[54]
     In its early stages the strike was both
confused and spontaneous.   Militant pits struck
before their leaders were prepared and moderate
pits refused to accept the advice of their branch
officials.   Panel leaders struggled hard to control
their pickets: at Glasshoughton in North Yorkshire,
for example, there was a nasty scene between branch
officials and Doncaster pickets and there were
persistent rumours of intimidation, fuelling
speculation that the Yorkshire Area was losing
control "and even the real power blocs in the coalfields, the Area Panels, are now finding that the
militancy they have nurtured .... has overtaken
them."[55]   The pickets attracted severe criticism
from Schofield who claimed there had been little

support for direct action in Council and that
"roving bands of pickets" were responsible for the
strike's spread.[56] Twenty-four pits were out and
it is unlikely all were out due to picketing:
Wheldale and Kellingley needed no prompting to
strike and only two pits (Barrow and Rockingham)
were working normally in Barnsley, so the Panel
accepted the situation and supported Doncaster
officially. After this the South Yorkshire Panel
also struck. Owen Briscoe remarked, "This is a
rank and file strike. The Officials did not lead
the men out ...."[57] The decision of Barnsley and
South Yorkshire marks the high-point of the strike.
Nevertheless, at the Council of 9 November some
delegates called for a special NEC meeting to
reverse the ballot decision and attempts were made
to unseat Bullough who, despite "many vociferous
urgings" refused to vacate the chair. Despite the
opposition within and 300 pickets outside a
compromise was achieved. Christmas was approaching
and some pits, particularly in Barnsley, were
drifting back, so the Chair agreed to accept a
resolution demanding a strike and a national
conference to reject the offer but only "on it being
made clear that (it) was only to indicate what
delegates felt, it was not to be regarded as a
vote for unofficial action ...." This was rejected
by 33 to 43 in favour of continuing the strike.[58]
      Schofield emphasised that this could not be
union policy and did not signify Yorkshire's support
for unofficial action.[59] However, the strike was
crumbling outside Doncaster: North Yorkshire
recommended a return and Barnsley was wavering. A
major blow came when Bentley and Hatfield in
Doncaster voted, against the Panel, to return to
work and the South Yorkshire Panel also agreed to
call   the strike. On 20 November Doncaster
accepted the inevitable.
      The weakness of the Panel system in unofficial
industrial action can be clearly seen in 1969 and
1970. Given an issue the Panel's could initiate
and organise industrial action, but it proved
impossible to mount an extended campaign without the
support and legitimacy conferred by official action.
Effective action was restricted by the provisions of
Rule 43 which made official industrial action
virtually impossible. Panel leaders knew that
without massive and general support throughout the
coalfield Doncaster and its allies would be
isolated, but they had to go along with the membership. Jim Millar, Kellingley branch secretary,

commented, "All the way along, it's been the story
of Tam O'Shanter, grabbing the horse's tail as it
bolted away."[60]   The continued right wing
dominance in the North Yorkshire, South Yorkshire
and Barnsley Panels prevented full scale action,
though the political balance of the last two was
changing.   The strike was not organised by "reds
under the bed";[61]   it was an expression of deeply
felt, but as yet diffuse grievances.
     An important facet of these strikes was the
hostility displayed to official leaderships.   Many
loyal branches were dismayed at the "betrayal"
by the NEC.   The Barrow branch, for example,
was fiercely critical of Area and National leaders:

>   Although we have supported them during the
>   recent conflict .... it was only because
>   of the Rules of the (NUM) that we did so.
>   We still wish to register our disgust,
>   and complain that we have no leadership
>   or advice from the officials of this
>   Union.   We deplore some of the action
>   taken by our National Officials, and hope
>   that in future .... our leaders will stand
>   by their convictions.[62]

Some sections of the Union only tolerated their
leaders because of their profound belief in
loyalty and unity.   This was a depreciating asset
soon exhausted unless the leadership responded.
Speculation went so far as to suggest that the
NUM might collapse because of internal tensions
unless Rule 43 was modified.[63]   The strikes were
the miners response to their treatment since 1958,
and in some respects since 1947, and were outbursts
of frustration.   The strikes were not political,
but were generated by politics.

The Climate of Militancy
In the late 1960s there were two critiques of the
NUM's political role. Lawrence Daly published a
pamphlet critical of the Labour Government's fuel
policy, arguing that Labour's election in 1964 had
been seen by the mineworkers as the guarantee of
their future.   The Government had reneged so the
task of the Union was to force the Government back
to its original policy.   Daly outlined a
comprehensive programme for the NUM covering wages,
hours, pensions, retirement, health and safety.
Little was new or original in this programme;   what
was new was the advocacy of industrial action.

The Unofficial Strikes and the Rise of the Left

Daly claimed the NUM had been too moderate:

> ....a Labour Government gives strength
> to the case for moderation. "Our Union
> is affiliated to the Labour Party - so
> let us be loyal to our own Government.
> Don't rock the boat, or we might get the
> Tories back. In any case, industrial
> action .... will chase away customers
> and lose miners jobs".

Thus, the NUM was trapped in a logic of
moderation: moderation and abandoning industrial
action led to the rapid closure of pits, reinforcing
the NUM's belief in its powerlessness. This logic
could be broken by industrial action to "make
the Government realise that the miners' loyalty
is not something to be coldly taken for granted."[64]
The Board and Government would only take the miners
seriously when "we demonstrate our determination to
take industrial action when other means have failed"
and, "Meakness on our part (has met) with no
response."[65] Daly was careful to emphasise that
industrial action must be within the NUM Rules and
it should not be used to damage a Labour Government.
The aim was to change policy.[66] The Miners and the
Nation struck a responsive chord in the coalfields
and it contributed materially to Daly's victory as
General Secretary. The left saw Daly's election
as representing a change in the NUM's orientation.
When these expectations were frustrated the miners'
sense of betrayal increased.
A manifestation of this frustration was a
pamphlet produced by the Yorkshire Strike
Committee.[67] This was a response to the Special
Conference of 31 October 1969 and to Daly's
earlier position. It emphasised the traditional
role of the miners as leaders of the working class
and that the 1969 strike demonstrated this still
to be so. The strike was seen as the result of
disappointment over nationalisation and the dismal
performance of the Union, expressing solidarity
with the plight of the surfaceworker.[68] This
pamphlet argued that the problems confronting the
miner were due to pressures on the   caused by the
absence of a fuel policy. This was consequential
on the NUM's inability to influence the Government.
There was bitter criticism for Union leaders and
the Government: "the Labour Government was elected,
and Lawrence Daly was elected, on the demands of
the miners for a fuel policy to take the place of

202

the competitive fuel market."[69]   Government policy
implemented by the NCB, was blamed for the state of
the industry and the inability of the Union to
respond effectively was blamed for the strike.
Unlike Daly's pamphlet, A Future For The British
Miners? did not emphasise a party-political
response, but urged a greater role for the miners
in actually running the industry: "we could bloody
well run the pits ourselves."[70]   The NCB had
bungled management, but this had not been challenged
by the Union because of "the incompetence and lack
of militancy of the National Executive."[71]   The
remedy was the periodic re-election of all union
officials.

These pamphlets represent differing responses
to the same problems.   Daly's advocacy of
industrial action was welded to the NUM's traditional political commitment to the Labour Party,
seeking to make that relationship function better.
The Yorkshire Strike Committee pamphlet was more
radical, devaluing party-politics in favour of a
more overtly industrial rank-and-file response by
calling on the NUM to rely upon its own resources
and fight its own battles.   Daly's strategy was to
become NUM policy after 1970 and was to guide the
NUM in 1972 and 1974, finally underpinning the
NUM's relationship with the Labour Government
elected in 1974.   The Yorkshire Area, however, was
profoundly influenced by the Strike Committee's
emphasis on the primacy of the industrial over the
political.

Why did Yorkshire become the militant nerve
centre of the NUM?   Unlike Scotland, Kent or South
Wales, Yorkshire never had a militant reputation.
Militancy was strong, but there existed powerful
countervailing tendencies which prevented
industrial militancy becoming part of the norms of
Area behaviour.   The strains within the Yorkshire
Area were, therefore, greater and more explosive
than in coalfields where either militancy or
moderation (for example, Nottingham) predominated.
During the 1960s the counter-vailing forces
weakened with the union's failure to influence the
Labour Government's fuel and pay policies, thus
shifting the internal balance of political forces
decisively to the left.

Secondly, Yorkshire was one of the major
Central Coalfields.   Up to the 1960s the closures
were confined mainly to the peripheral coalfields
which therefore lived with the reality of closure
for a decade.   Yorkshire only felt the full impact

in the mid-1960s, this had a tremendous psychological impact on the workforce. In the short-term pit closures prompted industrial quietism, but in the longer term bred frustration which turned to anger.

Third, after the reorganisation of the NCB in 1966-1967 there was no level of NCB authority equivalent to the Yorkshire Area (NUM). After 1967 there were four Area NCBs and the Panel system was modified accordingly. Reorganisation had the effect of raising the status of the Panels and reducing that of the Area, thus augmenting the disintegrative tendencies present in the coalfield. The Panels, closer to the membership than the Area, became an alternative union organisation which in 1969 and 1970 took over the leadership of the Yorkshire miners.

Fourth, before 1966 Yorkshire was one of the better paid Areas in the NCB. Under NPLA wage rates were stabilised and internal differentials reduced between 1966 and 1971 to allow lower paid Areas to catch up. This coincided with incomes policy. Hence, the enormous fund of discontent over wages. Further, NPLA had the effect of reducing the level of unofficial conflict. Paradoxically, small scale pit level unrest proved to be a valuable safety valve for industrial unrest. When each pit had its own price list the potential for minor disputes was high but the opportunity for major disputes was low as there was no common standard of measurement. NPLA reversed this and the number of adjourned pit meetings (disputes not settled at one meeting) fell as pay rates were standardised, as did disputes.[72] This was the result of "our members .... not having to argue so much with management on their wages and conditions".[73] In effect, NPLA had the effect of suppressing and generalising discontent after 1966.

It must be pointed out that Yorkshire was not opposed to NPLA per se or to the principle of national daywage rates; it opposed the method of implementation.

Finally, National and Area leaders misjudged the mood of the Yorkshire miners. After the disasters of the 1960s the membership was to some extent suspicious of the NEC's rapid conversion to industrial militancy in 1970. The Area leadership was in a dilemma: divorced from the branches by NCB reorganisation it was caught between its loyalty to the NUM and the membership. It failed to resolve this dilemma. Both groups of leaders

204

were motivated by their experience in, and memories of, an industry and communities which had suffered so much in the inter-war years and which after a brief period of post-war propserity, again sank into decline. This generation's abandoning of industrial action and the subsequent betrayal by Labour meant they had no response left. As the authority of the official leaders declined, that of the unofficial increased. In 1969 Panel leaders used their new legitimacy to call for the resignation of Ford and Daly, accusing "Sir Sidney of saying too much .... and Mr Daly of saying nothing."[74] Both strenuously denied their isolation from the membership but Will Paynter, Daly's predecessor, admitted candidly that once away from the coalfield "for any length of time that initmacy has gone."[75] During the 1969 strike eleven Yorkshire branches sent resolutions to Barnsley attacking the NEC, Ford and Daly, with the Corton-wood branch demanding the resignation of the Area Officials as well. They were convinced that the National Officials were isolated and actively ignoring the members. The NEC protested they were bound by the Rules (particularly Rule 43) and Daly argued in support of strike action stated it had to be official, via the Rules.[76]

The Rise of the New Leadership
In the election to replace Sidney Ford as National President, who resigned because of ill health, there were only two candidates: Joe Gormley, Secretary of the North West Area, and Mick McGahey, the President of the Scottish Area. Gormley projected the image of a blunt, down-to-earth miners' leader; he was on the right of both the NUM and Party (of which he was an NEC member) but his rhetoric suggested a man determined to defend his members. He stood unsuccessfully against Daly for General Secretary in 1968. McGahey, President of the Scottish Area, was member of the Communist Party executive and had been in office for only one year. Thus, he was not a good left candidate: he was not well known nationally, had only recently won a major Area post, and his election would have been unprecedented as then both senior national officials would have originated from the same NUM Area and both would have been left wing. Traditionally, a political balance was maintained between left and right at the highest level. This and the presence of one Scotsman at national level gave Gormley a major advantage.

Also Gormley had learnt from his 1968 experience
and used the resources and manpower of his Area to
finance his election and run his election campaign.
In the national ballot Gormley won by 117,663 to
McGahey's 92,883, a majority of 24,780.   Nationally, then, a clear victory but in Yorkshire the
vote was Gormley 21,747, McGahey 22,549 a majority
of 802 in favour of the left's candidate.[77]
    In common with most of the trade union movement
the Yorkshire Area pledged itself to resist "The
anti-democratic Tory Industrial Relations Bill by
all effective means, short of violence" and vowed
to have no truck with the Act or any institutions it
created, promising to support any union penalised
by the Act.[78]   There were a number of remarkable
expressions of verbal hostility to the Heath
Government.   For example, the Wheldale branch
proposed "That this Union calls upon the TUC to
call a General Strike with the express purpose
of forcing this Tory Government to resign and
enabling a·Labour Government to take office."
This received eight votes in Council.[79]   The
Yorkshire Area showed its hostility to the Heath
Government in a practical way by making a grant to
the workers at Upper Clyde Shipbuilders, and the
same Council meeting urged all tenants to resist
the Housing Finance Act.[80]   On the eve of the 1971
Conference the Yorkshire Area was espousing a vocal
political and industrial militancy.   The 1971
Conference approved a Yorkshire resolution origina-
ting from the Woolleybranch which sought a minimum
wage of £35 per week for those on NPLA face rates,
£28 for underground workers, and £26 for surface
workers.[81]   This was accepted by Conference and
was, therefore the casus belli of the 1972 strike.
    The 1972 strike prompted major changes in
the personnel and policies of the Yorkshire Area.
As we shall see, the strike was led and organised by
the branch and panel leaders, the most prominent of
whom was Arthur Scargill of the Barnsley Panel who
led the mass picket at Saltley.   After a mass
picket by the Barnsley Panel closed the Grimethorpe
Coalite Plant Scargill demanded official recognition
of this tactic, and this was agreed at national
level.[82]   It was from this local leadership,
which enjoyed the confidence of the membership, that
political change sprang.   Their prestige was
enhanced by the outcome of the 1972 strike and they
provided the new generation of leaders in the
Yorkshire Area.   During the strike Scargill rose to
prominence, first as leader of the East Anglian

pickets and then as the man who closed Saltley,
and this prominence and popularity was reflected
in his election in 1973 as Area Compensation
Agent.83   Eighteen candidates stood for election,
but the number was reduced to three by a branch
vote.   The result was: A Scargill, 28,050;
J Smart, 9,824; and, T Roebuck, 8,336.84   In
January 1973 Sam Bullough died.   Clearly Scargill
was the favourite to succeed him.   The voting was,
again, decisive, Scargill won with 28,362, over
J T Leigh's 7,126 and J Layden's 7,981.85   Also
in 1973 Sid Schofield retired due to ill health.
There were three candidates on the ballot paper:
W O'Brien (Glasshoughton), O Briscoe (Armthorpe),
and H Riley (Brodsworth).86   O'Brien and Briscoe
were the two major candidates, O'Brien was seen
as representing the right, and Briscoe the left.
Briscoe won by 19,736 over O'Brien's 12,758, and
Riley polled 6,386.   Briscoe's election confirmed
the rise to power of the political and industrial
left in the Yorkshire Area.
     After 1947 miners' leaders sought to secure
an industrial relations system in which conflict
with management was institutionalised and so
rendered less bitter.   This was a laudable
aspiration but it involved a cost: it enmeshed the
NUM in a cooperative framework which often entailed
putting other interests before those of the
mineworker.   The leadership's adherence to the
joint system of conciliation was often interpreted
as 'selling out' by their members, which in turn
contributed to the emergence of a climate of dissatisfaction and then militancy in the Yorkshire
Area.   New generations of mineworkers who had no
direct experience of the traumas of the inter-war
years and for whom nationalisation had none of the
tremendous symbolism it had for earlier generations,
became willing to challenge and confront their
leaders' interpretations of what constituted the
best interest of the men and their union.   By the
early-1960s the Yorkshire Area appeared stable
due to the dominance of the right-wing, but pit
closures, incomes policy, the implementation of
NPLA and the general malaise of the industry caused
the outbursts of 1969 and 1970.   These strikes
threw up new leaders and attitudes: these leaders
advocated militant industrial action to defend
the miners' interests, and they were to be vindicated by 1972.   Between 1971 and 1973 this new
generation came to power in the Yorkshire Area.
In so doing they profoundly affected the political

The Unofficial Strikes and the Rise of the Left

orientation of the NUM as a whole.

REFERENCES

1   JNNC; 9 October 1969.
2   JNNC; 17 October 1969.
3   Morning Telegraph; 1 October 1969.
4   Yorkshire Post; 10 October 1969
5   For example;
     Barnsley Chronicle; 11 October 1969.
6   Morning Telegraph; 29 September 1969.
7   Morning Telegraph: 4 October 1969.
8   YA(NUM); 6 October 1969.
9   Morning Telegraph; 8 October 1969.
10   YA(NUM); 11 October 1969.
11   Morning Telegraph: 13 October 1969. Only
     Bullough and two branch delegates dissented
     from the decision.
12   Morning Telegraph; 13 October 1969,
     The Times (Business News); 13 October 1969,
     and, The Times; 15 October 1969.
13   L Daly to S Schofield, 17 October 1969.
14   BS Circular 107/69 (18 October 1969)
15   NUM(EC); 21 October 1969.
16   The Times; 20 October 1969, and,
     Morning Telegraph; 22 October 1969.
17   Morning Telegraph; 24 October 1969.
18   Phone message from O Briscoe to J T Leigh,
     24 October 1969.
19   YA(NUM); 22 October 1969.
20   Morning Telegraph; 25 October 1969.
21   NUM: Special Conference Report, 30 October
     1969; p2.
22   Special Conference; pp14-15.
23   YA(NUM): 3 November, and 8 November 1969.
24   Morning Telegraph; 25 May 1970.
25   E Wigham, Strikes and the Government, 1893-
     1974 (London, Macmillan 1976); p156.
     G Dorfman, Government Versus Trade Unions
     in British Politics since 1968 (London,
     Macmillan 1979); pp50-52,
     C Crouch, The Politics of Industrial
     Relations (London, Fontana 1979); pp66-69.
     M Moran, The Politics of Industrial
     Relations (London, Macmillan 1977);
     pp77-98.
26   YA(NUM); NCB Coalfield Appraisal, July 1970.
27   BS Circular 23/70 (18 February 1970).
28   YA(NUM); 2 March 1970
29   NUM: Annual Conference Agenda, 1970.
30   NUM: Annual Conference Report, 1970; p138.

31   Annual Conference;   p139
32   Annual Conference;   pp87-88.
33   Annual Conference;   p153.
34   Annual Conference;   pp157-158.
35   Annual Conference;   p160.
36   JNNC: 6 August 1970.
37   JNNC; 16 September 1970.
38   NUM(EC); 17 September 1970,
          As Circular 118/70 (18 September 1970).
          BS Circular 198/70 (22 September 1970).
39   YA(NUM); 21 September 1970.
40   The NUM's claim was for minimum weekly wage
          rates of £20 (surface), £22 (underground)
          and £30 (NPLA). The NCB rejected this
          claim and offered £17-10s (surface),
          £10(underground) and £29-10s (NPLA)
          together with a 40 hour week (inclusive of
          20 minute meal breaks) for surface workers.
          The Union was tempted by the wages but
          was reluctant to see a linking of wages and
          hours. See;
          NUM(EC); 17 September 1970; and,
          JNNC; 6 August 1970.
41   All quotes form;
      Morning Telegraph; 5 October 1970.
42   Morning Telegraph; 8 and 9 October 1970.
          The Times; 8 and 9 October 1970, and,
          NUM(EC); 8 October 1970.
43   Morning Telegraph;   9 October 1970.
44   Morning Telegraph; 10 October 1970
45   YA(NUM); 26 October 1970; and,
          Morning Telegraph; 27 October 1970,
46   Morning Telegraph; 21 October 1970.
47   Morning Telegraph; 24 October 1970.
48   JNNC: 27 October 1970, and,
          NUM(EC); 27 October 1970.
49   NUM(EC); 27 October 1970.
50   YA(NUM); 29 October 1970.
51   YA(NUM); 29 October 1970, and,
          Morning Telegraph; 30 October 1970.
52   Morning Telegraph; 28 October 1970.
53   Morning Telegraph; 30 October 1970.
          Statement by Owen Briscoe.
54   Morning Telegraph; 2 November 1970.
      The North Yorkshire Panel was finding it
      difficult keeping some of their men at work.
      See;
      Letter from the Prince of Wales Branch
      (Pontefract), 4 October 1970.
55   Morning Telegraph; 3 November 1970.
56   Morning Telegraph; 4 November 1970.

57   Morning Telegraph; 5 November 1970.
58   YA(NUM); 9 November 1970.
59   Morning Telegraph; 10 November 1970.
60   Morning Telegraph; 6 November 1970.
61   The Times; 10 November 1970
62   YA(NUM); 30 November 1970.
63   Tribune; 20 November 1970 (Article by
        D Turner).
        Tribune; 27 November 1970 (Reply by
        L Daly).
        New Statesman; 20 November 1970 (John
        Torode, 'A Dusty Lesson for the Miners').
64   L Daly, The Miners and the Nation (NUM),
        Scottish Area 1968); p5 and p11.
        Daly was General Secretary of the Scottish
        Area and was seeking election to the post
        of national General Secretary on the
        retirement of Will Paynter.   This Pamphlet
        was widely interpreted in the NUM as a
        manifesto.
65   The Miners and the Nation; p16 and p17.
66   The Miners and the Nation; pp17-18.
        Daly had advocated guerrilla strikes -
        these had been proposed and rejected by the
        NEC (27 October 1970).
67   J Oldham, et al, 'A Future for the British
        Miners?', in,
        K Coates, et al, The Trade Union Register
        (London, Merlin Press 1970)
        This statement was a response to Daly's
        manifesto of 1968 and a second statement,
        'A Future for the Miners', in
        K Coates, et al, The Trade Union Register
        (London, Merlin Press, 1969); pp53-59)
68   A Future for the British Miners?; pp130-131.
69   A Future for the British Miners?; p132.
        Daly was bitterly attacked for abandoning
        the policies advocated in The Miners and
        the Nation (1968); see especially, p18.
70   A Future for the British Miners?; p133
71   A Future for the British Miners?; p133
72   YA(NUM): Annual Report of the General
        Secretary for 1968 (March 1969); p97.
73   YA(NUM): Annual Reports, 1970; p117.
74   Morning Telegraph, 20 October 1969.
75   T Lane, The Union Makes Us Strong (London,
        Arrow 1974); p231-2
76   The Miner (December 1969) for Daly's justifica-
        tion of his position.
77   AS Circular 120/71 (11 June 1971).
78   YA(NUM); 8 February 1971.

79 YA(NUM); 30-31 March 1971.
80 YA(NUM); 1 September 1971.
81 YA(NUM); 30-31 March 1971.
82 A Scargill, 'The New Unionism', in, New Left
        Review 92(1975); pp11-20. See also,
        NUM(EC); 12 January 1972 (Appendix I);
        and, Finance and General Purposes Committee,
        24 January 1972.
83 Scargill, 'The New Unionism', pp9-10, and,
        pp15-22.
84 YA(NUM); 15 May 1972, and, 22 June 1972.
85 YA(NUM); 7 May and 13 June 1973.
86 YA(NUM); 17 September, 8 October and
        29 October 1973.

Chapter Eight

THE NATIONAL COAL STRIKE OF 1972

The Significance of 1972

The spectacular political events surrounding the 1974 strike have obscured the importance of 1972. In 1972 the miners shook off the incubus of 1926 and the dead-hand of the nationalisation ethos which proscribed industrial action. Industrial decline created a groundswell of anger and frustration which erupted in the strikes of 1969 and 1970. The 1969 strike demonstrated that the miners were capable of industrial action; only reluctantly did the Union move in the same direction, sanctionning a strike ballot in 1970. The 1972 strike saw a coalescence of the Union leadership and members after the travails of the 1960s, a process helped by Joe Gormley's election as NUM President in 1971. Although on the right, Gormley's rhetoric was far more militant than that of his predecessors, enabling him to articulate the frustrations felt by his members. The strike demonstrated that despite the numerical decline of the miners the NUM was able to cause massive disruption by halting the production and distribution of coal. The dependence of the economy on centrally generated electricity and the dependence of the CEGB on coal gave the miners considerable potential power. The interdependence of coal and electricity production was crucial to the strike's outcome.

It should be emphasised that the overtime ban and strike were not motivated by any guarantee that the miners would win. The actions of the miners in 1972 are best seen as the last option open to a badly battered group of workers, a last gamble by those who believed they had nothing to lose by striking.

Preparing the Way

The 1971 NUM Conference was concerned with two problems: inadequate basic wage rates; and second,

the reform of Rule 43 to a simple majority to
facilitate industrial action. Gormley's rhetoric
in his first Presidential Address reflected the
anger felt by many members at policies of the
Heath and previous governments since 1947.[1]
Gormley committed himself and the NUM to making the
miners into the highest paid industrial workers in
Britain.[2]   Naturally, the central concern of
Conference was wages.   Composite Resolution II,
based on a Yorkshire resolution, demanded that "In
the event of an unsatisfactory response from the
(NCB) the (NEC) is to consult the membership with
regard to various forms of industrial action."[3]
This was moved by W Sykes from Yorkshire who
cautioned the delegates on the Government ("These
lads don't talk class warfare.   They practise it")
and emphasised that the militancy of 1970 had not
been dissipated:

> ....Last year's ballot on wages showed to
> some measure the feeling of our members on
> the wages question, a feeling of
> dissatisfaction and disenchantment, and
> we nearly saw a position .... where the
> tail was wagging the dog, and we saw it
> because of our members' total
> dissatisfaction with the wages that they
> were getting ....I want to remind you
> that the disenchantment has grown.   It
> has grown doublefold since then.[4]

Composite II was accepted unanimously.
      The second major issue was the reform of Rule
43.   Resolution 7 originated in the moderate
North Western NUM and was a product of the unrest
of 1970.   The resolution sought to reduce the
majority needed for national strike action from
two-thirds to 55%.   It was seconded by the militant
Kent Area and enjoyed the support of the NEC.
The change was opposed by Durham, the Midlands, and
COSA who claimed that it would make strike action
more likely, accelerating the industry's
contraction, whereas the two-thirds majority ensured
security from any dissension.   Resolution 7 was
passed by 215 votes to 98.[5]   Thus, the 1971
Conference laid the foundations for the 1972 strike
by removing the most important barrier to strike
action, the two-thirds rule.   The NEC submitted the
wage claim in the knowledge that strike action was
a realistic option.

Negotiation and the Overtime Ban

Immediately after Conference the NUM's negotiating
team on the JNNC met and decided to press for the
full and immediate settlement of £35/£28/£26 wage
claim under the terms of the resolution.   The
claim was presented on 14 September 1971.[6]   One
month later the NCB responded only £25m was
available for wage increases, which represented a
general increase of £1.60.   The NUM responded
angrily as "all they had heard had been most
interesting but it was basically the same that had
been heard in previous years .... on this basis
negotiations would be quite impossible."[7]   The
full NEC also expressed its strong resentment at the
offer.   Rejection was certain, so the NEC
considered how they should consult the membership.
It was decided to call a Special Conference to
approve a call for a national overtime ban and a
pithead ballot on strike action.   Should a strike
be called there would be no strike pay.[8]

The Special Conference unanimously approved the
overtime ban from 1st November and confirmed a
ballot.   The overtime ban was of pivotal importance
to the NEC's strategy.   Lawrence Daly stated:

> It is our intention, without waiting for
> the outcome of the ballot, to ensure that
> the overtime ban makes deep inroads into
> the stocks that the Coal Board talks about
> so we can consequently strengthen the
> bargaining position of our Union in the
> coming weeks.....[9]

The ban gave the NEC room to manoeuvre on the JNNC
whilst keeping open channels of communication to
the NCB and Government;   it increased the chances
of success should a strike be called by reducing
coal reserves;   it allowed NUM members to build
up resources as there would be no strike pay;   but
crucially, it would contribute to forging a higher
degree of national unity by demonstrating the real
level of earnings to all miners.   Under NPLA all
mineworkers doing comparable jobs in any coalfield
were paid the same daywage but overtime varied
from pit to pit and coalfield to coalfield, thus
disguising the national scales.   By reducing all
mineworkers to a comparable level, the low level
of wages would be revealed creating a national sense
of injustice.   Additionally, there was a tendency
for maintenance work to be done during overtime.
With a ban this would have to be done in production

time further reducing output.

No negotiations took place after 21 October,
only recommencing when the NEC was given authority
to call a strike. The margin of victory was small,
only 68.8% in favour, but there was a massive 75%
in Yorkshire. The NCB's offer had remained at
£1.80 for surface workers and £1.75 for all other
workers: the NEC voted to give the NCB one month's
notice of strike action, to begin on 9 January
1972 whilst expressing the hope that the Board would
make a satisfactory offer.[10] At this meeting
responsibility for the detailed preparation of the
strike was assigned to the General Purposes Sub-
Committee of the NEC.

Informal meetings were held between the NUM and
the NCB, but these contacts came to nought.[11] A
crucial encounter was a meeting between the Board
and the full NEC without the medium of the JNNC.
This had been requested by the NUM so as to give
the NCB the maximum opportunity for compromise.
The meeting was a failure as "there was no material
change in the Board's offer, thus the strike
notices remained in force." [12]

A Special Council Meeting on 22 October heard
Jock Kane report on the state of wage negotiations.
After he delivered his report the delegates voted
unanimously to impose the ban from 1 November and
approve the strike ballot.[13] The NEC and Area
Executive emphasised that branches must hereafter
obey all instructions issued by the union leadership. The aim of the ban was to reduce production
and stocks but safety and essential repair work
must be allowed and branches were not to interfere
with that work. To ignore these instructions
would be prejudicial to good discipline, order,
unity and might provoke dissension amongst the
workforce leading to a vote against strike action.[15]

Despite these warnings Barnsley received
complaints concerning "various incidents" involving
NUM members attempting to prevent overmen and
deputies (members of NACODS) and others from
conducting essential work. A Special Executive
decided that the Panels (the organisational basis
of the industrial action in Yorkshire) were to
warn their branches of the need for discipline.[16]
Warnings about "over-zealousness" fell on deaf ears
as a little under a week later a Special Council
Meeting was informed that certain branches were
going beyond the provisions of the ban. Council
declared itself to be "deeply disturbed",
ascribing any excesses to "misplaced loyalty and

discipline", warning that the ban was not a
weapon of last resort but a calculated attempt to
reduce coal stocks. It warned that continued
disobedience would not be tolerated and no financial
assistance would be given to any branch or member
guilty of disobeying instructions.[17] In this
period the strike ballot took place approving the
beginning of the strike on 9 January.[18]
      Between 9 December and 9 January there was a
hiatus whilst the NUM prepared for the coming
struggle. The press, nationally and locally, were
confident that a strike would be a disaster - but
only for the miners. The Economist, for example,
warned that a long strike would inevitably close
more pits and the miners "will have brought the
closures wholly on themselves."[19] This was a mis-
representation of the attitude of many miners who
felt that if the industry could not pay decent
wages then the pits should be closed.[20] The press
argued that the NUM was taking on more than it could
manage, that they lacked the numbers or weight to
do any real damage because of the coal stocks,
and that the strike was 'political' as some NUM
leaders regarded the strike as part of the class
war against the Heath Government and parallels were
drawn with 1926.[21] It was generally predicted by
the media that the miners would be defeated.
However, on 2 January Daly predicted that the NUM
would cripple the supply of electric power and
announced thatthe NUM had won the cooperation of
the railway and transport unions preventing the
movement of coal and other supplies to the power
stations.[22]

The New Politics of Industrial Conflict
The militancy of the membership soon expressed
itself. The Yorkshire coalfield was due to re-open
on 4 January, but this was threatened by the Barnsley
winders who were contemplating joining the strike.
This was the result of pickets interpreting strictly
the NEC guidelines and claims by winders of being
being intimidated by pickets ignoring NEC
instructions.[23] From the beginning of January to
the start of the strike there were persistent
rumours that a settlement might be reached between
Gormley and Sir Derek Ezra of the NCB.[24] This
was bitterly resented in Yorkshire, but the talks
went ahead in obedience to the accepted norms.
The NCB's final offer amounted to 7.9%, and was
rejected by the NEC by 23 votes to 2. The NEC also
rejected arbitration. Afterwards, the NEC met with

representatives of the TUC who recommended the
transport unions not to move coal or cross NUM
picket lines.[25]   Nevertheless, it was claimed
coal stocks were high and the strike would cause
"marginal disruption".[26]   A final attempt to stop
the strike by the Department of Employment (DE)
who offered talks about talks was rejected by the
NEC.   On 6 January NUM leaders met with Vic
Feather where it was suggested that the TUC as a
whole should formally support the NUM as the miners'
opposition to the pay norm was in the interest of
the whole Movement.   In particular, the NUM
wanted other unions to do nothing which might be
construed as strike breaking.   The NCB's response
to these overtures was to withdraw any offers made,
and Daly commented, "There will be a considerable
hardening of the miners' attitude.   They will be
all the more determined to fight for justice."[27]
On 10 January an emergency meeting of the TUC
General Purposes Committee heard a formal appeal
for help from the NUM.   Solidarity was expressed
but the committee felt that as NUR, ASLEF, and TGWU
had already promised their support there was no
point in an official TUC instruction.   However, the
TUC did insist that all unions observe the sanctity
of the picket line.   The NUM welcomed Feather's
assurances "that the Trade Unions would firmly
instruct their members not to cross such picket
lines in any circumstances."[28]
     The strike began in an atmosphere of bitterness
in the mining communities and the Yorkshire Area
Council greeted the strike with jubilation.   Sam
Bullough ended a noisy Council Meeting when
delegates tried to force him to adopt a resolution
withdrawing all mineworkers, even safety men, from
the pits.[29]   Other delegates and some branches had
demanded that pickets stop winders, NACODS and
management from entering the pits.[30]   An underground fire ("active heating") broke out at
Goldthorpe-Highgate, a combined unit employing
1,380 men, and the branch (with the support of
its members) refused to provide men to help
extinguish the fire.   The Doncaster Area Agent
commented, "The miners decided they had been black-
mailed long enough", and despite a plea from Gormley
the branch again refused to help.   This intransigence was seen as setting the tone for rest of the
dispute.[31]
     In the first few days of the strike the miners
concentrated on securing the support of the
transport unions and stopping the movement of coal.

This support was readily given.[32]   The weak spot
was road transport, not because the TGWU was lukewarm in its support, but because the industry is
not 100% unionised and there were considerable
numbers of 'cowboy' operators prepared to run
the picket lines.   The mass movement of coal could
only be prevented, as The Times pointed out in a
prophetic warning, "if the miners' union can post
pickets at points far from the coalfield."[33]   This
was exactly what was to happen.
     Mass picketing was thought to risk a government
response but this had not prevented the creation of
a comprehensive network of contacts between the
NUM and other unions to provide intelligence as to
when and where to have pickets.   The novel feature
of the strike was its high level of organisation.
The Yorkshire Area's strike effort was organised by
the four Area Panels whose prime targets were power
stations, coke ovens and coal dumps, as well as
transport in general.   Picketing began on
9 January, and the subsequent organisation of the
mass "flying pickets" by the Yorkshire miners was a
major refinement of picketing techniques.[34]   These
pickets completed the erosion of the overtime ban,
forcing the CEGB to consume their remaining stocks
to maintain output.   Of the 142 CEGB power stations
73.3% of total output was produced by coal or dual
coal/oil fired stations.   Coal stocks were high,
but badly distributed away from the point of
consumption.   Also a disproportionate number of
very large fuel efficient stations feeding the
National Grid were coal fired, situated on or near
the Yorkshire coalfield and were supplied by rail.
At the beginning of the strike these stations had
low stocks having been badly hit by the overtime
ban.   Pickets were instructed to stop deliveries of
oil as this was necessary to fire up coal burning
boilers.   The scale of picketing at power
stations was to be determined by their importance
to the National Grid and size of coal stocks.[35]
The ban had reduced deliveries to the power stations
by about 20% but as yet the winter had been mild
and electricity demand was not significantly
higher.   Low coal stocks coupled with a determined
attempt to stop the movement of coal meant that the
CEGB was vulnerable to a sudden change in the
weather.
     The first serious picketing clash in Yorkshire
occured at the Coalite Smokeless Fuel plant at
Grimethorpe in Barnsley.   Road tankers moving fuel
had been pelted with coke and the pickets from

Grimethorpe NUM branch reportedly stated their
determination to close the plant "by hook or by
crook".   It was also reported that the vast Ferrybridge power station complex was under "siege" by
pickets from the North Yorkshire Panel.[36]   By the
evening of 11 January the movement of coal was
virtually stopped.   The instructions issued by
the Yorkshire Area were brutally simple: "to
prevent the movement of coal and alternative fuels
between power stations, coal depots, and other coal
consumers."   NUR, ASLEF, and the TGWU would not
cross picket lines which "should therefore be
placed at strategic rail and road access points to
prevent the movement of coal and alternative
fuels ...."[37]   After a series of clashes between
pickets and drivers the police closed the
Grimethorpe plant.   The TGWU agreed to allow only
union labour to move fuel to destinations approved
by the NUM and the blacking of non-union haulage
firms began.[38]   Some 300 miners had been involved
in the Grimethorpe picket, and after this success
the tactic of the mass picket became the standard
weapon of the Yorkshire miners.[39]
     The organisation and deployment of the flying
pickets saw a qualitative change in the strike
as it became clear that it was not under the
detailed direction of the official union leaderships.   The refusal of the branches to undertake
safety work demonstrated depths of bitterness few
thought existed, and the flying pickets' effectiveness increased Government concern at the evolution
of the strike.[40]   Picketing successes and the
support of other unions led Schofield to declare
"I can envisage that at the outside - about four
weeks - there will be power cuts provided we
continue to receive the support we are receiving
from other unions."   Jack Leigh, the Vice-
President, forecast a six month strike and enhanced
picketing.[41]
     Information began to filter into the media on
the true state of coal stocks which revealed that
government estimates referred to the aggregate size
of national stocks of all types of coal, not all of
which were suitable for power station boilers.
Additionally, they were in the wrong places.   The
Government predicted it would take, on basis of
existing stocks, seven weeks for the strike to
bite.[42]
     On 18 January 121 pickets, known as the "flying
squad", left Barnsley for East Anglia to picket
power stations and ports.   By 20 January this 212

had grown to 1,000 and was described by one miner
as a "thousand bomber raid".[43]   Only oil remained
a problem: by the middle of January as increasing
numbers of tanker drivers were refusing to cross
NUM picket lines, so non-union drivers were used.
By the end of January, however, a number of key
industries, particularly steel, were beginning to
be affected by shortages of coke.[44]   At the end of
January the weather turned colder and electricity
demand increased, raising the likelihood of power-
cuts.   The CEGB maintained its power stations
were "under seige by mass pickets and a generating
capacity of 3,000MV (5% of national capacity) was
being lost." This was not so much a consequence of
a lack of coal but because the pickets were stopping
kindling oil, caustic soda, hydrogen gas and steel
piping from entering the power stations, forcing
the CEGB to reduce output to eke out existing
stocks.[45]
     Map 1 shows the power stations on, or near,
the Yorkshire coalfield.   Many of these were of the
most modern coal fired types,vital to the National
Grid supplying nearly 17% of total CEGB capacity.
These power stations generated 75% of the North
East Region's electricity.   Map 2 shows the power
stations in East Anglia.   Their pickets attracted
considerable attention but these power stations were
relatively unimportant, providing only 3% of
national capacity.

The Yorkshire Area's Strike Organisation
After three weeks of industrial action the miners
were having an impact beyond their wildest
expectations.   This was due to the effectiveness
of their pickets, organised by the Panels.[46]
There were over 1,000 pickets in East Anglia and
every pit, coal dump, port and coal installation
was covered by NUM pickets.[47]   The NEC issued a
circular on 21 January setting out targets but
the organisation and conduct of the strike lay with
the Area Unions, and in Yorkshire with the
Panels.[48]   The Yorkshire Area (NUM) HQ in Barnsley
acted as a clearing house and coordinator of
information.   The conduct of the strike was in
the hands of the branches who created a network of
contacts with other union branches which were so
vital to the miners' success.   Schofield wrote
to the Panels informing them of the transport
unions' commitments and advising them to create
closer liaison with the relevant union.   The Panels
then sent out requests for help to the local

branches of the TGWU, NUGMW, ASLEF,NUR, and the
AUEW.[49]   A Dawson (GMW Regional Secretary)
promised the closest cooperation; N P Pickles of
ASLEF wrote, "You can be assured of the support of
my members in your struggle"; and E Hayhurst of
the TGWU instructed his branches of the NUM's
position and that they do all in their power to
help.[50]   Yorkshire was allocated East Anglia and
the ports of Felixtowe, Harwich, Ipswich, Boston,
King's Lynn, Great Yarmouth and Colchester and
without the help of local trades councils they
would not have known where to begin.[51]   The Panels
in general organised all picketing teams on a
24 hour basis with a period allotted to a branch
who were responsible for providing the men.   There
was never any shortage of labour.   Even before
9 January the Panels had laid their plans and were
able to seal off coal supplies from the start.
The power stations were classified according to
capacity and picketed accordingly.[52]   The distribution of responsibility amongst the panels was:
Doncaster Panel - the major Yorkshire power
stations, the Barnsley Panel - the Barnsley area and
East Anglia, the North Yorkshire Panel - interme-
diate power stations and the Leeds-Wakefield area,
and the South Yorkshire Panel - the Sheffield and
Rotherham steel complexes, coke production plants,
coal and coke dumps and any power stations in the
area.   Barnsley was the basis of the East Anglian
pickets because the Panel organised and perfected
this type of picket, and more importantly there
were few coal using installations in Barnsley, so to
confine them to the Barnsley area would have been a
waste of resources.[53]

The Battle of the Power Stations
With the movement of coal halted, the pickets now
concentrated on stopping the movement of kindling
oil and other supplies into power stations.[54]
The Keadby power station, which was to be subject
of a trial of strength between the pickets and the
CEGB, had been stopped but re-started.   Panel
leaders learned from shop stewards that Keadby's
output was down by one-third but it could operate
on one-sixth of normal capacity for a considerable
period.   The power workers agreed to black any
supplies which crossed the picket line.[55]   Frequent
meetings were held at Thorpe Marsh with power
workers who gave the vital information that without
further supplies of oil the power station was in
danger of closing.   The pickets decided to stop all

tankers.[56]

On 24 January the East Anglian pickets
reported that all coal handling installations had
been blacked by the TGWU and were picketed.   Coal
supplies to the power station at Peterborough were
stopped, but pickets at Little Barford, Goldington
and Letchworth had been limited because of
accomodation problems.   Cliff Quay, closed by a mass
picket, was seen as a major victory.   South Denes
was a major problem.   It was oil fired and the
oil was pumped ashore from a sea terminal.
Generally, picketing was so effective pickets were
transferred to the Midlands.   ASLEF agreed not to
move coal into and within East Anglia.[57]

At Thorpe Marsh two road tankers carrying acid
and caustic soda had tried to run the pickets lines.
The Panel reported "It was necessary for the
pickets to lie in the road to stop the lorries.
At Flixborough barges carrying American coal for the
Anchor complex at BSC Scunthorpe were being unloaded.
Pickets were warned to check all road tankers by
turning on their valves as one, claiming to be
carrying distilled water, entered Keadby and power
workers reported it was carrying oil.[58]   The steel
workers federation instructed its members not to
move any coal in the Scunthorpe complex on the BSC's
private railway system.   There was now only 7,000
tons of coke in the entire complex.[59]   Thorpe
Marsh was still resisting but after a meeting
between pickets and shop stewards, the NUM achieved
the station's closure.   The picket was, however,
maintained so as to prevent a restart.[60]

The South Yorkshire Panel reported that of
their power stations, Mexborough had about 6,000
tons of coal left and the pickets had the
cooperation of the power workers;   at Blackburn
there was coal but no oil;   at Neepsend there was
both and the pickets were being maintained;   and
at Rotherham there was 500 tons at the main plant,
but 30,000 tons in stock half a mile away.   A
twenty-four hour picket was in force.   Main fuel
dumps had a twenty-four hour picket, while two
minor ones had only daylight cover.   Coke plants
were allowed to operate at a minimum level to keep
hot, but no coke was to leave.   Pickets were sent
to the Thorpe Marsh, Keadby and Doncaster power
stations.[61]

The North Yorkshire Panel enjoyed equal
success.   York power station was closed and the
picket moved on.   At Kirkstall (oil powered)
output was limited by an ASLEF agreement not to

move oil.   At Bradford power station there was a
twenty-four hour picket, as there was at Halifax,
Skelton Grange, Wakefield, Thornhill, Sculcoates
and Ferrybridge. The ports of Goole and Selby
were also covered.   The Panel paid tribute to
Leeds Trade Council and other unions, receiving
"tremendous support" from the NUR, ASLEF, TGWU and
GMWU.[62]
     The arrival of colder weather at the end of
January forced increasingly frequent power cuts
and lay offs in industry.   It was noticeable that
the miners' solidarity was undamaged and that they
enjoyed a considerable degree of public sympathy.[63]
Under the watchful eyes of the pickets Keadby and
Thorpe Marsh moved inexorably towards shut-down,
and shop stewards at BSC Scunthorpe reported output
was one-third of normal with management preparing
to shut the furnaces in three weeks.   In South
Yorkshire, two panel leaders, Abe Collins and
Eric Manns, persuaded the NUR to stop all coal
movements between BSC plants.[64]   The strike took
a tragic turn, however, with the death of a
picket, Frederick Mathews, at Keadby power station,
killed by a lorry which refused to stop.   He was
killed at the same time as arrests were made at
Stubbin and Wheldale as a result of increased police
activity to get NACODS men into the pits.[65]
Mathews' death raised the spectre of massive
retaliation from the miners: the Doncaster Panel
warned that their pickets were increasingly short
tempered and an emotional warning came from the NUM
sponsored MP, Alex Eadie.[66]   When Mathews was
killed it seemed that the Cabinet was seriously
contemplating a full State of Emergency.   Perhaps
the anger in the Commons and fears of the reaction
in the coalfields dissuaded the Cabinet from
taking any drastic action.[67]
     The other major event at this time was   "The
Battle of Saltley Gates".   On 7 February a report
was received in Barnsley that at the depot 600-700
police were allowing lorries to take away huge
amounts of coke.   There had already been four
arrests.[68]   The Yorkshire Area massed 700 pickets
mainly from the Barnsley Panel transferred from
East Anglia under Arthur Scargill.   The struggle
before the gates has now entered the mythology of
the union movement, and its symbolic importance
should not be denied.   Reinforcements were provided
by the Birmingham Trades Council, contingents were
sent by the TGWU and the engineers in the car plants
joined in the picketing.   The Cabinet, then,

presided over a steadily worsening and ugly
situation.   The NUM's appeals for help led to a
massive march on the depot which forced its eventual
closure.[69]   A State of Emergency was declared to
give the Government power to deal with the crisis,
but it was clear that it was too late.   Robert
Carr, the Home Secretary declared, these "sweeping
powers .... will be sensitively and sparingly
used" and would not involve the use of troops.[70]
In effect, the Government was powerless and the
strikers knew it.   The crippling of electricity
supplies and the emotions aroused by Saltley and
the death of Mathews would not be dampened by a
State of Emergency.[71]

Picketing at the Pits
As we have seen, official leaders emphasised the
need for cooperation with the NCB in safety and
emergency repair work, partly as a means of
keeping public sympathy.[72]   This had to be
reconciled with the need to win the strike and
pressure Government as quickly as possible to reach
a settlement.[73]   The pickets in Yorkshire instantly
closed the coalfield but a prime target became
those members of NACODS employed on safety, repair
and maintenance work.   Their continued activity
was seen by many, rightly or wrongly, as an affront
to the miners' solidarity.   A Council meeting three
days before the strike saw some dissent over the
NEC's instructions regarding safety and repair work.
Sam Bullough instructed that NACODS men be allowed
through picket lines without molestation.   Some
delegates, urging the principle of 'one out, all
out', tried to force acceptance of a resolution
demanding the removal of all labour, NUM or otherwise, from the pits.   Bullough refused.   The
suggestion was contrary to national policy: "I've
had to stick my neck out on this.   These pits have
got to be kept safe until the men get back to work.
This is one thing we've always done".[74]   The NEC
stated that pumpmen, winders, ventilation staff,
and telephone operators were to work and branch
committees, if asked for help, were to allocate
the minimum number necessary.[75]   Opponents argued
that if the NCB saw pits on the verge of collapse
they would be more willing to give in.   This
bitterness was symbolised by the branch's refusal
to help combat the fire at Goldthorpe-Highgate, a
decision supported by the Panel.[76]
        The Panels were bombarded with instructions
on the need for effective press relations, though

many miners were hostile to the media for quite
understandable reasons.   The Panels did, however,
do all in their power to ensure that fuel was
supplied to hospitals, schools, old people's homes
and cases of hardship and this allocation system
worked well.   The Panels were, however, less
willing to see NUM members remaining at work, no
matter how essential their services.[77]   Despite
NEC and Area instructions some pickets decided to
stop all work.   By early February police protection
for NACODS members was necessary, for example,
at Elsecar Main, Kiveton Park, Manvers Main, Cadeby
Main, Cortonwood, New Stubbin and Dinnington.
There was no safety cover at any of these pits
despite the NEC's and Area's strictures.[78]   This
intransigence came as a surprise given the miners'
traditional cooperation at work and their
interdependence in the pits for safety reasons.
However, it was, in fact, a facet of this occupational solidarity.   Nevertheless, this hostility
"as an unauthorised extension of official strike
action .... disconcerted both the Board and Union
leaders ...."[79]   In Yorkshire only three pits out
of 72 had any safety cover.   At Cadeby Main thirty
NACODS members went underground under a barrage of
bottles, bricks and stones which smashed thirty
windows in the pit yard; at Silverwood outside
Rotherham safety men were prevented from entering
the locker and lamp rooms and the approach roads to
Manvers and Stubbin were closed by road-blocks
defended by pickets.[80]   At Cadeby sixty hydraulic
jacks were crushed as no-one moved them despite an
NEC appeal for help.   The branch secretary, Tommy
Ryan, commented, "We are prepared to let the mining
industry decline of the Government does not think
it is important enough to solve the problem for
us."[81]   The imprudent attempt by Doncaster miners
to close Coal House, the NCB Area HQ, staffed mostly
by women and young girls (who were members of the
NUM), caused adverse publicity.   The Panel stopped
this picket.[82]
     As a consequence of these, and similar events,
claims were made that the coalfield was on the verge
of anarchy: Cadeby and Kilnhurst were under seige
by pickets and there were reports of brawling at
Silverwood.   The Cadeby miners, branded as the
Area's 'hard men', rejected this claiming violence
had been provoked by the 100 police on duty and by
the attitude of some NACODS members and management
who claimed there had been riots at Cadeby and
Kilnhurst where over 300 pickets were present.

A car had been overturned at Cadeby, at Kilnhurst
the pit entrance was blocked by a bonfire, and at
Silverwood there had been "street fighting" with
pickets chasing NACODS members through the village.
At Cortonwood ten men were injured on the picket
line.[83]   Some fears were expressed that the strike
was being infiltrated by 'outsiders' and the
Executive called for their rejection.[84]   The
Wheldale branch sought the extension of the strike
calling on the NUM and "on all other Unions to
mobilise their members on a united front with the
miners, to force this Tory Government to resign
and return a Labour Government pledged to implementing policies of a true and honest socialist
principle."   This was not accepted, but the death
of Frederick Mathews led to an outburst of anger.
The South Kirby branch moved "That this Council
Meeting calls upon the NEC to withdraw safety men,
including NACODS from all collieries, and it is
our opinion that this could force the Government to
concede sooner, rather than later."[85]   This was
approved by 58 votes to 21.
    An NCB announcement that four faces at Cadeby,
a pit in danger of closure, were about to collapse
and £500,000 of equipment would be destroyed was
greeted with indifference by the branch, and further
it redoubled its efforts to stop NACODS men
entering the pits despite a Panel decision.[86]   So
severe was the hostility that the NCB Area Directors
wrote to Joe Gormley complaining of the problems
at Cadeby, Cortonwood, Dinnington, Kilnhurst,New
Stubbin and Ackton Hall (with Cadeby as the worst
trouble spot) asking for his intercession.   Neither
he nor the Area were able to do anything, and at
Cortonwood the safetymen and winders joined the
strike.[87]   The Area continued to issue instructions
and warnings on offers of outside help and the
publication of pamphlets favourable to the miners,
whilst urging the branches to remember that the
media would focus on any violence on the picket
lines.[88]   Branches were warned that a refusal to
obey instructions would mean the ending of Union
money to finance picketing and disciplinary action
was threatened.[89]   By contrast, the South Yorkshire
Panel reported that its pickets at the coke plants
were becoming frustrated: "Pickets are considering
that it is pointless in these circumstances, a
feeling is growing 'that the gloves should be of'.
This is a very ticklish situation and will need
watching".   The Doncaster panel, angered by the
CEGB's use of a helicopter to fly supplies into

Thorpe Marsh   reported the "hotting up" of their
action, and the North Yorkshire Panel was
concentrating on stopping the few remaining NACODS
members at work.[90]   The Area's response fell
largely on deaf ears: "We feel no helpful purpose
can be served by picketing either colliery officials
or management .... such action may well have the
undesired and two-fold effect of stemming the rise
of public sympathy and providing evidence for the
Government and the Board of a growing conflict
between Trade Unions in the industry - a situation
they may well exploit."[91]   The mass pickets gave
the media all the copy they desired, their success
being portrayed as the opening of the floodgates
of anarchy:

> Already many people seem intent on shouting
> the Heath Government out of office whatever
> the voters at the polls might have said in
> 1970.... Arguments about the justice of the
> miners' claims now give way to fears for the
> security of the State.[92]

A member of the Barnsley strike committee was
quoted as saying: "I don't care what the NUM says
about pickets, the strike committee here will
decide when to reduce picket numbers."   The media
could not appreciate why miners were prepared to
see faces collapse and be sealed.   T Race, the
branch treasurer of Bentley branch, argued this was
because, "If we allowed the men in there would be a
split in our solidarity.   The men are bitter, and
are prepared to see the lid put on the pit if the
Coal Board are not prepared to pay them a decent
living."[93]   Despite this eloquence, the correspon-
dent doubted that Race really spoke for his members.
On 9 January few believed the miners would
win.[94]   Their victory was signalled by the appointment of the Wilberforce Inquiry which met during
massive power cuts, lay-offs of thousands of
workers and virtually no safety cover in the
Yorkshire coalfield.   Suggestions were made that
the NUM should now relax its action: this was
refused categorically.   The miners' success was
largely due to their pickets and the inability or
unwillingness of the authorities to deal with them.[96]
The police might have used the picketing provisions
under the 1875 and 1906 Acts, but without the
authority of the Government behind them, local
police forces responded by avoiding, where possible,
confrontation.   Mass pickets posed those same

problems associated with the mass arrests of miners
at Betteshanger in 1942 which made a bad situation
worse.[96]   The NEC accepted the Wilberforce Report,
though there were some fears of a militant
'blacklash', the coalfields accepted, and on
22 February picketing ended.[97]

The Wilberforce Report and Its Consequences

The NCB, as a nationalised undertaking, was not a
free agent in its relationship with the NUM.   Thus,
it was clear from the start that the strike would
be ended by Government intervention of one type or
another.   All attempts at a settlement foundered
on the NUM's demand for more on basic rates which
required Government approval.[98]   The NEC's
'negative' attitude, coupled with the Cabinet's
belief it could last out a strike stopped any
further talks.[99]   As the strike began to bite the
Government was pressured into settling: the power
cuts, Saltley, a picket's death, the lay-offs and
the miners' undiminished solidarity made a settlement imperative.   The Government's assumptions
concerning coal stocks had meant that no counter-
measures were ready and so they were forced to sit
back and watch the evolution of the strike.[100]
    On 9 February the NCB offered £2.75/£3.50
increases, phased over 18 months, costing them
£48m.   The NEC confidently rejected this.   The
Government denied they had sanctioned the new offer,
and on 10 February the CEGB announced that power
cuts would become operative.[101]   The Government's
response was to appoint a Court of Inquiry under
the Act of 1919 with the express purpose of finding
a settlement before the economy was damaged
further.[102]   The NUM used the inquiry to expose
mining's harshness and the level of low pay, just
as their predecessors had used earlier commissions
to expose the iniquities of private ownership.
Wilberforce's main conclusion was that miners were a
"special case" because of the importance of their
industry, the arduous nature of their work, and
their history of full cooperation with the NCB and
Government during the years of contraction.   Thus,

> We think it an essential part of the present
> settlement that the miners' basic claim for
> a general and exceptional increase should be
> recognised.   We believe this is accepted
> by public opinion and if it cannot be paid
> for out of the NCB's revenue account, in
> accordance with its statutory obligations,

> we think that the public, through the
> Government, should accept the charge.[103]

The strike was ended when the Government announced
its full and complete acceptance of the Report's
recommendations.[104]   Wilberforce could be seen
as nothing less than a crushing defeat of the Heath
Government's anti-inflation policy and a total
victory for the mineworkers.

The 1972 strike was officially described as
"the most important event of our lifetime":

> We were victorious because we had a just
> cause and we acquired the necessary
> ingredients: official leadership of the
> Union, official support from the TUC and
> the national Labour Party, and, last but
> not least, we had the overwhelming majority
> of the people behind us.[105]

Some of these factors were clearly vital: the
support of the TUC and public opinion for example,
but this account omits the role of the mass mobile
pickets.   Indeed, an attempt was made to divert
attention away from these new tactics.[106]   In
essence, the miners' victory was due to three
factors: first, the mineworkers' absolute commitment to victory.   During the 1972 strike bitterness
at their harsh treatment since the 1950s exploded.
This was well portrayed by Lawrence Daly:

> The miner has been persuaded to greater
> effort by successive governments, and he
> has responded.   He has been crushed by
> government policies which have obliterated
> whole mining communities in the national
> interest .... and he has accepted that
> tragedy in a manner born from years of
> living and working with imminent disaster.
> Many of those who survived these calamaties
> and worked on the industry moved round the
> country experiencing two or three further
> pit closures, wishing in desperation for a
> stable situation.   Those who remained in
> the areas of fairly secure employment were
> naturally uncertain about their future in
> the industry and consequently inhibited
> in their approach on matters relating to pay
> and conditions.[107]

In Yorkshire "acceptance" and "inhibition" gave away

in 1969 and 1970, and by 1971-1972 NPLA created
a common national unrest.   This, coupled with the
above frustrations, created the determination to
win the strike.
      Second, it was very simple for the NUM to stop
all coal production and the movement of coal from
the pitheads.   Of crucial importance were the fuel
dumps and power stations away from the pits.   The
NUM recognised this and secured the agreement of the
transport unions not to cross NUM picket lines.
Their solidarity was encouraged by a general
hostility to the Heath Government amongst the union
movement and the government, unwilling and unable
to coerce the miners, capitulated, using Wilberforce
to legitimise surrender.
      The final factor was the NUM's disruption of
power supplies.   The economy's dependence upon
centrally generated electricity was eloquently
demonstrated by the power workers work to rule in
1970:   the dispute began on 7 December and on
12 December a Court of Inquiry under Lord
Wilberforce was appointed to settle the dispute.
This demonstrated that to hinder electricity
production, which was dependent upon coal, would
disrupt the whole economy and that faced with such
a prospect the Government would not fight.
      The outcome of the strike gave a tremendous
boost to the miners' self-confidence.   The strike
was led and organised by the membership and their
immediate leaders and the miners were elevated into
the leaders of the Labour Movement, the symbol of
resistance to the Conservative Government.   For the
Yorkshire miners it led to the emergence of a new
generation of leaders committed to more militant
policies and in June 1972 Arthur Scargill was
elected Area Compensation Agent signalling the
left's arrival.

REFERENCES

1   NUM: Annual Conference Report, 1971;   p93
          (President's Address).
2   Annual Conference;   p88
3   Annual Conference;   Agenda;   p.xiii.   The
          figures were: £26 (surface), £28
          (underground) and £35 (NPLA).
4   Annual Conference;   pp134-135
5   Annual Conference;   pp173-181.
6   JNNC;   1st September and 14 September 1971.
7   JNNC;   12 October 1971.
8   NUM(EC);   14 October 1971.

9   NUM: Special Conference Report, 21 October
           1971; p9.
10   NUM(EC); 9 December 1971.
11   NUM(EC); 16 December 1971.
12   NUM(EC); 21 December 1971.
13   YA(NUM); 22 October 1971; and,
           BS Circular 107/71 (15 October 1971)
14   YA(NUM); 1 November 1971.
           The Branch vote on the overtime ban was;
           for, 1743; against, 0 with a turnout of
           94.3%.
           NUM(EC); 25 October 1971.
15   BS Circular 114/71 (25 October 1971)
16   YA(NUM); 4 November 1971.
17   YA(NUM); 9 November 1971.
           Council approved this statement by 28 votes
           to 4.
18   As Circular 285/71 (9 December 1971)
19   The Economist; 8 January 1972.
20   This point was made to me on numerous occasions
           in conversation with miners on the 1972
           strike.
21   The Economist; 8 January 1972.
     The Times (Business News); 3 January 1972.
22   The Times; 3 January 1972.
           See also;
           NCB: Annual Reports and Accounts, 1972-
           1973; para 46.   At this time the NCB
           claimed total coal stocks of 32.4m tons,
           50% of which was already distributed to
           power stations.   It was estimated this
           would last nine weeks.
23   Morning Telegraph; 3 January 1972.
24   The rumours of a compromise emanated from a
           Gromley-Ezra meeting at a Coal industry
           Society lunch.   The reaction of the
           Yorkshire miners to these rumours was
           "guarded, but with a hint of anger."
           Arthur Scargill commented; " There   must
           be no sell out, otherwise the miners will
           never forgive the leadership of this Union."
           Morning Telegraph; 4 January 1972.
           From reports of this meeting it is clear
           that there was no real hope of a settlement.
25   The Times; 6 January 1972, and,
           NUM(EC); 5 January 1972.
26   The Times; 6 January 1972 (Editorial: 'Miners
           on the Brink').
27   The Times; 8 January 1972.

28   <u>TUC</u>: Press Statements; 10 and 11 January
       1972; <u>and</u>,
       <u>The Times</u>; 7, 8, and 10 January 1972.
       The 10 January meeting with the TUC was of
       crucial importance in helping decide the
       outcome of the strike as it had soon
       become apparent that although coal stocks
       were large they were, in general, badly
       distributed: therefore the transport of
       these stocks was a crucial element in the
       strike. See:
       <u>The Times</u> (Business News), 8 January 1972.

29   <u>YA(NUM)</u>; 6 January 1972; <u>and</u>,
       <u>Morning Telegraph</u>; 7 January 1972.

30   <u>Morning Telegraph</u>; 8 January 1972 (Article:
       'The Law of the Fist!

31   This account is drawn from;
       <u>The Times</u>; 10 January 1972; <u>and</u>,
       <u>Morning Telegraph</u>; 10 January 1972.
       In the final analysis the fire was not as
       serious as was first thought. Neverthe-
       less, the hysteria the incident aroused in
       the press is an interesting comment on
       attitudes at the time.

32   <u>The Times</u>; 11 January 1972.

33   <u>The Times</u>; 11 January 1972.

34   <u>Morning Telegraph</u>; 12 January 1972.
       The same paper had noted that on the
       11th of January there were "no serious
       picketing clashes" in Yorkshire. For
       Yorkshire's picketing targets, see;
       <u>BS Circular</u> 5/1972 (6 January 1972); <u>and</u>,
       <u>AS Circular</u> 300/71 (30 December 1971).
       The above AS Circular described the creation
       of liaison committees with local trade
       unions.

35   <u>The Times</u> (Business News); 11 January 1972.
       For NUM preparations see;
       <u>AS Circular</u> 11/72 (January 1972); <u>and</u>,
       12/22 (12 January 1972).

36   <u>Morning Telegraph</u>; 12 January 1972.
       It was also reported that there was serious
       shortage of domestic coal in South
       Yorkshire.

37   <u>YA(NUM)</u>; 12 January 1972.

38   <u>Morning Telegraph</u>; 13 January 1972.
       It is at this point the first editorials on
       the new picketing tactics appear, for
       example, 'Anarchy and the Pit Head', which
       pointed out that the miners had broken the
       law but nothing could be done because of the

numbers involved.
39   Morning Telegraph;   14 and 15 January 1972.
40   The Economist;   15 January 1972.
         At this time the NCB made a fresh appeal to
         the NUM for arbitration.   Gormley's reply
         was;   "The day for arbitration is passed.
         It is money we want."   See also:
         The Times.   14 January 1972.
41   The Times;   15 and 18 January 1972;   and,
         Morning Telegraph;   15 and 18 January 1972.
42   Morning Telegraph: 22 January 1972.
43   The Times;   19 January 1972;   and,
         Morning Telegraph;   21 January 1972.
         For an account of the organisation of the
         East Anglian strike committee, see;
         Morning Star;   20 January 1972.
44   The Times;   24 January and 29 January 1972.
45   The Economist;   5 February 1972;   and,
         The Times;   31 January 1972.
46   On the 13 January the General Purposes Sub-
         Committee of the NEC   "Recommended that
         Areas should provide transport, food and
         accommodation" for pickets outside mining
         areas.   At a subsequent meeting of the
         Finance and General Purposes Sub-Committee
         it was agreed that initially Areas should
         finance picketing outside mining areas but
         at the conclusion of the strike these costs
         would be met from national funds.
         NUM(EC);   12 January 1972 (Appendix I);and,
         NUM(EC);   Finance and General Purposes
         Sub-Committee;   24 January 1972.
47   As Circular   22/72 (13 January 1972).
48   As Circular 35/72 (21 January 1972).
49   1972 Strike File: South Yorkshire Panel
         Correspondence, Letter from Sidney
         Schofield, 30 December 1971 (to all Panels).
50   1972 Strike File: Daily Report,
         3 - 5 January 1972.
51   1972 Strike File;   Miscellaneous Documents.
52   1972 Strike File: Miscellaneous Documents.
53   1972 Strike File;   General Report, 21 January
         1972.
54   1972 Strike File;   Panel Report, 19, 20, and
         21 January 1972.   The picketing was so
         effective that South Yorkshire Panel (for
         example) was able to send 55 men for duty
         in East Anglia.
55   1972 Strike File;   Doncaster Panel Report,
         22 January 1972.

56 1972 Strike File; Doncaster Panel Report,
      21 January 1972.
57 1972 Strike File; General Report,
      24 January 1972.
58 1972 Strike File; Letter File, 27 January
      1972.
59 1972 Strike File; Letter File, 28 January
      1972.
60 1972 Strike File; Panel Reports, 29 January
      1972. An illustration of the importance
      of Panel control can be seen in North
      Yorkshire's agreement to allow the
      movement of hydrogen by permit -- but only
      four were ever issued. In South Yorkshire
      it was reported that only 500 tons of
      boiler coal remained, plus 15,000 tons of
      Coalite solid fuel.
61 1972 Strike File; South Yorkshire Panel
      Report, 26 January 1972.
62 1972 Strike File; North Yorkshire Panel
      Report, 26 January 1972.
63 The Economist; 5 February 1972.
64 1972 Strike File; Panel Reports,
      31 January, 2 February, and 3 February 1972,
      Morning Telegraph, 26 January 1972.
65 The Times; 4 February 1972; and,
      Morning Telegraph: 2 February, and
      4 February 1972.
66 5s H C Debs 830 (February 1972); col. 677.
67 The Times; 4 February 1972.
      Pickets were now discussing how to stop
      convoys under military escort entering
      power stations.
68 1972 Strike File; Panel Report, 7 February
      1972.
69 The Times; 7 February and 8 February 1972.
70 The Times; 9 February 1972.
71 The Times; 10 February and 11 February 1972.
      See also;
      A Scargill, 'The New Unionism', in, New
      Left Review 92(1975); pp14-20. See also,
      Report of a Meeting between officials
      of the Yorkshire Area (NUM) and representa-
      tives of the EEPTU, TGWU and NUR at AUEW
      House, Sheffield 10 February 1982, in
      1972 Strike File.
72 The Miner 33 (October/November) 1971.
73 The Miner (Strike Issue): January 1972.
74 YA(NUM); 6 January 1972; and,
      Morning Telegraph; 7 January 1972.
      In a strike in 1919 the YMA had withdrawn

pumpmen from the pits and the Government responded by using naval ratings to operate the pumps.

75   As Circular 30/71 (30 December 1971).
76   YA(NUM); 14 January 1972.
77   As Circular 11/72 (10 January 1972).
78   Morning Telegraph; 3 February 1972; and,
      AS Circular 12/72 (12 January 1972).
79   The Times; 28 January 1972 (Leader).
80   Morning Telegraph; 8 February 1972.
81   The Times; 25 January 1972.
82   See, for example,
      Morning Telegraph; 22 January 1972; and,
      BS Circular 38/72 (29 January 1972).
      The Area Executive commented caustically
      there were more worthwhile targets than
      Coal House.
83   Morning Telegraph; 9 February 1972.
84   YA(NUM); 17 January 1972.
85   YA(NUM); 27 January 1972.
86   YA(NUM); 7 February 1972.
87   Correspondence in 1972 Strike File, and,
      Morning Telegraph, 24 and 25 January 1972.
88   BS Circular 35/72 (29 January 1972).
89   YA(NUM); 12 February 1972, and Morning
      Telegraph, 12 February 1972.
90   1972 Strike File: South Yorkshire Panel
      Report, 8 February; Doncaster Panel Report,
      8 February; General Report, 9 February;
      and North Yorkshire Panel Report,
      10 February 1972.
91   BS Circular 55/73 (15 February 1972), and,
      General Report, 12 February 1972.
92   Yorkshire Post, 17 February 1972 ('Britains
      Peril). The Area had instructed the Panels
      to use the minimum number of pickets, see,
      BS Circular 57/72 (16 February 1972). The
      Economist, 12 February 1972 was now under
      the control of the militants, a term left
      underfined.
93   Doncaster Evening Post, 17 February 1972.
94   The Times, 11 January 1972.
95   Morning Telegraph, 12 February 1972.
96   The Economist, 19 February 1972.
97   Morning Telegraph, 18 February 1972; YA(NUM),
      21 February 1972; and, Financial Times,
      22 February 1972.
98   Morning Telegraph 5 January and 6 January
      1972; and, The Times, 7 January 1972.
99   For an account of the DE's role at this stage
      see, AS Circular 11/72 (10 January 1972).

100 The Economist, 22 January 1972.
101 The Times 10 and 11 February 1972.
102 The Economist, 12 February 1972, and, Report
     of a Court of Inquiry Cmnd 4903
     (February 1972); para 8.
103 Report, para 42.   The NUM's case and evidence
     to Wilberforce is set out in, J Hughes &
     R Moore (eds), A Special Case?   Social
     Justice and The Miners (NUM/Penguin,
     Harmondsworth 1972).   See also, The Times
     and The Guardian, 14-17 February 1972.
104 The Times and The Guardian, 19 February 1972.
105 YA(NUM) Annual Report, 1972, pp98-99.
106 Annual Reports, p113
107 Hughes & Moore(eds), A Special Case?, p14-15.

Chapter Nine

THE NATIONAL COAL STRIKE OF 1974

The Aftermath to 1972

Victory not only increased the self-confidence of
the Yorkshire miners, but also, as we have seen,
transformed the Area's leadership with the
election of Arthur Scargill as Compensation Agent.
This new self-confidence, indeed truculence, can
be seen in their attitude to the Industrial
Relations Act.   The Grimethorpe and Barnburgh
branches put forward resolutions to Council which
sought to nullify the Act.   Barnburgh, for example,
urged the NEC to discuss the Act "with a view to
taking the strongest possible action including
strike action", and proposed total non-cooperation
with the Act.   Any person, or union, prosecuted
under the Act should be supported by strike
action.[1]   Similarly, the Glasshoughton branch, a
branch with a coalfield wide reputation for
moderation, urged the Yorkshire Area to actively
resist the implementation of the Housing Finance
Act (1972).[2]   However, miners' wages remained
the most important and sensitive issue.   The 1972
NUM Conference approved Composite Resolution VII
seeking wages rates of £30 (surface), £32 (underground), and £40 (NPLA).   This enjoyed the support
of the NEC and was passed unanimously.
        Historically, government has been a more or
less permanent factor in the politics of the coal
industry, a factor confirmed in 1972.   This strike
had demonstrated the enhanced economic and
political power of the NUM as coal had been the one
energy source that successive British governments
believed wholly reliable and dependable in a world
where Arab governments came and went.   The natural
response of the media to the miners' victory was to
question the dependence upon coal.[4]   Despite the
new self-confidence and the rise of the left, the
NUM as a whole was not fully reconciled to the NUM's
new role and feared it might overplay its hand.

239

Schofield warned of the temptations of 'political'
strikes:

> It would be fatal if we, through our
> impetuosity as trade unionists, took
> action of a kind that could change the
> attitude of millions of people, who
> would be prepared to support our cause
> at the next election .... I am of course
> referring to the possibility of a general
> strike to combat the Government's policy
> on pay and prices.   Of course the policy
> is unfair .... but a General Strike is the
> worst thing that could happen.[5]

The legacy of 1926 remained powerful.
    Whilst the Yorkshire miners were warned
against the deceptive attraction of direct action
they showed their solidarity with those engaged
in such action.   The imprisonment of the
'Pentonville Five' led to the calling of a special
NEC.   The TUC General Purposes Committee had met on
21 July and had voted by 18 to 6, with
6 abstentions, for a one day national strike.   The
NEC believed there was a possibility of unofficial
action in the coalfields, such calls coming
from Nottingham and Derbyshire, the South Wales
Area Conference recommended industrial action, and
so on.   Despite the release of the dockers the
NEC called on the TUC to organise a one day
national strike as the first step to breaking the
Act.[6]   The opposition to the Housing Finance Act
prompted Council to urge all NCB tenants to organise
themselves and "agrees to support and defend by
any means available those Socialist representatives
on Labour controlled Councils who may by subject
to penalties as a result of .... refusing to
implement the (Act) ..."[7]
    The NEC had a definite claim to present to
the NCB, but there was an awareness of the dangers
of repeating the 1972 negotiating process.   Before
presenting their claim, the NUM's negotiating team
on the JNNC requested that the submission of the
claim be deferred to allow papers to be prepared
on the cost implications of the claim before
they met again in October.[8]   The NEC, then, put
a brake on the negotiating process: why?
    After Wilberforce talks had been held between
the NUM, NCB and Government on the level of
financial support needed by the industry.[9]   Such
assistance was clearly vital if the NCB was to pay

the wages award. Consequently, the NEC was
concerned to ensure that the Government produced
a sympathetic Coal Industry Bill, hence the NEC's
reluctance to pursue agressively the wage claim.
In August 1972, Tom Boardman, the Minister of
Industry, received a report from the Committee
which urged both sides of the industry to secure
the future of the industry in return for Government
money.[10]   The Yorkshire Area was suspicious of
the JNNC decision of 13 September.   The Area
Executive wrote to the NEC reiterating Yorkshire's
total commitment to Conference decisions on wages
and that they expected the NEC to reflect this
total commitment.[11]   The October JNNC meeting
announced that the background papers were not
ready and would only be so in December.   The
JNNC decided to press ahead with those elements
of the claim relating to wages, hours and
differentials, reflecting a concern at a possible
adverse reaction from the membership over delay.[12]
The Union's team on the JNNC decided to modify
the claim in line with the finances of the
industry, formulating a list of priorities with
wages and hours coming first, and to hold talks
with the NCB and report to the NEC in December.[13]
      By November there was no sign of the Coal
Industry Bill.   Boardman, in response to NEC
pressure, agreed to publish a bill before the
Christmas recess.   This was done and referred
to the Economic Sub-Committee.[14]   Two informal
meetings were held with the NCB: the first saw
the presentation of the putative claim; and at
the second, the NCB stated it was "beyond the
Board's capability to achieve in one exercise."
In the spirit of cooperation the NCB suggested
a joint sub-committee to examine ways of paying
the wages sought by the NUM.[15]   The JNNC's
actions were considered and approved by the full
NEC and a full claim was to be submitted in
January 1973.[16]

The Failure of Cooperation, 1972-1973
In November 1972 the Government imposed a ninety-
day freeze on wages.   Phase 1 was to be replaced
by Phase 2 in the spring of 1973 with a pay limit
of £1 per week + 4%.   A Pay Board and Price
Commission was established to police the policy.
The NUM submitted its wage claim, which
clearly breached the policy in January.[17]

Government policy forced the NCB to emphasise
that only £25m was available for wage increases,
whereas the full claim would cost £105m and no
offer was made on hours.   The NUM responded
that "there was considerable pressure for improvement in wages throughout the coalfields and that
they intended to adhere to the decision taken
by the TUC General Council to oppose the
Government's Stage II proposals."[18]
     The death of Sam Bullough on 21 January
ushered in a new era for the Yorkshire Area.   At
a meeting of the Executive it was proposed that
Scargill become acting General Secretary as
Schofield was ill, whilst Jack Leigh acted as
President.   A proposal to make Scargill acting-
General Secretary received 17 votes, a counter
proposal, 4 votes.   Thus, Scargill was appointed
acting General Secretary.   At the same meeting
grave disquiet was expressed at pay policy, and
Council was asked to decide on policy.[19]
     Despite the rejection of the wage claim the
NEC decided to continue negotiations, whilst
reiterating opposition to Phase 2.   Resistance,
however, is "the larger question (and) was one
for the whole movement" and the miners did not
want to be isolated challenging the Government at
an unfavourable time of year.[20]   Several Yorkshire
branches vociferously attacked government policy
"as being grossly and unfairly weighted against
the working class" and Council called for a
Special Conference, the recall of the TUC and that
the NEC consider an immediate overtime ban to
emphasise the NUM's opposition to pay policy.[21]
The NUM's members on the JNNC, stressing "their
willingness to continue negotiations", again met
with the Board who reiterated that they were
forbidden to go beyond the provisions on Phase 2.
Despite this, and the attitude of some coalfields,
the NUM felt it had no other option other than
to negotiate.[22]
     In response to Phase 2 the TUC called a
Special Congress for 5 March.   The NUM'S stance
was to be decided by the NEC on 28 February.[23]
The TUC's response, in fact, offered no immediate
solution to the movement's problem but articulated
the long term aim of creating "the framework of
policies any Government would need to adopt to
obtain the support of workpeople in a joint
endeavour to control inflation."[24]   It was,
therefore, part of the TUC's longstanding attempt
to become an integral part of the Whitehall

economic policy machine, an aim accepted by
Heath after 1972.   The NEC accepted that this
document offered no positive response to Phase 2,
deciding that Gormley would move its reference
back.[25]   At Special TUC the policy was narrowly
rejected and the NUM delegation supported a
resolution calling on the TUC to force the
Government to abandon wages policy or call a
General Election.   Delegates, however, rejected
suggestions for a national day of action.
Gormley's speech is interesting and deserves
quoting at length as it reveals the pressures
within the NUM at this time;

> .... We can no longer carry on as a
> responsible organisation just
> expressing our opposition to
> Government policy and submitting
> alternatives without having the
> necessary ambition to do something
> positive if it does not change the
> Government's direction ... There
> will be many critics who will say that
> this would be an attempt to get the
> Trade Union Movement to use its
> industrial strength to defeat the
> Government and thereby bring about a
> General Election ... It is against
> the Government's policy and therefore
> can be termed a political strike ...[26]

Both left and right in the NUM were conscious
that any further dispute with the Heath
Government might necessitate a 'political strike'.
For the moment, however, negotiating remained
the only option.   Gormley and Ezra decided to
meet the Minister to find a way out.   The NCB
had offered a third week's holiday as part of the
settlement.   However, " Despite considerable
pressure .... the Minister was adamant that (this)
would be outside Phase 2 .... and could not be
allowed."   The NEC was left with an offer of
an average increase of £2.29 plus other
concessions.   After a lengthy discussion the NEC
agreed that the offer was unsatisfactory and that
the membership should be consulted in a ballot,
with a recommendation to support industrial
action.[27]   This was endorsed and approved by
Council.[28]   Yorkshire was committed to militant
opposition to Phase 2, but this was not reflected

nationally: 143,006 voted in favour of the
settlement, and 82,361 against. Only Yorkshire
and Scotland voted in favour of industrial
action. Of the 78 Yorkshire branches 40 votes
in favour of industrial action and 38 against.
The total vote was 25,683 (53%) for and 22,670
(47%) against. Upon recovening, the NCB pointed
out that the offer had been made under Phase 2
and any settlement implemented after 8 April might
be referred to the Pay Board. The NEC accepted
the offer.[29]

The NUM as a whole was clearly unhappy with
the experience of 1972-1973, particularly with
the role of the Government. The NEC's unanimous
acceptance of a strike call reflected the NEC's
animosity to the Cabinet over the long series of
negotiations and particularly their refusal to
concede the extra weeks' holiday.[30] Both the
NUM and Government were aware that the time was
long past for effective strike action. Nevertheless, the union's anger was real. In 1973
Scargill was elected Compensation Agent and later
President, also in 1973 Owen Briscoe was elected
General Secretary.[31] Scargill and Briscoe
occupied the two most important posts in the Area
and enjoyed mass support. There were some
remarkable expressions of verbal militancy from
this new leadership. For example, Owen Briscoe
wrote, "Ted Heath and his fascist dominated
government had been obsessed with hatred towards
the miners ever since the 1972 strike" and warned
the Yorkshire miners to expect them to seek
revenge.[32] When the NUM Conference met in July,
pay policy was governed by Phase 2; the NUM's
claim had been made under Phase 1 which had the
effect of extending Wilberforce by one month. The
NUM sought to return to the 1 November date.[33]
The NUM was determined to secure its wages demands
and Joe Gormley, in his Presidential Address,
repeated the sentiments made at the Special TUC:

> .... Never again will British miners be
> used during a period of energy shortage,
> never again will we say we shall be more
> loyal to the rest of the country than to
> our own members. We shall say to the
> country and the world that we will
> provide the coal they need .... but they
> are going to have to pay the right price
> for it.[34]

He gave the Union three aims: first, the
highest industrial wage; second, better sick and
injury pay; and finally, better retirement
provisions.   The Conference's centre-piece was
Composite Resolution IV(Scotland, the Power Group,
COSA, and the Midlands Area) demanding minimum
wages of £35/£40/£45 to be secured by strike action
if necessary.   The resolution was moved by Mick
McGahey who interpreted it as a direct assault on
the Government's pay policy.[35]   Arthur Scargill
cautioned Conference that "when we are discussing
the wages resolution, we are dealing with the most
immoral, the most corrupt government in living
memory .... They have been absolutely sincere and
dedicated to their class and to the people who
support them."[36]   Composite IV was passed
unanimously.   Speaking on the general situation
in the industry Daly stated, "We are going to face..
..a confrontation.   A confrontation not of our
making but of the making of 'Benito' Heath..... A
confrontation arises only when just and legitimate
demands are rejected...."[37]   Clearly, the NUM was
in no mood to repeat the experience of 1972-1973.

The Negotiation of the 1974 Wage Claim
The NUM's wage claim was submitted on 13 July, only
days after the conclusion of Conference.   The
most important elements were wage rates of £35/£40/
£45 and a return to the pre-Wilberforce settlement
date of 1 November.   The NUM stressed the deterioration of their wages relative to other groups since
1972, that the energy situation was increasingly
favourable to coal, and warned of the strong
feelings in the coalfields.   For its part, the
NCB reminded the NUM that the April 1973 settlement
was due to run until March 1974;   therefore the
1 November starting date was out of the question,
and that it had paid the maximum allowable under
Phase 2 to run for the minimum allowable time.[38]
After hearing a report on these negotiations the
Yorkshire Area Council demanded that the NEC
institute an overtime ban from 1 November, warning
"that a failure to implement a national overtime
ban could result in the Yorkshire Area imposing
a ban unilaterally."[39]
Not only was the NCB's offer within Phase 3,
Phase 3 had been formulated specifically with the
miners in mind.   The Board offered wage increases
amounting to about 7%, an increased shift allowance,
further wage concessions of 1% to account for
flexibility, one day's holiday, a productivity

agreement to be negotiated, and threshold agreements. The NEC agreed to consider the offer.[40] Subsequently, the NEC decided to seek a meeting with Heath and to reject the 7% as insufficient. It also agreed to meet the TUC to sound out its attitude and a Special Conference was called for the 26 October.[41]

The NEC met the TUC first on 16 October where they were informed that TUC policy was for unions to ignore Phase 3 in collective bargaining. On 23 October they met Heath. The NUM put its case in very strong terms and the Prime Minister agreed to consider it carefully, but his Government's main concern was the battle against inflation of which Phase 3 was the corner-stone. The NEC decided to recommend to the Special Conference the calling of an overtime ban, but it stressed it "should not follow the pattern of the previous overtime ban, but should be a complete ban on all overtime, which would mean that men would only work their normal five shifts a week regardless of circumstances."[42] The ban would begin when the NEC thought the time was right.

Significantly, when the NUM's claim had been rejected it did not argue with the Board: "They pay no attention to the statistics .... because (they fall) in line with Government policy ...."[43] The NEC's early decision to consult the membership during negotiations (albeit by a Special Conference which was bound to support militant action) together with recommending an overtime ban was to speed negotiations and encourage a settlement. A total overtime ban, plus coal's new market importance after the OPEC oil price rise and export embargo would, it was hoped, encourage the Government to relent. This was accepted by the Special Conference.

Two informal meetings were held between the NUM and NCB on 30 October and 6 November. The NCB regretfully insisted that it could not go beyond Phase 3 and had already made the maximum possible offer. The mineworkers representatives were forced to recommend the NEC formally reject the offer.[44] This was accepted: it was further decided to begin the ban on 12 November and withdraw all men except skeleton teams to keep the coke ovens hot. BACM and NACODS members were not to be hindered and an emergency committee was created to manage the ban nationally. [45] Manifestly, the crucial distinction between then and 1972 was that the NUM was directly

challenging a statutory incomes policy.
This caused some qualms: some NEC members
"suggested that the Union was being placed in a
position of opposing the law of the land not the
NCB or the Government. Therefore, such action
was political, not industrial." This was
countered by those who argued "it was the job of a
Trade Union to fight for its members if they were
not being fairly treated regardless of who must
be fought." Existing policy was re-affirmed.[46]
    On 28 November the NEC at its request met with
the Cabinet, and this meeting is important as it
set out both sides' positions and so helps explain
the strange evolution of the 1974 strike. Heath
emphasised his Government's three aims: to expand
the economy, to reduce inflation and to solve the
energy crisis. Achieving these aims depended on
avoiding a quarrel with the miners, thus Phase 3
had been formulated with the NUM specifically in
mind. Phase 3 had to stand as it was the basis
of the anti-inflation policy. The NUM accepted
the Government's good intentions, emphasising that
"the miners were not in the present excercise in
an attempt to bring down the Government" but were
seeking justice and a restoration of the position
established for mineworkers by Wilberforce. This
was prevented by Phase 3 and the NUM could only
defend its members by breaking it, thus Phase 3
lay at the root of the present crisis. At this
stalemate, the two sides adjourned to consider their
own and the other's positions. When the talks
resumed Heath emphasised "he would not relax
Phase 3", and on this the meeting ended. The NEC
regretted the Government's stance, arguing that
given its determination to adhere to Phase 3 there
could be no satisfactory settlement. They
reaffirmed their rejection of the offer and decided
to continue the overtime ban, but given the political implications of the situation refused to
sanction a strike ballot despite the urgings of
some NEC members.[47]
    On 13 November 1973 the Government declared a
State of Emergency with the aim of preserving
fuel stocks. This was primarily a response to the
Middle East War and OPEC, but its implications for
the NUM and miners were obvious. The NUM publicly
denied all responsibility for the measures but in
private saw them as a means of preserving CEGB
coal stocks in the event of a strike and possibly
predisposing public opinion against the miners.
Despite this it still refused to sanction a strike

ballot.48   These measures also increased the NUM's
already deep distrust of Heath.   Further emergency
regulations were announced on 18 December and these
were more closely connected to the dispute with
the miners, notably the three day week to begin on
1 January.   As the combined energy and miners
crisis deepened the NEC became convinced that
uppermost in the Cabinet's considerations was the
defeat of the NUM.   The TUC drew the same conclusions, enjoining its members not to blame the NUM
for the three-day week and other measures.49
        Two attempts were made to settle the dispute on
9 January.   The first was a meeting with the new
Secretary of State for Employment, William Whitelaw,
at his request (he was fresh from his post in
Ulster).   Whitelaw sought to assure the NUM that
the sole reason for the emergency measures was to
conserve fuel stocks and that the three day week
was not an attempt to turn public opinion against
the miners, likewise given the increases in oil
prices there had to be an anti-inflation policy
which, in effect, meant an incomes policy, Whitelaw
claimed that Phase 3 was "flexible and generous"
and must stand if inflation was not to sky-rocket.
He argued "that Phase 3 enabled the miners to be
offered a settlement in excess of that which could
be offered to most other groups of workers .... it
would restore the miners' position in the league
table and would make sure that the position could
not be eroded."50   If the NUM accepted the NCB's
offer he guaranteed talks with the newly created
Department of Energy on future investment in the
industry, so securing their members' long term
interests.   For the NUM the time for such offers
was long past, nothing new had been said, there had
been weeks of fruitless talks, suggestion and
counter-suggestion , and now the NUM refused to
depart from its publicly stated aims.   The NUM
did not want a confrontation and was prepared to do
all in its power to avoid one but it "could not
move unless they could obtain a fair basic wage for
their members.   The threat of a General Election
would not settle the problem facing the industry.
They had experienced this before, and their only
reward had been redundancies and pit closures".
Whitelaw accepted that the currently fashionable
solution of a General Election to decide 'who
governs' "would not solve any problems", but nothing
more could be conceded under Phase 3.   He did
suggest, however, that the NUM's claim might be
submitted to the independent Pay Board for analysis.

Politically, the NUM was in a crucial relationship to Phase 3 and the Government's whole anti-inflation policy as if they breached it, or were <u>seen</u> to breach it, the other unions would follow. The NUM agreed to consider carefully the points made at the meeting, but the one crucial point made - that there could be no more cash - needed little consideration.

The second settlement attempt sought to make the miners a 'special case'. This was a TUC initiative whereby if the Cabinet agreed to allow the NCB to settle outside Phase 3 by proclaiming the miners a special case, then the TUC would ensure that the settlement would not be quoted by other unions in their own negotiations. The Cabinet, though perhaps attracted by the offer, rejected it on the grounds that Phase 3 must stand and anyway, the TUC could not give a guarantee that no other union would seek to use miners' settlement as a justification. Unless the Government took up this offer, the NUM felt there was little point in further talks.[51]

On 23 January the Yorkshire Area Executive met in special emergency session to discuss negotiations. The Executive was under considerable pressure to escalate industrial action from Council and the branches which considered the high level of fuel stocks dangerous and which could only be neutralised by full strike action.[52] The overtime ban was not as successful as in 1972 because of the emergency measures and reports indicated that the CEGB "can easily continue with the present coal burn until the end of March, and as a result of the longer day and milder weather can immediately fulfil all its responsibilities, even if Britain returns to a full working week."[53]

In a final appeal Heath wrote to the NEC setting out the Government's position, asking the NUM to settle under Phase 3 and then join in tripartite talks on the industry's future, which because of the oil crisis was secure. Despite this the NEC felt that the rejection of the TUC's initiative on 9 January meant an honourable settlement was impossible. The NEC concluded that the emergency measures had been too successful, sanctioned increased action and authorised a strike ballot.[54] The ballot gave a resounding vote of confidence in the NEC: of 232,615 votes cast, 188,393 (80.9%) were in favour of strike action, with 44,222 (19.0%) opposed. In Yorkshire of 54,570 votes cast, 49,278 (90.3%) supported strike

action, only 5,292 (9.7%) were opposed. The NEC
resolved that "unless a satisfactory offer was
received all members of the NUM.... would be on
strike from midnight, 9 February 1974...."55

The Conduct of the Strike
The long, and ultimately fruitless, series of
negotiations between November and January demonstrates a concern to achieve a settlement by all
parties concerned.   Unfortunately, in making the
maximum offer under Phase 3 immediately, the NCB
committed a grave tactical blunder which made the
chance of a negotiated settlement almost impossible
given the Government's oft quoted determination to
adhere to Phase 3 no matter what.   The huge
majority in favour of strike action was, then, an
open challenge to Phase 3 and the Government.
Heath persisted in his attempts to achieve a
peaceful settlement up to 24 January despite
increasing pressure from the Conservative backbench
and some of his Cabinet (not counting the media)
for a General Election.   With the progressive
collapse of negotiations and the Cabinet's
reluctance to contemplate deploying the full
resources of the State against the miners, this
became an increasingly favoured option.   The
result of the NUM ballot meant that the only option
left, other than total capitulation, was to call
a General Election.   The three-day week made no
economic sense but it did save coal and it did
frighten millions of workers into settling under
Phase 3, possibly isolating the NUM.   Politically,
then it was astute.   However, it did not go
far enough as unless the miners backed off at the
last minute, were starved or coerced back to work
(politically and economically dangerous: as miners
say, "try digging coal with bayonets"), they would
have to be paid at some point, and given their
position in the economy, their strike was unlikely
to collapse before production stopped due to a
lack of electricity.   The publication of the
Relativities Report on the day before the ballot
was, potentially, a way out of the impasse but
the logic of the Government's position ruled out a
settlement until after a political victory over the
miners with a massive Conservative victory in a
'who governs' election.   On 7 February at 12.45pm
the General Election was announced for 28 February.
     At an emergency meeting of the NEC it was
suggested that as there would be no effective
government for the duration of the campaign there

was little point in going ahead with the strike as
there was no-one to negotiate with. However, to
call off the strike might be seen as an action
favourable to the Labour Party thus confirming
the Government's claim that this was a political
strike. The decision was then taken to continue
the strike: this was risky as the climate was
extremely unfavourable to the miners - a Conservative Government calling a 'who governs' election in
the middle of a three day week and blaming the
miners for the lay-offs. The NEC were aware that
their strike might be responsible for a Tory victory
which would damage the NUM and the rest of the
movement for a considerable period.[57] Again the
shadows of 1926 reached out: few . on the NEC
seemed really confident of victory.[57]

The 1972 strike 'ran away' from the official
leaderships but in 1974 they were determined this
would not happen: there would be no more Saltleys,
no more Frederick Mathews. In 1974 the political
aspects of the strike ensured far more visibility
for the NEC which was proportionately more concerned
with public relations and the miners' image.
Overall ccntrol was vested in the Finance and
General Purposes Committee of the NEC which was
renamed the National Strike Committee. This was
not the directing force behind the strike: as in
1972 the Areas were responsible for the conduct
of picketing, though this was supposed to occur
only after the NEC's approval had been sought and
given.[58]

The National Strike Committee's first task was
to contact the transport and power unions to secure
their support. The TGWU agreed to do nothing to
harm the NUM's strike effort but was lukewarm out
of a concern for its members' contractual obligations and the threat of the Industrial Relations
Act. The NUR and ASLEF (particularly the latter)
offered every assistance and agreed categorically
not to cross any NUM picket line. Similarly, the
power workers (both EEPTU and the EPEA) offered
their full cooperation. The Strike Committee set
out six major target groups: coal dumps, power
stations, ports, steel works, pits and coking
plants. There were to be covered twenty-four
hours a day, but with no more than six pickets so as
to avoid the opprobrium of mass picketing and
clashes with the police.[59]

The strike's organisation in Yorkshire was
decided by the Area Executive who met on the
evening of 8 February, where targets were allocated

to the Panels.   Their instructions were basically
those of 1972 coupled with the directives of the
National Strike Committee.   The maps, phone
numbers, and union contacts of 1972 were taken
from the Area archive and, if necessary, updated.
The instructions to deploy only six pickets excited
some adverse comment from the branches but, the
Executive wrote, "We know that this might dampen
enthusiasm, but be assured, there are very good
reasons"[60]   With the experience of 1972 to rely
upon the Area Panels had, by the evening of
9 February, covered every assigned target.[61]   A
special meeting of the TUC General Purposes
Committee had affirmed the miners' right to free
collective bargaining and noted that the NUM was not
seeking active TUC assistance but,

> It is of course normal trade union practice
> that the members of one union do not cross
> official picket lines established by
> another union and that members do not under-
> take other than normal work.   The Committee
> is confident that this practice will be
> observed by all trade unionists.[62]

The power and transport unions had already
responded favourably to NUM requests for support.
The trade union side of the National Joint Council
for the Electricity Industry met on 11 February and
"imposed a complete ban.... on all deliveries of
coal from whatever source", to prevent the
substitution of coal by other fuels, to use only
existing stocks at the power stations and to take no
action "which could be detrimental to the miners'
strike."[63]   Responding to TUC Circular 105 the
TGWU informed its Regional Secretaries of the TUC's
recommendations asking them to do all they could
to comply.[64]   On 6 February ASLEF's executive met
with representatives of the NEC adopting
resolutions giving full support to the NUM and
instructing that ASLEF members "must not take trains
conveying fuel past an official picket line set up
by members of the NUM."[65]   These national
arrangements had their local counterparts;   for
example, the South Yorkshire Panel wrote thus to
the local NUR,

> I am instructed to inform you that in
> addition to our picket lines at strategic
> railway points, we are now picketing
> all major steelworks in the Sheffield

and Rotherham area. The South Yorkshire
Strike Committee have declared that all
coal into steelworks .... is now black.
We ask that you support us and refuse
to move coal into the said steelworks.[66]

The support of these other unions was, again,
crucial and the Yorkshire Area used extensively
its connections with local trade union branches,
for example, to stop the movement of coke from the
Orgreave coking plant. Ray Buckton gave "an
assurance that no trains will cross our picket lines
and he will contact the depot at Rotherham to
instruct the members."[67] Similar requests were
made concerning TGWU drivers moving oil into power
stations.[68]
Not only did the Yorkshire Area ask for
help, local unions spontaneously gave help and
information. ASLEF, for example warned the Area
of the irregular movement of coal which had
increased to 50 to 60 per day; the NUR warned of
British Rail's attempt to move coal from New
Monckton, pickets were rushed there and the movement stopped; and, the ASLEF secretary at Tinsley
marshalling yards advised the NUM to place pickets
there as it was adjacent to a number of main lines
on which coal might be moved.[69] Such picketing
was costly in manpower terms and so the Area came
to an agreement with ASLEF: "There is now no need
for railway pickets to be on bridges, crossings,
embankments. ASLEF drivers will (if informed
by their Officials that there are NUM pickets in
the vicinity) stop the train."[70]
The CEGB had been hit badly in 1972 and in
1974 it noted with concern the NUM's intention to
picket the power stations. The CEGB warned the
NUM that this would cause them massive losses and
make them liable for breach of contract. The
CEGB therefore warned the NUM it was considering
legal action under the Industrial Relation Act for
any losses.[71] In effect, the NUM ignored this
threat and the power unions remained solidly
behind the NUM whilst committing themselves to
maintaining essential power supplies.[72] The scale
of picketing was less than in 1972, but it was no
less effective.
The Yorkshire Area was again responsible for
East Anglia and pickets were despatched.[73] On
18 February it was decided to send no more so
demonstrating the relative unimportance of the
area.[74] The cockpit of the strike in Yorkshire

was the Doncaster Panel's attempts to close the
BSC Anchor works at Scunthorpe.   At the beginning
of the strike the Panel reported that the complex
was covered by only 18 pickets divided into three
groups of six and that this was useless because
of the size of the complex.   The leaders of the
Panel visited the site to organise the picketing
and see exactly what resources were needed to seal
it up.[75]   The pickets had problems with trains;
Kellingley, for example, received a report of a
fuel train heading for Anchor but could not
establish whether it was NUR or ASLEF manned and as
a result missed it.   The Doncaster Area Agent
reported that lorries were crossing the picket lines
with fuel.[76]   A meeting was called between the
Panel and shop stewards to discuss how to close
Anchor, but even as late as 18 February there were
picketing problems.   The Panel contacted the Area
who sent reinforcements from the Barnsley Panel:
the Doncaster Panel commented, "It would seem we
are weak on steel works."   The size of Anchor
seemed to rule out effective picketing as total
coverage was almost impossible.   ASLEF, for
example, reported fuel trains leaving sidings and
being moved by BSC employees because no pickets
were present.   Greater success was enjoyed in
stopping road transport.[78]   To stop the movement
of coal in the entire Scunthorpe area the Yorkshire
Area met with the ASLEF district secretary and a
representative of the NUR and with their help and
cooperation Anchor was gradually sealed off.[79]
Output was already reduced to 50% because of the
three-day week and other regulations and by the end
of the strike if any coal did get through it was
whitewashed, the steel unions agreeing not to use
it.   Picketing was peaceful.[80]

The Election, Negotiation and Settlement
A miners' victory in 1974 was not a certainty.   If
the Conservatives had won in 1974 the miners might
well have become the pariahs of the Labour
Movement, responsible for giving Heath a renewed
mandate and four or five more years in power.
Once the election had been called and once the NUM
had refused to suspend its action, there could be no
negotiated settlement.   The outcome of the strike
would, the Government hoped, be settled by a massive
Conservative election victory.
     A referral of the NUM's pay claim to the Pay
Board offered a way out of the impasse for the
Government.   The Counter Inflation Act (1973)

allowed the Secretary of State for Employment to refer cases to the Pay Board for independent examination and recommendation. The referral was made on 8 February and the NEC spent a considerable amount of time discussing this, concluding that nothing material had changed.[81]   The Pay Board was instructed "to make recommendations as to the extent to which an <u>exceptional</u> increase would be justifiable, and it was to take into account the increase in relative importance of coal to the economy after 1973, as well as relevant social and economic factors.[82]

The Pay Board, working swiftly, noted the statistical and methodological problems in relating miners' pay to that of other industrial workers, but,

> ....there can be no doubt that the
> relative position of coalmining vis-a-vis
> manufacturing has changed considerably
> over the years.   It is also evident that
> the settlement following the Wilberforce
> Inquiry in 1972 was a temporary gain which
> has since been eroded.[83]

Once again the miners' case had been established. The Pay Board took into account NPLA which had compressed differentials whilst improving the pay of the lower paid resulting the relative decline of underground wages and **particularly,** face workers' pay.   The Pay Board asserted that pay had to be improved to encourage recruitment to a dangerous, but increasingly vital industry, and to increase productivity.   The Pay Board offered an increase of £1.20 per shift and 60p increase for ex-underground workers as a personal allowance, the November 1973 offer of £5.25 or 7%, and increase of the unsocial hours allowance, increased holiday pay, and the speedy implementation of a productivity deal.   The settlement date was to be 1 March 1974.[84]

Whilst the Pay Board was meeting the election campaign went ahead and pay negotiations could not take place until the result was decided.   When Heath failed to create his majority and Labour took office, pay negotiations began again, with the new Secretary of State, Micheal Foot.   At this meeting the contents of the Pay Board's report were revealed, the NUM and NCB was asked to re-open talks "unfettered by and previous government dictates or by the Pay Board's report."   It

could be used but "it was not a governing element
in the situation." The NEC decided to concentrate
on the basic wage claim, leaving other matters
affecting the coal industry to the tripartite
talks promised by Labour in its manifesto.[85] The
strike was settled at a long meeting of the JNNC on
the following day, the first full meeting since
October 1973. The basis of negotiation changed
with Labour's election and the NEC decided not to
depart from its basic wage claim and sought a
number of improvements. The meeting was adjourned
to allow the NCB to consult. On resumption the
sides were divided over differentials and basic
rates. To meet the NUM's claim the price of coal
would have to be increased by 50%, or massively
subsidised, thus the NCB offered £44.50/£35/£30
which would cost £43m giving an increase of £7.71
underground and £4.71 on the surface.

The NUM rejected the offer. The NCB conferred
with the Government who sanctioned increases to
£45/£36/£32, together with other concessions
including a long term review of the industry
involving a massive investment programme in new and
existing pits. The Union's side of the JNNC
agreed to recommend this offer to the NEC.[86] On
the same day the full NEC considered the JNNC report
and the negotiations and after a "very lengthy
discussion" the NEC agreed to accept the offer and
recommend the membership to accept. The return
to work would be 11 March, there would be no pit
head ballot to save time but there would be an
Area proxy vote.[87] The Yorkshire Area Council
considered the NEC's recommendations, only 12
delegates argued against acceptance and in the
final vote, only 5 voted against.

Despite protestations that they were not
engaged in a 'political' strike the fact that the
government was the NCB's paymaster meant the
politicisation of the two strikes. Power relations
in the coal industry are no different from those of
private industry. However, traditionally, coal
has been a 'political' industry enjoying a close
relationship with government. With the example of
1972 before them neither Gormley, Ezra or Heath
wanted a strike, albeit for different reasons, but
the dynamics of public sector pay bargaining and
the politics of inflation policy made conflict
inevitable when neither element in the relationship
was prepared to move from their positions. The
Heath Government's recognition of the miners'
importance can be seen in the provisions of Phase 3,

but these were insufficient for Gormley and the
other moderates on the NEC to manage the internal
politics of the NEC.   They were not helped by
the NCB making the full offer at the start of
negotiations.[88]   The strike was a major challenge
but the Government had only one response: an
election.   Of course, the Government could have
tried coercion or they could have capitulated by
either paying the miners or accepting the TUC's
9 January initiative but the logic of the Government's policy prevented such actions.

The miners' victory and Heath's defeat
invested the NUM with a tremendous aura of power.
1974 prompts two questions: was the strike
calculated to have a political effect, and, did the
strike force Heath from power?   That the NUM was
aware of the political sensitivity of their actions
can be seen in the NEC's reluctance to call the
strike ballot and in the greater national control
of the picketing.   Gormley consistently emphasised
that the strike was about wages, not an attempt to
bring down Heath;   even so, Area leaders such as
Mick McGahey and Arthur Scargill were in no doubt
that the miners were engaged in a political battle
and were seeking to shatter the incomes policy.
Once the Cabinet rejected compromise, coercion or
capitulation and when the ballot returned such a
vast majority, then confrontation was inevitable,
the confrontation being settled by a general
election.[89]

Did the miners bring down Heath?   The answer
is no governments lose elections, the strike was
the casus belli but it was largely fought on the
Government's record since 1970, a record which did
not inspire confidence.   Even if Heath had won he
would still have had to settle with the miners, what
if the miners had chosen to fight on as in 1926
after the ending of the General Strike?   The
Nuffield Election Study argues, "It is our
contention that in the last analysis the election
was called by the miners and that the circumstances
of its calling decisively affected the nature of the
campaign."[90]   This is overly simplistic, telling us
nothing of the Government's motives.   Heath held
off calling an election hoping a settlement could
be achieved;   once this became impossible the only
solution open was a general election to demonstrate
to the miners the legitimacy of his government's
policies, particularly the key Phase 3.   If 1974
was about "who governs?" political calculation
suggest it should have been held in late-January or

early-February and Heath would probably have won.
The election was not fought over 'who governs?'
but on the Government's record since 1970.
Initial support for the government faded: on
10 February Marplan registered its support at 54%,
by polling day this had fallen to 36.23%.91   The
Government's record coupled with embarassing
revelations such as those of 21 February released
by the Pay Board which showed that the miners could
have been offered more under Phase 3 and which
suggested that the NCB did not understand its own
pay system and that the whole conflict was unnecessary.   The Conservatives lost the election,
rather than Labour winning and the miners emerged
victorious with an enhanced reputation.
    In the late-1960s and early-1970s the NUM was
transformed from a union reluctant to accept
industrial action to one of the leading exponents
of, and practicioners of militant industrial action.
The Yorkshire Area played a crucial role in this
metamorphosis.

REFERENCES

1   YA (NUM);   24 July 1972.
        The official NUM attitude to the Industrial
        Relations Act had been decided at the 1971
        Annual Conference, and the policy decided
        had been put into effect by a Special
        Conference of the 11 February 1972.
2   YA (NUM);   1 May 1972
3   NUM;   Annual Conference Report 1972; pp126-
        130.
4   The Economist;   19 February 1972, and
        The Guardian;   19 February 1972, article by
        V Keegan.
5   YA (NUM);   Annual Reports 1972;   Report of the
        General Secretary, p98 and p101.
6   NUM (EC);   27 July 1972.   Special Meeting.
        The TUC reply was that no action could be
        taken, see:
        NUM (EC);   12 October 1972.
7   YA (NUM);   25 September 1972.
        The NEC rejected industrial action on the
        grounds that policy had been determined by
        Resolution 42 of the 1972 Annual Conference,
        and the matter had been referred to the
        Labour Party on the 13 July.   The NEC
        felt, "that the matter (should) be dealt
        with through the political wing of the
        movement".   See: NUM(EC);   12 October 1972.

8   JNNC;   13 September 1972.
9   See: NCB: Annual Reports and Accounts
        1972-1973;   para 6-10.
10   NUM(EC);   30 September 1972 (Special Meeting);
        Minutes of a Joint Meeting;   29 August 1972,
        Minutes of a Meeting with the Minister;
        31 July 1972.
        The NUM inserted the following paragraph
        in the joint report: "The industry has
        agreed that wage negotiations should be
        persued within the terms of the agreed
        conciliation procedures and in the event of
        disagreement the fullest consideration would
        be given to arbitration to avoid industrial
        action if possible.   Nevertheless, it is
        understood that, in accordance with the
        rules of the Unions concerned, the right to
        resort to industrial action remains."
11   YA(NUM);   9 October 1972.
12   JNNC ;   11 October 1972 (Union's Side).
13   JNNC;   7 November 1972.
14   NUM (EC);   8 November and 14 December 1972.
15   JNNC;   7 December 1972.
16   NUM (EC);   14 December 1972.
17   JNNC;   10 January 1973.
18   JNNC;   24 January, and NUM (EC);
        8 February 1973.
19   YA(NUM);   29 January 1973.
20   JNNC;   30 January 1973.
21   YA (NUM);   6 February 1973.
22   JNNC;   7 February 1973.
23   NUM (EC);   15 February 1973.
24   TUC;   Economic Policy and Collective Bargaining
        in 1973;   para 37.
25   NUM(EC);   28 February 1973 (Special Meeting).
26   NUM (EC);   7 March 1973 (Report of a Special
        TUC).   The NUM also supported the reference
        back of para 116: "Affiliated unions
        are and always have been free to seek advice
        and support from the General Council when
        faced by a problem ... If a union makes such
        an approach to the General Council, in the
        context to guidelines of the application of
        the Government pay policy, the General
        Council will examine its request in the
        light of the circumstances and merits of
        the particular case."
        The reference back was rejected by 3,280,000
        to 4,585,000.   See also:
        The Miner;   March 1973, for Gormley's
        speech.

27 NUM (EC); 16 March 1973.
28 YA(NUM); 19 March 1973, and BS Circular
        29/73 (5 March 1973). At the same time
        Council decided to support NUPE in their
        opposition to the pay policy, but the
        Yorkshire Area was unable, as an Area, to
        join in a day of action because of union
        rules, but Council did urge the branches to
        join NUPE's day of protest, to be held on
        the 23 March.
29 NUM (EC); 3 April 1973.
        For the reaction of the Yorkshire Area, see:
        YA (NUM); 4 April 1973, and
        BS Circular 52/73 (9 April 1973) for details
        of the settlement.
30 The Miner: March 1973.
31 YA (NUM); 7 May 1973, and 13 June 1973.
32 YA (NUM); 16 April 1973, and Annual Reports
        1973; p109.
33 NUM: Report of the NEC, May 1973; p27.
        For the controversy over the extra holiday
        see: pp30-31. The outcome of the
        negotiations were:

NUM Claim	NCB Offer (£1 + 4%)
£30	£28.16½
£32	£29.74
£40	£36.79

34 NUM: Annual Conference Report 1973;
        President's Address; p88.
35 Annual Conference Report; p163.
36 Annual Conference Report; p168.
37 Annual Conference Report; p246.
38 JNNC; 12 September 1973.
39 YA (NUM); 17 September 1973.
40 JNNC; 10 October 1973.
41 NUM (EC); 11 October 1973.
        The Yorkshire Area organised a lobby of
        this meeting; see;
        BS Circular 137/73 (8 October 1973).
42 NUM (EC); 25 October 1973 (Special Meeting).
        The majority was 18 to 17.
43 NUM: Special Conference; 26 October 1973; p5.
        The Yorkshire Area accepted and welcomed
        the decision of the Conference, but sought
        a definite starting date - the 12 November.
        See:
        YA (NUM); 29 October 1973.
44 JNNC; 7 November 1973 (Union's Side).
45 NUM (EC); 8 November 1973.
        A Special Council Meeting agreed to

implement the ban and arrangements were
made to organise the ban in the Yorkshire
coalfield. See:
YA (NUM): 10 November 1973 (Special
Meeting), and
BS Circular 164/73 (9 November 1973).

46   NUM (EC); 21 November 1973.
47   NUM (EC); 21 November 1973.
48   NUM (EC); 13 December 1973.
49   TUC Circular 72 (1973-1974); 19 December
        1973.
50   NUM (EC); 9 January 1974. Report of a
        Meeting with the Secretary of State for
        Employment.
51   NUM (EC); 10 January 1974.
52   YA (NUM); 23 January 1974 (Special Council
        Meeting).
53   BS Circular 17/74 (28 January 1974).
54   NUM (EC); 24 January 1974.
        The Union's negotiating team recommended a
        strike ballot as although power output was
        being hampered, "the effect on the stocks
        appears not to be as drastic as had been
        desired". The bulk of information on the
        size of coal stocks came from the EPEA and
        the EEPTU. See also,
        JNNC; 23 January 1974 (Union's Side).
55   NUM (EC); 8 February 1974.
56   A Gamble, The Conservative Nation, (London,
        RKP, 1974); pp225-28).
57   NUM (EC); 8 February 1974 (Special Meeting).
58   NUM (EC); 5 February 1973.
59   National Strike Committee; 7 February 1974.
60   BS Circular 27/74 (9 February 1974).
61   1974 Strike Documents; Phone message from
        J Smart to Area HQ; 9 February 1974.
        six pickets were stationed at each point.
62   AS Circular 48/74 (13 February 1974), and
        TUC Circular 105 (1973-1974); 12 February
        1974.
63   NJIC 18/74 (12 February 1974, and
        AS Circular 51/74 (13 February 1974).
64   TGWU: Regional Secretaries; 8 February 1974,
        and
        AS Circular 30/74 (11 February 1974).
65   ASLEF to Branches (Resolution 136/303);
        7 February 1974, in
        AS Circular 18/74 (11 February 1974).
66   South Yorkshire Panel Secretary to A Wild (NUR
        Secretary at Tinsley); 12 February 1974.
        This was agreed.

South Yorkshire Panel: Picketing Lists;
February 1974.
Daily Report; 12 February 1974.

67   Letter File: Message 12 February 1974, and
National Strike Committee; 13 February 1974
Jack Jones indicated that there would be
no contractual problems for TGWU members who
refused to cross NUM pickets lines.

69   Letter File (Messages); 12 February 1974 and
21 February 1974.

70   Message from A Scargill to all Area Strike
Committees and HQs; 15 February 1974.

71   A L Wright to L Daly; 8 February 1974, and
AS Circular 44/74 (9 February 1974).
The response of the NUM was to seek advice
on the ability of CEGB to sue for damages;
See:
National Strike Committee; 18 February
1974.

72   AS Circular 36/45 (15 February 1974).

73   YA (NUM); 15 February 1974.
Pickets were in action in East Anglia as
early as 11 February.
See
Message from A Rigby (nd), and Daily Report;
13 February 1974.

74   Daily Report; 18 February 1974.

75   Daily Report; 11 February 1974.

76   Daily Report; 13 February 1974.

77   Daily Report; 18 February 1974.   Barnsley sent
30 pickets.

78   Daily Report; 15 February 1974.

79   Daily Report; 14 February 1974.

80   Morning Telegraph: 15 February 1974.

81   NUM (EC); 12 February 1974.

82   Pay Board (Special Report), Relative Pay of
Mineworkers, Cmnd 5567 (March 1974);
para 1, emphasis added.

83   Relative Pay of Mineworkers; para 55.

84   Relative Pay of Mineworkers; para 81-93.
For a discussion of 'The Theory of
Relativities', see;
Sunday Times; 3 February 1974, article by
J Fryer.

85   NUM (EC); 5 March 1974.

86   JNNC: 6 March 1974.

87   NUM (EC); 6 March 1974.
The Area votes were in favour of the offer;
See:
NUM (EC); 14 March 1974.

88   For the background see:
        S Fay and H Young, The Fall of Edward Heath
        (London, Sunday Times 1975); pp6-10, and,
        D Butler and D Kavanagh, The British
        General Election of February 1974 (London,
        Macmillan 1974), pp27-44.

89   For the NUM's attitude to the February Election
        see: NUM General Election Manifesto
        published in The Miner (General Election
        Issue); February 1974.
        The overall position of the NUM was:
        "The (NEC) expressed its full support for
        the Labour Party and undertook to fight for
        the return of a Labour Government pledged
        to operate joing TUC and Labour Party
        policies." NUM: Report of the NEC,
        May 1974; p9.

90   Butler and Kavanagh, The British General
        Election.... p29.

91   Butler and Kavanagh, The British General
        Election.... p34
        This study shows surprisingly, that only
        54% of Conservative candidates mentioned
        the question 'Who Governs?' in their
        election address (p62).

Chapter Ten

THE LEFT IN POWER

Even though the Yorkshire Area moved to the left
after 1973-4 the political problems confronting
the new leadership were basically those of the
past, amplified by the miners' enhanced reputation.
This chapter explores the policies and attitudes
of the Area leadership, particularly the Area's
relationship with the Labour Government and a
right-wing dominated NEC.   How would the miners
react to their position?   Significantly, the 1974
NUM Conference saw the re-emergence of the familiar
subordination of industrial militancy to the
maintenance of Labour in office.

    The second purpose of this chapter is to
examine the inexorable slide of the mineworkers and
the NUM after 1977-78 towards crisis and then
confrontation over the size of the industry as
recession inevitably reduced the demand for coal.
History dictates that this crisis will come under
a Conservative government with Margaret Thatcher
as Prime Minister, and with Arthur Scargill as
NUM President.   The final reaction of the miners
is unknown, but what is known is that the left,
though in power, have thus far found their
prescriptions often rejected by the mineworkers. In
writing this chapter the author found it impossible
to confine the analysis to Yorkshire: the crisis
facing the Yorkshire miners is that of the British
miners (and vice-versa), hence the final section.

    As is so often the case with mining and miners,
history seems to be repeating itself, but history
never truly repeats itself.   This time the left,
who rode to power on a wave of revulsion against pit
closures and low pay, are called upon to defend the
industry against pit closures.   However, the miners
of 1982 are not those of 1972:   conditions have
changed and many of the elements which created the

national consciousness of the early-1970s no
longer apply.   Resistance cannot be guaranteed.
The rise of the left was the mineworkers' response
to the crises of the late-1950s and 1960s;   what
will be their response to the crisis of the
1980s?   The leadership, committed to resistance,
know what that response should be: their task
was to convince the mineworker.

Wages Militancy and the Social Contract

Having taken power in the Yorkshire Area the left
saw its main task as maintaining and expanding the
consciousness of the Yorkshire miners: consciousness had led to action, and action to further
consciousness.   This new political style placed
enormous emphasis upon active leadership and it saw
the task of leadership as being to offer the member a
clear policy, explain their advocacy of that policy
and ask the men for their support.[1]   The new stance
of the Yorkshire Area had three aspects: the
militant defence of miners' wages and conditions,
the promotion of party and union democracy to
institutionalise the left's influence, and finally,
promoting an awareness that the mineworkers'
influence was based on, perhaps, shifting sands.
Thus, the miners needed allies and needed to be
ready to defend themselves.
      The public face of this new leadership was
characterised by the clear determination that never
again would miners' wages and conditions be bartered
or held hostage to the political interests of a
Labour Government.   This was of crucial importance
as the philosophy of the social contract was
predicated upon wage restraint, and the miners
(perceived as the leaders of the union movement)
had to support, and be seen to support, that
philosophy if the social contract was not to
collapse.   After 1974, with the Yorkshire Area
unequivocally part of the NUM left, it was more
difficult for the NUM's support to be delivered
to the Labour Government.[2]   The Yorkshire Area's
attitude to the social contract was unequivocal:
total opposition.
      The energy crisis, the escalating cost of oil
and the economy's dependence on coal fired power
stations increased the potential power of the
miners.   The Yorkshire Area drew two conclusions
from this: 1972 and 1974 represented a break-
through in pay and conditions which must be exploited further.   Thus, the "Trade Union Movement must
at all times insist on the right to free collective

bargaining".[3] Second, though recognising and
accepting the need for party-political action to
secure the industry's future and expressing a
willingness to cooperate with the NCB and
government for the industry's good, "this does not
mean that we sacrifice everything to do this. This
was the policy adopted .... after the Second World
War, which led to the drastic decline ....we must
never allow this to happen again".[4] Thus, the
miners should support a Labour Government, but that
Government should never interfere with the Union's
first task -- the defence of its members' interests.[5]
The Yorkshire miners must also be aware of the
NUM's wider destiny:

> Socialist pioneers understood that it was
> necessary to have a political perspective
> in order to ensure that the industrial
> demands could not only be achieved but
> retained on a permanent basis (we must)
> play our part politically as well as
> industrially (but) this union will not
> be used as a mere vehicle for ironing out
> our problems as and when they arise in the
> capitalist system.[6]

Whilst the Labour Government pursued policies
in the interests of the miners and the working
class and adhered to the principles and commitments
of the February 1974 manifesto, the miners would
support that Government. Should the Government
betray those principles and commitments the miners
and their union had the right and duty to defend
themselves, by strike action, if necessary.[7] Such
a posture meant, inevitably, a deep suspicion of,
and then rejection of, the entire concept of the
social contract.
     This is not to suggest that the supporters of
the social contract such as Joe Gormley were
actively prepared to 'sell out' the miners to keep
Labour in office. They too accepted the need to
defend the miners' wages and conditions: they were
concerned at the method of defence while securing
the trade unions general interests.[8] Thus, the
fundamental cleavage in the NUM, and a crucial
source of instability in its relationship with the
Government, was selecting the means of defending its
members without jeopardising the Government. The
right argued that militancy was in the interests of
neither the miners nor the Government, whereas the
social contract offered the prospect of real and

and substantial gains in the form of a massive
investment programme. The NUM had been seeking
such a commitment since the late-1950s and the
moderates were determined not to endanger this
commitment (which depended on keeping Labour in
office) by the aggressive pursuit of wage
increases.9   Tripartism, fundamental to the
philosophy of the social contract, was portrayed as
an effective surrogate for militancy and to be
more effective in defending miners' wages. The
support of the miners was essential for the
Government, not only because of their intrinsic
power but also because of the solidarity miners had
evoked from other workers. Under no circumstances
could miners be allowed to become the focal point
of resistance to Government policy. The
circumstances and outcome of the February election
saw the re-emergence of familiar attitutes and
policies in the NUM-Government relationship.10
The attitude of the Yorkshire Area was unequivocal:
"If a claim for a wage increase is justified, then
it should be prosecuted by the Union irrespective
of the Government of the day".11   Nationally, the
NUM was in the same political quandary as between
1945-1951 and 1964-1970. Hitherto, the Yorkshire
Area had been subject to the same dilemma, but the
political change of 1969-1974 had largely resolved
this.
      The miners' political importance can be seen
in Labour's manifesto which promised to work with
the miners, securing their services for the
benefit of the whole nation by investment in the
coal industry and the social contract.12   The
tripartite review of the industry, The Coal
Industry Examination, sought to educate the mineworkers and their leaders in the realities of power,
pointing out the benefits to be secured by
cooperation with Government. The Examination and
the resulting Plan For Coal (1975) committed the
Government to a massive investment programme in new
and existing pits.13   The political function of
this exercise was to secure the cooperation of the
NUM, negating the possibility of industrial action.
Nevertheless, the distrust forged between 1964-1970
meant that despite these undertakings, the Yorkshire
Area was sceptical. Prophetically, Arthur Scargill
warned Council that there was no point in pursuing
improved wages and conditions if the industry was
to be decimated and "We must ensure that the
coalmining industry never again faces the trauma of
a pit closure programme along the lines experienced

in the 1957-1970 period".[14]
Between 1974 and 1979 the traditional political
relationships of 1964-1970 reasserted themselves,
but with an important difference. Opposition to
the NUM's policy of cooperation with the NCB and
Government (even Conservative ones) was hitherto
largely outside the official structure of authority
in the NUM. After 1971 this was challenged at
Area, then national level, as the Yorkshire Area
moved decisively to the left. This proved a major
source of instability in the NUM-Government relationship, but for the principle of equal
representation of the Areas on the NEC the left
would have been in a majority. The mere existence
of a Labour Government, then, had little effect
on the attitude of the Yorkshire Area which had
declared its intention of militantly defending the
miners. As early as February 1975 the Area
Executive accepted an emergency resolution calling
on the NEC to pursue aggressively a realistic wage
claim. This was recommended to Council for its
acceptance. The settlement of 1975, though well
below the claim approved by the NUM Conference, was
hailed by the Yorkshire Area as a victory as it
breached the social contract's wage provisions, and
that more would have been conceded if the NEC had
displayed a more determined attitude to the
Cabinet.
Clearly, then, the NUM was beset by a contradiction which, it was feared, might split the NUM
dividing it from the Government. Therefore, the
NEC decided to seek a definitive decision on the
membership's attitude to the social contract,
something made all the more important by the introduction of incomes policy in 1975. To resolve
this contradiction the NEC decreed a pithead
ballot on accepting (or otherwise)the £6 pay policy,
a policy rejected by the Yorkshire Area Council.
The ballot approved government policy by 116,076 to
75,743, and in Yorkshire there was a small majority
in favour of acceptance: 21,555 to 21,694, a
majority of 821. One year later Yorkshire
reaffirmed its hostility to pay policy, with Council
expressing total rejection of Stage 2 and the NEC's
acceptance. Yorkshire's response to incomes
policy was to sponsor a resolution in March 1976 for
the NUM Conference demanding £100 per week for
those on NPLA Grade A (with appropriate
differentials) to be paid from 1 November. If
the claim was refused, the NEC were to consult the
membership on industrial action. Council again

rejected pay restraint in February 1977, recording
its opposition to any continuation of the social
contract which, it claimed, had cut miners'
living standards. This was accompanied by a call
for a return to free collective bargaining.[15]
Given the Yorkshire Area's political perspective,
Stage 1 of incomes policy, the public expenditure
cuts which followed the Sterling Crisis of 1976
and the intervention of the IMF, showed that once
again a Labour Government had chosen to rescue
capitalism at the expense of the working class,
therefore the miners were free to defend themselves
in whatever way necessary. Nationally, however,
the perspective was somewhat different. To avoid
a possible split between militant and moderate
Areas, leaders such as Joe Gormley were compelled
to abandon formal pay restraint, but they were
also anxious to avoid a confrontation over pay with
the Government. For the NUM and Government there
remained the vexing question of how to pay the
miners more without destabilising the social
contract.

Thus, by 1977 the political need for a productivity incentive scheme was irresistible. The
onset of recession made it apparent that the coal
industry would need substantial financial help and
declining demand for energy forced the NCB, supported by the Cabinet, to emphasise cost control and
the maximisation of productivity. Some type of
incentive scheme would satisfy these economic and
political criteria, so avoiding a clash with the
Government. In 1975 the miners' external wage
differential with manufacturing industry stood at
20%; by 1977 it had fallen to 5% and Handy
estimates that by April 1978 this critical differential would have been reduced to the pre-1972
strike level.[16] To move such a solution, however,
was politically dangerous as the NUM was deeply
divided on incentives: many miners (not only those
on the left) saw them as a return to piecework, of
pit against pit, man against man, and the threat of
'blood on the coal'.

After 1972 an incentive scheme had been on the
fringes of official NEC thinking. A scheme had
been prepared in 1974 but was rejected (on the
recommendation of the NEC) by 123,615 to 77,199.
Nevertheless, the political justification for such
a scheme remained and became increasingly
imperative, with Gormley advocating openly such a
scheme as a panacea for the NUM-Government
dilemma.[17] When voting on the NEC's Report the

1977 Conference approved that section dealing
with the possibility of an incentive scheme. At
the September 1977 meeting of the NEC this purely
formal approval was used as a pretext by the
supporters of such a scheme to begin negotiations
with the NCB. Gormley ruled out of order demands
for a further national ballot on the principle of
a scheme.

Yorkshire's opposition to any such scheme was
absolute. An incentive scheme, it was argued,
would lead to a further round of pit closures,
an increase in the accident rate and would cripple
the national unity so central to victory in 1972
and 1974.[18]   An angry Council meeting on
26 September rejected the NEC's decision, demanding
a strict adherence to Conference decisions which
vetoed on successive occasions any move to
incentive schemes. Council insisted that the 1974
ballot and the 1977 Conference decision forbad
such schemes and Council called on the Officials
to organise a mass demonstration at the next NEC.

The 1 September decision led to the negotiation
of a national scheme and strenuous efforts were
made to persuade the miners to accept by promising
them substantial increases in pay.[19]   The conflict
over the scheme was particularly bitter: the
Yorkshire Area had already called on its members
to resist national policy and claimed that the
proposed scheme would result in "Death, disease and
more pit closures".[20]   Council also agreed to
support the Kent Area in any and every way in their
efforts to secure an injunction restraining the
NEC.   The injunction was however, refused.[21]   Yet
again there was a majority against such a scheme:
nationally, 87,901 for,110,634 against, and in
Yorkshire a massive 76% were opposed, 36,564 to
11,080.   Despite two national votes and clear
Conference decisions incentive schemes were,
nevertheless, implemented.

At the November NEC meeting Gormley ruled out
of order suggestions that the ballot result be
declared null-and-void because of the actions of
some Areas in trying to block the scheme.   The
ballot result, he ruled, had to be accepted, there
could be no national scheme but in response to a
suggestion from the South Derbyshire Area, he
ruled that the NEC had no objection should Areas
wish to negotiate local incentive schemes.   In
those Areas which voted for the scheme negotiations
began immediately, though it has been suggested
that such negotiations had been proceeding

informally for sometime.   The policy of Yorkshire
and the left was to resist any attempt by the
NEC, or individual Areas, to introduce incentive
schemes.   On 19 December Council reiterated its
earlier decisions and decided to ballot the Area's
members on giving the Area Officials the power to
call industrial action to preserve the principle
of the daywage.   Council voted by a large majority
in favour, but in the ballot there was a majority
of 10,770 (26,451 to 15,681) to accept an Area
scheme.   In January 1978 the Area Officials were
empowered by Council to sign such a scheme.[22]   As
most other Areas had signed or were negotiating
agreements, for Yorkshire to reject them would
have meant fighting alone.
      For the remaining year of incomes policy, as
the Government moved inexorably towards the
'Winter of Discontent', the Yorkshire Area remained
consistently and bitterly opposed to pay restraint.
In February 1978 Council declared its opposition to
"the 10% pay freeze", which the NEC agreed to
support by 14 votes to 10 despite a Conference
decision and at the end of 1978 it rejected the
proposed 5% pay limit.[23]   Throughout the latter
part of the Labour Government Arthur Scargill and
the Yorkshire Area warned that an incomes policy
would cost the government working class support at
the next election.   The effect of pay restraint
"has been devastating.   Strike after strike has
been taking place in industry.   The effect in
terms of ordinary people has been staggering.   Yet
it was as predictable as night follows day".[24]
In his annual report for 1976 delivered in
March 1977 Scargill declared:

      "The last time a Labour Government
      introduced an incomes policy, it
      resulted in the defeat of the Labour
      Government in the 1970 General
      Election.... the last few weeks have
      demonstrated...the fact that the British
      working class are fed up with the
      imposition of the Social Contract...The
      Labour Government are rushing headlong,
      like lemmings towards self-destruction.
      Unless there is a reversal of policy,
      and the introduction of socialist
      commitment, I can see no alternative but
      defeat at the next General Election.[25]

      Socialism and free collective bargaining were

seen as Labour's only hope.   After 1974 the
Yorkshire Area and its allies were steadfast
opponents of the social contract and wage restraint.
Yet, Yorkshire and the left were uninfluential in
deflecting the moderates led by Gormley from their
support of the Government.   The moderates, or as
they preferred to be known 'those who took the
decisions', were able to pursue this policy because
of the unrepresentative nature of the NEC which
entrenched a right-wing majority and because of
Gormley's skills in interpreting the NUM Rulebook
and Conference standing orders.   Although the left
moved the NUM decisively against formal incomes
policy, the NUM remained, in effect, supporters
of pay restraint.   Despite the nightmares of the
Cabinet after 1974 it was not the miners who sealed
the fate of the Callaghan government.

Solidarity and Consciousness
The leaders of the Yorkshire Area felt the miners
had an obligation to show solidarity with any other
group of workers engaged in a dispute with their
employers, either public or private.   Although
there was no industrial action over miners' pay, the
Yorkshire Area displayed an increased willingness
to support industrial action in defence of themselves and other unions.   Highly visible expressions
of solidarity were, therefore, a major element in
the left's platform.
     Miners' pay dominated industrial politics, yet
the membership of the NUM had other interests which
the Yorkshire Area was prepared to defend by
industrial action.   In early 1975, for example, in
a dispute over miners' fuel allowances ('home coal')
industrial action was threatened if a national
agreement on home coal led to a reduction in
allowances made to Yorkshire miners. Similarly,
Council recommended industrial action in November
1976 over the early retirement scheme which
threatened to exclude large numbers of surface
workers.   An NEC decision to recommend a settlement
offering less than that approved by Conference and
which did indeed exclude surface workers led to
threats of unofficial industrial action and a
promise of determined opposition from the Yorkshire
Area.   There is little point in multiplying
examples: after 1974 the Yorkshire Area became the
militant core of the NUM, but to what extent was
this reflected amongst the Yorkshire miners?

Table 1: Yorkshire Area Voting, 1974-1979

Issue	Yes (%)	No (%)	Area Recommendation
Social Contract (July 1975)	22,555(51)	21,694(49)	Vote No
Langwith Overtime Ban (March 1976)	20,292(49)	21,375(51)	Vote No
Early Retirement (January 1977)	16,875(37)	28,694(63)	Vote No
Concessionary Coal (July 1977)	4,167(9)	42,068(91)	Vote No
Incentive Scheme (November 1977)	11,080(24)	36,564(76)	Vote No
Wage Offer (March 1979)	27,176(59)	19,277(41)	Vote No
Industrial Action (November 1979)	14,741(27)	40,363(73)	Vote No

The results in this table testify to the divergence
of Area from National policy, a divergence seen all
the more clearly in the speeches of the Area
leadership in public, at Conference and on the NEC.
To draw an analogy from the study of political
parties: the 'activists' traditionally support
more militant policies than those generally acceptable to a party's voters. The danger is that if
the gap between the policy demands and preferences
of the activists and those of the voter diverge
drastically, the result will be an erosion of
support from the electorate.[26] This phenomena is
present in the relationship between union leaders
and their members and, clearly poses a threat to the
coherence and stability of the union's political
posture. It is a particular problem for left-
wing union leaders advocating policies outside the
traditional mainstream of union politics. Hence,
the importance placed by the Yorkshire Area on
communication and leadership. The voting pattern
displayed does not demonstrate a direct
reciprocity between leaders and led. Nevertheless,
the three votes of 1977 (which nationally went
against the NEC) were particularly important
as they were interpreted (as a whole) by
national leaders to mark the end of the .
membership's acquiescence in the social contract.

The vote in support of the social contract is
notable for its narrowness, whilst the result in
March 1979 reflects the recognition that the time
of the year ruled out effective industrial action.
In the November 1979 ballot and nationally the
corrosive effect of incentive schemes can be seen:
the result was quite close: 107,656 (48.75%) to
113,160(51.25%), a majority against strike action
of 5,504.   The result in the Yorkshire Area was
hailed by the leadership:

> In voting the way you did, you displayed
> a degree of understanding, commonsense
> and far-sightedness fully worthy of
> the country's leading coalfield.   You
> proved beyond doubt that the damage and
> the divisiveness of the incentive
> scheme can be conquered.   The struggle
> was lost nationally.   In Yorkshire you
> won.   And you were magnificent.[27]

So far we have emphasised the Yorkshire
miners' own strong sectional consciousness, but
their leaders saw them as having a wider role.
Reciprocating for 1972 and 1974 the Yorkshire
Area pledged its support for the NUR in 1975,
prohibiting the movement of coal by road which
was normally moved by rail and it promosed not to
cross NUR picket lines.   The most publicised
example of the Yorkshire Area's solidarity was
the Grunwick dispute.   In June 1977 an emergency
resolution expressing support for the locked-out
Grunwick workers and APEX and calling for the
despatch of NUM pickets and the re-call of the
TUC was approved by Council.   Further pickets were
sent after the farce of the Scarman Inquiry on
17 October and the Area agreed to finance the
legal costs of any arrested NUM picket.[28]   Despite
the trade unions failure at Grunwick the picketing
was seen as one further example of the Yorkshire
miners' willingness to help other workers.[29]   The
firemen's strike of 1977-1978 secured the Area's
financial support and moral backing.   Council
not only approved of the strike as a challenge to
the social contract but sanctioned a substantial
donation to the FBU's strike funds as well as
individual pit collections.   In the 'Winter
of Discontent' the Area received and supported
an appeal for help from the TGWU.   It also
responded favourably to requests from other
unions in the local authority manual workers'

dispute.   In the 1980 steel strike the Area gave
help and advice to inexperienced ISTC strike
organisers and participated in a number of mass
pickets, notably at the private steel company,
Hadfields, in Sheffield.   Finally, on more than
one occasion the coalfield had undertaken one day
strikes in support of nurses' pay claims, the most
recent being September 1982.

      Again the militancy and the commitment of the
Yorkshire miners cannot be doubted.   Obviously,
those who participated in the Grunwick or Hadfield
picket lines were an activist minority but the
sympathy of the broad membership for other workers
be they firemen, council workers, nurses or railwaymen is apparent and testifies to a powerful
awareness of the value of solidarity.   Yet, the
outcome of the Grunwick dispute demonstrated
eloquently that unless the disciplined solidarity of
the miners and others was coordinated and directed
its impact would be blunted.

Labour Party and Trade Union Democracy
The Yorkshire Area's scepticism of the Party
leadership's commitment to socialism seemed
confirmed by the social contract.   The failure of
Party leaders to implement the manifesto and
Conference decisions could only be remedied by
making them accountable for their actions.

      Criticism of the Party's internal processes,
though always present, first emerged with force
during the controversy over the EEC Referendum when
the Area Executive expressed support for Benn in
his campaign for the supremacy of Conference
decisions.   The crucial change in the Area's
position came with the 1976 Sterling Crisis and the
final abandoning of the 1974 manifesto in return
for the IMF loan.   The crisis and its resolution
was held to demonstrate the need for democracy
and accountability in the Party if there was to be
"a real socialist alternative".   Thus,

      The National Conference of our Party must
      become the supreme body.   The leader of
      the Party, as well as the people elected
      to Cabinet, must be answerable and
      accountable to the Annual Conference.
      They should be elected by that
      Conference and not selected by one
      individual.   Our Union should pledge
      itself to campaign for the automatic
      reselection of MPs, the object being

> to ensure that the Annual Conference of
> the Party not only adopts resolutions,
> but carries them out when it is the
> Government of the day 30.

The election of Party leaders by Annual Conference
became Area policy.   In February 1978 Council
voted to support the Campaign for Labour Party
Democracy and the reselection of MPs.   It also
voted to oppose the Campaign for Labour Victory.
The Yorkshire Area was also a committed supporter
of Tony Benn for the leadership and then deputy-
leadership of the Party.
        The Yorkshire Area did not confine itself to
passing resolutions.   The Area's political
strategy was to penetrate and transform the Party
from within.   The scrapping of the proscribed
organisations list facilitated left-wing unity
which sought to use the bloc vote to secure left
wing policies at Conference.   This conception of
intra-party democracy allots a special role to
the unions who control the necessary votes and
resources.[31]   Loyalty to Conference decisions was
therefore, the key political touchstone.   Those
who rejected this supremacy and sovereignty at
whatever level of the Party should, in the Area's
view, be expelled.[32]   Such attitudes are deeply
hostile to parliamentary elitism,   "Our Party
does not belong to a select bunch of MPs.   It was
created out of the womb of the trade union
movement and belongs to all of its members."[33]
The delegate principle is both stronger and more
legitimate than the representative principle, which
means that any MP who accepts union money must
respect that union's wishes "on issues which are
particular and peculiar to this Union".[34]
Speaking at the South Wales Miners' Gala immediately
after the May 1979 election Arthur Scargill
demanded the democratisation of the Party "to enable
a leadership to be elected which truly reflects
the grassroots of the membership".[35]   The
mandatory re-selection of MPs was vital, providing
a mechanism whereby any recalcitrant right-winner
might be held accountable to his CLP.[36]   In the
coalfield this power would be weilded by the NUM
and their allies, hence the campaign after 1979
to revitalise the Area's influence in the coalfield
CLPs.   The message was addressed to the Union and
party activist who are held to be the essence of
the Party: the MP is merely the agent and servant
of the Party and should defer to the membership.[37]

Despite its hostility to the Wilson-Callaghan
governments the Area did, in May 1979, commit
itself to the Labour Party. At the beginning of
the campaign the Executive and Council pledged
their full support for the Party, but Labour's
defeat was ascribed to the frustrations of the
social contract and led to demands that the
Party pursue fully socialist policies as the only
sure way of returning to power.[38]
    Intra-union democracy was part of the same
demand for accountability to the rank and file.
We have seen through this book that the left's
view of the 1944 Rulebook was that it was unde-
mocratic because it created an unrepresentative
NEC which could then override Conference. As
with the Party, so with the union: the legitimate
and final voice in deciding union policy was the
membership organised in an annual conference and
that the task of the national leaders was to carry
out its decisions.[39] If the left could control
Conference they believed they could control the
NUM: events after 1974 disproved this assumption
pointing to the importance of the NEC's composition
and the role of the national President.[40] Writing
in The Yorkshire Miner Scargill argued that the
NEC's machinations over incentive schemes were a
betrayal of the membership; he was particularly
angry at their rejection of the pithead ballot
result and Conference decisions. This, he claimed
proved the case for reform.[41]
    Attempts were made to change the composition of
the NEC. At the 1972 Conference, for example, a
Yorkshire Area resolution argued that as the whole
union operated on the basis of simple majorities,
why not the NEC? Reform, it was asserted, was
resisted by the right as they interpreted such
resolutions as a bid for power by the left who
would then impose their will on the moderate
majority. This, it was argued, was the existing
situation in reverse: the smaller Areas imposing
policies on the larger.[42] This resolution was
passed by 153 to 148, but a rule change requires
a two-thirds majority of Conference. In 1973,
1974 and 1975 Joe Gormley as Conference chairman,
ruled out of order reform resolutions on what were,
in reality, technicalities.[43] Gormley argued that
restructuring the NUM was the NEC's responsibility
under Rule 7 and only after full consultation with
Areas and after each had given their consent. A
resolution from the Derbyshire Area at the 1978
Conference sought to compel the NEC to implement

Conference resolutions, arguing that it was anomalous that NEC decision making was distorted by
unequal representation.[44]   The seconder, from
Yorkshire, commented on the inequity of Cumberland
having one NEC representative for its 1,033 members
whilst Yorkshire had 3 for 60,000:   "We have on a
Monday and Friday more absentees.... than you are
representing".[45]   The smaller Areas, rallied by
Nottingham who saw these reorganisation proposals
as the start of a left wing takeover, secured the
defeat of the resolution by 126 to 145.[46]   Clearly,
whilst the ancien regime remained in office there
would be no reform of the NEC as this was a major
bulwark against the left.

Long Live The King
Gormley's retirement from the Presidency of the
NUM was important not because Arthur Scargill was
the left's contender, but because his likely
election promised the extension of the leadership
style and policies which had won him power in
Yorkshire to the national level, and this presaged
a far more 'political' role for the miners.[47]
     Gormley's indecision over his retirement after
1979 was to ensure that Mick McGahey was too old
to run for President and to prevent the left
winning one of the NUM's seats on the TUC.   This,
however, could not prevent Scargill from running
for President;   indeed Gormley's actions made it
inevitable (not that there was much doubt anyway)
that the national left would unite behind
Scargill.[48] The right's strategy was confused
(a measure of how much things had changed) as can be
seen at the 1980 Conference.   This saw the
emergence of Ray Chadburn, the Nottinghamshire Area
President, as Gormley's likely heir apparent.
Gormley had to retire not later than July 1982.
The right believed that Scargill had begun his
campaign too early, giving them sufficient time to
project their contender and take the political
initiative.[49]   The 14 member right-wing caucus on
the NEC was, however, split.   A majority were
thought to favour Trevor Bell (COSA), a close
confidante of Gormley and the former head of the
NUM research department.   Bell was, on Gormley's
initiative, elected general secretary of the white-
collar section of the NUM and so on to the NEC in
1979, but electorally he was a dubious candidate.
Though a Yorkshireman and an ex-underground fitter
(he had once worked with Roy Mason) Bell was
essentially a union bureaucrat unknown in the

coalfields.   Thus, the right had two unknown
candidates supported by little in the way of
organisation, opposing a highly visible charismatic leader with a massive Area power base and
nationwide support.

The right's eventual candidate was Bell, with
Chadburn, at first, withdrawing.   Chadburn was
unknown outside Nottinghamshire, whereas Bell had
national experience (he was credited, somewhat
unfairly, with the authorship of the NUM's evidence
to the Wilberforce Enquiry whereas in fact a
considerable amount of work was done by the Trade
Union Research Unit at Ruskin College, Oxford) if
not exposure.   He had had some underground
experience and had fought mid-Bedfordshire for
Labour in 1964 and 1966.   The right believed that
these qualities gave sufficient scope to project
Bell as a national not a sectional figure.   His
main disadvantage was his 'office boy' image.[50]
The right also tried to use Scargill's demand that
the campaign be about policies not personalities
against him: Bell's campaign was based on 'common
sense';   on him being portrayed as a Joe Gormley
Mk II;   on the assumption that, historically, the
miners prefer moderates as national leaders;   on
his promising "to try to emulate the Gormley style
of wheeler-dealing", and on his playing on real
fears of political and industrial confrontation if
Scargill were elected.[51]   This strategy had been
formulated in December 1980 at a meeting at
Gormley's home, where a consensus emerged in favour
of Bell, who was initially discarded because of
his bureaucratic background only to be restored.[52]
This demonstrates the startling lack of unity and
purpose within the right: Chadburn was an underground man but unknown;   Bell had national
experience and was in an Area sense 'neutral' but
he was glaringly vulnerable to the left pointing
out that the last time a COSA man (Sid Ford) was
President 400 pits and 300,000 jobs were lost in
ten years.   The right had no effective challenger
to Scargill.

Scargill's campaign began in March 1979.[53]
He undertook a massive speaking campaign throughout
every coalfield, steering it away from his militant
politics and emphasising bread and butter issues of
concern to all miners irrespective of their
politics.   However, as his campaign progressed the
threat of a further massive round of pit closures
became the centre-piece of his speeches as the
Conservative Government demanded financial rectitude

from the NCB.[54]
The campaign began in earnest with Gormley's
announcement in July 1981 of his intention to
retire in the following spring. The right were in
disarray and increasingly anxious as Scargill
was having an unexpectedly strong impact in the
moderate Areas.[55] Hence, the re-entry of Chadburn.
His candidacy raised the possibility of splitting
the right wing vote but the Single Transferable
Vote system might, it was thought, still prevent
Scargill's election. In a straight fight Bell's
votes would have nowhere to go and sufficient
moderate miners might vote for Scargill because of
Bell's COSA background. Scargill could win on the
first ballot only with right-wing votes, thus
Chadburn's presence would probably attract these
votes, blocking Scargill. Three candidates would,
in this view, prevent Scargill's victory on the
first ballot and the more ballots the greater the
chance of votes transferring away from Scargill.
However, the right's strategy, a desperate one
at best, received an embarassing blow when Chadburn
was not even nominated by his own Area whose Council
voted by 15 to 9 to endorse Scargill. By
November 1981 Scargill was endorsed by 12 NUM Areas,
representing 200,000 out of 240,000 members.[56]
Scargill's victory in December 1981 was total,
though the right claim one further month of
campaigning would have given them victory.
Scargill won with 70% of the votes cast. Then
aged 43 he could be NUM President until 2004 -- in
response the Financial Times Share Index fell by
11.8 points. At his victory press conference,
held in an interval between wage negotiations with
the NCB, Scargill thanked the miners for their
support and confidence: he had stood on a left-
wing platform, he had been elected and these
policies would now be implemented.

The Advent of Thatcherism
The advent of a Conservative Government committed
to free market capitalism, the curbing of union
power and reductions in public expenditure was a
direct threat to the mineworkers and the coal
industry. At a Labour Party rally in Leeds Owen
Briscoe called for a one day general strike against
public spending cuts and attempts to weaken the
unions: "But like Heath, Thatcher's plans can be
defeated if the full power of the unions is brought
to bear against them".[58] Similar calls were made
for the miners to defend their industry against

closures, with Arthur Scargill urging a national campaign to force an early general election.[59]

The Area's hostility to Conservatism is, of course, part of a historical tradition -- calls to defend the welfare state became increasingly ritualistic but a harder element was present in the Area's opposition to Thatcher: preventing pit closures. This was a particularly important issue as the left's rise to power was, in part, occasioned by the NUM failure to deflect the post-1958 closure programme, firing a determination that this would never happen again. At the 1979 Area Demonstration Scargill warned his audience that free market economics meant pit closures on a massive scale. The South Wales miners' change of heart over strike action over the closure of Deep Duffryn, placed an even greater emphasis upon the leadership convincing   the union membership that united they could win.[60]   Despite a 20% pay offer the Yorkshire Area recommended rejection as it was essential for the miners self-confidence that they fight back immediately. Nationally, the ballot was 107,656 for industrial action to 113,160 against: In Yorkshire this was reversed, 40,363 for to 14,741 against, and the loss was ascribed to weak and ambivalent national leadership. Area policy was collective unity in the face of resurgent individualistic-capitalism, symbolised by the Area's support of the steelworkers. This support showed enormous grassroots vitality but the outcome showed that the steelworkers and possibly the miners were not facing a second Heath, but a Cabinet determined to resist union power and winning public support in so doing. In retrospect the 1980 steel strike was crucial event for the miners' consciousness.

Scargill's 1980 Presidential Address concentrated upon attacking government policy, their attacks on the unions and the threat of pit closures.   These themes were repeated at the 1980 Annual Demonstration but with a change of emphasis: " Jobsecurity...must now be the major aim of the (NUM)... We must be prepared to fight to defend the gains of the past few years".[61]   The miners were on the defensive, but the Area Council recommended that should any Yorkshire pit be threatened with closure as a result of government policy (a commitment extended to any pit anywhere in the United Kingdom) the coalfield be balloted on strike action.   To close one pit was to threaten every pit and the NCB's tactics of divide and rule

should be resisted from the outset.[62]
     The Coal Industry Bill (1980) imposed on the
NCB the target of financial viability by 1982-1983
with the ending of all government grants to cover
loss making pits.   The consequence could only be
massive pit closures and the outburst of anger
led to the miners' last victory in March 1981.[63]
Despite the Cabinet's humiliating surrender its
long term policy remained unchanged with the NCB
pursuing a 'softly-softly' approach to pit
closures.   Additionally the slump in demand made
more pits uneconomic and this coincided with
Scargill's election as national President precisely
when the industry was on the verge of a protracted
crisis over pit closures that he had pledged himself
and the NUM to resist.   The events of 1981 implied
that the NUM could block government policy if it
was united in favour of resistance.   The task of
the Area and National leaderships was to create such
a national consciousness.

The Miners In Retreat?

Writing in Marxism Today Professor Allen looked
forward to the politicisation of the miners, with
the election of Arthur Scargill as national
President as a signal contribution to this process.
Politicisation was not concerned simply with wages,
conditions or strikes "but whether they achieve a
political awareness which would lead them to shape
their own destinies in and beyond the coal
industry".[64]   In these terms, the miners have
opted to play a waiting role in the present crisis
of British capitalism.   Surely, this is what we
would expect: the ideological hegemony of the
crisis is extremely powerful and one of the first
casualities of recession is energy demand, and the
miners knew this.   The psychological impact of
growing coal stocks cannot be lightly dismissed.
Miners as a group are, however, dismissive of
Thatcherite orthodoxy, but such is the ideological
weight of the recession, there seemed no credible
response.   Recession has induced a crisis of
confidence within the unions exacerbated by the
changing composition of the workforce, the gap
between leaders and led, the proliferation of
bargaining centres and the ever present tendency
towards sectionalism.[65]   Why should the miners
be immune to these influences?
     Allen concentrates on the key question of
consciousness, nothing its complexity and unpredic-
tability.   Prophetically, he wrote, "Intensive

political activity may produce no tangible changes in the consciousness of workers", but, he continued, "in other situations workers may suddenly, with little prompting, express a heightened awareness of their political position".66   This equates consciousness with militancy and lack of militancy with a lack of consciousness.   However, the recent behaviour of the miners indicates not a lack of consciousness but rather an acute awareness of their present political and economic vulnerability.

After their victories in 1972 and 1974 the miners enjoyed, as we have seen, the reputation as the steafast militant core of the organised working class, a reputation enhanced by the Cabinet's retreat over pit closures in 1981.   The November 1982 ballot on pay and pit closures was seen as part of a resurgence of consciousness but only 39% of the membership who voted supported the NEC.   Many factors contributed to the result. Coal stocks were high at the power stations and the CEGB (with the experience of 1972 and 1974 to draw upon) were confident of lasting out the winter. Additionally, it was unlikely that the power workers and engineers would give the NUM the same degree of support as in 1972 and 1974.   The Triple Alliance of miners, steelworkers and railwaymen, whilst powerful on paper was weak in practice.67   The general atmosphere of gloom and despondency engendered by the recession created a public opinion unsympathetic to industrial action and the Thatcher Government seemed a far more resolute opponent than the Heath Government.   The failure of the miners to support the NEC can be explained in economic terms: the overtime ban was costing some miners £30-£40 per week, the NCB's offer was above the current rate of inflation, and so on.   Yet, between 1969 and 1972 the miners challenged the economic 'facts of life' and the government.   Why not this time?

The miners' refusal to support the NEC was not because of a lack of publicity.   The NEC transmitted its case (even against the opposition of some members) in The Miner and Arthur Scargill undertook a wide-ranging speaking tour.   These activities were mirrored at Area level.   These meetings testified to the impact of Scargill and his message upon his audience but it was not these miners who needed to be convinced; it was the vast majority who did not attend.   They obviously failed to respond.   With hindsight the linking of pit closures and pay in the ballot was a mistake.

If there had been separate questions the miners
might have accepted the wages offer and approved
the NEC's line on pit closures. Linking the two
make it likely that the wages would be accepted,
thus ensuring the rejection of resistance to pit
closures. A further defect was the short time
allowed for negotiation between the presentation
of the claim on 15 July and the settlement date of
1 November. This gave the NCB ample opportunity to
prevaricate and force a crisis (serious negotiations
did not begin until September) whilst emphasising
the level of coal stocks and precarious nature of
coal demand.
     The mining industry is in a state of confusion
and this contributed to this and subsequent results
rejecting the NEC's stances. Four broad groups of
pits can be identified: first, pits with a long
life but which are facing temporary problems
(eg. geological). Strike action in this instance
might be seen as jeopardising long term investment.
Second, those pits with a short life but which were
doing well. Here strike action might contribute to
speedy closure. Third, pits with a long life
facing no immediate problems. Again, there was
little reason to strike as the future seemed secure;
equally, it could be argued that this group of
pits could strike with little risk. Finally, pits
with a short life doing badly and facing severe
problems; here strike action might result in
rapid closure. Although as closure was assured,
these pits might be said to have nothing to lose by
striking. These are not rigid categories, but they
do show the complex cross pressures in the coal
industry. Each group of pits can be said to have
a compelling reason for not striking. However, such
explanations and immediate factors disguise the
importance of other elements.
     A factor rarely considered in the behaviour of
miners is the NCB. Yet, power relations in the
nationalised coal industry are not, in reality,
significantly different from those of private
industry and as an employer the NCB is increasingly
subject to the same market forces as private
industry. Norman Siddal, NCB Chairman, saw the
Board's main problem as one of finance, and the
solution lay in bringing supply into line with
demand. While high-cost pits remained in production
there would be less money for investment and halting
investment in all but the most productive pits would
force up costs so making more pits vulnerable to
closure. By selective investment the NUM's

determination to protect jobs could then be portrayed as threatening future employment prospects.68
   The problem was how to close pits without provoking an explosion in the NUM. The NCB did this by arguing doggedly and persistently that there was no national 'hit list' of closures, these were a matter for the various NUM and NCB Areas to discuss. To acknowledge the existence of a national pit closure programme was to risk uniting the NUM, this could be avoided by adhering rigidly to the colliery review procedure and by claiming that it was 'common knowledge' in the coalfields which were the vulnerable pits on the basis of the monthly computer print-outs. NCB Area Directors were instructed to acknowledge that there would have to be closures, but that those miners who took neither early retirement or redundancy would be redeployed. Logically, then, there could be no national 'hit list' because closures were a local matter and the process would be relatively painless as the victims would be provided for. This strategy sought to prevent the emergence of a national consciousness by pursuing 'salami tactics', whilst the strategy of the NUM was the opposite: the creation of a national consciousness. Siddal's line was to argue constantly and consistently that the industry would not be butchered, but that the industry's problems would not go away. The NUM's publication of an internal NCB paper and the NCB's evidence to the Monopolies Commission, both of which suggested an embryonic closure programme existed, embarrassed both the NCB and Scargill's critics.69 However, the NCB's interpretation of the crisis facing the industry (endorsed by the media), the policy of localisation, high pay and high severance payments all had their impact.
   The NCB's projection for the industry to 1991 assumed the rapid closure of high cost pits at the rate of 2m tonnes capacity per year for ten years. Between March 1974 and March 1982, 29,700 jobs were lost in mining. In 1981-1982 employment fell by 12,000. If the NCB's assumptions were fully implemented this would mean job losses on the scale of 1981-1982 every year for the next nine years, with the bulk of the closures coming in periphery coalfields. Given such a closure rate is it likely that the labour not made redundant or retiring could be absorbed back into an industry pressing ahead with automated new-technology mining techniques?70

In its defence the NCB argued that this closure
rate is less than that envisaged in the Plan For
Coal, but this was to be balanced by continued
high investment in new and existing pits.   Under
the impact of recession and cash limits the NCB
has reduced the rate of capital investment.[71]   In
aggregate terms investment remains high.   However,
two points should be noted: first, the rate of
investment has declined since 1974-1975 and
dramatically between 1979-1981.   The implication is
that the NCB is seeking a reduction on the planned
long-term capacity of the industry and planned
future investment has fallen from £620m (1980-1981)
to £552m (1981-1982).   Second, high aggregate
investment disguises regional disparities.   These
measures have been adopted despite the fact that
coal has maintained its share of the energy market
(about 36%) since 1973, has improved its overall
performance, and that the long-term future for
coal is bright.   Coal consumption is less than in
1973 because of more efficient fuel use and the
recession: domestic consumption has fallen from
131.2m to 118.4m tonnes between 1973-1981.   The
future of the industry may be sacrificed to short
term financial expediency.   The profit and loss
account of a pit is only of secondary importance
compared to whether or not it is classified as
having a long or short life (up to 10 years), but
this categorisation may depend on whether or not
there is investment to exploit coal reserves.
      The miners' acceptance of the NCB's interpre-
tation of the industry's problems was encouraged by
two important events.   In early December 1982 it
was rumoured that the CEGB wished to reduce coal
purchases by £400m and cancel existing contracts
which committed the CEGB to taking 65m tonnes,
amounting to 60% of the NCB's output.[72]   Whilst
concerned at the CEGB's attitude this was a great
help in the NCB's own cost-cutting campaign as it
enabled the NCB to reiterate coal's market weakness.
The new contracts signed between the NCB and CEGB
means that the CEGB would take less coal but pay
more or less the same price.
      The brief inquiry into pit closures by the
Energy Select Committee in November 1982 rejected
the NUM's claims of a 'hit list'.   It urged the
NCB to speed up closures whilst recommending
greater openness with the NUM.   The Committee
accepted the Board's case, describing the NUM's
position as perverse: capacity had to be brought
into line with demand and the taxpayer could not be

expected to subsidise pits and coal stocks.[73]

Perhaps the final blow of the left's hopes of an immediate resurgence of miners' consciousness came with the failure of the South Wales, Kent and Scottish miners to generate opposition to proposed closures (either partial or total) in their Areas. These failures and the later failure over the closure of Lewis Merthyr demonstrated eloquently that the miners accepted there was no alternative to pit closures. Right wing union leaders cannot be blamed this time.

The history of the miners since 1947 is dominated by their adaptation and that of their industry to dramatically changing market conditions. Handy has demonstrated that a downturn in strike action coincided with a downturn in the demand for coal, whereas when demand strengthens (as in the early-1970s), there tends to be an upsurge in industrial action. As demand weakened in the early-1970s there was a greater willingness to negotiate and bargain.[74]

Over the last ten years the workforce as a whole has been remarkably quiescent. Taking the post-war period as a whole the militancy of 1969-1974 is an aberration and in the strike ballots between 1972 and 1982 the miners have voted for moderation on all but three occasions, albeit with significant regional variations. Wage movements exert a powerful influence on the miners. From the late 1950s the daywagemen maintained their position relative to wages in manufacturing industry, but the relative position of the piece-worker (generally, the faceworkers)was substantially eroded. After 1960 they fell further and further behind. Coal's market weakness made effective opposition difficult, but the change in coal's market position and the two strikes of 1972 and 1974 enabled faceworkers to improve their relative position. Other mineworkers were then pulled along under NPLA.

Under the piecework system localised disputes were frequent, industrial conflict (albeit unoffi-cial) was an integral part of the work situation. NPLA was, as we have seen a major landmark: it gave the NCB greater control over costs and was compatible with low demand. For the NUM it standardised pay and preserved jobs (albeit at the cost of low pay) and in ending local piece rates helped forge the national unity of the early 1970s.

The introduction of Area incentive schemes had two
important effects.   First, they weakened national
solidarity by removing common wage rates.
Solidarity is now far harder to forge: miners are
well paid and key groups are doing well out of the
schemes.   Second, they have not generated the same
gut hostility as the piecework system.   Payment
is not dependent on the individual effort of the
miners, but on a team achieving a set task.   Thus,
in terms of effort by the individual miner the
cost of these schemes is small compared to the
payments.   Allen has claimed that the incentive
schemes have not broken the national unity of 1972
and 1974.   The evidence denies this, and even if
we accept Allen's contention this does not alter
the fact that they are a dis-unifying force in the
NUM which make it harder to secure national unity.
This effect has been amplified by recession.[75]
More importantly, these schemes have so far
enabled miners as a group to maintain their external
differential with the rest of industry.   This, as
we have seen, is crucial.   The present crisis in
the industry came not at the end of a period of
massive deterioration in pay and rapid pit closures
but at the end of a period when the miners had
maintained their relative position.   Some NUM Areas
(for example, Nottingham) have so far benefited
from the restructuring of the industry.
         It should be remembered that the labour force
is in a state of flux.   During the rundown of the
industry the percentage of miners under 40 fell
from 50% in 1958 to 36% in 1971;   it was an
ageing workforce.   In 1972 the average age of the
workforce was 44.2, by 1981 this had fallen to 39.4.
Juvenile recruitment (under 18) has increased from
36% of new entrants in 1971-1972 to 44% in 1980-81.
Adult new entrants have increased from 19% to
25%, and total new recruitment has increased from
55% to 69%.   Re-entry recruitment was 45% in 1971-
72, peaked at 62% in 1973-74 and halved to 31% of
total recruitment in 1980-81.   On average, over
the past ten years, 58% of recruits were new to the
industry.   This percentage is all the more
important when we remember that in the last ten
years the total workforce has fallen by 50,000(18%),
of the 274,000 employed in 1972, 22% have left the
industry.[76]
         In 1974-75 manpower increased by 6,200, the
first increased since 1957-1958, and recruitment was
concentrated amongst the younger age groups.   In
August 1977 the early retirement scheme came into

operation and 9,200 miners left the industry.   Such
a loss of experienced and skilled workers caused
both a labour shortage and a fall in productivity.
This was remedied by increased recruitment and
the biggest increase was in adult recruits with no
previous mining experience, the so-called 'green"
miners.   In the last ten years the workforce has
become younger and substantial numbers of miners
have no direct experience of the struggles of the
early-1970s.[77]   Such rapid change was not a
problem when mining was a family trade handed down
from father to son and when the younger miner was
socialised from birth into the mores and traditions
of the mining industry and mining communities.
However, as with other working class occupational
communities this process of labour reproduction
has been eroded, weakening industrial if not
electoral solidarity.   The ecology of the mining
communities has been disrupted: for example, pit
closures mean that many miners travel considerable
distances to   work, technological   change at the
point of production has weakened or broken up the
cohesive work-teams, and the erosion of the coalfields' relative geographical and social isolation
has weakened the reinforcing cycle of pit, community
community, union.   The miners have been subject
to those forces which have eroded the traditional
basis of working class politics and culture.[78]
The ecology of the mining communities was based on
occupational communities where work and non-work
life reinforced each other creating a political-
cultural pattern crucial for the evolution of the
Labour Movement.   The nature of mining, relative
isolation and the power of history have, to some
extent, insulated the mining communities but they
have not been immune from the forces of change.
     An activist consciousness is not easy to
create, even amongst a group of workers with a
reputation for such a consciousness.   The behaviour
of the miners in recent years owes much to the
general impact of recession but other factors
peculiar to the mining industry have also been at
work.   Paradoxically, because of their success
in 1972 and 1974 measures promoted to maintain
their relative position have reduced the miners'
willingness to act in concert.   This is not to
argue that the miners are a spent force (the
influences which have generated quiescence could
also generate militancy,) but after 1981 the miners
were reluctant to respond to their leaders.
While they continue to appeal to a militancy which

has fragmented since 1981 the perception of the miners' power will weaken further and their influence along with it.   Yet, history shows that there will come a point, as their leaders predict, where the miners will take a collective decision to retreat no further and to stand their ground and fight.

REFERENCES

1   The emphasis upon consciousness and leadership
     was one of the main reasons for the
     founding of the Area' monthly newspaper,
     The Yorkshire Miner in 1976. Distributed
     free at the pits the paper had the effect
     of taking the leadership's message
     directly to the mass membership.
2   I have examined the complexities of the NUM-
     Government relationship in my unpublished
     paper, The Miners and the Labour Government,
     1974-1979, presented to the PSA Conference,
     University of Hull, April 1980.
3   President's Address to Council, in, YA(NUM)
     Annual Report, 1973;   p6.
4   Annual Report, 1973;   p9.
5   Annual Report, 1975;   p18
6   Annual Report: 1976; p21.   The Objects of the
     NUM include the aspirations "to join with
     other organisations for the purpose of and
     with a view to the complete abolition of
     Capitalism".   NUM Rules 1976, Rule 3(s).
7   Annual Report, 1976;   p7.
8   See, for example, NUM: Annual Conference
     Report, 1974; pp94-98.   At this Conference
     Gormley declared, "whatever we do we must
     ensure a succession of Labour Governments..
     .."(p98).
9   NUM: Report of the NEC, May 1973;   pp11-12,
     and, National Energy Policy (NUM, October
     1972) for the union's policy and LPCR 1973;
     pp130-138 for the Party's acceptance of a
     coal based energy policy.
10   For the NUM's attitude to the February election
     see, The Miner (General Election Issue),
     February 1974, and Report of the NEC, May
     1974;   p9.   NUM(EC): Economic-Sub
     Committee, 9 April and 9 May 1974 contains
     the NEC's acceptance of the scoial
     contract's voluntary incomes policy
     accompanied by economic and social reform.
11   YA(NUM): Annual Reports, 1975; p12 (my

emphasis).

12 Labour Party Manifesto, February 1974; pp1-3
    and pp9-10.
13 Coal Industry Examination, Interim & Final
    Reports (1974), and, The Plan For Coal
    (1975).
14 YA(NUM): Annual Report, 1975; p7.
15 The Yorkshire Miner (Ferbuary-March 1977).
    1977 saw an upsurge in opposition to incomes
    policy and the social contract throughout
    the whole NUM. See, for example, The
    Miner (February-March) 1977, p 5 for
    Nottinghamshire's rejection of incomes
    policy, and, S Vincent, 'How the Labour
    Government Can Save Its Skin', in, The
    Miner (May-June) 1977, p7.
16 H L Handy, Wages Policy in the British Coal-
    mining Industry (Cambridge UP 1981); p287.
17 For his continued advocacy of incentive
    schemes see, J Gormley, Battered Cherub
    (London, Hamish Hamilton 1982), pp149-153.
18 The Yorkshire Miner (May-June) 1977.
19 The Miner (Special Ballot Issue) October 1977;
    The Guardian, 2 September 1977, and The
    Sunday Times, 6 November 1977.
20 The Yorkshire Miner (August/September) and
    (September/October) 1977.
21 High Court (Chancery Division) Group A, 1977-
    N-No 2345 (19 October 1977) for the
    judgement and details of the injunction.
22 The Yorkshire Miner (January) 1978.
23 The Yorkshire Miner (February) 1978, and, The
    Miner (February-March) 1978 for Lawrence
    Daly's acknowledgement of the political
    motives underpinning the NEC's decision.
24 YA(NUM): Annual Reports, 1978; p8.
25 YA(NUM): Annual Reports, 1976; p7.
26 D Butler, 'The Paradox of Party Difference',
    in, American Behavioral Scientist (1960),
    and, R Rose, 'The Political Ideas of
    English Party Activists', in, American
    Political Science Review (1962) for this
    phenomenon.
27 The Yorkshire Miner (December) 1979.
28 Information from participants.
29 YA(NUM): Annual Reports, 1977; p71, and
    J Dromey & G Taylor, Grunwick: The Workers'
    Story (London, Lawrence & Wishart 1978);
    p123 contains an account of the fate of the
    first group of pickets at the hands of the
    Special Patrol Group on 23 June.   On

23 June both Arthur Scargill and Morris Jones, then editor of The Yorkshire Miner, were arrested.   It was this incident which caused Jones to flee to the GDR with his wife and family claiming police had threatened them.   In addition, p141 describes the Area's decision to send a second contingent for the mass demonstration of 11 July, and p146 contains a moving description of the visual and emotional impact of the miners "disciplined solidarity".

30   YA(NUM): Annual Reports, 1977;   p16.

31   A Scargill, 'The New Unionism', in New Left Review, 92 (July-August) p31.

32   The Sheffield Star, 28 August 1975.

33   The Sheffield Star, 12 January 1981.

34   The Sheffield Star, 28 August 1975, and, 11 March 1980 (source of quote).   Such sentiments led to the Committee on Privileges hearing.

35   Sheffield Morning Telegraph, 11 June 1979. See also, The Sheffield Star, 18 June 1980.

36   The Sheffield Star, 6 November 1979.

37   The Sheffield Star, 13 January 1981.

38   The Yorkshire Miner (May) 1979

39   It should be pointed out that this conception of leadership places an obligation on the membership to support elected leaders trying to implement democratically determined policies.   The left's firm belief that if a policy was put clearly before the membership and fully explained this support would be forthcoming.   Again we see the heavy emphasis upon active leadership.

40   The power structure of the NUM has already been described in Chapter 6.

41   The Yorkshire Miner (December) 1977, and, (March) 1978 for similar sentiments.

42   NUM: Annual Conference Report, 1972;   p166.

43   NUM: Annual Conference Report, 1973;   Agenda p.xx;   1974 Agenda p.xiv and p105 (Business Committee) and 1975;   pp21-213.

44   NUM: Annual Conference Report, 1978;   p486.

45   Annual Conference Report, p488.

46   Annual Conference Report, pp492-493.

47   Scargill arouses emotion, never indifference. Doubt as to whether his Yorkshire persona and politics could be 'nationalised' to appeal to the broad membership as opposed to the national left was not considered at

the time.   There was never any doubt on the left that he would be the candidate and would be elected: the vicissitudes of being national President would, obviously, only become apparent after the election.

48   Daily Telegraph, 22 May 1979.
49   The Guardian, 11 July 1980.
50   The Guardian, 5 March 1981.
51   The Sunday Times, 5 July 1981.   Bell's election material, a tabloid newspaper-type manifesto, 'Britain's Miners -- The Way Ahead', of 4 sides contained 3 pictures of Bell in miners helmet and lamp either underground or on the pit top.   Even a cartoon of Arthur Scargill had Bell in underground equipment.
52   The Times, 12 December 1980.
53   The Yorkshire Miner (March/April) 1979.
54   The Guardian, 21 November 1981.   Scargill's manifesto, Miners in the Eighties was published in September 1981.   For an examination, see my, 'The Miners in the Eighties: An Analysis', in, Political Quarterly 53(2) 1982; pp218-221.
55   The Guardian, 10 July 1981.
56   The Yorkshire Miner (November) 1981.   There was a fourth candidate, Bernard Donaghy (President of the North-West Area).   His candidacy was interpreted by the left as a measure of the right's disarray.
57   The Voting was;   A Scargill   138,083(70.4)
                       T Bell   34,075(17.3)
                       R Chadburn   17,979 (9.1)
                       B Donaghy   6,442 (3,3)
                                       197,229
     The Guardian, 5 and 9 December 1981.
58   The Yorkshire Miner (December) 1979.
59   The Yorkshire Miner (January) 1980.
60   The Yorkshire Miner (June) and (July) 1979.
61   The Yorkshire Miner (June) 1980.
62   NUM: Annual Conference Report, 1980; pp483-495, and The Yorkshire Miner (September) 1980.
63   T Hall, King Coal (Harmondsworth, Penguin 1981); pp253-267.
64   V Allen, 'The Miners on the Move', in, Marxism Today (February) 1982, p21.
65   R Taylor, The Workers and the New Depression (London, Macmillan 1982) and, T Lane, 'The Unions: Caught on the Ebb Tide', in, Marxism Today (September) 1982, and

R Currie, Industrial Politics (Oxford, Clarendon Press 1979).

66   Allen, 'The Miners on the Move', p19.

67   See, Report of a Joint Conference Between the NUM, ISTC and NUR, 23 January 1981; What Is the Future? (ISTC, NUR, NUM January 1981); and the NUM's, The Miners and the Battle For Britain (1980).

68   The Guardian, 2 December 1982.

69   The Guardian, 10 November 1982, 24 November 19 1982.   Both before and after the 1983 General Election further evidence of a pit closure programme emerged, given credence by MacGregor's appointment as NCB chairman, See, Daily Mirror, 6 June 1983, The Guardian 16 June and 12 July 1983.

70   The Monopolies and Mergers Commission Report (Cmnd 8920) forecast continuing heavy losses(confirmed by the 1983 NCB Report) unless pits were closed.   10% of the NCB's output added £260m to the 1981-1982 deficit of £428m.   These pits are concentrated in already high unemployment areas - - Scotland, South Wales and the North East.

71   Capital Expenditure on the Coal Industry (£5m)

74-75	75-76	76-77	77-78	78-79	79-80	80-81	
131	211	266	334	454	617	736	
	+46	+21	+20	+26	+26	+16	(%)

Source: NCB: Annual Reports & Accounts.

72   The Guardian, 1 December and 7 December 1982. Sunday Times (Business News), 5 December, and The Guardian, 16 December for the negotiation of the final agreement.

73   HC 135 Second Report from the Energy Committee confirmed what the NUM had already claimed in leaking Cabinet documents that the Government nuclear power programme was motivated (partly) by a desire to create a 'Scargill free-zone' and end electricity's dependence on coal.   HC 114-1.   First Report from the Energy Committee (1980-1981): The Government's Statement on the New Nuclear Power Programme, Vol.1 (Report), para 20(p19).

74   Handy, Wages Policy ...., p226.

75   Allen, 'The Miners on the Move', p20.

76   Calculated from information in the NCB's Annual Report & Accounts.   The NCB has ceased to publish detailed information on

the age composition of the labour force.
77   At the 1983 NUM Conference Peter Heathfield
(North Derbyshire) urged the delegates to
"Stop basking in the glory of 1972 and
1974.   It's a completely different ball
game".   The Guardian, 7 July 1983.
Heathfield estimated that 50% of the present
workforce were not involved in the disputes
of the early-1970s.
78   The best known example of this argument is,
J Seabrook, What Went Wrong? (London,
Gollancz 1978) and on a wider canvass see,
A Gorz, Farewell to the Working Class
(London, Pluto Press 1983).   Interestingly,
though the voting in the 1983 election
showed a further erosion in Labour's
electoral base, the most secure areas were
the old established industrial heartlands
such as the Yorkshire coalfield.   See,
The Economist (Post-Election Survey)
18 June 1983; pp36-27; A Ryan 'The Slow
Death of Labour England', in, New Society
16 June 1983; pp419-421; P Kellner,
'Anatomy of a Landslide', in, New Statesman,
17 June 1983; pp7-8; and, D Massey,
'The Contours of Victory', in, Marxism
Today (July 1983); pp16-19.

CONCLUSIONS

The Miners and Politics: An Overview
The Labour Party's supra-class electoral strategy
has proved to be an enormously valuable resource for
Party leaders and ministers in their dealings with
the trade unions. Despite loyalty and commitment
the miners found this electoral perspective enabled
Labour to resist 'sectional' demands. This was
compounded by the miners' political dependence on
Labour and their apprehension at the prospect of
Conservative rule. These factors inhibited the
miners from challenging a Labour Government.
Acquiescence provoked controversy on the extent to
which the NUM ought to support a Labour Government
to the detriment of its own interests. To the
question: under what circumstances should the
miners refuse to support a Labour Government and
what sanctions should be taken?, no authoritative
answer was found.
     It is a myth that the miners dominate
absolutely coalfield CLPs. The Party is
responsible for electoral activity and the miners,
though numerically and financially significant,
were supportative of the CLPs whose responsibilities
were wider than those of the miners. Considerable
historical, financial and personal links exist, but
the relationship is one of functional separation and
organisational independence.
     The sponsored MPs have a small role in the
political activity of the miners. They do play an
intelligence-propagandist role, and have a symbolic
importance in the PLP but when faced by a choice
between the miners or loyalty to Party leaders,
the majority chose the latter. Sponsorship confers
little influence: cocooned by parliamentary
privilege MPs can withstand extra-parliamentary
pressure.
     The political activity of the Yorkshire miners
was profoundly influenced by the outcome of the

controversy over how best to defend the miners'
interests.   The policies of the leadership
resulted in the unofficial strikes of 1969 and 1970
which were a repudiation of the 'moderate and
responsible' policies pursued since 1947 and which
resulted in change in the Area's policies and
leadership.   The consequences of the rise of the
left for the NUM as a whole were considerable.
However, their influence was limited by the mal-
representation of the Areas on the NEC which
conferred a majority on the right-wing.

The coal strikes of 1972 and 1974 represent
the end of an epoch for the miners.   Their
organisation, the economy's dependence on coal and
the solidarity displayed by other workers transformed the miners' political influence.   A
remarkable aspect of the strikes was their organisation: they were run by an increasingly self-
confident membership and they demonstrated that
trade union power is not a simple function of
size for despite decline the miners disrupted an
economy dependent on electricity generated by coal.
Militancy was amplified by the enhanced market
position of coal consequent on the rise of OPEC --
an unforseeable and fortuitous confluence of
events.   Despite determination and market power the
miners' victories were not guaranteed, they needed
the solidarity of other unions.   Without this the
miners' fight would have been longer and harder.

The Miners and Labour Governments

It is assumed frequently that the more loyal a
trade union is to a political party the more
responsive it will be to a union's desires.
Loyalty does bring rewards but also disappointment
and frustration.   The miners' commitment to the
Labour Party cannot be doubted, yet this has rarely
been reciprocated in full measure precisely
because of the miners' loyalty to and reliance upon
Labour.

The Labour Party originated as a means of
increasing working class representation, and on to
this was grafted the socialist objective of
Clause 4.   One of Labour's central aims is the
reform of British society in the interests of the
working class, but this has never dominated
aboslutely.   The theory and practise of British
socialism emphasised the rejection of the class
struggle in favour of altruistic reform and governing in 'the national interest'.   The miners
affiliated to the Labour Party because it offered

Conclusions

a more satisfactory party-political instrument
than the Liberals, particularly when nationalisation
became the key item on the miners' 'shopping list'.
Before the mines could be nationalised Labour had
to form a government. With the failure of direct
action in 1919 legislation became the only hope and
defeat in 1926 confirmed the miners' leaders
acceptance of the pre-eminence of Labour's electoral
strategy: that of taking power by becoming the
largest single party in the House of Commons. This
was to be achieved by appealing to all "workers by
hand or brain" and politically this enabled Labour
to claim responsibilities wider than those of the
unions or the working class. This strategy seemed
to offer the miners their best chance of securing
a sympathetic government, hence their deference to
the Party leadership's definition of Labour's
electoral interests. The weakness of minority
governments confirmed that only a majority government could achieve real advances. Party leaders
rejected an exclusivist class appeal in favour of
an inclusivist supra-class appeal as the best means
of winning power. This was accepted by the Union
on both ideological and pragmatic grounds.
      This strategy seemed vindicated when the 1945
Labour Government nationalised the mines.   In
return, the NUM pledged its full support to 'their'
Government. The Government asked for their cooperation in producing cheap coal to fuel recovery, and
as wages were the largest single cost in the price
of coal, union leaders endeavoured to restrain
wage demands. They supported Government incomes
policy, claiming it was the duty of the miners as
well as in their long term interests, to support
fully the Attlee government. Though grateful for
nationalisation the miners became increasingly
reluctant to accept that government policy or the
'long term' should dominate their immediate
interests. The result was the decisive rejection
of incomes policy in 1949-1950.
      Despite working with the Conservative
Government elected in 1951, the policy of the NUM
and Yorkshire Area was to secure the re-election of
Labour as quickly as possible, both to complete
the work of 1945-1951 and to defend the miners and
their industry. During the 1950s there was a
community of interest between the miners' leaders
and the Party leadership. The latter saw unions
like the NUM as a bulwark against left-wing
factionalism, and NUM leaders opposed factionalism
as it ran counter to the dominant ethic of trade

unionism (unity), and because it damaged the
Party's electoral attractiveness. Yorkshire Area
leaders were bitterly hostile to any group or
ideology which threatened the unity of the Movement
and its electoral prospects, seeing their supporters
as misguided allies of the Conservative Party.

Thus, loyalty to Labour was fundamental to the
political activity of the miners in the 1950s.
This activity can be divided into two phases:
between 1945 and 1957 coal enjoyed a strong market
position. Nationalisation enhanced the role of
the Union, and the NUM believed it could achieve
its industrial aims by pressure group politics and
collective bargaining. Gradually, however the
NUM became aware of the political impositions on
the coal industry, particularly the government's
refusal to halt the rundown after 1958. The
second phase (1958-1964) saw the political and
industrial policies of the Area (and the NUM)
being motivated by a determination to secure the
election of a majority Labour Government committed
to reversing the policies of the Conservative
Government. The NUM persuaded (apparently
successfully) the Party and TUC to adopt a target of
a 200m ton coal industry. Industrial decline
seemed to confirm two axioms: that Conservative
governments were anti-coal and could not be trusted;
and the defence of miners' interests could not be
secured solely by institutionalised collective
bargaining or group politics, but needed a
sympathetic, and therefore Labour, government.

The miners found it easy to persuade the Party
in Opposition to accept a 200m ton industry but
they were to find it impossible to persuade the
Wilson Government to adhere to this commitment.
The Attlee Government had sometimes ignored and
acted against the miners' interests when they were
not felt to be congruent with wider responsibilities, but it had nationalised the mines. The
Wilson Government seemed to take and give nothing.
The Cabinet declared that coal would remain the
basic fuel in the economy but they would not
guarantee a 200m ton industry. Union leaders
supported the Government, accepting an incomes
policy which rapidly became pay restraint despite
opposition from the membership. No sanctions
were taken: why?

It is a myth that a Labour government must be
dominated by the unions. There is a 'special
relationship': the Party proclaims its unique
ability to work with the unions, and the unions see

the Party as more sympathetic and responsive than
Conservative governments.   Yet, Labour has two
resources for resisting 'sectional' demands from
the Unions: primordial sentiments of loyalty, and,
fear of the Conservatives.   Both were deployed
against the miners.
    First, a caveat: the miners must not be seen
as a monolithic bloc.   The NUM-Government
relationship was complicated by the inability of
union leaders to extend their bargains with government to the members.   It had proved possible
to secure acquiescence on wage restraint for two
years (more or less); then internal opposition
forced union leaders to abandon their bargains.
Area and National leaders were obsessively loyal to
'their' government, whilst the vast bulk of the
members were content to take the advice of their
leaders.   Yet, there were substantial minorities
within the Yorkshire and other Areas who were
bitterly critical of union and government, arguing
that party-political activity was a blind alley and
that the miners should rely on their industrial
resources.   Until 1969-1970 they had little impact.
Miners leaders were in a dilemma: they naturally
preferred Labour to Conservative, but Labour was
pursuing policies inimical to the immediate
interests on their members.   They wanted to change
those policies but felt unable to take sanctions.
The result was paralysis   Yet resistance was
possible.
    The miners have rejected the policies of the
Party leadership on five occasions: incomes policy
(1949 and 1966), Clause 4 (1960), fuel policy
(1968) and industrial relations legislation (1970).
Opposition to some policies was inevitable as they
struck at the vitals of the union.   The NUM, as
the foremost advocate of nationalisation, had to
oppose Gaitskell's attempt to expurgate Clause 4
despite supporting Gaitskell as leader and the
political strategy of Revisionism.   Similarly,
union leaders could do nothing other than oppose In
Place of Strife, even though Wilson proclaimed it
as vital for Labour's electoral prospects and as
in the national interest.   The NUM's support was
simply not negotiable.   On fuel and incomes policy,
however, compromise was negotiable.   In both
1945 and 1964 the NUM accepted the Government's
case for wage restraint: that inflation would
destroy the government.   Despite mounting
opposition they attempted to deliver support for
government policy, even to the point of ignoring an

NUM conference resolution and Union Rules.   Despite
considerable pressure the NUM was unable to change
government fuel policy from continuing the rundown
of the industry.   This decline was believed to have
destroyed the industrial power of the miners and,
in any case, a political strike against a Labour
Government (or any government for that matter) was
inconceivable.   Thus, in return for higher
redundancy payments and government funding of the
social costs of pit closures, the union acquiesced.
      Political impotence, then, was the result
of three factors.   First, the inhibitions born of
history, sentiment and political calculation
decreed inaction against Labour.   Second, the
ethos of nationalisation which proscribed industrial
action and elevated cooperation as an article of
faith.   Finally, the quantitative reduction of
the industry convinced many miners and their leaders
that they had no effective sanction to deploy.
The rundown and the uncertainty it generated broke
the confidence of the miners until the late-1960s
when the orthodoxy, maintained since 1947,
collapsed.
      The conclusion must be that the miners' loyalty
to Labour led to a lack of influence over government policy.   The disdain showed by the Government
for the miners led to some disillusionment, but
for the threat of a Conservative Government committed to industrial relations reform and free market
economics, the drift from Labour might have been
more severe.   Before the 1970 election there was
a remarkable reconciliation between the NUM and
Labour but there was also a deep discontent
manifested in the unofficial strikes of 1969 and the
1970 election.
      The miners' relationship with the Labour
Government confirms the hypothesis that any union
which places support of a government above the
interests of its members risks internal conflict
and, ultimately, schism.

The Miners and Electoral Politics
The role of the miners in grassroots politics has
rarely been examined, yet there is a powerful
image of that role: that the miners are the Labour
Party in the coalfields.   Except for a brief period
after 1918, the miners and the CLPs were
organisationally distinct and independent of the
Union.   This is not to say that the miners and the
Union played no role in the CLPs: the branch
official who is also a CLP official is a familiar

figure and one which still exists. Similarly,
the Union provided and provides candidates, but it
does not run the CLPs in a 'Tammany Hall' fashion.
The Yorkshire Area regarded these seats as 'theirs'
only in the sense that the miners were unrivalled
and provided the bulk of political finance. The
CLPs were, however, of the Party, not the Union,
and the miners saw it as their duty (as well as in
their interest) to support the CLP's electoral
efforts.
    The influence of the miners in coalfield CLPs
was not based on any intrinsic organised strength
but largely on the concentrated number necessary in
the coal industry. Other groups of workers and
the ward parties lacked the numbers and cohesion of
the miners. Post-war social change led to the
emergence of new groups of professional workers, new
light industries and new unions which created in
some parts of the coalfield a more differentiated
and complex style of politics. Many of these
groups were based on a mining background, their
members coming from mining families, but in some
constituencies (for example, Rother Valley) this
social change resulted in changed perceptions of
what constituted a 'good' MP. There was no
organised challenge to the miners: they remained
the largest single group in CLP politics and their
secondary influence (ex-miners, miners' wives and
miners children) should not be discounted. The
appearance of these new elements demonstrated
the relative weakness of the Yorkshire Area in the
CLPs. Even in those selection processes where
the miners were successful the Area Executive
commented on the shortcomings of political organisation.
    The miners exhibited a marked reluctance to
join the Party as individual members and, more
seriously, a failure to mobilise their full delegate
entitlement. These problems were exacerbated by
the decline of the industry and changes in Party
standing orders which made individual membership
the criteria for full participation. The miners'
political commitment and consciousness has been
noted frequently, but in the Yorkshire coalfield it
did not lead to mass participation in CLP politics.
The reason for this can be found in the dynamics of
one-party dominance, the legacy of history and the
weakness of political organisation.
    These CLPs enjoy electoral security, and thus
there is no incentive to create a mass, vote
mobilising-maximising party organisation. Commit-

Conclusions

ment and support can be expressed by voting Labour
and paying the political levy. Voting has an
importance beyond that of registering support for
Labour and turnout is, historically, high for safe
seats. A proportion of miners do join the Party
but partisan commitment is not felt to be dependent
on individual participation or membership.

The historical dominance of the miners and the
absence of rivals, made it difficult for the union
to respond adequately to their decline. These were
miners' seats; they always had been and always
would be. However, as the Yorkshire Area and other
Areas began to lose nominations, union leaders
exhorted their members to join and participate but
with little effect. Why?

The crucial linkage between the miners and the
CLP are the branch secretaries. Branch office is
a trade union office concerned overwhelmingly with
the immediate work environment. Political matters,
when raised at branch level, tend to be referred via
the branch delegate, to Area Council, not the
branch's CLP. A further problem is that of the
mobility of labour. This means a branch may have
members in several constituencies which reduces
the impact of the branch in CLP politics. Branch
secretaries are generally too busy with industrial
affairs to be deeply involved in CLP affairs,
although there are a number of exceptions.

As these are safe seats the real political
process is not election but candidate selection.
How influential is the Yorkshire Area and the miners
in candidate selection? Despite losing only two
seats between 1944 and 1974 union influence has
declined. In interviews with participants it was
emphasised frequently that the image of miners'
influence was buttressed by the longevity of MPs
and, therefore, the infrequency of selection
conferences. It was asserted that the generation
of MPs selected in the 1950s/1960s would not be
replaced by miners. Rother Valley was, then, a
harbinger of future coalfield politics, with the
Yorkshire miners reduced to perhaps two MPs. This
has been disproved by events. The miners remain
the largest single group in coalfield politics,
which gives them considerable potential influence,
but to have an impact influence must be organised.

All studies of working class politics note the
electoral role of the miners. Since 1874 they
have been at the forefront of sponsoring and electing
miners as MPs - why?, and what use have they made
of them? The why of parliamentary representation

is obvious.   During the nineteenth century the
mining unions were too weak to secure concessions
through collective bargaining.   Legislation seemed
the only sure way of improving the miners' lot.
Parliamentary spokesmen were therefore invaluable in
persuading government to pass mining legislation.
Today, when the NUM enjoys 100% membership and is
accepted as a legitimate part of the industry,
what is the role of the sponsored MP?   Why bother
when the miners enjoy direct access to government?
     Originally, miners' MPs had no formal political
affiliations, though they were in fact Liberals.
In return for miners' votes the Liberals in
Yorkshire conceded two seats to miners and offered
a sympathetic ear to their grievances.   This
altered after the miners affiliated to the Labour
Party.   Labour placed far more party demands on
the MPs and they ceased to be miners' MPs in any
proprietorial sense, becoming the miners' contribution to the political wing of the Labour Movement.
These MPs are miners, sit for coalfield constituencies are supported financially by the NUM and are
expected to 'represent' the miners, but first and
foremost they are Labour MPs representing a
geographical area not an occupational group or even
a class.   The miners wanted, and want, a propa-
gandist voice in the Commons whilst subscribing to
and accepting the Burkesan doctrine of independence.
This both augments and supports the imperatives of
party government.   Sponsored MPs are the fossilised
remains of early Labour politics, when the Party was
impoverished, lacked constituency organisation and
when the unions saw MPs as a natural extension of
their industrial activities.
     How influential is the union in the MPs
political behaviour?   Sponsored MPs follow the
Party not the union line, as the 1975 EEC dispute
showed and the Yorkshire Area had no means of
bringing them to account.   Their importance is
purely secondary, outweighed by the NUM's direct
contacts with government and the Whitehall
bureaucracy.   The NEC and the Miners Group
cooperate amicably when needed and there is never
any attempt to dictate to the MPs.   The attempt by
the Yorkshire Area to censure those MPs who rejected
Area policy on the EEC demonstrated the impotence
of the Union.   Although the NUM does have the
power to withdraw its financial support (this is
accepted by the tenets of parliamentary privilege),
to do so after an MP, or MPs, have opposed Union
policy, or, to threaten to withdraw it unless the

MP or MPs speak and vote in a certain way, will be regarded as a breach of privilege. The power of withdrawal, in any case, lay with the National Union, not the Area in which the MP sat. MPs are in a difficult position: they are Party men but also feel a loyalty to the communities from which they come. This problem was brought into sharp relief by the 1967 Fuel Policy White Paper: only reluctantly could the miners MPs bring themselves to oppose a policy responsible for the devastation of so many mining communities. The Yorkshire Area might be influential in the selection of MPs, but once in Parliament it cannot withdraw sponsorship and MPs with safe seats need not worry about their futures. He who pays the piper does not call the tune.

Internal Union Conflict and Political Change
It is customary to regard the Yorkshire Area as a militant coalfield. Yet, for the bulk of the post-war period Yorkshire was on the right of the NUM. How did this change come about?

The political change of 1971-1973 was the consequence of, and reaction to, successive union and government policies. After the reorganisation and nationalisation of the MFGB in 1944 the NUM's internal politics was dominated by two inter-locked aims; to defend nationalisation and to avoid industrial action by relying upon institutionalised collective bargaining and direct contact with government to defend miners' interests. Internal conflict and political change was produced by a conflict over means and ends. Unions leaders sought to maintain the highest possible level of employment in the industry (a legacy of the inter-war years) by extending union influence into managerial functions. The concomitant was the abrogation of all forms of industrial action both in principle (it offended against the ethos of nationalisation) and because it placed marginal pits in danger of closure. Union leaders sought to ease the rundown of the industry but they accepted, apparently with equanimity, the policy of contraction as well as low wages as part of their attempt to maintain employment. This enmeshed the NUM in a 'logic of moderation': industrial action was out of question because of nationalisation, because it would close pits, and later because the rundown was held to have destroyed the miners' industrial power. This logic of moderation was buttressed by a political process dominated by the right wing.

Opposition to this style always existed in the Yorkshire Area but it remained a minority view and relatively unorganised despite the existence of the Doncaster Panel. This opposition consistently argued that the NUM should not surrender the right to strike and should seek to defend actively miners' conditions. They also came to advocate industrial action as a method of changing unfavourable government policies as well as increasing wages. Absent was a generalised discontent and an eruptive factor to begin the process of political change.

A long term cause of political change was disappointment with aspects of nationalisation. It soon became clear that the Morrisonian model of public industry adopted by the Labour Party changed ownership not control. Although the miners gained from nationalisation the fundamental power relations of private industry did not change. Nationalisation was held to necessitate a change of attitude on the part of both management and men; thus the NUM was sometimes compelled to support management. The result was an increase in unofficial industrial action and, at times, vociferous opposition to union policy.

A second factor contributing to political change was the decline of the industry. The Yorkshire coalfield escaped relatively lightly from the early round of closures, the bulk coming in the 1960s. Widespread closures were something which happened to other Areas. Yorkshire has always accepted closure on the grounds of seam exhaustion, but closure on economic grounds had always been resisted. This was the main reason for closure and many miners seemed to expect vigorous opposition. Initially the closures had the effect of creating a quiescent workforce. However, uncertainty gradually bred frustration and the feeling that something had to be done. The something was the unofficial strikes of 1969 and 1970.

A third factor was the failure of pressure group politics and more particularly, the anger felt by the miners at their betrayal by Labour. Both Conservative and Labour governments rejected the miners' prescriptions for the industry and their arguments that it was economically foolish and political imprudent to base the economy on temporarily cheap oil from a politically unstable

Middle East.   Rapid contraction was dangerous as
once a pit was closed it was too expensive to
re-open, to which should be added the financial cost
of redundancy, the social costs of pit closures
and the drain on national finances of massive crude
oil imports.   Once these arguments had been
rejected the Union concentrated on preserving the
maximum number of jobs.   The miners did not expect
to be treated fairly by a Conservative Government,
but they did expect fair treatment from a Labour
Government, particularly one they believed was
committed to a clear policy.   When the NUM found
that the Government was not so committed, there
was growing disenchantment with the Labour Government, with union leaders, and with conventional
lobbying which, in turn, led to a willingness to
contemplate industrial action.

The problems and dilemmas facing the miners
can be seen in the complex restructuring of wages
in mining under NPLA after 1966.   NPLA sought the
equalisation and standardisation of wage rates
throughout the industry.   This was wholly laudable,
but implementation generated a series of problems.
First, equalisation was not achieved by the NCB
increasing wages to the level of the highest paid
coalfields but by restraining their wages and using
the surplus created by increased productivity to
raise wages in the lowest paid coalfields.   Second,
it slowed but did not stop the rundown.   As
marginal and high-cost pits were closed and as
productivity increased, further pits became vulnerable to closure.   Up to 1966 and NPLA coal
production was to be concentrated on low cost, high
productivity coalfields; under NPLA it was to be
concentrated on low cost, high-productivity pits.
Third, as NPLA was a 'rational' wage system it
demanded the destruction of many past practises and
placed an increased burden on mineworkers.   As
such, it contributed greatly to the uncertainty in
the industry.   Finally, NPLA was envisaged as a
means of avoiding pay policy as it was a productivity deal.   It offered the prospects of regular pay
increases beyond the Government's norm, but as NPLA
institutionalised low pay, percentage increases
were given on low basic rates.   Miners pay was thus
squeezed from two directions: by Government pay
policy and by NPLA.

Unrest over pit closures, the failure of
traditional policies, hostility to existing leaders,
hostility to the Labour Government, low pay and
poor conditions led to the outburst of unofficial

strikes in Yorkshire.   The importance of these
strikes was that they were organised by the branch
leadership via the Panel system.   The 1969 strike
was a response to, and product of, the accumulated
frustrations and tensions, not only of the previous
ten years, but to the history of the industry
since 1947.   1969 and 1970 were a critical juncture
in history of the Yorkshire Area: the Yorkshire
miners threw off the uncertainties of the 1960s,
challenged their leaders and forced a number of
changes in union policy and leadership which
paved the way for 1972.   The strike of 1972
demonstrated that miners were still capable of
militant industrial action and that there was an
alternative to party-political action, an alternative which avoided the debilitating and
enervating effect of dependence on untrustworthy
governments.   The Panels obtained vital experience
in organising mass, coalfield-wide industrial
action and the strikes were led by a younger,
vigorous, more militant branch leadership.   This
new leadership advocated the militant defence of
miners' wages and conditions and they, and their
members, were determined that the miners and their
industry would never again be treated as they had
been between 1958 and 1972.

The Miners Resurgent: 1972 and 1974
The official strikes of 1972 and 1974 marked the
end of a chapter in the history of the miners,
a chapter which began in 1926.   For the Yorkshire
Area the 1972 strike was far more important than
1974 for three reasons: first, it demonstrated what
many miners had known instinctively -- that
effective industrial action was feasible.   Second,
it demonstrated the economic and political power
of the miners, and finally, the miners' victory
increased their influence as a pressure group
with government.   In retrospect, dazzled by the
miners' victory, it is easy to forget that many
miners also saw the 1972 strike as a last desperate
gamble: they were told by the media and the NCB
that they could not win and that a prolonged strike
would close pits.   The miners' reply -- 'if the
industry cannot pay decent wages then close the
pits' __ was incomprehensible to the media,
reflecting their traditional failure to understand
the miners, so reinforcing the miners' feelings
of separateness.   Indeed, the uncertainly amongst
the membership can be seen from the narrowness of
the majority.

Conclusions

The Yorkshire miners quickly emerged as the chief exponents of a new style of industrial action. Official union leaders in Barnsley knew what had to be done, but the conduct of the strike lay with the Panels. 1972 was, in effect, a rank and file strike. The production of coal was easily stopped; the crucial step was stopping the consumption of that already mined. The major weakness of miners' industrial action in the past had been immobility. The impact of the miners solidarity was wasted by their unwillingness and inability to move away from the pit-heads. Tactics changed in two important respects; first, mobility, and second, size. The Yorkshire miners perfected the tactics of mass, mobile picketing: assembling large numbers of pickets and providing them with logistical support and blockading a target until it closed. A token picket was then left and the main body moved to the next target. These pickets could only have been dispersed by direct police action, precipitating escalation.

The miners' commitment and solidarity was important in sustaining their struggle and the mass pickets were vital, but their impact was amplified by other factors. First, preventing the movement and consumption of existing fuel stocks was absolutely crucial as the Government were confident there were sufficient stocks to outlast the strike. In tonnage terms this was true, but the stocks were badly distributed and had to be moved to the power stations. The commitment from the NUR, ASLEF and the TGWU that their members would respect NUM picket lines was a major contribution to victory. A second factor was the pattern of fuel use. The dependence of industry upon centrally generated electricity, produced by relatively few coal burning power stations amplified the miners' ability to disrupt the economy. Industry depended on electricity and electricity depended on coal, thus the interdependence characteristic of modern industrial society greatly aided the miners. A final factor was the attitude of the British state and its rulers. The events of 1972 and 1974 suggest that, compared to 1926, a psychological change had taken place in governing circles. Under the twin impact of competitive electoral politics and the traditional governing style of compromise and consensus, post-1945 politics became characterised by a willingness to conciliate powerful corporate forces. The strength of the miners and the Heath Government's growing predilection for

consensus politics after the blood-letting of the
Industrial Relations Act reduced its ability and
willingness to confront the miners. No attempt
was made to break the NUM as Baldwin broke the
MFGB in 1926 and despite the rhetoric of 'standing
up to the miners' the Government sought a negotiated end to the strikes. The members of the Heath
Cabinet were aware of the social and political
damage that would be caused by an attempt to smash
the strikes. The members of the Cabinet had come
into politics in the post-war period and were
deeply imbued with consensus politics. Thus, they
were unable and unwilling to try and repeat the
actions of the Baldwin Government.
     The 1972 strike transformed the relationship
between the miners and politics. Before 1972 the
miners were regarded as a spent force, the
unofficial strikes being the death throes of an
industrial giant. The 1972 strike changed this:
the miners' industrial power was seen in their
disruption of the economy, and their political
power in forcing a Conservative Government to meet
their demands. The strike led to changes in both
leadership and policy in Yorkshire, but at national
level there was a sharper awareness of the dangers
of confrontation. In response to 1972 the Heath
Government attempted to involve the NUM in tripartism as a means of promoting industrial and
economic stability.
     These attempts were a failure. The wages
resolution passed by the 1973 Conference presaged a
further confrontation, but conflict was not
inevitable. Both the NUM and the Government were
anxious to avoid a strike as can be seen in the
negotiations between Gormley, Heath and Sir William
Armstrong (Head of the Home Civil Service) which
had the aim of making Phase 3 fit the NUM's
requirements. This strategy foundered because of
the NCB's ignorance of the NUM's internal politics.
Believing a settlement was guaranteed the Board
tabled the entire offer at once, ensuring that the
moderates on the NEC were unable to fight for
further concessions. The Government refused to
make more money available, Gormley was bound by a
Conference decision (militant Areas like Yorkshire
was keeping a sharp watch for any betrayal) and
the result was a strike. Unable to coerce the
miners Heath called an election which he lost,
further investing the miners with an aura of power.

The Yorkshire Miners and Politics: The Transformation

By 1974 the Yorkshire Area, the largest in the NUM, was unequivocally in the 'militant' camp of the union.   The new Yorkshire leadership were determined that never again would miners' wages and conditions be bartered or held hostage to the political interests of a Labour Government.

The transformation was in response to the experience of the coal industry after 1947.   From the vantage point of 1974 the Yorkshire Area's leaders noted how the industry had moved from indispensibility to impotence and back again.   They saw that Union leaders had refused to wield the miners' devastating economic power, arguing that nationalisation would guarantee prosperity and security without the costs of strike action.   The result was the butchery of the industry and the devastation of countless mining communities. Union leaders had failed to formulate an adequate response: the policy of acquiescence, of preserving jobs at the cost of low was interpreted by them, and many miners, as a sell-out.

The response to this political and industrial bankruptcy came in 1969 and 1970, and as a result of these strikes the Yorkshire miners became identified as the most important in the NUM. Yorkshire had never been part of the NUM left, but it did contain a considerable and well organised reservoir of left wing activists and sympathisers who led and organised the growing frustration of the late-1960s.   This new group of leaders provided the leadership in 1972 and 1974. Men such as Arthur Scargill organised the miners into a highly effective force, introducing new tactics to win the strikes.   As a result of the events of 1969-1973 a new generation of left-wing leaders emerged and took power in Yorkshire.   In doing so they shifted the distribution of power in the NUM.   After 1974 the Yorkshire Area and Yorkshire miners played a leading role in opposing the return to pre-1971 policies of avoiding industrial action and relying on a sympathetic Labour Government. Thus, the Yorkshire Area and the Yorkshire miners played a crucial role in the resurgence of the NUM in the 1970s, making the NUM one of the most important elements in the political system.   From being an ignored relic of Britain's industrial and political past the miners, their Union and their product, underwent a political renascence.

312

Appendix

MAP 1

POWER STATIONS ON THE YORKSHIRE COALFIELD

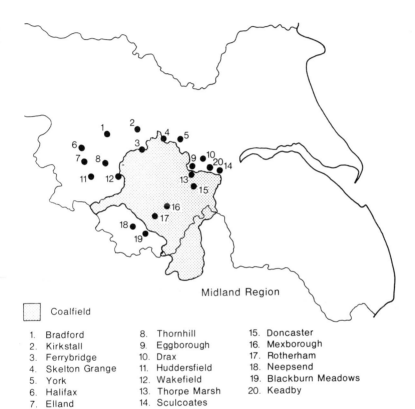

Midland Region

☐ Coalfield

1. Bradford
2. Kirkstall
3. Ferrybridge
4. Skelton Grange
5. York
6. Halifax
7. Elland

8. Thornhill
9. Eggborough
10. Drax
11. Huddersfield
12. Wakefield
13. Thorpe Marsh
14. Sculcoates

15. Doncaster
16. Mexborough
17. Rotherham
18. Neepsend
19. Blackburn Meadows
20. Keadby

Appendix

MAP 2

POWER STATIONS IN THE EAST ANGLIA AREA

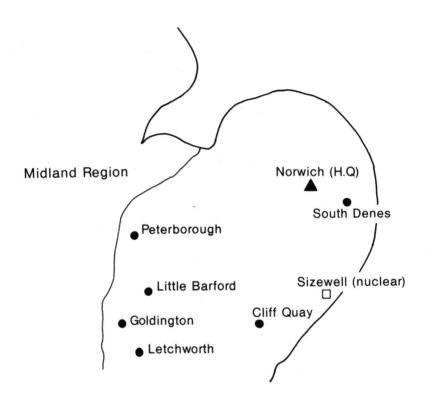

Appendix

MAP 3

YORKSHIRE COALFIELD PARLIAMENTARY CONSTITUENCIES

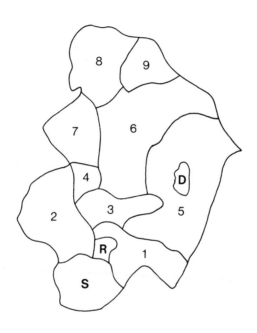

D — Doncaster   1. Rother Valley   6. Hemsworth

R — Rotherham   2. Penistone   7. Wakefield

S — Sheffield   3. Dearne Valley   8. Normanton

  4. Barnsley   9. Pontefact and Castleford

  5. Don Valley

Appendix

MAP 4

THE YORKSHIRE COALFIELD IN 1970

SOUTH YORKSHIRE

Cortonwood
Wath
Barnburgh
Manvers
Denaby
Elsecar
Cadeby
Kilnhurst
New Stubbin
Silverwood
Maltby
Rotherham
Thurcroft
Sheffield
Treeton
Dinnington
Orgreave
Firbeck
Brookhouse
Kiveton Park
Shireoaks
Steetley
Manton

NORTH YORKSHIRE

Middleton Broom
Waterloo
Peckfield
Leeds
Ledston Luck
Rothwell
Primrose Hill
Water Haigh
Allerton Bywater
Gomersal
Savile
Fryston
East Ardsley
Newmarket Silkstone
Wheldale
Lofthouse
Whitwood
Glass Houghton
Kellingley
Shaw Cross
Wakefield
St. Johns
Prince of Wales
Manor
Park Hill
Ackton Hall
Sharlston
Thornhill
Walton
Nostell

● Collieries

0   5   10   15

miles

MAP 4 (continued)

DONCASTER

BARNSLEY

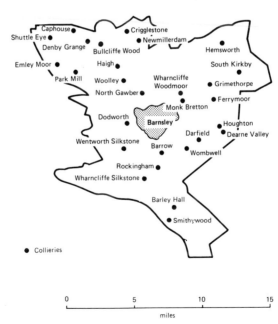

● Collieries

```
0           5          10          15
|_____|_____|_____|
                miles
```

SELECT BIBLIOGRAPHY

1   The Yorkshire Area (NUM)

Minutes of the Area Executive Committee, 1944-
     1974
Minutes of the Area Council Meetings, 1944-1974
Minutes of Executive Sub-Committees, 1944-1974
Annual Reports of the Area Officials
Circulars issued by the Area to Branch Secretaries
The Yorkshire Miner, 1959-1960 and 1976 to date
Rules of the Yorkshire Area (NUM), 1976
Miscellaneous Papers relating to the 1972 and 1974
     Strikes

2   The National Union of Mineworkers

Minutes of the National Executive Committee
Annual Conference Reports
Annual Reports of the NEC
Circulars issued by the NUM to all Area Secretaries
The Miner, 1969 to date
Special Conference Reports (dates and purpose
     cited)
NUM General Election Manifestoes
NUM Rules, 1972
National Power Loading Agreement, 1966
Reports of the Miners' Parliamentary Group
Wage Claim Research Papers 1 - 5 (Prepared by the
     Trade Union Research Unit, Ruskin College
     Oxford, 1971)

3   Official Publications

Coal Mining: Report of the Technical Advisory
     Committee, Cmd 6610, 1945
Industrial Relations Handbook, 1961 (Revised
     Edition)
The National Plan, Cmnd 2764, 1965
Fuel Policy, Cmnd 2798, 1965
Fuel Policy, Cmnd 3438, 1967
Royal Commission on Trade Unions and Employers
     Associations 1965-68; Report, Cmnd 3623,
     1968
Report of a Court of Inquiry, Cmnd 4903, 1972
The Pay Board: A Guide To Its Work, 1973
The Pay Board: Relativities, Cmnd 5535, 1974
The Pay Board (Special Report): The Relative Pay
     of Mineworkers, Cmnd 5567, 1974
Committee of Privileges (2nd Report) HC634, 1974-75
Report of the Committee on Financial Aid to

Political Parties, Cmnd 6601, 1976

4   National Coal Board

Annual Reports and Accounts
Plan For Coal, 1950
Investing In Coal, 1956
The First Ten Years, 1957
Revised Plan For Coal, 1959
The Question of Pit Closures in the Yorkshire
        Division (NCB) in the Next Five Years,
        1965
The Coal Industry Examination (Interim & Final
        Report), 1974 and 1975
The Plan For Coal, 1975

5   Newspapers

a)   National
The Economist, The Guardian, The Times, Tribune
b)   Local
The Collier, Barnsley Chronicle, Sheffield Morning
        Telegraph, The South Yorkshire Advertiser,
        South Yorkshire Times, The Yorkshire Post.

6   Books and Articles

(All books published in London unless otherwise
        stated)
Abrams M, Rose R, and Hinden R Must Labour Lose?
        (Penguin,   Harmondsworth 1960)
Allen V Trade Union Leadership (Longmans, 1957)
----   Trade Unions and the Government (Longmans,
        1960)
----   Militant Trade Unionism (Merlin Press, 1972)
----   The Militancy of British Miners (The Moor
        Press, Shipley 1981)
Amsden J and Brier S 'Coal Miners on Strike: The
        Transformation of Strike Demands and the
        Formation of a National Union' Journal of
        Interdisciplinary History VII(1977)
Baldwin G B 'Structural Reform in the British
        Miners Union' Quarterly Journal of Economics
        67(1953)
Banks J A Marxist Sociology in Action (Faber &
        Faber 1970)
Barrat Brown M 'What Will the Miners Do Now? New
        Society,   23 November 1970
---- What Really Happened To the Coal Industry?
        (Institute for Workers Control, Nottingham
        1971)

Baxter R 'The Working Class and Labour Politics'
     Political Studies 20(1972)
Beackon S 'Labour Party Politics and the Working
     Class' British Journal of Political Science
     6(1976)
Bealey F(ed) The Social and Political Thought of
     the Labour Party (Weidenfeld, 1972)
---- and Pelling H Labour and Politics, 1900-
     1906 (Macmillan, 1958)
Beer S H Modern British Politics, second edition
     (Faber & Faber, 1969)
Berkovitch I Coal on the Switchback (G Allen and
     Unwin 1977)
Birch A H 'The Habit of Voting' The Manchester
     School 18 (1950)
Blondel J Voters, Parties and Leaders, revised
     edition (Penguin, Harmondsworth 1974)
Bulmer M I 'Sociological Models of the Mining
     Community' Sociological Review 23 (1975)
----(ed) Mining and Social Change (Croom Helm,
     1978)
Burgess K The Origins of British Industrial
     Relations (Croom Helm 1975)
Butler D and Stokes D Political Change in Britain
     (Penguin, Harmondsworth 1969, and, second
     edition, Macmillan 1974).
Child J, Loveridge R, and Warner M 'Towards an
     Organisational Study of Trade Unions'
     Sociology 7 (1973)
Clegg H The Changing System of Industrial
     Relations in Great Britain (Basil Blackwell,
     Oxford 1980)
---- , Fox A and Thompson A A History of British
     Trade Unionism Since 1889: Volume 1,
     1889-1910 (Clarendon Press Oxford 1964)
Coates D The Labour Party and the Struggle for
     Socialism (University Press, Cambridge
     1975)
Coates K (ed) Democracy in the Mines (Spokeman
     Books, Nottingham 1974)
Crewe I 'The Politics of Affluent and Traditional
     Workers in Britain' British Journal of
     Political Science 3 (1973)
Crossman R H S Diaries of a Cabinet Minister:
     Volume 2, Leader of the House (Cape, 1976)
Crouch C Class conflict and the Industrial
     Relations Crisis (Heinemann 1977)
----The Politics of Industrial Relations (Fontana,
     1979)
----Trade Unions: The Logic of Collective Action
     (Fontana, 1982)

Select Bibliography

Daly L The Miners and the Nation (Scottish Area
    NUM, 1968).
---- 'A Future for the Miners', Trade Union
    Register (Merlin 1969)
---- 'Protest and Disturbance in the Trade Union
    Movement' in Crick B and Robson W(eds)
    Protest and Discontent (Penguin,
    Harmondsworth 1970)
Dennis N Henriques F and Slaughter C Coal Is Our
    Life (Tavistock 1968)
Dorfman G Government Versus the Trade Unions in
    Britain Since 1968 (Macmillan, 1979)
Edelstein J D 'Countervaling Powers and the
    Political Process in the British Mineworkers
    Union' International Journal of Comparative
    Sociology 9 (1968)
---- and Warner M Comparative Union Democracy
    (G. Allen and Unwin 1975)
Farnham D 'The Labour Alliance: Reality or Myth'
    Parliamentary Affairs 29 (1976)
Fay S and Young H The Fall of Edward Heath (The
    Sunday Times, 1976)
Ferris P The New Militants (Penguin, Harmondsworth
    1972)
Finer S E 'The Political Power of Organized Labour'
    Government and Opposition 8 (1973)
Flanders A 'Collective Bargaining: A Theoretical
    Analysis'
    British Journal of Industrial Relations 5
    (1968)
---- Trade Unions, seventh edition (Hutchinson
    1968)
---- Management and Unions (Faber & Faber 1970)
Foa V 'Incomes Policy: A Crucial Problem for the
    Unions' International Socialist Journal
    (January) 1964
Forester T The Labour Party and the Working Class
    (Heinemann 1976)
Fox A 'Trade Unions and Defence' Socialist
    Commentary 25 (1961)
Giddens A The Class Structure of the Advanced
    Societies (Hutchinson 1973)
Gormley J Battered Cherub (Hamish Hamilton, 1982)
Gregory R The Miners and British Politics, 1906-
    1914 (Clarendon Press, Oxford 1968)
Griffin A R The British Coalmining Industry
    (Moorland Press, Buxton 1977)
Hall T King Coal: Miners, Coal and Britain's
    Industrial Future (Penguin, Harmondsworth,
    1981)
Handy L J Wages Policy in the British Coalmining

Industry(University Press, Cambridge 1981)

Harrison M The Trade Unions and the Labour Party
    Since 1945 (G Allen and Unwin 1960)

Harrison R(ed) Independent Collier (Harvester
    Press, Brighton 1978)

Haseler S The Gaitskellites (Macmillan 1969)

Hemingway J Conflict and Democracy (Clarendon
    Press, Oxford 1978)

Hindess B The Decline of Working Class Politics
    (Paladin 1971)

Hobsbawm E J 'Trade Union History' Economic
    History Review (2s) 20(1967)

Horner A Incorrigible Rebel (Macgibbon and Kee,
    1960)

Howell D British Social Democracy (Croom Helm,
    1976)

Hughes J and Moore R A Special Case? Social
    Justice and the Miners (Penguin/NUM,
    Harmondsworth, 1972)

Hyman R Marxism and the Sociology of Trade
    Unionism (Pluto Press, 1971)

---- Strikes (Fontana, 1971)

---- Industrial Relations: A Marxist Analysis
    (Macmillan, 1975)

Ingham G K Strikes and Industrial Conflict
    (Macmillan, 1974)

Jencks C 'Britain Coal: Labour Relations Since
    Nationalisation' Industrial Relations 6 (1966)

Jevons S H The British Coal Trade, new edition
    (David and Charles, Newton Abbot, 1969)

Kirby M W The British Coalmining Industry, 1870-
    1946 (Macmillan 1976)

Laslett J 'Why Some Do and Some Don't: Some
    Determinants of Radicalism amongst British and
    American Coal Miners, 1872-1914' Society for
    the Study of Labour History Bulletin 28
    (1974)

Lenin V I On Trade Unions (Progress Publishers,
    Moscow, 1970)

Lipset S M, Trow M and Coleman J Union Democracy
    (Anchor Books, New York, 1956)

Lovell J British Trade Unions, 1875-1933
    (Macmillan, 1977)

McKenzie R 'Labour Party Organisation' Fabian
    Journal 16 1955)

---- British Political Parties, revised edition
    (Mercury Books, 1963)

McKibbin R I The Evolution of the Labour Party,
    1910-1924 (Clarendon Press, Oxford, 1974)

McKormick B 'Strikes in the Yorkshire Coalfield'
    Economic Journal (1965)

Select Bibliography

---- Industrial Relations in the British Coal Industry (Macmillan, 1978)

---- and Williams J E 'The Miners and the Eight Hour Day' Economic History Review (2s) 12 (1959-1960)

Macdonald D The State and the Trade Unions, second edition (Macmillan, 1976)

Mac Dougall I(ed) Militant Miners (Polygon Books, Edinburgh, 1981)

Machin F The Yorkshire Miners, volume 1 (Yorkshire Area NUM, Barnsley, 1958)

Mann M Consciousness and Action Amongst the Western Working Class (Macmillan, 1973)

Martin R M 'Union Democracy: An Explanatory Framework' Sociology 5 (1968)

May T C Trade Unions and Pressure Group Politics (Saxon House, Farnborough, 1975)

Michels R Political Parties (Free Press, New York 1962)

Middlemas K Politics in Industrial Society (Deutsch, 1979)

Miliband R Parliamentary Socialism, second edition (Merlin Press, 1972)

---- The State in Capitalist Society (Quartet, 1972)

Minkin L 'The British Labour Party and the Trade Unions: Crisis and Compact' Industrial and Labour Relations Review 28 (1974)

---- 'The Party Connection: Divergence and Convergence in The British Labour Movement' Government and Opposition 13 (1978)

---- The Labour Party Conference (Allen Lane, 1978)

Moore E The Emergence of the Labour Party, 1880 - 1924 (Hodder and Stoughton, 1978)

Moore R Pitmen, Preachers and Politics (University Press, Cambridge 1974)

Moorhouse R 'The Political Incorporation of the British Working Class' Sociology 7 (1973)

Moran M The Politics of Industrial Relations (Macmillan, 1977)

Muller W D The Kept Men? (Harvester Press, Brighton 1977)

Nairn T The Left Against Europe? (Penguin, Harmondsworth, 1973)

Oldham J etal 'A Future For the British Miners' Trade Union Register (Merlin Press, 1971)

Page Arnot R The Miners: Volume 1

---- The Miners: Volume 2, Years of Struggle

---- The Miners: Volume 3, In Crisis and War

---- The Miners: Volume 4, One Union, One Industry

(G Allen and Unwin, 1949, 1953, 1961 and
    1979)
Panitch L 'Ideology and Integration: The Case of
    the British Labour Party' Political Studies
    19 (1971)
---- Social Democracy and Industrial Militancy
    (University Press, Cambridge 1975)
Paterson P The Selectorate (MacGibbon and Kee, 1967)
Paynter W 'Nationalisation Betrayed?' Labour
    Monthly (June) 1962
---- British Trade Unions and the Problem of
    Change (G Allen and Unwin, 1972)
---- My Generation (G Allen and Unwin, 1972)
Peace K 'Some Changes in the Coalmining Industry
    of Southern Yorkshire' Geography 58 (1973)
Pelling H A History of British Trade Unionism
    (Penguin, Harmondsworth, 1965)
---- The Origins of the Labour Party, second
    edition(Clarendon Press, Oxford, 1965)
Pitt M The World On Our Backs (Lawrence and
    Wishart, 1979)
Ranney A Pathways To Parliament (Macmillan, 1965)
Rawson D W 'The Frontiers of Trade Unionism'
    Australian Journal of Politics and History 1
    (1956)
---- 'The Life Span of Labour Parties' Political
    Studies 17 (1967)
---- 'The Paradox of Partisan Trade Unionism'
    British Journal of Political Science 4
    (1974)
Richter I Political Purpose in Trade Unions
    (G Allen and Unwin, 1973)
Rimlinger G 'The Legitimation of Protest: A
    Comparative Studies in Society and History 2
    (1960)
Robens A Ten Year Stint (Cassell, 1972)
Rose R The Problem of Party Government (Penguin,
    Harmondsworth 1976)
Rush M The Selection of Parliamentary Candidates
    (Nelson, 1969)
Rutledge I 'Changes in the Mode of Production and
    the Growth of Mass Militancy in the British
    Mining Industry, 1945-1974, Science and
    Society XLI (1977-78)
Saville J 'Notes on the Ideology of the Miners
    Before 1914', Society for the Study of
    Labour History Bulletin 23 (1970)
---- 'Labourism and the Labour Government'
    Socialist Register (1971)
---- 'The Ideology of Labourism', in R Benewick(ed)
    Knowledge and Belief In Politics (G Allen and

Unwin, 1973)

Scargill A   'The New Unionism' New Left Review 92
      (1975)

Scott W, Mumford E, McGivering I and Kirby J
      Coal and Conflict (University Press,
      Liverpool, 1963)

Simpson B   The Trade Unions and the Labour Party
      (G Allen and Unwin, 1973)

Simpson E   Coal and the Power Industries in Post
      War Britain (Longmans 1966)

Slaughter C   'The Strike of the Yorkshire Miners
      in May 1955' Sociological Review 6 (1958)

Taylor R   The Fifth Estate   revised edition (Pan
      Books, 1980)

Trice J E 'Methods of and Attitudes to Picketing'
      Criminal Law Review 1975

Turner H A   Trade Union Growth, Structure and
      Policy (G Allen and Unwin 1962)

Warner M 'Unions, Integration and Society'
      Industrial Relations Journal 1 (1966)

Webb S and B   Industrial Democracy, revised edition
      (Longmans, 1913)

Wedderburn K   The Worker and the Law (Penguin,
      Harmondsworth, 1974)

Wigham E   Strikes and the Government, 1893-1976
      (Macmillan, 1976)

Williams (Tom) Lord Digging For Britain (Hutchinson
      1965).

Wilson H   The Labour Government, 1964-1970
      (Penguin, Harmondsworth, 1971)

Index